Understanding
Macroeconomics

Understanding Macroeconomics

SIXTH EDITION

ROBERT L.
HEILBRONER

LESTER C.
THUROW

PRENTICE-HALL, INC. Englewood Cliffs, N. J. 07632

Library of Congress Cataloging in Publication Data

HEILBRONER, ROBERT L
    Understanding macroeconomics.

    Includes index.
    1. Macroeconomics. I. Thurow, Lester C., joint
author. II. Title.
HB171.5.H392 1978b   339   77-28332
ISBN   0-13-936575-3

UNDERSTANDING MACROECONOMICS, 6th edition
by Robert L. Heilbroner and Lester C. Thurow

Cover design by Felix Cooper, from a photograph supplied by Mobil Oil Corporation.

10 9 8 7 6 5 4 3 2 1

Prentice-Hall International, Inc., *London*
Prentice-Hall of Australia Pty. Limited, *Sydney*
Prentice-Hall of Canada, Ltd., *Toronto*
Prentice-Hall of India Private Limited, *New Delhi*
Prentice-Hall of Japan, Inc., *Tokyo*
Prentice-Hall of Southeast Asia Pte. Ltd., *Singapore*
Whitehall Books Limited, *Wellington, New Zealand*

Contents

1

The trend of things—a first look at macroeconomics, 1

2

The market mechanism, 24

3

Wealth and output, 38

4

Gross national product, 49

5

Supply of output, 59

6

Demand for output, 77

7

Saving and investment, 96

8

Consumption demand, 112

9

Investment demand, 128

10

Motivation of investment, 145

11
Government demand, 159

12
Deficit spending, 177

13
The determination of GNP, 190

14
Money, 208

15

Money and the macro system, 232

16

The problem of inflation, 249

17

The problem of unemployment, 267

18

Problems of economic growth, 284

19

Gains from trade, 300

20

Mechanism of international transactions, 319

21
The international monetary problem, 332

The trend of things— a first look at macroeconomics

How shall we begin to study macroeconomics? The best way is to get acquainted with the thing that macroeconomics is about—the overall working of the economy as it generates growth and prosperity or inflation and unemployment. Therefore we are going to jump right into the center of the main problems with which macroeconomics is concerned. Later we shall study the nature of these problems in careful detail. But it will give use a sense of familiarity if we start off by acquainting ourselves with the big issues and pressing problems of our subject. When you have finished this first chapter you will not really have begun your study of macroeconomics. But you will be ready to begin.

The Trend

Let us imagine that we could look at a series of photos of our national economy— a series that started back in 1900 and that showed us the changing scene, as a photo album would show the changes in a family. There is no doubt about the first impression we would gain. Everything would be getting larger. Business firms would be growing in size. Labor unions would be bigger. There would be more households, and each household would be

1

richer. Government would be much larger. And underlying all of this, the size of the economic system itself would be steadily increasing.

Growth is not, of course, the only thing we would notice. Businesses are different as well as bigger when we compare 1975 and 1900: there are far more "incorporated" businesses now than in the old days, far more "diversified" businesses, fewer family firms. Households are different because more women work outside the home. Labor unions today are no longer mainly craft unions, limited to one occupation. Government is not only bigger but has a different philosophy.

Total output   Nonetheless, it is growth that first commands our attention. The camera vision of the economy gives us a picture that keeps

widening. It *has* to widen, to encompass the increase in the sheer mass of output. **Hence the first major impression we gain is that growth lies at the center of our macroeconomic concerns.**

This gives us a foretaste of problems to come. Clearly we must trace the sources of the tremendous increase in our total output. We will have to look into the reasons why growth proceeds faster in some periods, slower (or not at all) in others. We will have to consider whether growth can go on forever. But at this juncture it is enough to identify the fact of growth as the main subject of our study. *We can also take a moment to learn the name for the flow of total output whose trend we are about to study. We call it gross national product* (GNP), a term we will define more carefully in our coming chapters. Here we need only note that it

FIG. 1·1   Value of GNP, 1900–1975, current prices

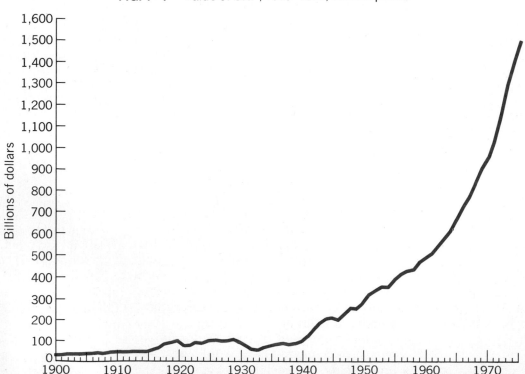

VOLUME AND VALUE

You should be warned that there is no entirely satisfactory way of wringing price increases out of the hodgepodge of goods and services called GNP, because different items in this collection of goods rise or fall in price in different degrees. There is always a certain element of arbitrariness in correcting GNP for price changes. Different methods, each perfectly defensible, will yield somewhat different measures of "corrected" GNP.

Isn't there some way of getting around the problem of dollar values when we compare GNPs? One way is to measure actual physical volumes. When certain kinds of outputs, such as foodstuffs, bulk very large in GNP, as they do in India or China, we sometimes measure growth just by adding up the tonnages of food production.

The problem, of course, is that the composition of these tonnages may change—more wheat one year, more rice another—which gets us into another comparison problem. And then such a measure ignores entirely the outputs of nonagricultural goods. (We meet the same problem if we try to measure growth by tonnages of freight, metal production, etc.)

A more defensible way might be to consider GNP as a sum total of labor time, the embodiment of so many million hours of work. Even this does not get us around the measurement and comparison problem, for we use different kinds of labor as time goes on. Therefore, we have to make the difficult assumption that all kinds of labor, skilled and unskilled, trained and untrained, can be "reduced" to multiples of one "basic" kind. That basic labor, in turn, would have to boil down to some constant unit of "effort." But does the unit of "effort"—of human energy—remain constant over time?

In the end, the task of measuring an aggregate of different things can never be solved to our complete satisfaction. Any concept of GNP always has an element of unmeasureableness about it. Growth is a concept that we constantly use, but that remains tantalizingly beyond precise definition.

refers to the dollar value of our annual production of final goods and services.

Figure 1.1 gives us a graphic representation of this increase in yearly output.

Correcting for inflation

As we can see, the dollar value of all output from 1900 to 1975 has grown by a factor of almost 100. But perhaps a cautionary thought will have already struck you. If we measure the growth of output by comparing the dollar value of production over time, what seems to be growth in actual economic activity may be no more than a rise in prices. If the economy in 1975 produced no more actual tons of grain than the economy in 1900, but if grain prices today were double those of 1900, our GNP figures would show "growth" where there was really nothing but inflation.

To arrive at a measure of real growth, we have to correct for changes in prices.

How we do so is a complicated matter that you can study in a course on statistical methods. But the basic idea is simple. Essentially, we take one year as a *base* and use the prices of that year to evaluate output in all succeeding years.

Here is an elementary example. Suppose that our grain economy produces 1 million tons in 1900 and 2 million tons in 1975, but wheat sells for $1 in 1900 and $2 in 1975. Our GNP in the current prices of 1900 and 1975 is $1 million for 1900 and $4 million 75 years later. But if we evaluate the GNP using only the 1900 prices (i.e., $1 per bushel), our GNP is reduced to $2 million in 1975. This constant dollar GNP is often referred to as the real GNP, while the current dollar GNP is called the nominal GNP. We can use the prices of any year as the "base." The important thing is that all outputs must be evaluated with only one set of prices.

Figure 1.2 shows us the much reduced growth of output when output is measured in 1958 dollars.

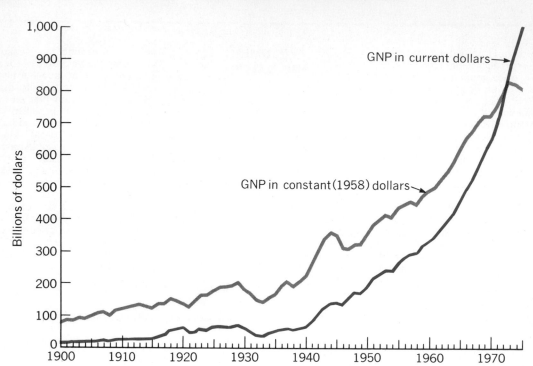

FIG. 1·2   GNP in constant (1958) and current dollars

Per capita growth   As we can see, growth in real (or constant dollar) terms is much less dramatic than growth in current dollars that make no allowance for rising prices. Nonetheless, the value of 1975 output, compared to that of 1900, with price changes eliminated as best we can, still shows a growth factor of eight.

But there still remains one last adjustment to be made. The growth of output is a massive assemblage of goods and services to be distributed among the nation's households, and the number of those households has increased. In 1900, United States population was 76 million; in 1975 it was 214 million. **To bring our constant GNP down to life size, we have to divide it by population, to get GNP per person, or per capita.**

The normal range in growth rates for capitalist economies does not seem to be very great. How much difference does it make, after all, if output grows at 1.7 or 2.7 percent?

The answer is: an amazing difference. This is because growth is an *exponential* phenomenon involving a percentage rate of growth on a steadily rising base. At 1.7 percent, per-capita real income will double in

THE DIFFERENCE THAT GROWTH RATES MAKE

about 40 years. At 2.7 percent, it will double in 26 years.

Recently, Professor Kenneth Boulding pointed out that before World War II no country sustained more than 2.3 percent per-capita growth of GNP. Since World War II,

Japan has achieved a per-capita growth rate of 8 percent. Boulding writes: "The difference between 2.3 and 8 percent may be dramatically illustrated by pointing out that [at 2.3 percent] children are twice as rich as their parents—i.e., per capita income approximately doubles every generation—while at 8 percent per annum, children are six times as rich as their parents."

Basic importance of growth

As Fig. 1.3 shows, between 1913 and 1972 real per capita growth ranged be-tween 1.7 and 2.0 percent per year. That may not seem very much, but growth rates compound, like interest in a bank. A rate of 1.8 percent was enough to give the average citizen in 1975 six times as large a volume of goods and services as the average citizen got in 1900. Whether or not average happiness multiplied six times is another question. We will look into the relation between GNP and personal well-being in Chapters 4 and 18.

Sources of growth

How will we explain this long upward trend? Here we can give only a brief summary of the causes that we will study more systematically as we go along. Essentially, we grew for two reasons:

1. The quantity of "inputs" going into the economic process increased.

In 1900 our labor force was 27 million. In 1975 it was 95 million. Obviously, larger inputs of labor produce larger outputs of goods and services.

Our inputs of capital increased as well. In 1900 the total horsepower energy delivered by "prime movers"—engines of all kinds, work animals, ships, trains, etc.—was 65 million horsepower. In 1975 it was 25 *billion.*

Land in use also increased. In 1900, there were 839 million acres of land used for farming purposes, and over 1,000 million acres for nonfarm purposes such as grazing. By 1975, land in farms had increased to over 1,000 million acres, and land in nonfarm use had also increased: we had reclaimed "virgin land" and made it economically productive.

2. The quality of inputs improved.

The population working in 1975 was not only more numerous than in 1900, it was better trained and better schooled. The best overall gauge of this is the amount of education stored up in the work force. In 1900, when only 6.4 percent of the working population had gone beyond grade school, there were 223 million man-years of schooling embodied in the popu-

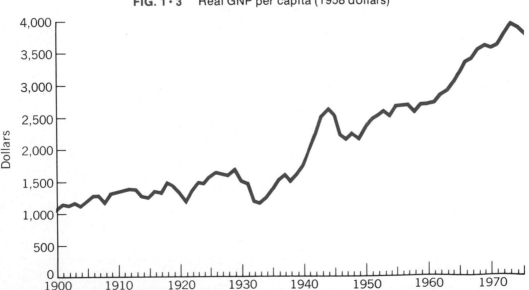

FIG. 1·3   Real GNP per capita (1958 dollars)

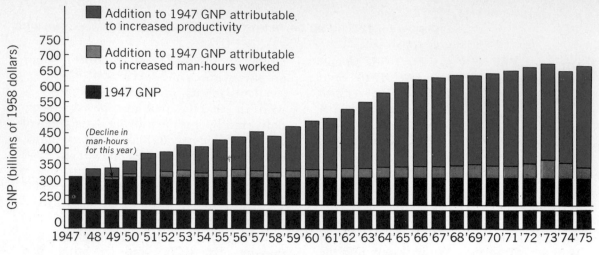

FIG. 1 · 4   Source of GNP increases, 1947–1975

lation. In 1975, when over two-thirds of
the population had finished high school,
the stock of education embodied in the
population had grown to 991 million man-
years.

The quality of capital has also
increased, along with its quantity. As an
indication of the importance of the changing quality of capital, consider the
contribution made to our output by the
availability of surfaced roads. In 1900
there were about 150,000 miles of such
roads. In 1975, there were almost 4 million
miles. That is an increase in the "quantity"
of roads of over 25 times. But that increase
does not begin to measure the difference
in the transport capability of the two road
systems, one of them gravelled, narrow,
built for traffic that averaged 10 to 20 miles
per hour; the other, concrete or asphalt,
multilane, fast-paced.

Productivity   There are still other
sources of growth,
such as shifts in occupations and
efficiencies of large-scale operation, but
the main ones are the increase in the
quantity and the quality of inputs. Of the
two, improvements in the quality of
inputs—in human skills, in improved
designs of capital equipment—have been
far more important than mere increases in
quantity. **Better skills and technology en-**

able the labor force to increase its productivity, the amount of goods and services it
can turn out in a given time. Figure 1.4
shows how this increase in productivity
has overweighed the increase in sheer
man-hours during the last 25 years.

Some Major Economic Problems

We have begun to acquaint ourselves with
the trend of growth that plays such a
central role in macroeconomics. But we
have yet to complete our first examination
of our economic photo album. For
everyone studies economics not just to
learn about the forces that move us ahead,
but to study the forces that set us off
course. Let us therefore look at the economic trend from a different perspective,
paying less heed to its forward momentum, and more attention to the problems that have disturbed it, yesterday and
today.

Inflation   There is no question
where to start. For the
last decade, the pollsters tell us, inflation
has headed the list of the public's worries.
What should we know, to begin with,
about this major issue?

FIG. 1 · 5   Inflation in perspective

Inflation in retrospect

Inflation is both a very old problem and a very new one. If we look back over history, we discover many inflationary periods. Diocletian tried (in vain) to curb a Roman inflation in the fourth century A.D. Between 1150 and 1325, the cost of living in medieval Europe rose fourfold. Between 1520 and 1650, prices doubled and quadrupled, largely as a result of gold pouring into Europe from the newly opened mines of the New World. In the years following the Civil War, the South experienced a ferocious inflation. Finally, during World War I, prices in the United States rose 100 percent.

Let us focus closer on the U.S. experience up to 1950 (Fig. 1.5). Two things should be noted about this chart. **First, major wars are regularly accompanied by inflation.** The reasons are obvious enough. War greatly increases the volume of public expenditure, but governments do not curb private spending by an equal amount through taxation. Invariably, wars are financed largely by borrowing; and the total amount of spending, public and private, rises rapidly. Meanwhile, the amount of goods available to households is cut back to make room for war production. The result is the classic description of inflation: *too much money chasing too few goods.*

Second, U.S. inflations have always been relatively short-lived in the past. Notice that prices fell during the long period 1866 to 1900, and again from 1925 to 1933. The hundred-year trend, although generally tilted upward, is marked with long valleys as well as sharp peaks.

Recent inflationary experience

Now examine Fig. 1.6, which shows the record of U.S. price changes since 1950. Once again we notice that the outbreak of war has brought price rises, albeit relatively small ones. But in a vital way, contemporary experience differs from that of the past. Peaks of inflationary rises have not been followed by long, gradual declines. Instead, inflation seems to have become a chronic element in the economic situation. Only in late 1975 did the rate of inflation begin to abate substantially, al-

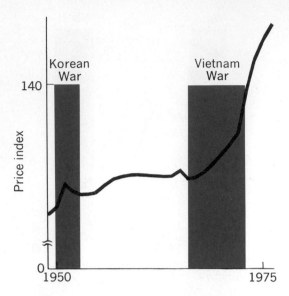

FIG. 1·6 Wholesale prices since 1950

though it did not come to a halt. The slowdown was achieved only by the application of economic policies that resulted in severe economic hardship for many.

Causes of inflation

What causes inflations? Many things. We know that we are likely to suffer from inflation if our banking system creates too much money (we will study that in Chapters 14 and 15). The trouble is, we don't know exactly how much money is "too much."

We also know that inflation always results when the spending of households and businesses and governments presses against the limits of our capacity to produce goods and services—the "money-chasing-goods" problem. Here, the trouble is that inflation sometimes begins *before* we've reached operating "capacity."

We know that price rises can be brought on by accidents of nature such as massive crop failures or by political actions such as an oil embargo. But we also know that inflation can occur without these accidents.

Finally, we know that inflation will break out if wages or other payments to factors of production are raised more rapidly than productivity, so that costs per unit of output are pushed up. But we don't know why inflation happens even when costs don't seem to be "pushing"— indeed, when wages in many areas are lagging behind the cost of living.

We will not be able to inquire more deeply into these causes of inflation until we have learned something more about the way our economy works. Yet we already know enough to enable us to follow a few general arguments about its origins.

The shift to services

One fact that we notice in all industrialized nations is the movement of an ever larger fraction of their work forces into the service industries. In the U.S., as we have seen, almost 70 percent of the labor force works in offices, shops, classrooms, municipal and state and federal buildings, producing the "services" that are ever more in demand in a highly urbanized, high-consumption society.

WAGES AND COSTS

It isn't higher wages that make prices rise, but higher wages per unit of output. Suppose a factory pays $1 million a year in wages and makes 1 million units of clothing. Wage cost *per unit* is $1. Now suppose that wages go up 25 percent *but productivity rises 50 percent.* Wage cost is now $1.25 million. Output is 1.5 million units. Wage cost per unit is $1,250,000 ÷ 1,500,000 = $0.83. *Wage costs per unit have actually fallen.*

Could this happen? Yes, if higher wages cause workers to work harder, or simply if technology has improved and boosted output.

Professor William Baumol has suggested that *this shift to services may have important inflationary implications.* Productivity in many areas of the service sector probably lags behind productivity in most industrial tasks. (We say "probably" because service productivity is often bafflingly difficult to measure.) But wages in the service sector tend to be drawn up toward the levels established in the great industrial enterprises. Thus wages in many service businesses or government agencies may rise faster than output, pushing up prices. Between 1967 and 1975, when the consumer price index rose by 61 percent, the price index of services rose by 67 percent, whereas that of manufactured goods rose by only 50 percent.

Increasing power in the marketplace

We have already noted that one of the most striking differences between modern inflations and those of the past is that in former days, inflationary peaks were followed by long deflationary periods when prices fell. Why did they fall? One reason is that it was not unusual, in the nineteenth and early twentieth centuries, for large companies to announce across-the-board wage cuts when times were bad. In addition, prices declined as a result of technological advances and as the consequence of sporadic "price wars" that would break out among industrial competitors.

Most of that seems a part of the past beyond recall. Technology continues to lower costs, but this has been offset by a "ratchet tendency" shown by wages and prices since World War II. A ratchet tendency means that prices and wages go up, but they rarely or never come down. This characteristic is probably due to the increasing presence of concentrated big industry, to stronger trade unions, and to a business climate in which wage cuts and price wars are no longer regarded as legitimate economic policies. These changes have undoubtedly added to our inflationary propensities.

Expansionist influence of governments

A third change, equally visible throughout the Western world and Japan, *is the much larger role played by the public sector in generating demand.* This does not mean that government spending by itself is inherently inflationary. As we will learn, *any* kind of spending can send prices up, once we reach an area of reasonably full employment. Rather, the presence of large government sectors and the knowledge that governments are dedicated to policies of economic growth help bring about inflation by influencing *private* expenditures in an inflation-producing way.

In the old days, when governments were minor contributors to GNP, and when large-scale government policies against recession were unknown, the public expected bad times as well as good and behaved accordingly. At the first sign of an economic storm, sails were furled. Businesses cut back on expansion programs; people meekly accepted wage cuts; consumers gave up "luxuries." As a consequence, private spending of all kinds dwindled, lessening the pressure on prices.

That has also changed. **Corporations, labor leaders, and the public now expect governments to prevent recessions.** Accordingly, they no longer trim their sails at the first sight of trouble on the horizon. The willingness to maintain private spending serves to set a floor under the economy, adding to the ratchet-like movement of incomes and prices.

Effects of affluence

A last suggestion is closely related to the previous ones. *The staying power of labor is now vastly strengthened compared with its prewar days.* Only a generation ago, a strike was essentially limited by the meager savings of working families or the pittance of support that unions could offer. There was no unemployment compensation, no welfare, no large union treasury. Today, strikes are backed by very substantial staying power, and both corporations and municipalities know it. Thus there is a tendency to settle for higher wages than would be granted if the employer felt that by waiting a few weeks he could enforce a better bargain.

Add to that a change that affluence makes in the expectations of the public. Strikes of teachers, transportation workers, sanitation workers, and others who were formerly resigned to low wages have added impetus to the inflationary surge of industrial nations. A policeman in New York City in 1920 did not think that he had a "right" to earn as much as a worker in the Ford plant in Detroit. A policeman today sees no reason why he should not. **In an affluent society, where personal aspirations are encouraged and the constraints of poverty are lessened, the established "pecking order" of an old-fashioned society gives way to a free-for-all, in which each group tries to exploit its economic strength to the hilt.** This may be good for the group concerned and may lead to a more equitable distribution of income, but it also lends its momentum to the forces that push our society toward a seemingly unstoppable inflation.

A last word

It is clear that the causes of inflation are many and deep-seated. Inflation is not an economic tendency that we are likely to be able to reverse or even to control with mild

policies. Most economists today expect a chronic, endemic inflation at annual rates of between 3 to 8 percent a year as the "price" of running a reasonably fast-moving, reasonably fully-employed economy. Later, in Chapter 16 we will explore some of the possibilities for slowing inflation, but it is a bitter truth that no one today expects to see the process come to a halt.

Unemployment

Ask American citizens what is their *second* most worrisome economic problem, and you will likely get agreement that it is unemployment. Unlike inflation, however, unemployment has not been high on the public's complaints for ten years. This is because large-scale unemployment is a fairly recent problem, the consequence of the economic recession of 1973–1975.

Recessions and unemployment

Because unemployment and recession are so closely linked, we had better begin by asking: what is a recession? The answer is very simple. **A recession is a drop in the gross national product that lasts for at least 6 months.** The word *depression* is used to refer to a severe drop in GNP, but there is no generally accepted definition of when a recession becomes a depression. People generally call a downturn a recession if their neighbor is unemployed, but a depression if they are unemployed.

Although recessions always bring unemployment, we can suffer from unemployment even without recession, if our growth is too slow. Each year our productivity increases by about 3 percent and our labor force by about 1 percent (on the

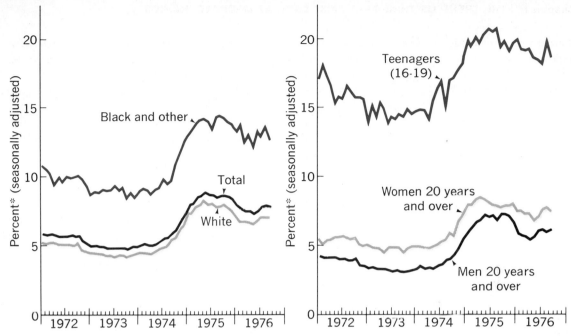

*Unemployment as percent of civilian labor force in group specified.
Source: Department of Labor

FIG. 1·7 Impact of recession on employment

average). This means that each year we have the ability to turn out about 4 percent more goods. *Unless our GNP grows by at least that rate, we will not be able to keep up with our rising productivity capacity. The consequence is that there will be unsold goods and workers who are let go or not rehired.*

Impact of recession

Let us trace exactly what happens when GNP falls or lags. The pace of business activity slows down. There is less demand for consumer goods and services, less demand for plant and equipment and other business items. Some businesses fire people, other businesses hire fewer new workers. Because our labor force is steadily growing as our population swells, even a small decrease in the willingness to take on new workers spells a sharp rise in unemployment for certain groups, such as young people.

When a recession really deepens, as in 1975, it is not just the young who cannot find work, but experienced workers find themselves thrown out of work, as Fig. 1.7 shows.

Unemployment vs. inflation

Unemployment is a problem that has to be judged differently from the way we judge inflation. Rising prices affect everyone, although some kinds of wage earners or profit-receivers gain while others lose. Unemployment, however, is a sharply focused economic ill. As we can also see from Fig. 1.7, some groups, such as teenagers or blacks, bear the brunt of unemployment much more painfully than others.

Meanwhile, within the ranks of the unemployed, suffering is also concentrated. When we state that 8 percent of the (white) labor force is unemployed, this does not mean that every

11

white worker is laid off for 8 percent of the year. It means that some workers are unemployed for long periods. In mid-1975, for example, 15 percent of all the 7.8 million jobless had been without work for over *half a year*. Many of them had exhausted all unemployment insurance and had to go on welfare. Another 15 percent of the unemployed had been without work for more than 15 weeks. Another 30 percent had experienced unemployment for more than 5 weeks.

Curing unemployment

How can unemployment be cured? That, too will have to await a fuller discussion of economics, but we can anticipate the main points.

1. To cure unemployment, we must raise GNP. Additions to GNP may come from increased consumer outlays, increased business outlays, or increased government outlays.

2. In remedying unemployment, an increase in spending may lead to a faster inflation. The issue, therefore, is to determine how much inflation the public will bear in order to eliminate excess unemployment. We have seen that unemployment affects some individuals or families much more harshly than inflation affects any family. Yet, the general feeling of the public is that inflation is a more serious economic ailment than unemployment! The reason is clear. Most people feel hurt by inflation, even if they aren't. Only a small minority of people feel the full brunt of recession.

3. Some groups will experience high unemployment, even if we have a high level of GNP. Men and women who do not

THE GREAT DEPRESSION

The Great Depression was probably the most dangerous economic episode in American life. GNP fell precipitously from $104 billion in 1929 to $56 billion in 1933. Unemployment rose from 1.5 million to 12.8 million: one person in every four in the labor force was out of work. Residential construction fell by 90 percent; nine million savings accounts were lost as banks closed their doors. Eighty-five thousand businesses failed. Wages fell to 5 cents an hour in sawmills, 6 cents in brick and tile manufacturing, 7½ cents in general contracting. As the stock market crashed, $30 billion in financial assets vanished. By 1932 nearly one in five of all Detroit schoolchildren was officially registered as seriously undernourished.

What caused the Great Depression? To this day we do not have a wholly convincing account. In part it was the consequence of a general decline in business expansion: investment expenditures fell by 88 percent from 1929 to 1933. But underlying this collapse were a number of contributory factors. Farm incomes had been steadily falling for years. The distribution of income was worsening, with profits booming at the same time that wage income was basically unchanged. Compounding and aggravating these weaknesses in the economy was a devastating collapse in credit. Whole structures of companies, pyramided one atop the other, fell like so many houses of cards when the stock market fell. And to worsen matters still further, the monetary authorities pursued policies of "prudence" and "caution" that unwittingly weakened the economy still further.

Can another Great Depression devastate the economy? Most economists would doubt it. Most bank accounts are today insured by the Federal Deposit Insurance Corporation, so that the wholesale wiping out of household assets would not happen again. The stock market, although still subject to wide swings, is unlikely to drag households or businesses into insolvency, because stocks can no longer be bought on the thin "margins" (partial payments) characteristic of the 1930s. Most important of all, the sheer size of government expenditure today makes a total collapse almost impossible. Moreover, if a severe depression were to begin, government would pursue policies of expansion either unknown or unthinkable in those days of laissez-faire economics. We will be studying all these matters later.

have the right skills or training will not be able to fill existing jobs. Members of groups who are discriminated against or people with undesired characteristics (such as teenagers who quit jobs casually) will have trouble finding work. To cure this "structural" unemployment requires special programs. We will discuss some of them in Chapter 17.

4. A big issue for the future is how much the government should do about unemployment. Should the government become an "employer of last resort," offering guaranteed work to all who seek work? Should the government impose price controls in order to curb inflation, while spending more? We will come back to these issues many times.

Running Out of Growth

One last problem remains for our consideration. We have seen that growth has been the great central trend of American capitalism; indeed, of all capitalist systems. As we have just mentioned, a necessity to continue growth is a prime requirement if we are to maintain a

high level of employment. Now we must face the fact that growth is a destructive as well as constructive process and that sooner or later, perhaps within a generation, growth may have to taper off substantially or even come to a halt.

Exponential growth and resources

Why do we face such an unprecedented challenge? The reason is that growth of the kind that has carried forward both capitalism and industrial socialism is a process that converts the raw materials of the planet into commodities that men use for their consumption or for further production. Thus along with growth has come a steady rise in the volume of raw materials that man has extracted from the planet and an even more rapid increase in the energy he has harnessed, both for the extraction and the processing of those raw materials.

What is alarming is that the rate of use of resources rises with frightening rapidity because growth is an exponential process. Today, global industrial output is rising about 7 percent a year, thereby doubling every 10 years. If we project this rate of growth for another 50 years, the rate of use of resources would double 5 times (assuming that today's technology of industrial production is essentially unchanged). Thus 50 years hence we would need 32 times as much material input as we need today. A century hence, when output would have doubled 10 times, we would need over 1,000 times the present volume of output, and this gargantuan volume of extraction would still be relentlessly doubling.

Resource availability

Does this mean that we will run out of resources? Table 1.1 shows a 1972 estimate of the number of years that then known and estimated future resources would supply us at present growth rates.

At first glance, the figures are sobering, to say the least. Yet we must be careful before we take them at face value. Resources are not so "fixed" as the table shows, for these reserves include only those deposits of minerals that are available with today's technology. They do not include minerals that exist in levels of concentration that are not "economic"; that is, too costly to utilize with existing

Table 1·1   Global resource availability

Years of global resource availability at present growth rates (1972)		
Resource	If present resources stocks are used	If resource stocks are quintupled
Aluminum	31	55
Coal	111	150
Copper	21	48
Iron	93	173
Lead	21	64
Manganese	46	94
Natural gas	22	49
Petroleum	20	50
Silver	13	42
Tin	15	61
Tungsten	28	72

Source: Meadows, *et al.*, *The Limits to Growth* (Washington, D.C.: Potomac Associates, 1972).

techniques. But techniques change, and with them, the volume of "economic" resources. Consider the fact that taconite, the main source of iron today, was not even considered a resource in the days when the high-grade ores of the Mesabi Range provided most of our ore.

THE EXPONENTIAL FACTS OF LIFE

Exponential growth is a startling phenomenon. It is illustrated in the famous parable about the farmer who has a lily pond in which there is a single lily that doubles its size each day. After a year, the pond is completely covered. How long did it take for the pond to be *half* covered? The answer is—364 days. In the last day the doubling lily will completely fill the pond.

Exponential examples such as these must always be used with great care. Their mathematical logic does not take into account the feedback mechanisms that inhibit explosive behavior of exponential series. Long before the lily covered half the pond it would probably have used up the nutrient matter in the pond and ceased growing. Long before the horrendous projections of exponential population growth, in which human beings will stand on one another's shoulders in a few centuries, feedbacks would have slowed down or halted or reversed population trends. Exponential trends show the *potential* growth of variables, but this potential is rarely realized.

One last point. There is a convenient way of figuring how long it takes for any quantity to double, if we know its exponential growth rate. *It is to divide the growth rate into the number 70.* Thus if population is growing at 2 percent a year, it will double in 35 years (70 ÷ 2). If the growth rate rises to 3 percent, the doubling time drops to 23+ years (70 ÷ 3).

Some economic resources, such as oil, may be exhausted within a relatively short time. In general, however, resources exist in vast quantities, especially if we consider the gigantic amounts of minerals locked into the earth's crust or present in "trace amounts" in its seas. Given the technology and the energy, we could literally "mine the seas and melt the rocks" to provide ourselves with "unlimited" resources.

The technological factor

We are therefore essentially engaged in a race between technology and the exponentially rising demands for raw materials. Technology enters this race in many different ways. It may enable us to recycle existing wastes, so that we do not need to extract as much new material. It may enable us to get more usable resources from a given quantity of raw material. It may open up new modes of production that enable us to shift production techniques away from materials that are becoming scarce (and therefore expensive) to those that remain abundant and therefore cheap. It gives us new sources of energy that enable us to use materials that are now too "low-grade" for economic production.

A primary question in estimating the "limits" to growth is therefore the rate at which we will develop the appropriate technology. Unfortunately, the link between research and development and economically usable technology is not clearly understood. We do not really know whether we will find an appropriate technology to run a vast private automobile fleet in the year 2000 or whether we will be able to turn out enough high quality steel to support global industrialization 50 years hence. More important, we do not know if a technology that permitted us to "mine the seas and melt the rocks" will be perfected or whether such a technology would be compatible with other ecological and environmental considerations.

The heat problem

Mention of the environment opens a last problem of great importance. To extract resources on the scale required to sustain industrial growth on its present path will require the application of tremendous amounts of energy. Production of this energy, if it uses the combustion of conventional fuels or nuclear power (including fusion power) is associated with the generation of heat. This man-made heat may be our most serious long-run environmental barrier. A number of scientists have expressed concern that the massing of industrial processes is already capable of throwing off so much heat that it can alter the climate patterns of the world in disastrous ways. They fear that at today's growth rates, the continued exponential generation of man-made heat would, in a matter of about a century, approach the danger zone. Man-made heat would then be generated in such quantities that it would begin to warm up the atmosphere—a process that would be fatal if allowed to go on unchecked for another century or so.

Doomsday?

Projections such as these can give rise to Doomsday attitudes, beliefs that we are racing hell-bent on an unalterable disaster course. This is not what economists who are concerned about the growth problem have in mind. A terrible resource shortage or a climatic disaster is possible, but by no means inevitable. Sources of energy such as solar power generators or wind machines can utilize the existing heat and

ZERO GROWTH?

The long-term outlook for industrial societies implies that very low or zero industrial growth lies ahead. But here it is very important to recognize that even zero industrial growth in itself is not an answer to all problems. *A zero growth society may still pollute the atmosphere.* It may still be adding unacceptable amounts of heat or other harmful wastes, even though the flow of those pollutants into the air is not increasing over time. Zero industrial growth is not an end in itself,

any more than positive growth was an acceptable end in itself. Zero growth is useful only insofar as it leads to *zero pollution,* including heat pollution.

From this, another conclusion follows. A society may still enjoy a growth in output if that output does not contribute to pollution. A society that draws its power from the wind and tides and sun can safely enlarge its volume of energy. A society that increases its technical efficiency, perhaps by recycling, can permit growth to occur if that growth will not be ecologically harmful. A society that seeks to grow through the enrichment of the *quality* of output need not impinge on the constraints of ecological safety.

energy in the atmosphere to provide us with substantial amounts of power that do not pour man-made heat into the air. Moreover, if we begin to encroach seriously on our resource base, we can expect resource prices to rise, thereby providing an incentive to conserve raw materials. Further, a shift toward "safer" consumption, such as human services, opens an avenue for nonpolluting, nonresource-using growth.

For all these and still other reasons, a Doomsday attitude is not warranted. The frightening picture of a world running out of resources or fatally overloading its environment is a projection of what would happen if growth continued at its present rate, unabated and uncontrolled, but the very dangers we have cited make such a fatally self-destructive course highly improbable.

That is not, however, an end to our analysis. The worry about growth is not that it will lead the world into a catastrophe. It is simply that our present kind of industrial growth must slow down. We cannot yet give a very clear timetable for when it must slow down or by how much or in exactly what industries and fields, but few would deny that safe industrial expansion will be more and more difficult to achieve in the coming decades. Significantly, a number of industrial countries have already officially adopted growth policies that are less than the maximum possible rate.

Global inequality

Two problems must be squarely faced if we contemplate the consequences of limiting growth. The first problem has to do with the unequal distribution of income (and resources) among the nations of the world. Standards of living in underdeveloped nations today are far below even the poorest levels in advanced countries. Thus the prospect of an enforced slowdown in the rate of industrial output raises the specter of *an international struggle for resources* as the poor countries attempt to build modern industrial structures and as developed nations continue along their present course.

The question of an impending slowdown for industrial growth therefore poses a major economic problem for international relations. How are the remaining easily available resources of the world to be shared? As the advanced nations continue to build up their industrial systems, will they leave the underdeveloped regions on a permanently lower level of well-being? Will the poorer countries, many of which already have (or will have) The Bomb, acquiesce in such a two-class world?

Stationary capitalism?

Second, we must ask whether a very low rate of industrial growth is compatible with capitalism.

Economists from Adam Smith through Karl Marx down to the present day have pointed out that such a "stationary state" would pose very great difficulties for a capitalist system. As we have seen, even a slowing of growth can set into motion a downward spiral of incomes and employment. A permanent slowdown might plunge capitalism into severe depression.

Moreover, the end of growth would mean that the struggle among various social groups for higher incomes for themselves would take place in a fixed or even shrinking economic system. There would no longer be more available for all. One group's gain could only come at another's loss. Whether capitalism can make that adjustment—or whether industrial socialism can make it better—are questions that our analysis raises but cannot answer.

A spaceship economy

What is certain, is that *all* industrial systems, socialist as well as capitalist, will eventually have to change their attitudes toward growth. In the long run there is no alternative to viewing the earth itself as a spaceship (in economist Kenneth Boulding's phrase) to whose ultimately finite carrying capacity its passengers must adjust their ways. From this point of view, production itself suddenly appears as a "throughput," beginning with the raw material of the environment and ending with the converted material of the production process, which is returned to the environment by way of emissions, residuals, and so on. In managing this throughput, the task of producers is not to maximize "growth," but to do as little damage to the environment as possible during the inescapable process of transformation by which man lives. If growth enters man's calculations in this period of rationally controlled production, it can be only insofar as he can extract more and more "utility" from less and less material input; that is, as he learns to economize on the use of the environment by recycling his wastes and by avoiding the disturbance of delicate ecological systems.

Such a spaceship economy is still some distance off, although by no means so far away that our children or grandchildren may not encounter its problems. Much depends on the rate at which the Third World grows in population and productivity and on the technological means of lessening pollution in the advanced countries. Not least, a true spaceship earth would require a feeling of international amity sufficiently great so that the industrialized peoples of the world would willingly acquiesce in global production ceilings that penalized them much more severely than their poorer sister nations.

These longer perspectives begin to make us aware of the complexity of the problem of growth. Growth is desperately needed by a world that is, in most nations, still desperately poor. Yet, growth is already beginning to threaten a world that is running out of "environment." If growth inevitably brings environmental danger, we shall be faced with a cruel choice indeed. Today we have only begun to recognize the problems of pollution-generating growth, and we are engaged in devising remedies for these problems on a national basis. Ahead lies the much more formidable problem of a world in which growth may encounter ecological barriers on a worldwide scale, bringing the need for new political and economic arrangements for which we have no precedent. The true Age of Spaceship Earth is still some distance in the future, but for the first time the passengers on the craft are aware of its limitations.

FOCUS

This is a first of a series of chapter endings, where we try to sum up the main ideas of the chapter as a guide for your study. We don't attempt to cover every issue in these reviews, but rather—as the name Focus suggests—to remind you of core problems on which you should concentrate your attention. Following these ideas, you will find a short list of Words and Concepts. This is a somewhat more detailed review of the items of new vocabulary and ideas that you should also know. It's wise to see if you can murmur to yourself a good short definition of these terms. If not, look them up on the indicated pages. Last, there are questions to be thought about or worked out. Don't skip them. They are a great help in mastering the subject.

In this first chapter there are two big things to learn. The first is the central importance of economic growth as a main theme of macroeconomics. This introduces you to gross national product (GNP) as the measure of growth, and to changes in the quantity and quality of land, labor, and capital as the main sources of growth. Right away, productivity leaps to the fore as a major source of increased output.

Second, we focus on three major problems: inflation, unemployment, and the "limits" to growth. We shall have to wait until we know more about the economy before we can discuss these in greater detail. But perhaps you can quickly see that there is a crucial connection between inflation and unemployment—a connection that exists because policies that lessen unemployment may worsen inflation, and policies that lessen inflation may worsen unemployment. There will be much more about this as we go along. Finally, we take a look at growth as a potentially dangerous process. Here we see that technology plays a vital role, determining for us the availability of resources and the amount of pollution that growth generates. Sooner or later, growth will have to slow down, although this time may still be a few decades ahead. But the idea of Spaceship Earth cautions us against the attitude that growth is always a good thing in itself.

WORDS AND CONCEPTS YOU SHOULD KNOW

QUESTIONS

No questions this time. This is a chapter to reflect on, not so much one to "master" in terms of answers. The big questions are spelled out in the "Focus" above. Answers lie in being more questioning about our usual answers.

Capitalism

We have raised many big problems but remained silent on the biggest one of all. Surely some of you have asked whether the root problem is not the economic system itself: capitalism. Here is an effort to open a discussion on that profoundly serious but extremely elusive query.

WHAT IS CAPITALISM?

We had better begin with definitions. If we are now to ask whether America's troubles are due to capitalism, we should know what we mean by that crucial word.

It is surprisingly difficult to find a succinct definition of capitalism. All shades of opinion, however, from right to left, would agree that its essential characteristics are these:

1. The legal right to private ownership of the means of production.

Under capitalism, the productive equipment of society is owned by a minority of individuals (capitalists) who have the right to use this property for private gain.

2. The market determination of distribution.

Capitalism relies primarily on the market system, not only to allocate its resources among various uses but also to establish the levels of income (such as wages, rents, profits) of different social classes.

WHAT IS SOCIALISM?

As we might expect, socialism is something of a mirror image of capitalism. "In its primary usage," writes Paul M. Sweezy, a leading Socialist theoretician, "the term 'socialism' means a social system which is differentiated from other social systems by the character of its property relations. . . . Capitalism recognizes a relatively unrestricted right of private ownership in the means of production, while socialism denies this right and reserves such ownership to public bodies."[1]

Thus Sweezy, like most Socialists, makes the crucial distinction between capitalism and socialism the question of *property ownership*—to which most Socialists would also add that socialism, unlike capitalism, depends primarily on *planning,* rather than on the market, both for its overall allocation of resources and for its distribution of income. Underlying these differences in conceptions of property, or in market vs. planning, we can also see a profound rift between societies that are based on private ownership and those that are not.

IDEAL TYPES VS. REAL CASES

These definitions are what the sociologist Max Weber called "ideal types." They are meant to summarize and abstract out of the enormous variety of actual institutions and historical experiences those essential elements that make up a pure model of the

---

[1]Paul M. Sweezy, *Socialism* (New York: McGraw-Hill, 1948), p. 3.

institution or activity in which we are interested. The emphasis on public vs. private property, on market vs. planned distribution, or on economic individualism vs. economic community-mindedness, serves to sharpen our conception of the "irreducible" elements of capitalism and socialism that are to be discovered behind their many variations in actual history.

No sooner do we create these ideal types than we find ourselves in something of a quandary. The question arises: what practical function do these models of capitalism and socialism serve? If one asks a dedicated humanitarian Socialist if socialism is better than capitalism, he will unhesitatingly tell you that it is because he believes in the superiority of public over private ownership or prefers planning over the market or group rather than individual economic rights.

The same humanitarian Socialist, however, recoils in horror at the repressiveness of Russia and looks with approval on the humaneness of (capitalist) Denmark. How does he reconcile this contradiction? By telling you that Russia is not "really" socialist but only a grim travesty of socialism, and that Denmark is not "really" capitalist but a modified socialist version of capitalism. Yet, unquestionably, the Soviet Union has public ownership of property, a thorough-going system of planning, and group "rights." Denmark has private ownership of property, a general market determination of incomes and outputs, and a great deal of economic individualism.

The point of this disconcerting confrontation is clear. It is that the elements that all agree are decisive in defining capitalism and socialism as "ideal types" do not necessarily tell us very much about the societies that display those characteristic elements. As a matter of fact, thinking about the differences among capitalist nations—compare Sweden and the Union of South Africa—or among socialist countries—contrast Russia and China—we begin to wonder if the words *capitalism* and *socialism* mean anything at all.

CAPITALISM AND SOCIALISM AS ECONOMIC SYSTEMS

The terms *do* mean something, although, as we shall see, there are crucial areas of life to which they add little if any understanding. In other areas they add a good deal, and it is to these that we now direct our attention.

The first such area is that of economics proper. *Capitalism and socialism as ideal types identify for us a series of economic problems that we find among all members of each type.*

What are these problems? For capitalism, we have but to refer to the chapter we have just completed. Whether we look to Japan or Sweden, the Union of South Africa or the United States, we see inflation and unemployment, worries about growth.

Can we find problems common to socialism? To a certain extent our comparison is muddied by the fact that so many socialist systems are still in (or only very recently out of) a period of backwardness. Hence we do not really have "mature" socialisms to compare with mature capitalisms.

Nonetheless, there seems to be a set of common economic problems built into socialism in much the same fashion as the problems that are intrinsically part of the capitalist mechanism. As we would expect, these are problems of public ownership and planning—in particular, the problem of controlling unwieldy state bureaucracies and avoiding inefficient production and distribution directives. Indeed, one of the most brilliant Socialist economic theoreticians, the late Oskar Lange, wrote presciently in 1938: *"The real danger of socialism is that of the bureaucratization of economic life. . . ."*[2]

PROBLEMS AND SOLUTIONS

Our discussion suggests that the ideal types of "capitalism" and "socialism" *are* useful because they indicate different kinds of problems that the two systems tend to generate. Now let us ask an extremely important question that our findings pose. Granted that capitalism and socialism have common problems, *does this mean that they all find similar solutions to these problems?*

To ask the question is to answer it. Obviously, different capitalisms respond to their economic and social and political problems in very different ways, as do different socialisms. Take capitalism as an example. Two well-known Marxist critics of capitalism have written that genuine planning or resolute action to provide housing would be impossible in America because "such planning and such action . . . will never be undertaken by a government run by and for the rich, as every capitalist government is and must be."[3] They have obviously concentrated on the lack of an effective social sector in the U.S., and overlooked the planning and housing undertaken by Norway, Sweden, Denmark, New Zealand, Netherlands, and other governments presumably run by and for the rich, since they are certainly countries where private ownership of the means of production prevails.

Nor does it follow that because all capitalist systems suffer from economic instability, all will therefore have the same degree of unemployment. During the 1970s when unemployment here reached levels over 8 percent, in West Germany unemployment never rose over two percent of the labor force. In New Zealand it was considerably less than that.

This same variety of responses can be found in socialist economies. Oskar Lange's diagnosis of bureaucracy has proved true within all socialisms, but some have responded with a reliance on market socialism (Yugoslavia or pre-invasion Czechoslovakia). In others, efforts have been made to solve the problem with better computer planning (U.S.S.R.). Still others have searched for "moral incentives" (Cuba or China).

CAPITALISM ABROAD

All this has an obvious relevance to the central issue with which we began this chapter. We can see now that whereas many of the problems that beset America undoubtedly have their roots in our capitalist institutions, the fact that we often cope with them inadequately is not a matter that can be blamed solely on capitalism as such.

[2]Oskar Lange and Fred M. Taylor, *On the Economic Theory of Socialism* (New York: McGraw-Hill, 1956), p. 109.
[3]Paul Sweezy and Paul Baran, *Monopoly Capital* (New York: *Monthly Review Press,* 1966), p. 300.

Take, for example, the question of social neglect that is so dismaying an aspect of American life. If we compare the United States with Norway in terms of various indicators of social well-being, there is no doubt that we show up poorly. Infant mortality in the United States is a full 50 percent higher than it is in Norway. Norway spends a higher proportion of its GNP on education than we do, and did so even when it had a smaller GNP per capita than we have. Norway has more hospital beds per thousand population than we have. It allocates a larger proportion of its GNP to social security expenditures than does the United States. Its cities are essentially free of all slums. Poverty as a result of social neglect has been virtually eliminated in Norway. Yet, by the criteria of property ownership or the market distribution of income or the presence of economic individualism, Norway is unquestionably a "capitalist" society.

The same superior social performance can be found in other European capitalist nations. Denmark, Sweden, Netherlands, Austria, West Germany, England, and still other nations have managed to cope with, or to get rid of, many aspects of social life that plague the United States.

CAPITALISM OR AMERICAN CAPITALISM

All this has chastening, as well as encouraging, implications. It is that much of what troubles America seems to be related to factors that, however much exacerbated by our economic system, cannot be uniquely attributed to capitalism as such. The poor level of social services in America, the powerful role played by the military, the "rat-race" tempo of American big-city life, the extent of our slums, the callous treatment of criminals, the obsession with "communism," and other unlovely aspects of our social system are not predominant in many other capitalist systems.

The problem, in other words, resides as much in those elements of our society that are American as in those that are capitalist. To put it differently, the significant question for us is to understand why capitalism here has not achieved a number of possibilities realized by capitalism elsewhere. Unless we understand and correct these failures, a change of economic systems in this country might produce only an *American* socialism that would manifest many of the very failings of American capitalism.

The market mechanism

This is a chapter that some students will wish to skip. Anyone who has already mastered the ideas of supply and demand can turn directly to Chapter 3, where we begin to study the macro economy at work. Some students, however, may not yet have learned what the important words *supply and demand* mean, and they should certainly take the time to read this basic introduction to the subject. WARNING: there is much, much more to supply and demand than this chapter covers, but it should serve to explain some basic terms.

Prices and behavior

The first attribute of a market system that we must examine is how prices take the place of tradition or command to become the guide to economic behavior.

The answer lies in the fundamental principle of maximization. Through prices, individuals learn what course of action will maximize their incomes or minimize their expenditures. This means that in the word *price* we include prices of labor or capital or land prices that we call wages, profits, interest, or rent. Of course, within the category of prices we also include those ordinary prices that we pay for the

2

goods and services we consume and the materials we purchase in order to build a home or to operate a store or factory. In each case, the only way that we can tell how to maximize our receipts and minimize our costs is by "reading" the signals of price that the market gives us.*

Therefore, if we are to understand how the market works as a mechanism—that is, how it acts as a guide to the solution of the economic problem—we must first understand how the market sets prices. When we say the market, we mean the activity of buying and selling, or in more precise economic language, *demand and supply.* Let us discover how demand and supply interact to establish prices.

Demand

When you enter the market for goods and services (almost every time you walk along a shopping street), two factors determine whether or not you will actually become a buyer and not just a window-shopper. The first factor is your taste for the good. It is your taste that determines in large degree whether a good offers you pleasure or utility, and how much. The windows of shops are crammed with things you could afford to buy but which you simply do not wish to own, because they do not offer you sufficient utility. Perhaps if some of these were cheaper, you might wish to own them; but some goods you would not want even if they were free. For such goods, for which your tastes are too weak to motivate you, your demand is zero. *Thus taste determines your willingness to buy.*

*In the real world, reading prices can be very complicated, for it involves not only how much we know about the market, but how much we *think* we know about it. Here we simplify matters and assume, to begin with, that we all have perfect knowledge.

On the other hand, taste is by no means the only component of demand. Shop windows are also full of goods that you might very much like to own but cannot afford to buy. Your demand for Rolls Royces is also apt to be zero. *In other words, demand also hinges on your ability to buy—on your possession of sufficient wealth or income as well as on your taste.* If demand did not hinge on ability as well as willingness to buy, the poor, whose wants are always very large, would constitute a great source of demand.

Budgets   Note that your demand for goods depends on your willingness and ability to buy goods or services *at their going price.* From this it follows that the amounts of goods you demand will change as their prices change, just as it also follows that the amounts you will demand change as your wealth or income changes. There is no difficulty understanding why changing prices should change our ability to buy: our wealth simply stretches further or less far. **In economic language, our budget constraint is loosened when prices fall and tightened when they rise.**

Diminishing marginal utility   Why should our *willingness* to buy be related to price? People are maximizing creatures, but they do not want ever more of the *same* commodity. On the contrary, as we saw, economists take as a plausible generalization that additional increments of the same good or service, within some stated period of time, will yield smaller and smaller increments of pleasure. These increments of pleasure are called *marginal utility,* and the general tendency of marginal utility to diminish is called the *law of diminishing marginal utility.* Re-

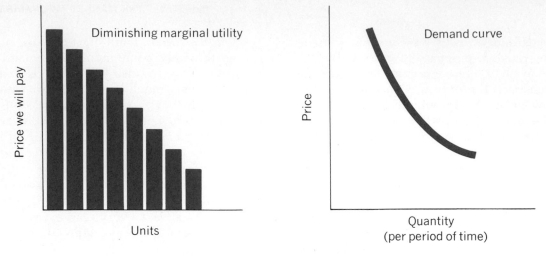

FIG. 2·1 Diminishing marginal utility and a demand curve

member: diminishing marginal utility refers strictly to behavior and not to nature. The units of goods we continue to buy are not smaller—only the pleasure associated with each additional unit.

Demand curves In the bar chart on the left of Fig. 2·1, we show the ever-smaller amounts of money we are willing to pay for additional units of some good or service, simply because each additional unit gives us less utility than its predecessor. In the graph on the right, we have drawn a *demand curve* to generalize

this basic relationship between the quantity of a good we are interested in acquiring and the price we are willing to pay for it.

Figure 2·1 deserves a careful look. Note that each *additional* unit affords us less utility, so we are not willing to pay as much for the next unit as for the one we just bought. This does not mean that the *total utility* we derive from 3 or 4 units is less than that derived from the first. Far from it. It is the *addition* to our utility from the last unit that is much lower than the *addition* of the first or second.

UTILITIES AND DEMAND

Does diminishing marginal utility really determine how much we buy? The idea seems far removed from common sense, but is it? Suppose we decide to buy a cake of fancy soap. In commonsense language, we'll do so only "if it's not too expensive." In the language of the economist this means we'll only do so *if the utilities we expect from the soap are greater than the utilities we derive from the money we have to spend to get the soap.*

If we buy one or two cakes, doesn't this demonstrate that the pleasure of the soap is greater than the pleasure of holding onto the money or spending it for something

Price of soap = marginal utility of the money it costs

else? In that case, why don't we buy a year's supply of the soap? The commonsense answer is that we don't want *that much* soap. It would be a nuisance. We wouldn't use it all for months and months, etc. *In the language of the economist, the utilities of the cakes of soap after the first few would be less than the utilities of the money they would cost.*

In the accompanying diagram we show these diminishing marginal utilities of successive cakes. The price of soap represents the utility of the money we have to spend. As you can see, if soap costs *OA*, we'll buy three cakes; no more.

The puzzle of bread and diamonds

The notion of diminishing marginal utility also clears up another puzzle of economic life. This is why we are willing to pay so little for bread, which is a necessity for life, and so much for diamonds, which are not. The answer is that we have so much bread that the marginal utility of any loaf we are thinking of buying is very little, whereas we have so few diamonds that each carat has a very high marginal utility. If we were locked inside Tiffany's over a long holiday, the prices we would pay for bread and diamonds, after a few days, would be very different from those we would have paid when we entered.

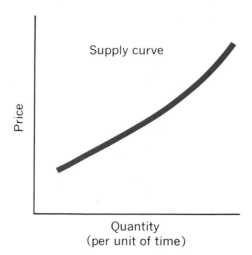

FIG. 2·2   The short-run supply curve

Supply

What about the supply side? Here, too, willingness and ability enter into the seller's actions. As we would expect, they bring about reactions different from those in the case of demand.

At high prices, sellers are much more *willing* to supply goods and services because they will take in more money. They will also be much more easily *able* to offer more goods because higher prices will enable less efficient suppliers to enter the market, or will cover the higher costs of production that may result from increasing their outputs.

Therefore, we depict supply curves as rising in the short run. These rising curves present a contrast to the falling curves of demanders: sellers eagerly respond to high prices; buyers respond negatively. Figure 2·2 shows such a typical supply curve.

Supply and demand

The idea that buyers welcome low prices and sellers welcome high prices is hardly apt to come as a surprise. What is surprising is that the meaning of words *supply* and *demand* differs from the one we ordinarily carry about in our heads. It is very important to understand that when we speak of demand as economists, we do not refer to a single purchase at a given price. **Demand in its proper economic sense refers to the various quantities of goods or services that we are willing and able to buy at different prices at a given time.** That relationship is shown by our demand curve.

The same relationship between price and quantity enters into the word *supply*. When we say *supply*, we do not mean the amount a seller puts on the market at a given price. We mean the various amounts offered at different prices. Thus our supply curves, like our demand curves, portray the relationship between willingness and ability to enter into transactions at different prices.

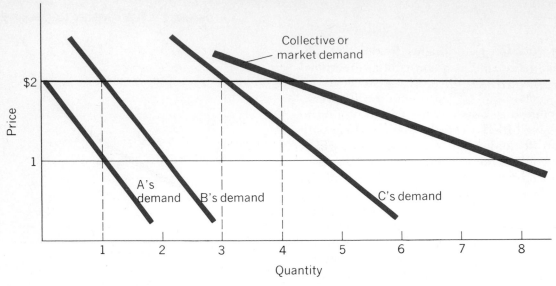

FIG. 2·3 Individual and market demand curves

Individual and collective supply and demand

We must add one last word before we investigate the market at work. Thus far we have considered only the factors that make an *individual* more willing and able to buy as prices fall or less willing and able to sell. Generally when we speak of supply and demand we refer to markets composed of *many* suppliers and demanders. That gives us an additional reason for relating

price and behavior. If we assume that most individuals have somewhat different willingnesses and abilities to buy, because their incomes and their tastes are different, or they have unequal willingnesses or abilities to sell, then we can see that *a change in price will bring into the market new buyers or sellers:* **As price falls, it will tempt or permit one person after another to buy, thereby adding to the quantity of the good that will be purchased at that price. Conversely, as prices rise, the number of**

FIG. 2·4 Individual and market supply curves

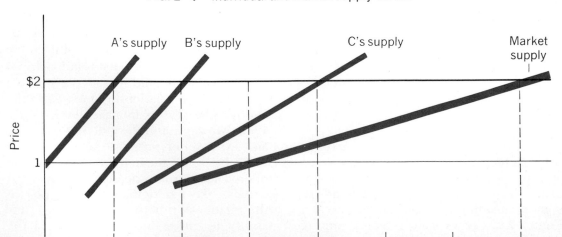

sellers drawn into the market will increase, and the quantity of goods they offer will rise accordingly.

We can see this graphically in Fig. 2 · 3. Here we show three individuals' demand curves. At the going market price of $2, A is either not willing or not able to buy any of the commodity. B is both willing and able to buy 1 unit. C buys 3 units. If we add up their demands, we get a *collective or market demand curve*. At the indicated market price of $2, the quantity demanded is 4 units. What would it be (approximately) for each buyer, and for the group, at a price of $1?

The same, of course, applies to supply. In Fig. 2 · 4 (bottom left) we show individual supply curves and a collective or market supply curve that is 7 units at $2 market supply. What would total supply be at a price of $1? What would seller A's supply be at $1?

Balancing supply and demand

We are now ready to see how the market mechanism works. Undoubtedly you have already grasped the crucial point on which the mechanism depends. *This is the opposing behavior that a change in prices brings about for buyers and sellers. Rising prices will be matched by an increase in the willingness and ability of sellers to offer goods, but in a decrease in the willingness and ability of buyers to take goods.*

It is through these opposing reactions that the market mechanism works. Let us examine the process in an imaginary market for shoes in a small city. In Table 2 · 1 we show the price-quantity relationships of buyers and of sellers: how many thousand pairs will be offered for sale or sought for purchase at a range of prices from $50 to $5. We call such an array of price-quality relationships a *schedule* of supply and demand.

Table 2 · 1   Demand and supply schedules

Price	Quantity demanded (1,000 prs.)	Quantity supplied (1,000 prs.)
$50	1	125
$45	5	90
$40	10	70
$35	20	50
$30	25	35
$25	30	30
$20	40	20
$15	50	10
$10	75	5
$ 5	100	0

As before, the schedules tell us that buyers and sellers react differently to prices. At high prices, buyers are either not willing or unable to purchase more than small quantities of shoes, whereas sellers would be only too willing and able to flood the city with them. At very low prices, the quantity of shoes demanded would be very great, but few shoe manufacturers would be willing or able to gratify buyers at such low prices.

If we now look at *both* schedules at *each* price level, we discover an interesting thing. *There is one price*—$25 in our example—*at which the quantity demanded is exactly the same as the quantity supplied.* At every other price, either one schedule or the other is larger, but at $25 the amounts in both columns are the same: 30,000 pairs of shoes. We call this balancing price the *equilibrium price.* We shall soon see that it *is* the price that emerges spontaneously in an actual market where supply and demand contend.*

---

*Of course we have made up our schedules so that the quantities demanded and supplied would be equal at $25. The price that actually brought about such a balancing of supply and demand might be some odd number such as $24.98.

Emergence of the Equilibrium Price

How do we know that an equilibrium price will be brought about by the interaction of supply and demand? The process is one of the most important in all of economics, so we should understand it very clearly.

Suppose in our example above that for some reason or other the shoe retailers put a price tag on their shoes not of $25 but of $45. What would happen? Our schedules show us that at this price shoe manufacturers will be pouring out shoes at the rate of 90,000 pairs a year, whereas customers would be buying them at the rate of only 5,000 pairs a year. Shortly, the shoe factories would be bulging with unsold merchandise. It is plain what the outcome of this situation must be. In order to realize some revenue, shoe manufacturers will begin to unload their stocks at lower prices. *They do so because this is the rational course for competitive maximizers to pursue.*

As they reduce the price, the situation will begin to improve. At $40, demand picks up from 5,000 pairs to 10,000, while at the same time the slightly lower price discourages some producers, so that output falls from 90,000 pairs to 70,000. Shoe manufacturers are still turning out more shoes than the market can absorb at the going prices, although the difference between the quantities supplied and the quantities demanded is smaller than it was before.

Let us suppose that the competitive pressure continues to reduce prices so that shoes soon sell at $30. Now a much more satisfactory state of affairs exists. Producers will be turning out 35,000 pairs of shoes. Consumers will be buying them at a rate of 25,000 a year. Still there is an imbalance. Some shoes will still be piling up, unsold, at the factory. Prices will therefore continue to fall, eventually to $25. At this point, the quantity of shoes supplied by the manufacturers—30,000 pairs—is exactly that demanded by customers. There is no longer a surplus of unsold shoes hanging over the market and acting to press prices down.

The market clears

Now let us quickly trace the interplay of supply and demand from the other direction. Suppose that prices were originally $5. Our schedules tell us that customers would be standing in line at the shoe stores, but producers would be largely shut down, unwilling or unable to make shoes at those prices. We can easily imagine that customers, many of whom would gladly pay more than $5, let it be known that they would welcome a supply of shoes at $10 or even more. They, too, are trying to maximize their utilities. If enough customers bid $10, a trickle of shoe output begins. Nevertheless, the quantity of shoes demanded at $10 far exceeds the available supply. Customers snap up the few pairs around and tell shoe stores they would gladly pay $20 a pair. Prices rise accordingly. Now we are getting closer to a balance of quantities offered and bid for. At $20 there will be a demand for 40,000 pairs of shoes, and output will have risen to 20,000 pairs. Still the pressure of unsatisfied demand raises prices further. Finally a price of $25 is tried. Now, once again, the quantities supplied and demanded are exactly in balance. There is no further pressure from unsatisfied customers to force the price up further, because at $25 no customer who can afford the going price will remain unsatisfied. The market "clears."

Characteristics of equilibrium prices

Thus we can see how the interaction of supply and demand brings about the establishment of a price at which both suppliers and demanders are willing and able to sell or buy the same quantity of goods. We can visualize the equilibrating process more easily if we now transfer our supply and demand schedules to graph paper. Figure 2·5 is the representation of the shoe market we have been dealing with.

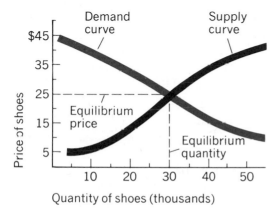

FIG. 2·5   Determination of an equilibrium price

The graph shows us at a glance the situation we have analyzed in detail. At the price of $25, the quantities demanded and supplied are equal: 30,000 pairs of shoes. The graph also shows more vividly than the schedules why this is an *equilibrium* price.

Suppose that the price were temporarily lifted above $25. If you will draw a horizontal pencil line from any point on the vertical axis above the $25 mark to represent this price, you will find that it intersects the demand curve before it reaches the supply curve. In other words, *the quantity demanded is less than the quantity supplied at any price above the equilibrium price, and the excess of the quantity supplied means that there will be a downward pressure on prices, back toward the equilibrium point.*

The situation is exactly reversed if prices should fall below the equilibrium point. Now the quantity demanded is greater than that supplied, and the pressure of buyers will push the price up to the equilibrium point.

Thus equilibrium prices have two important characteristics:

1. **They are the prices that will spontaneously establish themselves through the free play of the forces of supply and demand.**
2. **Once established, they will persist unless the forces of supply and demand themselves change.**

Equilibrium prices, emerging from the wholly unsupervised interaction of competing buyers and sellers, are now a part of our understanding. These prices, once formed, silently and efficiently perform the necessary social task of allocating goods among buyers and sellers. Yet our analysis is still too static to resemble the actual play of the marketplace, for one of the attributes of an equilibrium price, we remember, is its lasting quality, its persistence. Things are different in the real world around us, where prices are often in movement. How can we introduce this element of change into our analysis of microeconomic relations?

The answer is that the word equilibrium *does not imply changelessness. Equilibrium prices last only as long as the forces that produce them do not change. To put it differently, if we want to explain why any price changes, we must always look for changes in the forces of supply and demand that produced the price in the first place.*

Shifts in Demand and Supply

What makes supply and demand change? If we recall the definition of those words, we are asking: What might change our willingness or ability to buy or sell something at any given price? Having asked the question, it is not difficult to answer it. If our incomes rise or fall, that will clearly alter our *ability* to buy. Similarly, a change in the prices of other commodities will alter our real income and thus our ability to buy. When food goes up, we go to the movies less often. Finally, a change in tastes will change our *willingness* to buy.

On the seller's side things are a bit more complicated. If we are owners of the factors of production (labor, land, or capital), changes in incomes or tastes will also change our ability and willingness to offer these factors on the market. If we are making decisions for firms, changes in *cost* will be the main determinant.

Shifts in curves vs. shifts along curves

Thus changes in tastes or prices or in income or wealth will shift our whole demand schedule. The same changes, plus any change in costs, will shift our whole supply schedule.

Note that this is very different from a change in the quantity we buy or sell when *prices* change. In the first case, as our willingness and ability to buy or sell is increased or diminished, *the whole demand and supply schedule (or curve) shifts bodily.* In the second place, when our basic willingness and ability is unchanged, but prices change, our schedule (or curve) is unchanged, but *we move back or forth along it.*

Here are the two cases to be studied carefully in Fig. 2•6 (p. 33). Note that when our demand schedule shifts, we buy a *different amount at the same price.* If our willingness and ability to buy is enhanced, we will buy a larger amount; if they are diminished, a smaller amount. Similarly, the quantity a seller will offer will vary as his willingness and ability are altered. Thus demand and supply curves can shift about, rightward and leftward, up and down, as the economic circumstances they represent change. In reality, these schedules are continuously in change, since tastes and incomes and attitudes and technical capabilities (which affect costs and therefore sellers' actions) are also continuously in flux.

Price changes

How do changes in supply and demand affect prices? We have already seen the underlying process at work for shoes. Changes in supply or demand will alter the *quantities* that will be sought or offered on the market at a given price. An increase in demand, for instance, will raise the quantity sought. Since there are not enough goods offered to match this quantity, prices will be bid up by unsatisfied buyers to a new level. At that level, quantities offered and sought will again balance. Similarly, if supply shifts, there will be too much or too little put on the market in relation to the existing quantity of demand, and competition among sellers will push prices up or down to a new level at which quantities sought and offered again clear.

In Fig. 2•7, we show what happens to the equilibrium price in two cases: first, when demand increases (perhaps owing to a sudden craze for the good in question): second, when demand decreases (when the craze is over). Quite obviously, a rise in demand, other things being equal, will

CHANGES IN QUANTITIES
DEMANDED OR SUPPLIED vs . . . . . . CHANGES IN DEMAND OR SUPPLY

**A change in price alone changes the
QUANTITY we demand or supply**

**A change in our willingness or ability changes
our whole DEMAND SCHEDULE**

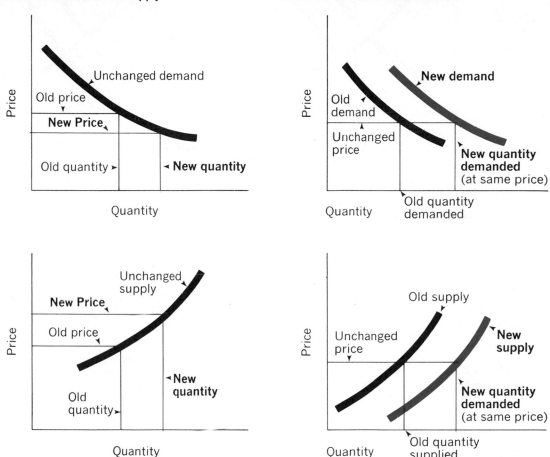

FIG. 2·6   Changes in quantities demanded or supplied
vs. changes in demand or supply

FIG. 2·7   Shifts in demand change equilibrium prices

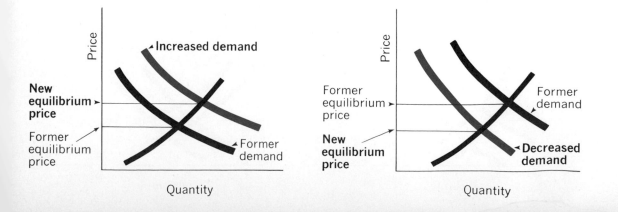

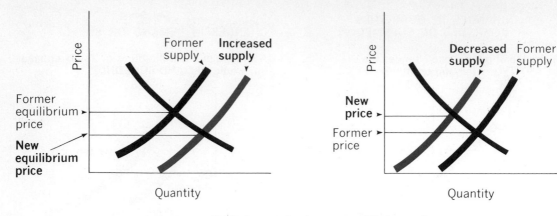

FIG. 2·8   Shifts in supply change equilibrium prices

cause prices to rise; a fall will cause them to fall.

   We can depict the same process from the supply side. In Fig. 2·8, we show the impact on price of a sudden rise in supply and the impact of a fall. Again the diagram makes clear what is intuitively obvious: an increased supply (given an unchanging demand) leads to lower prices; a decreased supply to higher prices.

   And if supply and demand *both* change? Then the result will be higher or lower prices, depending on the shapes and new positions of the two curves; that is, depending on the relative changes in the willingness and ability of both sides. Figure 2·9 shows a few possibilities, where S and D are the original supply and demand curves, and S′ and D′ the new curves.

FIG. 2·9   How shifts in both supply and demand affect prices

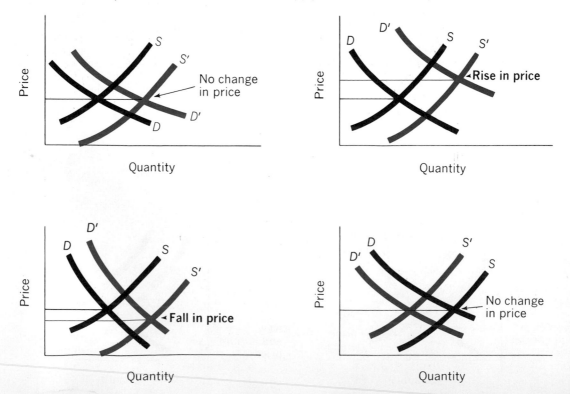

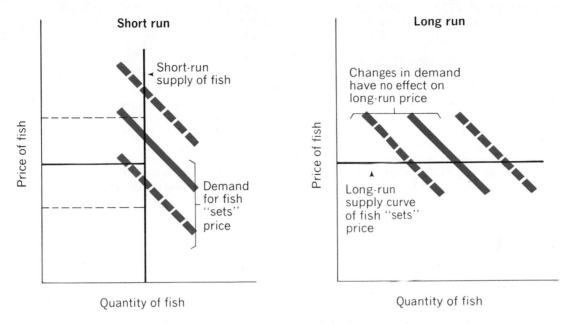

FIG. 2·10 Short- and long-run supply curves

Long and short run

There is one point we should add to conclude our discussion of supply and demand. Students often wonder which "really" sets the price—supply or demand. Alfred Marshall, the great late-nineteenth-century economist, gave the right answer: *both do,* just as both blades of a scissors do the cutting.

Yet, whereas prices are always determined by the intersection of supply and demand schedules, we can differentiate between the *short run,* when demand tends to be the more dynamic force, and the *long run,* when supply is the more important force. In Fig. 2·10 we see (on the left) short-run fixed supply, as in the instance of fishermen bringing a catch to a dock. Since the size of the catch cannot be changed, the supply curve is fixed in

place, and the demand curve is the only possible dynamic influence. Broken lines show that changes in demand alone will set the price.

Now let us shift to the long run and draw a horizontal supply curve representing the average cost of production of fish (and thus the supply price of fish) in the long run. Fluctuations in demand now have no effect on price, whereas a change in fishing costs that would raise or lower the supply curve would immediately affect the price.

In all cases, do not forget, *both* demand and supply enter into the formation of price. In the short run, as a rule, changes in demand are more likely to affect changes in prices, whereas in the long run, changes in supply are apt to be the predominant cause of changes in price.

Focus

What are you supposed to gain from this chapter? Above all, an understanding of how a market works. Here two basic questions you should be able to answer.

● What is meant by an equilibrium price?

● How do equilibrium prices change?

In answering the first question, you will have to learn to think about the relationship between the quantities we demand or supply at different prices. Here the demand and supply curve stays fixed, and only the lines indicating p's and q's will change.

The second question asks you to think about the forces that change the supply and demand curves themselves. Nothing is more important than understanding the difference between a shift *along* the supply curve or demand curve and the shift of the supply curve itself or the demand curve itself.

● Why do price changes signal different things to buyers and sellers?

● Why is it necessary to specify both willingness and ability in talking about supply and demand schedules?

● Why is marginal, not total, utility so important in determining our demand schedules?

● Why is the meaning of the word "demand" not the same as "quantity demanded"? (Ditto for "supply" and "quantity supplied.")

● Why does an equilibrium price "clear" a market?

● Why is competition a double battle—between buyers and sellers, and among buyers themselves and sellers themselves? Why do we need both battles to have a working market system?

In the end, there is also one exercise everyone should do. Insert reasonable numbers in the table for question 1, and graph them on the axes below your table.

WORDS AND CONCEPTS YOU SHOULD KNOW

Demand, 25
Total vs. marginal utility, 25
Diminishing marginal utility, 25
Demand curves, 26

Supply, 27
Equilibrium price, 29–31
Clearing the market, 30
Shifts in demand or supply curves, 32–34

QUESTIONS

1. Fill in reasonable numbers for quantities demanded and supplied and graph your answers. What is the equilibrium price of books in your example?

2. Choose some arbitrary price above equilibrium. How will maximizing behavior lead this higher price back to the equilibrium price? Be sure to describe the contest that will take place among sellers and among buyers.

3. Now go through the same exercise with a price lower than the equilibrium. Once again, trace the return of the price to equilibrium.

4. Subtract the quantities in your supply schedule from those in your demand schedule. There will be a plus or minus difference at all prices except one. Why is that? Does that help explain why equilibrium prices clear markets?

5. Why are so many necessities of life, such as salt, so cheap, since they are indispensable?

6. Whatever quantity is sold must, by definition, be bought. Then why do we not say that the market will clear at any price? (Hint: look again at question 2.)

SUPPLY AND DEMAND FOR BOOKS

Price of books	Quantity demanded	Quantity supplied
$10		
9		
8		
7		
6		
5		
4		
3		
2		
1		

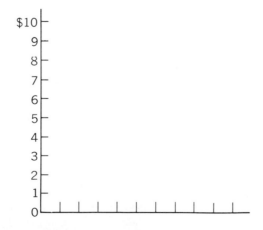

Wealth and output

We have taken a first overview of our economic system and briefly viewed problems of supply and demand. Now to start our systematic studies, to learn new words and ideas that will really open up to us the subject of macroeconomics. The place to begin is surely with the word itself. Exactly what is *macroeconomics?* The word derives from the Greek *macro* meaning "big," implying that it is concerned with bigger problems than those in microeconomics (*micro* = small). Yet microeconomics wrestles with problems as large as those of macroeconomics. The difference is really not one of scale but of approach, of original angle of incidence. *Macroeconomics begins from a viewpoint that initially draws our attention to aggregate economic phenomena and processes,* such as the growth of total output. Microeconomics begins from a vantage point that first directs our analysis to the workings of the marketplace. Both views are needed to comprehend the economy as a whole, just as it takes two different lenses to make a stereophoto jump into the round. Since we can learn only one view at a time, we now turn to the spectacle of the entire national economy as it unfolds to the macroscopic gaze.

3

The macro perspective

What does the economy look like from this perspective? The view is not unlike that from a plane. What we see first is the fundamental tableau of nature—fields and forests, lakes and seas, with their inherent riches; then the diverse artifacts of man—cities and towns, road and rail networks, factories and machines, stocks of half-completed or unsold goods; finally the human actors themselves with all their skills and talents, their energies, their social organization.

Thus our perspective shows us a vast panorama from which we single out for special attention one process that we can see taking place in every corner of the economy. This process is a vast flux of buying and selling that makes up the complex web of transactions we call the *market system*. Not all economic activity is brought into being or regulated by the market, because government plays a critical role in the economic picture. But there is no doubt that the buying activities of households and businesses are the immediate cause of much of the great flow of output we have already identified as our gross national product, or GNP.

Here is another good place to distinguish between micro and macroeconomics. In microeconomics we look directly into the motives and activities of *individual* households and *individual* businesses as they engage in the buying and selling process, and we also examine the consequences of their actions on the *kinds* of goods and services the economy produces. A macro perspective studies the market process somewhat differently. We will look into the motives of *all* households and *all* businesses as "sectors" (or groups with common motivations), and we will examine how their collective activities affect the total *volume* of output, rather than its composition.

Following the flow of output

We can start to follow this overall flow of output if we now return to our aerial view of the economy, and imagine that each and every good and service that is produced—each loaf of bread, each nut and bolt, each doctor's service, each theatrical performance, each car, ship, lathe, or bolt of cloth—can be identified in the way that a radioactive isotope allows us to follow the circulation of certain kinds of cells through the body. Then if we look down on the economic panorama, we can see the continuous combination of land, labor, and capital giving off a continuous flow of "lights" as goods and services emerge in their saleable form.

Intermediate goods

Where do these lights go? Many, as we can see, are soon extinguished. *The goods or services they represent are* intermediate goods *that have been incorporated into other products to form more fully finished items of output.* Thus from our aerial perspective we can follow a product such as cotton from the fields to the spinning mill, where its light is extinguished, for there the cotton disappears into a new product: yarn. In turn, the light of the yarn traces a path as it leaves the spinning mill by way of sale to the textile mill, there to be doused as the yarn disappears into a new good: cloth. Again, cloth leaving the textile mill lights a way to the factory where it will become part of an article of clothing.

Final goods: consumption

And what of the clothing? *Here at last we have what the economist calls a* final *good. Why "final"? Because once in the possession of its ultimate owner, the clothing passes out of the active economic flow.* As a good in the hands of a consumer, it is no longer an object on the marketplace. Its light is now extinguished permanently; or if we wish to complete our image, we can imagine it fading gradually as the clothing "disappears" into the utility of the consumer. In the case of consumer goods like food or of consumer services like recreation, the light goes out faster, for these items are "consumed" when they reach their final destination.*

We shall have a good deal to learn in later chapters about the macroeconomic behavior of consumers. What we should notice in this first view is the supreme importance of this flow of production into consumers' hands. By this vital process, the population replenishes or increases its energies and ministers to its wants and needs. If the process were halted very long, society would perish. That is why we speak of consumption as the ultimate end and aim of all economic activity.

A second final good: investment

Nevertheless, for all the importance of consumption, if we look down on the illuminated flow of output we see a surprising thing. Whereas the greater portion of the final goods and services of the economy is bought by the human agents of production for their consumption, we also find that a lesser but still considerable flow of final products is not. What happens to it?

If we follow an appropriate good, we may find out. Watch the destination of steel leaving a Pittsburgh mill. Some of it, like our cotton cloth, will become incorporated into consumers' goods, ending up as cans, automobiles, or household articles. Some will not find its way to a consumer at all. Instead, it will end up as part of a machine or an office building or a railroad track.

Now in a way, these goods are not "final," for they are used to produce still further goods or services. The machine produces output of some kind; the building produces office space, the rail track produces transportation. **Yet there is a dif-**ference between such goods, used for production, and consumer goods, like clothing. The difference is that the machine, the office building, and the track are goods that are used by business enterprises as part of their permanent productive equipment.** In terms of our image, these goods slowly lose their light-giving powers as their services pass into flows of production, but usually they are replaced with new goods before their light is totally extinguished.

That is why we call them *capital goods* or *investment goods*, distinguished from consumers' goods. *As part of our capital, they will be preserved, maintained, and renewed, perhaps indefinitely. Hence the stock of capital, like consumers, constitutes a final destination for output.*

Gross and net investment

We call the great stream of output that goes to capital gross investment. The very word *gross* suggests that it conceals a finer breakdown; and looking more closely, we can see that the flow of output going to capital does indeed serve two distinct purposes. Part of it is used to replace the capital—machines, buildings, track, or whatever—that has been used up in the process of production. Just as the human agents of production have to be replenished by a flow of consumption goods, so the material agents of production need to be maintained and renewed if their contribution to output is to remain undiminished. **We call the part of gross investment, whose purpose is to keep society's stock of capital intact, replacement investment, or simply replacement.**

Sometimes the total flow of output going to capital is not large enough to maintain the existing stock; for instance, if we allow inventories (a form of capital) to become depleted, or if we simply fail to re-

---

*In fact, of course, they are not *really* consumed but remain behind as garbage, junk, wastes, and so on. Economics used to ignore these residuals, but it does so no longer.

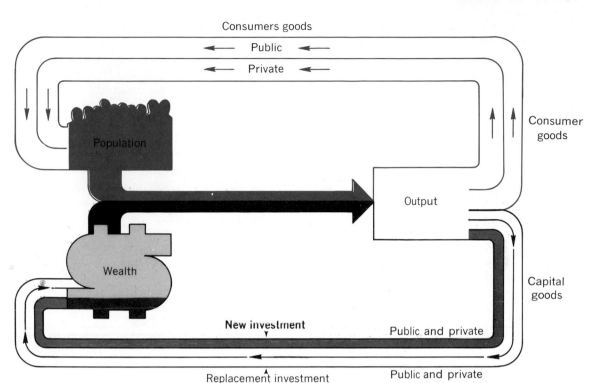

FIG. 3 · 1   The circular flow, view 1

place wornout equipment or plant. This running-down of capital, we call *disinvestment,* meaning the very opposite of investment. Instead of maintaining or building up capital, we are literally consuming it.

Not all gross investment is used for replacement purposes, however. Some of the flow may *increase* the stock of capital by adding buildings, machines, track, inventory, and so on.* If the total output consigned to capital is sufficiently great not only to make up for wear and tear but to increase the capital stock, we say there has been new or net investment, or net capital formation.

*Note carefully that increased inventory is a form of investment. Later this will receive special attention.

Consumption and investment

A simple diagram may help us picture the attributes of the flow of final output that we have been discussing. Figure 3 · 1 calls our attention to these paramount attributes of the output process:

1. The flow of output is circular, self-renewing, self-feeding. This circularity, which we have encountered before, is one of the dominant elements in the macroeconomic processes we will study.

2. Societies must make a choice between consumption and investment. At any given level of output, consumption and investment uses are rivals for the current output of society. Furthermore, we can see that so-

ciety can add to its capital only the output that it refrains from consuming. Even if it increases its output, it cannot invest the increase except by not consuming it.

3. **Both consumption and investment flows are split between public and private use.** Like consumption and investment, these are also rival uses for output. A society can devote whatever portion of output it pleases to public consumption or public investment, but only by refraining from using that portion for private consumption or investment.

4. **Output is the nation's budget constraint.** Our output is the total quantity of goods and services available for all public and private uses (unless we want to use up our past wealth). More goods and services may be desired, but if output is not large enough, they cannot be had.

Wealth

The flow of output interests us for many reasons. Perhaps we can already see that many macroproblems—the level of GNP, volume of employment, rate of growth— will depend directly on the size of the flow of total production. It must also be apparent that our standard of living as consumers will depend very largely on the size of that part of the total flow of output that goes into private or public consumption.

Not so obvious, perhaps, is the strategic role of another aspect of the overall flow: the portion of total output that goes into the creation of new capital goods. This investment flow is the main source of our stock of national wealth.

Kinds of wealth What exactly is our wealth? In Table 3·1 we show the most recent inventory

of our national wealth. Note that it consists of the value of those physical objects we noticed in our aerial overview: land, buildings, equipment, and the like. Yet a closer examination reveals some odd things.

To begin with, our wealth does not include *all* our material goods. Immense economic treasures such as the contents of the Library of Congress or the Patent Office cannot be accurately valued. Nor can works of art, nor military equipment— not any of them included in the total. Much of our public land is valued at only nominal amounts. Hence at best this is the roughest of estimates of the economic endowment at our disposal.

Table 3·1   U.S. national physical wealth 1975 value

	Billions of dollars, rounded
Structures	
Residential	$ 953
Business	857
Government	745
Equipment	
Producers (machines, factories, etc.)	544
Consumers durables (autos, appliances)	497
Inventories, business	707
Monetary gold and foreign exchange	16
Land	
Farm	336
Residential & business	706
Public	243
Net foreign assets	78
Total	**5,682**

What is more important, the table omits the most important constituent of our wealth: the value of skills and knowledge in our population. If we estimate the value of those skills for 1976 they come to $8.9 trillion—more than the value

HUMAN WEALTH

Why do we not include the value of human skills in our inventory of wealth? The reason is that all our inventory consists of *property* that can be sold; that is, marketable goods. When our economy included slaves, they were part of our wealth; but in today's market system, people are not property. They can sell their labor but not themselves.

Ideally, our inventory of wealth should therefore include the "asset value" of that labor, or the human capital that gives rise to the various

tasks, skilled and unskilled, that people perform. How could we estimate that value? The method is much the same as that used to estimate the value of a machine. If a lathe produces a flow of output worth, say, $1,000 a

year, we can "capitalize" the value of that flow of output to arrive at the current value of the machine itself.

In the same way we can capitalize the flow of output of humans. The value of human output is measured by the *incomes* that the factor of production labor earns. In 1976 that stream of income was worth $890 billion. If we capitalize it at 10 percent—a rough and ready figure that is comparable to the rate at which we might capitalize many assets—the value of our human capital was therefore $8.9 trillion.

of the material equipment with which they work! For reasons that we explain in the box, "Human Wealth," we do not usually include human wealth along with physical wealth, although we shall return again and again to this strategic element of our economic system. Here we shall familiarize ourselves with the material side of our national balance sheet, leaving the human side for later.

Capital   One portion of the endowment of a nation's physical wealth has a special significance. *This is its national* capital—*the portion of its productive wealth that is* man-made *and therefore* reproducible. In Table 3 • 1 we can see that our own national capital in 1975 consisted of the sum total of all our structures, producers' equipment and consumer durables, inventories, monetary gold and foreign assets—$4,397 billion in all.

We can think of this national capital as consisting of everything of use that has been preserved out of the sum total of everything that has ever been produced from the very beginning of the economic history of the United States up to a certain date—here December 31, 1975. Some of

that capital—inventories for example— might be used up the very next day. On the other hand, inventories might also be increased. In fact, our national capital changes from date to date, as we do add to our inventories or to our stocks of equipment or structures, etc., or more rarely, as we consume them and do not replace them. At any date, our capital still represents *all the output that the nation has produced*—yesterday or a century ago—*and has not used up or destroyed.*

The reason that we identify our national capital within the larger frame of our wealth is that it is constantly changing and usually growing. Not that a nation's inheritance of natural resources is trivial. Indeed, the ability of a people to build capital depends to no small degree on the bounties or obstacles offered by its geography and geology. Think of the economic limitations imposed by desert and ice on the Bushman and the Eskimo. The point in singling out our capital is that it represents the portion of our total national endowment over which we have the most immediate control. As we shall later see, much of a nation's current economic fortune is intimately related to the rate at which it is adding to its capital wealth.

Wealth and claims

There remains to be noted one more thing before we leave the subject of wealth. *Our table of national wealth omits two items that would be the very first to be counted in an inventory of personal wealth: bank accounts and financial assets such as stocks or bonds or deeds or mortgages.* Why are these essentials of personal wealth excluded from our summary of national wealth?

The answer to this seeming paradox is that we have already counted the *things*— houses, factories, machines, etc.,—that constitute the real assets behind stocks, bonds, deeds, and the like. Indeed these certificates tell us only who *owns* the various items of our national capital. Stocks and bonds and mortgages and deeds are *claims* on assets, not those assets in themselves. The reality of General Motors is its physical plant and its going organization, not the shares of stock that organization has issued. If by some curious mischance all its shares disintegrated, General Motors would still be there. If the plants and the organization disintegrated instead, the shares would not magically constitute for us another enterprise.

So, too, with our bank accounts. The dollars we spend or hold in our accounts are part of our personal wealth only insofar as they command goods or services. The value of coin or currency as "objects" is much less than their official and legal value as money. But most of the goods over which our money exerts its claims (although not, it must be admitted, the services it also buys) are already on our balance sheet. **To count our money as part of national wealth would thus be to count a claim as it if were an asset, much as in the case of stocks and bonds.**

Why, then, do we have an item for monetary gold in our table of national wealth? The answer is that foreigners will accept gold in exchange for their own real assets (whereas they are not bound to accept our dollar bills). Therefore, monetary gold gives us a claim against *foreign* wealth* In much the same way, the item of *net foreign assets* represents the value of all real assets such as factories located abroad and owned by U.S. citizens, less the value of any real wealth located in the United States and owned by foreigners.

Real wealth vs. financial wealth

Thus *national wealth is not quite the same thing as the sum of personal wealth.* When we add up our individual wealth, we include first of all our holdings of money or stocks or bonds—all items that are excluded from our national register of wealth. The difference is that as individuals we properly consider our own wealth to be the *claims* we have against one another, whereas as a society we consider our wealth to be the stock of material *assets* we possess, and the only claims we consider are those that we may have against other societies.

National wealth is therefore a *real* phenomenon, the tangible consequence of past activity. Financial wealth, on the other hand—the form in which individuals hold their wealth—is only the way the claims of ownership are established vis-à-vis the underlying real assets of the community. The contrast between the underlying, slow-changing reality of national wealth and the overlying, sometimes fast-changing financial representation of that wealth is one of the differences between economic life viewed from the vantage

---

*Gold has, of course, a value in itself—we can use it for jewelry and dentistry. However, in the balance sheet of our national wealth, we value the gold at its formal international exchange price, rather than merely as a commodity.

point of the economist and that same life seen through the eyes of a participant in the process. We shall encounter many more such contrasts as our study proceeds.

Wealth and output

Why must we pay so much attention to national wealth? Exactly what is the connection between the wealth of nations and the well-being of their citizens?

The question is not an idle one, for the connection between wealth and well-being is not a matter of direct physical cause and effect. For example, India has the largest inventory of livestock in the world, but its contribution to Indian living standards is far less than that of our livestock wealth. Or again, our national stock of capital goods in 1933 was not significantly different from that in 1929, but one year was marked by widespread misery and the other by booming prosperity.

Clearly then, the existence of great physical wealth by itself does not guarantee—it only holds out the possibility of—a high standard of living. It is only insofar as physical wealth interacts with the working population that it exerts its enormous economic leverage, and this interaction is not a mechanical phenomenon that we can take for granted but a complex *social* process, whose motivations we must now start to explore.

FOCUS

The essential point of this chapter is to bring a macroeconomic perspective into sharp focus. We do so by beginning to examine the flow of output, a subject that will occupy us for many more chapters, and by learning something about our treasury of national wealth.

Studying the flow of output introduces us to a number of concepts and vocabulary items that we will be using regularly from now on. This is the time to learn very carefully the difference between intermediate goods and final goods. Be sure you understand why we divide all final goods into two broad categories: consumption and capital. As part of that learning process, pay attention to the ideas of gross and net investment, which will also recur frequently in the chapters to come.

Finally, In learning about the output, pay close heed to Figure 3 · 1 on page 41 and the accompanying 4 attributes of the output process. You want to understand why output is self-renewing. Notice how it replenishes the factors of production and the worn-out wealth of the economy. Make sure you see how output divides twice: once between consumption and investment; the other between public and private.

A look at our national wealth is interesting in its own right, but it is especially useful because it enables us to see how the flow of output into investment becomes part of our stock of wealth. Because we tend to think of "wealth" as consisting of money or financial assets, we take a moment to separate "real" wealth from claims. That's an important idea to grasp. And now we are ready to move into a study of how output is generated.

WORDS AND CONCEPTS YOU SHOULD KNOW

Remember that each chapter of our text is followed by a "Focus"—not a full-scale review of the chapter, but a section that will help you center your attention on main issues and set for yourself central learning objectives. Beyond these issues remains the always necessary, always tricky business of learning the new vocabulary that you encounter in each chapter, a vocabulary that you must eventually master in order to "speak economics."

That is the purpose of these Words and Concepts sections. Sometimes they repeat terms or phrases that you will already have met in the "Focus," sometimes not. All these words and ideas are important for you to know. Thus you should pause for a moment to see if you can give a clear, short definition of each term. If in doubt, look back to the page or pages indicated. Make a note opposite the items about which your memory failed you. Then in a few days look over the section again and see if you have added these words and concepts to your working knowledge.

Macroeconomics, 38
Intermediate goods, 39
Final goods, 39–40
Consumption goods, 39–40
Investment goods, 40–41
Gross investment, 40–41

Replacement, 40
Disinvestment, 41
Capital, 43
Wealth vs. claims, 44
Financial vs. real wealth, 44–45

QUESTIONS

1. Why is capital so vital a part of national wealth? Why is money not considered capital? Why are stocks and bonds not part of national wealth?

2. Explain how the "circularity" of the economic process means that the outputs of the system are returned to it as fresh inputs.

3. What is meant by net investment? How is it different from gross investment? How is investment related to wealth?

4. Why is investment considered a final rather than an intermediate good?

5. What is the physical relation between the stock of wealth and the flow of output? Is it the same as the social relationship? Can a society be "rich" yet "broke"? How do you think that can happen? (This is one of the main subjects that we will be studying. You might think about it now, even if you're not sure of the answer.)

Public vs. private goods and services

What is the right division of the national output between public and private goods and services? This question has been debated since the first economists began to study society, but it has recently been the focus of even more than the normal amount of attention. Is government too big? Do we have too many public goods and services relative to private goods and services? Too little? Here are some facts.

In the post-World War II period there has certainly been an upward trend in the share of GNP going to government. Surprisingly, President by President, the largest increase in the share of the GNP going to government occurred in the Nixon-Ford administration.

Table 3 · 2   Share of GNP originating in federal government expenditures

	Percent
Truman, 1946–1952	17.0–20.5
Eisenhower, 1952–1960	20.5–18.4
Kennedy-Johnson, 1960–1968	18.4–20.8
Nixon-Ford, 1968–1976	20.8–23.0
Carter, 1976–	23.0–

In addition to buying goods and services, government also reallocates private goods and services by taxing some individuals and giving transfer payments, such as social security, to others. Transfer payments do not require public production of goods and services, but they do represent a government intervention in the economy. The biggest growth in government expenditures has not been in public production but in transfer payments. From 1948 to 1976 these have gone from 4.1 to 10.9 percent of the GNP. Many of those who object to the size of government are not really talking about the division between the public and private output of goods and services, but about the extent to which governments should reallocate incomes among individuals.

Big government is also usually taken to mean federal government. In fact, the federal government's purchases of goods and services have grown from 6.3 percent to 7.8 percent of the GNP from 1950 to 1976, but purchases of state and local governments have grown from 6.8 percent to 13.7 percent of the GNP. The governments that have grown have in fact been little governments, at least relative to the federal government. Thus the issue is not really big government, but government in general.

The issue arises because we have no concrete way of measuring gains or losses of social welfare. We often do not know whether public or private expenditures yield more benefits. Each of us may have an opinion, but we have not agreed upon a way of deciding which opinion is correct. Lacking a better means of deciding the question, we rely on the political process. Thus public expenditures grew because, as a society, we wanted them to grow.

What economics does tell us, however, is that the correct allocation of the national output cannot be made by debating what fraction of the GNP should go to "government." The question must be decided at a more disaggregated level. Do we have too much education or too little? Do we have too many roads or too few? Too many or too few sewage treatment plants, missiles, post offices, policemen? Advocates of budget cuts often find a general agreement to cut expenditures in the abstract, but no agreement on which individual expenditures should be cut. To be more truthful, each of us believes that those expenditures which benefit *others* should be cut, but not those which benefit us. The litmus test of a serious budget cutter is to be willing to cut expenditures that he enjoys.

It is also well to remember that in many cases, public and private purchases of goods and services are not substitutes for each other; they complement each other. Private cars need public roads; private boats need public lakes; private farms use public weather forecasters; national defense exists at least in part to defend private property.

Gross national product

We have had a first view of the overall flow of national output that will play so large a role in our macroeconomic studies. Now we want to look into the flow more closely. Here we can begin by using a term that is already familiar to us from Chapter 1. **We call the dollar value of the total annual output of final goods and services in the nation its gross national product.** The gross national product (or GNP as it is usually abbreviated) is thus nothing but the dollar value of the total output of all consumption goods and of all investment goods produced in a year. We are already familiar with this general meaning, but now we must define GNP a little more precisely.

Final goods   We are interested, through the concept of GNP, in measuring the value of the *ultimate* production of the economic system; that is, the total value of all goods and services *enjoyed by its consumers or accumulated as new or replacement capital.*

Hence we do not count the intermediate goods we have already noted in our economic panorama. We do not add up the value of the cotton *and* the yarn *and* the cloth *and* the final clothing when we

4

49

compute the value of GNP. That kind of multiple counting might be very useful if we wanted certain information about our total economic activity, but it would not tell us accurately about the final value of output. When we buy a shirt, the price we pay includes the cost of the cloth to the shirtmaker. In turn, the amount the shirtmaker paid for his cloth included the cost of the yarn. In turn, again, the seller of yarn included in his price the amount he paid for raw cotton. Embodied in the price of the shirt, therefore, is the value of all the intermediate products that went into it.

Thus in figuring the value for GNP, we add only the values of all final goods, both for consumption and for investment purposes. Note as well that GNP includes only a given year's production of goods and services. Therefore sales of used car dealers, antique dealers, etc., are not included, because the value of these goods was picked up in GNP the year they were produced.

Types of final goods

In our first view of macroeconomic activity we divided the flow of output into two great streams: consumption and gross investment. Now, for purposes of a closer analysis, we must impose a few refinements on this basic scheme.

First we must pay heed to a small flow of production that has previously escaped our notice. That is the net flow of goods or services that leaves this country; that is, the total flow going abroad minus the flow that enters. This international branch of our economy will play a relatively minor role in our analysis for quite a while. We will largely ignore it until Chapter 10, then Chapters 19–21. But we must give it its proper name: *net exports*. Because these net exports are a kind of investment (they are goods we produce but do not

consume), we must now rename the great bulk of investment that remains in this country. We will henceforth call it *gross private domestic investment.*

By convention, gross private domestic investment refers only to investments in physical assets such as factories, inventories, homes. Personal expenditures on acquiring human skills, as well as expenditures for regular use, are considered *personal consumption expenditures*—the technical accounting term for *consumption.* As these accounting terms indicate, *public* consumption and investment are included in neither personal consumption expenditures nor gross private domestic investment. Here is our last flow of final output: all public buying of final goods and services is kept in a separate category called *government purchases of goods and services.*

Four streams of final output

We now have four streams of "final" output, each going to a final purchaser of economic output. **Therefore we can speak of gross national product as being the sum of personal consumption expenditure (C), gross private domestic investment (I), government purchases (G), and net exports (X), or (to abbreviate a long sentence) we can write that**

$$\text{GNP} \equiv C + I + G + X$$

This is a descriptive identity that should be remembered.

It helps, at this juncture, to look at GNP over the past decades. In Fig. 4•1 we show the long irregular upward flow of GNP from 1929 to the present, with the four component streams of expenditures visible. Later we will be talking at length about the behavior of each stream, but first we need to be introduced to the overall flow itself.

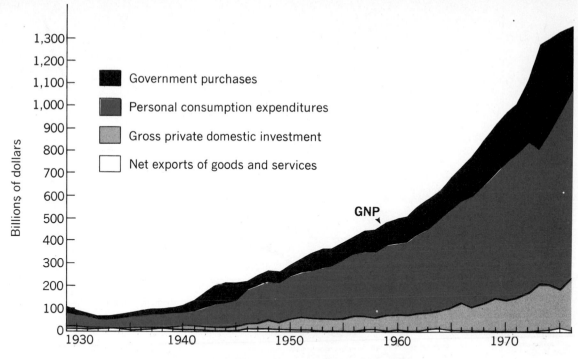

FIG. 4 · 1   GNP and components, 1929–1976

Stocks and flows   One final point should be made about our basic identity. All through our discussion of GNP we have talked about *flows* of output. We do so to distinguish GNP, a "flow concept," from wealth or capital (or any asset) that is a *stock,* or a sum of wealth that exists at any given time.

A moment's reflection may make the distinction clear. When we speak of a stock of business capital or of land or structures, we mean a sum of wealth that we could actually inspect on a given date. GNP, however, does not "exist" in quite the same way. If our gross national product for a year is, say $1.5 trillion, this does not mean that on any day of that year we could actually discover this much value of goods and services. Rather, GNP tells us the rate, for that year, at which production was carried out; so that if the year's flow of output had been collected in a huge reservoir without being consumed, at the end of the year the volume in the reservoir would

indeed have totaled $1.5 trillion. GNP is, however, constantly being consumed as well as produced. Hence the $1.5 trillion figure refers to the value of the *flow of production over the year* and should not be pictured as constituting a given sum of output existing at any moment in time.

GNP as a Measure

GNP is an indispensable concept in dealing with the performance of our economy, but it is well to understand the weaknesses as well as the strengths of this most important single economic indicator.

1. **GNP deals in dollar values, not in physical units.**

That is, it does not tell us how many goods and services were produced; only what their sales value was. As we know from Chapter 1, trouble then arises when we

51

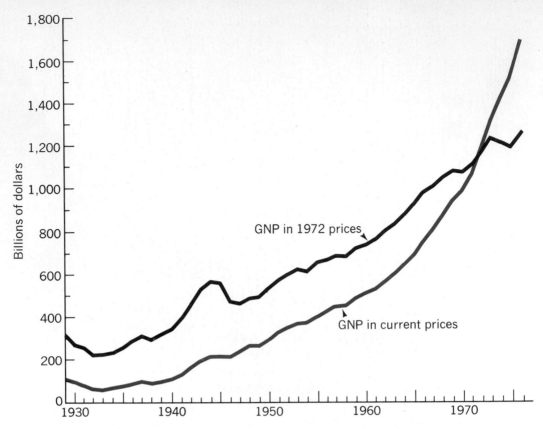

FIG. 4·2 GNP in constant and current prices, 1929–1976

compare the GNP of one year with that of another, to determine whether or not the nation is better off. If prices in the second year are higher, GNP will appear higher, even though the actual volume of output is unchanged or even lower!

We could correct for this price change very easily if all prices moved in the same degree or proportion. Then it would be easy to speak of "real" GNP—that is, the current money value of GNP adjusted for price changes—as reflecting the actual rise or fall of output. The price problem becomes more difficult, however, when prices change in different degrees or even in different directions, as they often do. Then a comparison of "real" GNP from one year to the next, and especially over a long span of years, is unavoidably arbitrary to some extent.

Figure 4·2 shows us the previous

totals for GNP corrected as best we can for price changes. In this chart, 1972 is used as the "base," and the GNP's of other years use 1972 prices, so that the price changes are eliminated to the greatest possible extent. One can, of course, choose any year for a base. Choosing a different year would alter the basic dollar measuring rod, but it would not change the profile of "real" year-to-year changes.

2. Changes in the quality of output may not be accurately reflected in GNP.

The second weakness of GNP also involves its inaccuracy as an indicator of "real" trends over time. The difficulty revolves around changes in the utility of goods and services. In a technologically advancing society, goods are usually improved from one decade to the next, or even more rapidly, and new goods are

52

constantly being introduced. In an urbanizing, increasingly high-density society, the utility of other goods may be lessened over time. An airplane trip today, for example, is certainly highly preferable to one taken 20 or 30 years ago; a subway ride is not. Television sets did not even exist 40 years ago.

Government statisticians attempt to correct for changes in the quality of goods and services. Committees composed of government statisticians and industry representatives meet to decide on the extent to which price increases represent quality improvements. It is very difficult to determine whether these committees over- or under-adjust for quality improvements. In the 1950s these committees counted the cost of putting "fins" on cars as a quality improvement rather than as a price increase. The fins did not affect the performance of the car, but they were thought to improve its beauty.

Completely new goods, such as the picture phones that have been demonstrated in some part of the country, present an even more difficult problem. Clearly, a picture phone is not an ordinary telephone. Yet, how much of a quality improvement is it? Since there is no satisfactory answer to this question, picture phones will be valued at their selling price in any given year. If picture phones fall in price as they are introduced into the mass market, an evaluation of GNP in 1980 prices will give a much higher "weight" to picture phones than an evaluation of GNP in 1990 prices. This is a prime reason why base years and deflating formulas are periodically reconsidered.

REAL AND CURRENT GNP

It's worth a moment to review the ideas on p. 38.

How do we arrive at a figure for "real" GNP? *The answer is that we "correct" the value of GNP (or any other magnitude measured in dollars) for the price changes that affect the value of our dollars but not the real quantities of goods and services our dollars buy.*

We make this correction by applying a *price index.* Such an index is a series of numbers showing the variation in prices, year to year, from a starting or *base year* for which the price level is set at 100. Thus if prices go up 5 percent a year, a price index starting in year one will read 105 for year two, 110.25+ for year three (105 × 1.05), 115.8 for year four, and so on.

In correcting GNP we use a very complex price index called a GNP *price deflator.* This index, constructed by the Department of Commerce, allows for the fact that different parts of GNP, such as consumers goods and investment goods may change in price at different rates. The present price deflator uses GNP price levels in 1972 as a "base." In 1975, the value of the deflator was 126.37. That is, the price index was up 26% from 1972.

Now let us work out an actual example. *To arrive at a corrected GNP, we divide the current GNP by the deflator and then multiply by 100.* For example, GNP in current figures was $1,171 billion for 1972; $1,306 billion for 1973; $1,413 billion for 1974; and $1,499 billion for 1975. The deflators for those years were 100, 106, 116, and 127. Here are the results:

$$\frac{\$1171}{100} = \$11.71 \times 100 = \$1,171 \text{ billion}$$

$$\frac{\$1306}{106} = \$12.32 \times 100 = \$1,232 \text{ billion}$$

$$\frac{\$1413}{116} = \$12.18 \times 100 = \$1,218 \text{ billion}$$

$$\frac{\$1499}{127} = \$1180 \times 100 = 1,180 \text{ billion}$$

Thus the "real value" of GNP in 1974 was $1218 billion, *in terms of 1972 prices,* rather than the $1413 billion of its current value. Two things should be noted in this process of correction. First, the "real value" of any series will differ, depending on the base year that is chosen. For instance, if we started a series in 1975, the "real value" of GNP for that year would be $1,413, the same as its money value.

Second, the process of constructing a GNP deflator is enormously difficult. In fact there is no single "accurate" way of constructing an index that will reflect all the variations of prices of the goods within GNP. To put it differently, we construct different kinds of indexes, with different "weights" for different sectors, and these will give us differing results. The point then is to be cautious in using corrected figures. Be sure you know what the base year is. And remember that complex indexes, such as the GNP deflator, are only approximations of a change that defies wholly accurate measurement.*

3. GNP does not reflect the purpose of production.

A third difficulty with GNP lies in its blindness to the ultimate use of production. If in one year GNP rises by a billion dollars, owing to an increase in expenditure on education, and in another year it rises by the same amount because of a rise in cigarette production, the figures in each case show the same amount of "growth" of GNP. Even output that turns out to be wide of the mark or totally wasteful—such as the famous Edsel car that no one wanted or military weapons that are obsolete from the moment they appear—all are counted as part of GNP.

The problem of environmental deterioration adds another difficulty. Some types of GNP growth directly contribute to pollution—cars, paper or steel production, for example. Other types of GNP growth are necessary to stop pollution—sewage disposal plants or the production of a clean internal combustion engine. Still other types of GNP have little direct impact on the environment. Most personal services fall into this category.

As we know from Chapter 1, growth is not a process without its dangers, and nobody would count all kinds of output as being equally compatible with safe, long-term growth. But the sheer measure of GNP tells us nothing with respect to such a problem. For example, our conventional measure of GNP makes no allowances for the harmful goods and services that are often generated by production. Actually, all forms of pollution and congestion diminish individual pleasure or utility and should be *subtracted* from GNP. Yet under our accounting procedures, they are included in GNP! So too, we fail to factor out of GNP those expenditures taken to repair the damage caused by other elements in the total. For instance, the cleaning bills we pay to undo damage caused by smoke from the neighborhood factory become part of GNP, although cleaning our clothes does not increase our well-being. It only brings it back to what it was in the first place.

These costs of cleaning up the harmful effects of economic growth are just one of a large number of *defensive expenditures* in GNP. Defensive expenditures are designed to prevent bad things from happening or to offset the impacts of adverse circumstances, rather than to cause good things to happen. In addition to environmental expenditures, other major examples include military and police expenditures, flood control, repair bills, many medical outlays. These outlays are not desired in their own right; they are simply forced on us by man-made circumstances.

4. GNP does not include most goods and services that are not for sale.

Presumably GNP tells us how large our final output is. Yet it does not include one of the most useful kinds of work and chief sources of consumer pleasure—the labor of women in maintaining their households. Yet, curiously, if this labor were paid for—that is, if we engaged cooks and maids and babysitters instead of depending on wives for these services, GNP *would* include their services as final output, since they would be purchased on the market. The labor of wives being unpaid, it is excluded from GNP.

The difficulty here is that we are constantly moving toward purchasing "outside" services in place of home services. Laundries, bakeries, restaurants, etc., all perform work that used to be performed at home. Thus the process of *monetizing* activity gives an upward trend to GNP statistics that is not fully mirrored in actual output.

A related problem is that some parts of GNP are paid for by some members of the population and not by others. Rent, for

IMPUTED INCOMES

Imputed rents are calculated by determining the rent a homeowner would have to pay for the home he or she occupies. This hypothetical rent is added into the GNP to maintain consistency in the treatment of the nation's housing stock. The produce grown in personal vegetable gardens is handled in a similar fashion.

Given the precedent of imputed rents, why haven't government statisticians imputed the value of homemakers' services into GNP?

Actually, the Social Security Administration has tried to estimate the market value of the services of women who keep house. The calculation is far from simple, for two reasons. First, the amount of housework varies greatly as children appear or as families get older and acquire more appliances. Second, it is very hard to know what dollar value to put on a housewife's services as cook, babysitter, laundress, etc.

And then imputing values to housewives' services opens a Pandora's box for men. What about *their* unpaid labor as carpenters, plumbers, bartenders, etc.?

For all these reasons, government statisticians have shied away from trying to impute unpaid household labor as part of GNP. The consequences of this omission are not small. If we evaluated the labor of full-time housewives at the same rate of pay as full-time female workers, the value of GNP would be raised by about 18 percent.

example, measures the services of landlords for homeowners and is therefore included in GNP, but what of the homeowner who pays no rent? Similarly, what of the family that grows part of its food at home and therefore does not pay for it? In order to include such items of "free" consumption into GNP, the statisticians of the Commerce Department add an "imputed" value figure to include goods and services like these not tallied on a cash register.

5. GNP does not consider the value of leisure.

Leisure time, enjoyable in its own right, is also *necessary* in order to consume material goods and services. A boat without the time to use it is of little consumption value. Over the years, individual enjoyment and national well-being go up because each person has more leisure time, *but leisure time does not show up in GNP.*

Leisure time has not been integrated into measured GNP, since economists have not managed to find either a good technique for measuring its extent or for placing a value upon it. What should be subtracted from the 24-hour day to indicate hours of leisure?

If you were asked to divide your own day into the hours that give pleasure

(utility) and the hours that give you pain (disutility), how would you divide your day? Most of us would find many ambiguous hours that we could not really categorize one way or another. If you cannot do it yourself, economists cannot do it for you.

Consequently, GNP suffers as a realistic measure of our changing true standard of living.

6. GNP does not indicate anything about the distribution of goods and services among the population.

Societies differ widely in how they allocate their production of purchasable goods and services among their populations. A pure egalitarian society might allocate everyone the same quantity of goods and services. Many societies establish minimum consumption standards for individuals and families. Few deliberately decide to let someone starve if they have the economic resources to prevent such a possibility. *Yet to know a nation's GNP, or even to know its average (per capita) GNP, is to know nothing about how broadly or how narrowly this output is shared. A wealthy country can be composed mainly of poor families. A poor country can have many wealthy families.**

GNP and economic welfare

These problems lead economists to treat GNP in a skeptical and gingerly manner, particularly insofar as its "welfare" considerations are concerned. Kenneth Boulding has suggested that we relabel the monster *Gross National Cost* to disabuse ourselves once and for all of the notion that a bigger GNP is necessarily a better one. Paul Samuelson suggests a new measure—Net Economic Welfare, or NEW—to supplement GNP, the difference being mostly the maintenance or defensive or negative outputs we have mentioned. Economists Tobin and Nordhaus propose MEW—Measure of Economic Welfare—for much the same purposes, subtracting the outputs that contribute nothing to the sum of individuals' utilities and adding back other sums, mainly housewives' services, that are conventionally omitted. (We might note in passing that MEW, as calculated by Tobin and Nordhaus, grows much less rapidly per capita than does GNP. From 1929 to 1965, real per capita GNP mounted at 1.7 percent per year; MEW, at 1.1 percent.)

All these doubts and reservations should instill in us a permanent caution against using GNP as if it were a clear-cut measure of social contentment or happiness. Economist Edward Denison once remarked that perhaps nothing affects national economic welfare so much as the weather, which certainly does not get into the GNP accounts. Hence, because the U.S. may have a GNP per capita that is higher than that of say, Denmark, it does not mean that life is better here. It may be worse. In fact, by the indices of health care or quality of environment, it probably *is* worse.

Yet, with all its shortcomings, GNP is still the simplest way we possess of summarizing the overall level of market activity of the economy. If we want to summarize its welfare, we had better turn to specific social indicators of how long we live, how healthy we are, how cheaply we provide good medical care, how varied and abundant is our diet, etc.—none of which we can tell from GNP figures alone. But we are not always interested in welfare, partly because it is too complex to be summed up in a single measure. For better or worse, therefore, GNP has become the yardstick used by most nations in the world. Although other yardsticks are sure to become more important, GNP will be a central term in the economic lexicon for a long time to come.

FOCUS Here is a chapter that is essentially definitional. Its purpose is to introduce you, at a technical level, to the nomenclature and basic conceptual problems of gross national product.

Accordingly, that is the thing to study. What you want to understand is:

1. **Why GNP is a measure of final output (not final plus intermediate output).**
2. **The four kinds of final goods or services.**
3. **What we mean by GNP as a "flow" and by wealth as a "stock."**
4. **The main conceptual difficulties with GNP: the problem of prices, of qualities, of purpose, of nonmarketed output, of leisure, and distribution. Perhaps the best way to sum up this whole problem is to ask you to reflect carefully on why GNP may not accurately measure *welfare*.**

WORDS AND CONCEPTS YOU SHOULD KNOW

Gross national product, defined, 49
Gross private domestic investment, 50
Government purchases, 50
Net exports, 50

Stocks vs. flows, 51
Real GNP, 52–53
Imputed incomes, 54–55

QUESTIONS

1. Write the basic identity for GNP and state *carefully* the exact names of each of the four constituents of GNP.

2. Suppose we had an island economy with an output of 100 tons of grain, each ton selling for $90. If grain is the only product sold, what is the value of GNP? Now suppose that production stays the same but that prices rise to $110. What is the value of GNP now? How could we "correct" for the price rise? If we didn't, would GNP be an accurate measure of output from one year to the next?

3. Now suppose that production rose to 110 tons but that prices fell to $81. The value of GNP, in terms of current prices, has fallen from $9,000 to $8,910. Yet, actual output, measured in tons of grain, has increased. Can you devise a price index that will show the change in real GNP?

4. Presumably, the quality of most products improves over time. If their price is unchanged, does that mean that GNP understates or overstates the real value of output?

5. When more and more consumers buy do-it-yourself kits, does the value of GNP (which includes the sale price of these kits) understate or overstate the true final output of the nation?

6. What is an intermediate good, and why are such goods not included in the value of GNP? Is coal sold to a utility company an intermediate good? Coal sold to a homeowner? Coal sold to the army? What determines whether a good will or will not be counted in the total of GNP?

7. A bachelor pays a cook $100 a week. Is this part of GNP? He then marries her and gives her an allowance of $100 a week. Allowances do not count in GNP. Hence the measure of GNP falls. Does welfare fall?

8. Do you think that we should develop measures other than GNP to indicate changes in our basic well-being? What sorts of measures? After thinking about this, see the "Extra word" at the end of this chapter.

Social indicators

Many people object to the gross national product on the grounds that it focuses our attention on too narrow a band of human activity. Many of the things that improve or degrade our society are left out. Worse still, because they are left out they are ignored. These are not the previously mentioned items, such as imputed income for housewives or negative economic outputs in the form of pollution, that might be added to the GNP to make it a more comprehensive measure of economic *output*. These omissions are measurements of life expectancy, morbidity, mental illness, crime, social unrest and other areas of human activity.

The Social Indicators "movement" is an effort to expand our system of social accounts to measure progress (or the lack of progress) in these other dimensions. The GNP would not be eliminated but would be just one of a number of measurements in an expanded set of social accounts, some of them listed in Table 4 • 1.

Table 4 • 1 Some social indicators

Life expectancy at birth	71.1 years (1971)
Days of disability	24 days per year per person (1969)
Violent crimes	397.7 per 100,000 (1972)
Property crimes	2,432 per 100,000 (1972)
High school graduate rate	76.2 percent (1972)
Job satisfaction	3.44 on scale of 1 to 4 (1973)
Substandard housing units	7.4 percent (1970)

Ideally, such a wide-ranging set of social accounts would give us a better indication of the trend of general welfare than that provided by simple GNP measurements. Yet, although the federal government now issues a social report every other year, the Social Indicators movement has never had the impact that was imagined when it started in the mid1960s. There are two fundamental reasons for its weakness.

First, there are many aspects of human existence that are important to welfare but *unmeasurable.* Consider friendship. Without doubt, social relationships influence our welfare; but could we measure whether the average American has more or fewer friends, better or less helpful friends? Clearly we cannot. Unfortunately, the Social Indicators movement has been so closely linked to the idea of measurement that such problems have led to less and less political interest in the idea.

Second, there is the aggregation problem. We have seen that dollar values are used as the common denominator to aggregate different economic goods and services. What is to be the common denominator used to aggregate life expectancy, crime, and mental illness? Nothing obvious suggests itself. Although there is nothing wrong in presenting three dozen different indices of social progress, one cannot easily say, if indicators point in different directions, whether society is improving.

Lacking an aggregate measure of general welfare, social indicators have had very little impact on public opinion. A declining GNP is front-page news. General welfare may also be declining, but no one social indicator is able to show us this. The net result is that the GNP, for all its shortcomings, is not about to be eclipsed by a more general indicator of social welfare in the near future.

Supply of output

We have already stressed that macroeconomics is essentially concerned with growth. At the center of its focus is the question: How does an economy expand its output of goods and services? Or if it fails to expand them, why does growth not take place? Chapter 1 opened a discussion of the long upward trend of U.S. output and the reasons for this trend. In Chapter 3, we began to analyze this process by familiarizing ourselves with the way our stock of wealth interacts with our labor force to yield a flow of output that we call gross national product.

Now we are going to push forward by learning much more about the underlying trends and causes of growth in the American economy. That will set the stage for the work that still lies ahead, when we will narrow our focus down to the present and inquire into the reasons for the problems of our macrosystem—unemployment and inflation, booms and busts.

Historical record In Fig. 5·1 we see the American experience from the middle of the nineteenth century, in terms of real per capita GNP in 1929 prices. Viewed from the long perspective of history, our average rate of growth has been astonishingly consistent.

5

59

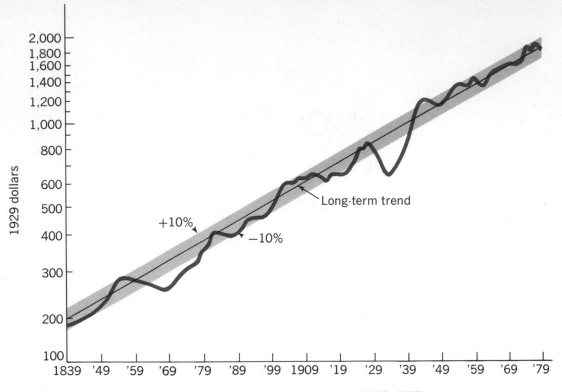

Fig. 5·1 Trend in real GNP per head, 1839–1977

This holds true for an average over the past thirty-odd years since the Great Depression or back to the 1870s (or even 1830s). As the chart shows, the swings are almost all contained within a range of 10 percent above or below the trend. The trend itself comes to about 3.5 percent a year in real terms, or a little over 1.5 percent a year per capita. Although 1.5 percent a year may not sound like much, remember that this figure allows us to double our real per capita living standards every 47 years. If we could raise the rate to 2.0 percent, real living standards could double every 35 years.

What determines our rate of growth? As with so many economic processes, we can think of growth as the outcome of a contest between two forces: an active driving force of demand and a constraining, limiting force of supply. We shall learn more about the driving force when we arrive at the study of business investment

and government expansionary policy. Here, we focus on the question of supply, equally important in determining our final growth rate. That leads to a fundamental question from the supply side: How much can an economy produce?

Production-possibility curve

If the economy produced only a single good, like wheat, the answer would be simple. Maximum output would be some number of bushels that result from the use of every available acre, every tractor, every hour of work.

Obviously, economies produce many kinds of goods. Thus we cannot answer the question in terms of a single figure, but in terms of a range of possibilities, depending on which goods we produce. It would be difficult to represent this range of possibilities in a simple graph, so we abstract the range of possible outputs to two goods,

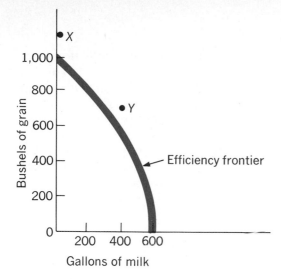

FIG. 5·2   Production-possibility curve

say grain and milk, and *we then show what combinations of outputs are possible, using all factors. We call such a schedule of alternative possibilities a production-possibility curve,* and we draw such a curve in Fig. 5 • 2.

Efficiency frontier   The production-possibility curve shows us a number of things. First it makes vivid the material meaning of the word *scarcity. Any point outside the frontier of the curve is unattainable for our community with its present resources.* If the economy uses all available inputs in the most efficient manner, it can produce 1,000 bushels of wheat or 600 gallons of milk. If it had more inputs or were more productive, it could produce more; but with its present supply of inputs and its present level of productivity, it cannot. That is why we call the boundary of the production-possibilities curve *the efficiency frontier.*

It is easy to see that point X is unattainable, but look at point Y. This is an output that represents roughly 700 bushels of grain and 400 gallons of milk. Either one of these goals, taken separately, lies well within the production possibilities of the economy. *What the curve shows us is that we cannot have both at the same time. If we want 700 bushels of grain, we must be content with less than 400 gallons of milk. If we want 400 gallons of milk, we will have to settle for about 600 bushels of grain.*

Importance of the frontiers   Such a two-commodity diagram may seem unreal, but remember that "milk" and "grain" can stand for consumption and investment (or any other choices available to an economy). In fact, with a little imagination we can construct a three-dimensional production-possibility *surface* showing the limits imposed by scarcity on a society that divides its output among three uses such as consumption, investment, and government. Figure 5 • 3 shows what such a diagram looks like.

FIG. 5·3   A production-possibility surface

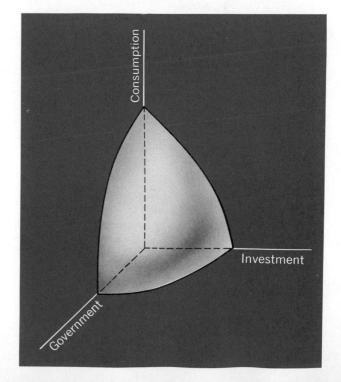

Note how the production-possibility surface swells out from the origin like a windfilled spinnaker sail. Any place on the sail represents some combination of consumption, investment, and government spending that is within the reach of the community. *Any place "behind" the efficiency frontier represents a failure of the economy to employ all its resources. It is a graphic depiction of unemployment of men or materials.*

Very few economies actually operate on their efficiency frontiers. Most economies have at least *some* unemployed inputs or are not using their inputs with all possible efficiency. Perhaps only in wartime do we reach the frontiers of our production-possibility map. Nonetheless, we can see that a major job of economic policy makers is to move the economy as close to its frontiers as possible, under normal conditions.

Law of increasing cost

One point deserves clarification before we move on. The alert student may have noticed that all the production-possibility curves have bowed shapes. The reason for this lies in the *changing efficiency* of our resources as we shift them from one use to another. This is a basic constraint we first met in Chapter 1. *We call this changing efficiency, represented by the bowed curve, the* **law of increasing costs.** *Note that it is a law imposed by nature, rather than behavior.*

What would it mean if the curve connecting the two points of all-out grain or milk production were a straight line as in Fig. 5·4 *It would mean that as we shifted resources from one use to the other, we would always get exactly the same results. The last man and the last acre put into milk would give us exactly as much milk, at the loss of exactly as much grain, as the first man and the first acre.*

Such a straight-line production-possibility curve is said to exhibit constant returns to specialization. Except perhaps in a very simple economy, where a population might choose between hunting or fishing, constant returns to specialization is an unrealistic assumption, for it implies that there is no difference from one man or acre to another, or that it made no difference as to the *proportions* in which factors, even if they were homogenous, were combined.

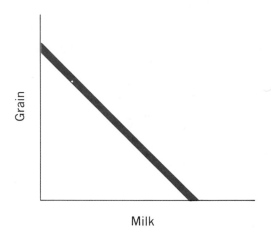

FIG. 5·4   Constant returns to specialization

That is a very unrealistic assumption. Men and land (and any other resource) *are* different. Different products *do* utilize them in different proportions. Hence, as we shift them from one use to another, assuming that we always choose the resources best suited for the job, society's efficiency changes. *At first we enjoy a very low opportunity cost in terms of what we must give up for what we get. Thereafter we pay an increasing opportunity cost.* (see box p. 63). Although the shapes of production-possibility curves may have considerably different contours, the unevenness of nature's gifts make most of them bowed, or concave from below.

The production-possibility curve gives a new meaning to *cost*. Suppose we were producing both grain and milk, as shown by the lines *OA* and *OA'*. If we move a given quantity of resources *AB* out of grain and into milk, grain production will fall by the length of the line *AB*. Milk production will rise by *A'B'*. Now imagine that we continue to concentrate on milk at the expense of grain, until we are producing only *OC* worth of grain and *OC'* worth of milk. Once again we move the *same amount* of resources from grain to milk (*CD* = *AB*). Look how much smaller is the gain in milk production: *C'D'* compared with *A'B'*.

Note that the cost of a given quantity of milk is the amount of grain we have to give up to get that milk. The cost of producing a quantity of grain is the amount of milk we would have to give up to get that much grain. **We must trade off gains in one commodity against losses in another.**

A VERY IMPORTANT LOOK AT OPPORTUNITY COST

Economists call this trade-off *opportunity* **cost. The term drills home a fundamental truth: there is no economic activity that does not have a cost.** That cost is the measure of other actions we might have taken but could not, because we were engaged in the course we chose. As the saying goes, economics teaches us that there is no such thing as a free lunch. Everything that utilizes labor or resources has a cost, whether a charge is levied or not.

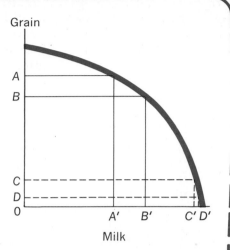

The cost is the alternative benefits that could have been enjoyed by using those resources for some other purpose. *Costs are foregone opportunities.*

Shifting frontiers outward

One last point about production-possibility curves will relate them more specifically to growth. P-p *curves are not static. Changes in factor supplies can move* *frontiers to the right.* If all factors grew at the same rate, the p-p frontier would shift evenly outward as in Fig. 5•5, panel I. If only the factors that specialized in milk production increased, it would shift as in panel II.

FIG. 5•5   Shifts in the production frontier

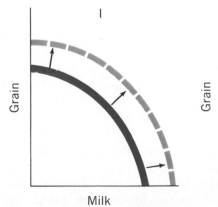

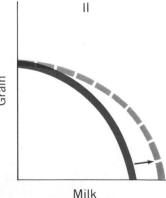

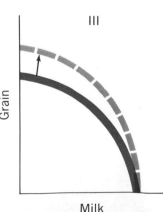

Exerting more influence, as we know, technical progress or changes in skill increase the amount of output we can derive from a given input. These changes also move the *p-p* frontier out. In panel I we enjoy a general increase in productivity that enables us to have both more grain and milk, whereas in panels II and III, productivity has increased only in one area of production, so that the maximum output available for the other good remains the same, regardless of increases in the output of the first.

Thus, changes in the quantity or quality—in sheer volume or productivity—of the factors of production is once again highlighted as the two sources of economic growth. We say "once again," for we first made the acquaintance of these two sources of growth in Chapter 1 (pp. 5–6). Now we must look into them further.

The Supply of Growth

Labor input and production   Output depends on work, and work depends on people working. Thus, the first source of growth that we study is the rise in the sheer numbers of people in the *labor force*. As we shall see, this is a more complicated matter than might at first appear.

Figure 5·6 gives us a picture of the population and the labor force over the past almost half-century. As we would expect, the size of the force has been rising because our population has been rising. One might expect that as our society grew richer and more affluent, fewer people would seek employment, but that is not the case. Looking back to 1890 or 1900, we find that only 52 out of every 100 persons over 14 sought paid work. Today about 60 out of every 100 persons of working age seek employment. Looking forward is more uncertain; but if we can extrapolate (extend) the trend of the past several decades to the year 2000, we can expect perhaps as many as 65 persons out of 100 to be in the labor market by that date.

Participation in the labor force   How can we explain this upward drift of the labor force itself? The answer is to be found in the *different labor participation trends* of different ages and different sexes. Figure 5·7 shows the different participation rates more clearly.

Thus the overall trend toward a larger participation rate for the entire population masks a number of significant trends.

1. **Young males entering the labor force are older than were those who entered in the past.**

A larger number of young men remain in high school now or go on to college. Only a third of elementary school pupils now go on to college, but the ratio is steadily growing.

2. **Older males show a dramatic withdrawal from the labor force.**

Almost 7 out of 10 older males used to work. Now only 2 to 3 work. The reason is the advent of Social Security and private pension plans. It is probable that the proportion of older males in the labor force will continue to fall as the retirement age is slowly reduced.

3. **Counterbalancing this fall in male participation is a spectacular rise in total female participation. Indeed, the overall trend toward an increasing**

search for work within the population at large is entirely the result of the mass entrance of women into the labor force.

This surge of women into the labor market reflects several changing factors in the American scene (many of these changes can be found abroad, as well). One factor is the growth of nonmanual, as contrasted with manual, jobs. Another is the widening cultural approval of working women and working wives. The average American girl who marries today in her early twenties and goes on to raise a family will nevertheless spend *25 years* of her life in paid employment after her children are grown. Yet another reason for the influx of women is that technology has released them from household work. Finally there is the pressure to raise living standards by having two incomes within the household.

FIG. 5·6   United States labor force, 1929–1975

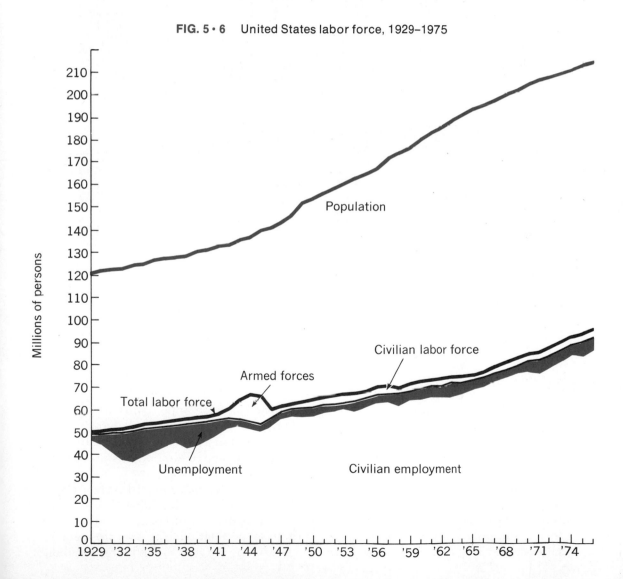

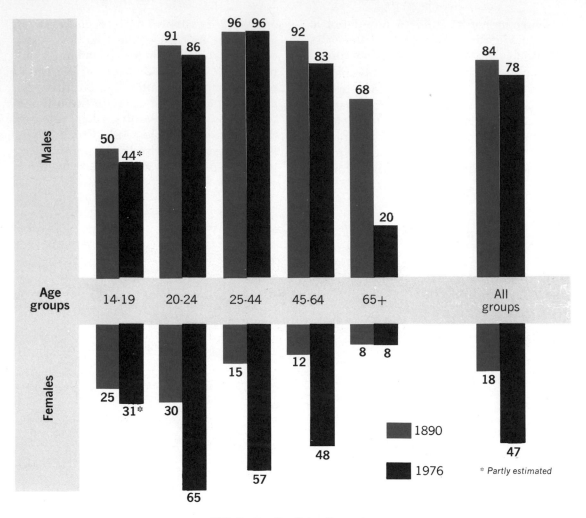

FIG. 5·7   Participation rates

Monetization of work   Actually, the upward trend of female participation does not imply an increasing amount of labor performed within society. Rather, it measures a larger amount of *paid* labor. In the 1890s, many persons worked long and hard hours on a family farm or in a family enterprise, and above all within a household, *without getting paid* and, therefore, were not counted as members of the "labor force." To a very considerable extent, the rising numbers of female participants in the labor force mirror the transfer of these unpaid jobs onto the marketplace where the same labor is now performed in an economically visible way. There is every likelihood this process will continue.

These are not, of course, the only factors that bear on the fundamental question of how many persons will seek work out of a given population. The drift from country to city, the decline in the number of hours of labor per day expected of a jobholder, the general lengthening of life, the growth of general well-being—all these changes bear on the decision to work or not. *Overall, what the complex trends seem to show is that we are moving in the direction of a society where employment absorbs a larger fraction of the life (but not of the day) of an average woman, and a diminishing fraction of the life and of the day of an average man.*

Hours of work

In addition to deciding whether to participate in the labor force, individuals decide how much labor they wish to contribute as members of the labor force. That is, they must decide how many hours of work they wish to offer during a week or how many weeks they wish to work in a year.

Had we asked this question in the days of Adam Smith, it would have been relatively simple to answer. Wages were so close to subsistence that someone in the labor force was obliged to work extremely long hours to keep body and soul together. Paid vacations were unknown to the employees of the cotton mills. Unpaid vacations would have been tantamount to starvation.

MEASURING PRODUCTIVITY

As the accompanying table shows, the average increase in productivity of 3.5 percent masks wide swings from year to year. Compare 1950, when productivity per man grew at 9.2 percent, with 1956, when it actually declined by 0.1!

There is a caution here. These sharp ups and downs do not so much reflect real variations in output per man-hour as they reflect the way in which we measure productivity. *Productivity is measured by dividing total output by total man-hours.* When recessions occur and output falls, businesses reduce their labor forces as much as possible, but they find considerable numbers of overhead workers who cannot profitably be let go simply because output is down. If General Motors' production falls by 25 percent, it does not reduce the working time of its president by 25 percent.

Hence, in recession years, a smaller output is divided by a number of man-hours that has been "kept high." The underlying normal growth in productivity of the labor force may still be occurring, but it is masked by the overhead labor that is not reduced as much as output. In booming years, just the opposite occurs. Output increases faster than employment, since the company does not need to add overhead as rapidly as output. Result: *year-to-year productivity figures must be interpreted with great care.*

	Productivity index (GNP/ man-hour)	% change in productivity per man-hour in the private economy
1947	100	
1948	103.4	3.4%
1949	105.9	2.4
1950	115.7	9.2
1951	121.0	4.6
1952	124.5	2.9
1953	130.2	4.6
1954	133.7	2.7
1955	139.5	4.3
1956	139.5	−0.1
1957	143.3	2.7
1958	146.6	2.3
1959	152.5	4.0
1960	154.2	1.1
1961	158.4	2.7
1962	166.8	5.3
1963	172.3	3.3
1964	178.7	3.7
1965	184.6	3.3
1966	193.1	4.6
1967	197.0	2.0
1968	204.9	4.0
1969	207.1	1.1
1970	206.8	1.0
1971	214.6	4.1
1972	222.2	3.8
1973	227.9	2.9
1974	221.5	−3.4
1975	222.2	2.1
1976	231.6	5.8

With the slow rise in productivity, working men and women gradually found their income rising above "subsistence," and a new possibility came into being: the possibility of deliberately working less than their physical maximum, *using part of their increased productivity to buy leisure for themselves instead of wages.* Thus, beginning in the early nineteenth century we find that labor organizations (still very small and weak) sought to shorten the workweek. In England, in 1847 a signal victory was won with the introduction of the Ten (!) Hour Day as the legal maximum for women and children. In America, in the prosperity of the 1920s, the 48-hour week finally became standard. More recently, the two-day weekend has become the general practice. Now we hear of the coming of the three-day weekend.

Thus the total supply of labor-time has not risen as fast as the labor force, because a decline in average hours has offset the rise in participation rates and population. On balance, the total supply of labor-hours has increased, but the supply of labor-hours *per employee*, male and female, has fallen.

Labor productivity   As we have seen, we can trace part of our long-term growth to increases in the total supply of man-hours of production. But this is by no means the main source of growth. Far outpacing the growth in the sheer volume of labor-time has been the increase in the amounts of goods and services that each hour of labor-time gives rise to.

Economists measure the productivity of the labor force by dividing the total output of goods by the total number of man-hours. *In Chapter 1, p. 6, we saw the wide margin by which changes in labor productivity outweigh changes in labor-time as a source of increased output.*

Over the post World War II period, the *average* increase in productivity per man-hour has been growing at about 3½ percent a year (see box). At that rate, productivity per man-hour doubles in just under 20 years. Of course, this increase varies from one sector to another. Over the last two decades it increased by 80 percent in manufacturing and *tripled* in agriculture.

Sources of Labor Productivity

What is the explanation for this tremendous and persistent increase in the ability of labor to turn out goods? Here are the most pertinent answers.

1. Growth of human capital

By human capital, as we know, we mean the skills and knowledge possessed by the labor force. Even though the measurement of "human capital" is fraught with difficulties, we cannot ignore this vital contributory element in labor productivity. Ferenc Jánossy, a Hungarian economist, has suggested a vivid imaginary experiment to highlight the importance of skills and knowledge.

Suppose, he says, that the populations of two nations of the same size could be swapped overnight. Fifty million Englishmen would awake to find themselves in, say, Nepal, and 50 million Nepalese would find themselves in England. The newly transferred Englishmen would have to contend with all the poverty and difficulties of the Nepalese economy. Newly transferred Nepalese would confront the riches of England. Yet the

Englishmen would bring with them an immense reservoir of literacy, skills, discipline, and training, whereas the Nepalese would bring with them the very low levels of "human capital" that are characteristic of underdeveloped countries. Is there any doubt, asks Jánossy, that growth rates in Nepal with its new skilled population would in all likelihood rise dramatically, and that those of England would probably fall catastrophically?

One way of indicating in very general terms the rising "amount" of human capital is to trace the additions to the stock of education that the population embodies. Table 5 · 1 shows the change in the total number of years of schooling of the U.S. population over the past three quarters of a century, as well as the rise in formal education per capita. While these measures of human capital are far from exact or all-inclusive, they give some dimensions to the importance of skills and knowledge in increasing productivity.

Table 5 · 1   Stock of education, U.S.

	1900	1976
Total man-years of schooling embodied in population (million)	228	2098
Percent of labor force with high-school education or more	6.4%	71%
Percent of high-school graduates entering college	17.0	45%

2. Shifts in the occupations of the labor force

A second source of added productivity results from shifts in employment from low productivity areas to high productivity areas. If workers move from occupations in which their productivity is low relative to other occupations in which output per man-hour is high, the production possibility curve of the economy will move out,

even if there are no increases in productivity *within* the different sectors.

A glance at Table 5 · 2 shows that very profound and pervasive shifts in the location of labor have taken place. What have been the effects of this shift on our long-term ability to produce goods?

Table 5 · 2   Percent distribution of all employed workers

	1900	1976
Agriculture, forests, and fisheries	38.1	3.8
Manufacturing, mining, transportation, construction, utilities	37.7	36.1
Trade government, finance, professional and personal services*	24.2	60.1

Source: Calculated from *Historical Statistics*, p. 74; also from *Statistical Abstract*.

*It is customary to include transportation and utilities among the third, or service, area of activities. In this analysis, however, we group them with goods-producing or goods-handling activities, to highlight the drift into "purely" service occupations. Since domestic servants, proprietors, and the self-employed are omitted (owing to inadequate statistics), the table under-represents the labor force in the service and trade sector.

The answer is complex. In the early years of the twentieth century, the shift of labor out of agriculture into manufacturing and services probably increased the overall productivity of the economy, since manufacturing was then the most technologically advanced sector. In more recent years, however, we would have to arrive at a different conclusion. Agriculture is now a highly productive though very small sector, in terms of employment. Moreover, the proportion of the labor force employed in manufacturing is roughly constant, up or down only a few percentage points year to year, from its long-term level of 35 to 40 percent of all workers.

Today, growth in employment takes place mainly in the congeries (collection) of occupations we call the service sector: government, retail and wholesale trade, professions such as lawyers, accountants, and the like. The growth of output per capita is less evident in these occupations.* **Thus the drift of labor into the service sector means that average GNP per worker is growing more slowly today than if labor were moving into manufacturing or agriculture.**

Why is this growth-lowering shift taking place? The reason has to do with the changing pattern of demand in an affluent society. There seems to be a natural sequence of wants as a society grows richer: first for food and basic clothing, then for the output of a wide range of industrial goods, then for recreation, professional advice, public administration, and enjoyments of other services.

3. Economies of large-scale production

A third source of increasing productivity is the magnifying effect of mass production on output. As we have seen, when the organization of production reaches a certain critical size, especially in manufacturing, economies of scale become possible. Many of these are based on the possibility of dividing complex operations into a series of simpler ones, each performed at high speed by a worker aided by specially designed equipment. It is difficult to esti-

---

*It is only proper to note that we cannot measure productivity of output in the service sector nearly so unambiguously as in the goods sector, and there is no doubt that the *quality* of many services has increased substantially. Compare, for example, the "productivity" of a surgeon operating for appendicitis in 1900, 1930, and 1960. On the other hand, insofar as we are interested in increases of measurable output per capita, there seems little doubt of the considerable superiority of the goods-producing branches of the economy.

mate the degree of growth attributable to these economies of size. Certainly during the era of railroad-building and of the introduction of mass production, they contributed heavily to growth rate. In a careful study of the contemporary sources of U.S. growth, Edward F. Denison estimates that economies of large-scale production today are responsible for about one-tenth of our annual rate of productivity increase.

4. Increases in the amount of capital

A fourth basic reason for the rising productivity of labor again harks back to Adam Smith's day. It is the fact that each additional member of the labor force has been equipped with at least as much capital as earlier members had; and that all members of the labor force have worked with a steadily more productive stock of capital.

We call the first kind of capital growth a *widening* of capital. It consists of matching additional workers with the same amounts and kinds of equipment that their predecessors had. The streams of additional part-time women workers coming into offices and stores, for example, would not be able to match the productivity of those who preceded them if they did not also get typewriters, cash registers, or similar equipment.

But we must also notice a *deepening* of capital as a source of increased labor productivity. This means that each worker receives *more* capital equipment over time. The ditch digger becomes the operator of a power shovel; the pencil-and-paper accountant uses a computer.

Over the long course of economic growth, increased productivity has required the slow accumulation of very large capital stocks per working individual. Thus investment that increases capital per worker is, and will probably continue to

MASS PRODUCTION IN ACTION

Allan Nevins has described what mass production techniques looked like in the early Ford assembly lines.

Just how were the main assembly lines and lines of component production and supply kept in harmony? For the chassis alone, from 1,000 to 4,000 pieces of each component had to be furnished each day at just the right point and right minute; a single failure, and the whole mechanism would come to a jarring standstill. . . . Superintendents had to know every hour just how many components were being produced and how many were in stock. Whenever danger of shortage appeared, the shortage chaser—a familiar figure in all automobile factories—flung himself into the breach.

Counters and checkers reported to him. Verifying in person any ominous news, he mobilized the foreman concerned to repair deficiencies. Three times a day he made typed reports in manifold to the factory clearing-house, at the same time chalking on blackboards in the clearing-house office a statement of results in each factory-production department and each assembling department.[1]

Such systematizing in itself resulted in astonishing increases in productivity. With each operation analyzed and subdivided into its simplest components, with a steady stream of work passing before stationary men, with a relentless nevertheless manageable pace of work, the total time required to assemble a car dropped astonishingly. Within a single year, the time required to assemble a motor fell from 600 minutes to 226 minutes; to build a chassis, from 12 hours and 28 minutes to 1 hour and 33 minutes. A stopwatch man was told to observe a 3-minute assembly in which men assembled rods and pistons, a simple operation. The job was divided into three jobs, and half the men turned out the same output as before.

[1] *Ford, the Times, the Man, the Company* (New York: Scribner's, 1954), 1, 507.

be, one of the most effective levers for steadily raising output per worker. Unlike the steady widening of capital, however, the deepening of capital is not a regular process. Between 1929 and 1947 there was no additional capital added per worker! This was, of course, a time of severe depression and thereafter of enforced wartime stringencies. Since 1947, the value of our stock of capital worker has been growing at about 2.7 percent a year. As we shall see immediately following, however, the *size* of this additional stock of capital is less crucial than the *productivity* of that capital—that is, its technological character.

5. Technology

We have already implied the fifth and last main source of increases in productivity: technology. Even during the 1929–1947 era, for instance, when capital stock per worker remained fixed, the output of GNP per worker grew by 1.5 percent per year!

Part of this growth can be attributed to some of the sources of growth that we have itemized above, such as improvements in the skills of the labor force. But contemporary economic investigation increasingly attributes the bulk of the bonus rate of growth to the impact of new technology. In the long run, our real standard of living depends upon advances in applied knowledge rather than simply on increases in the supply of capital with which each laborer works (see box).

What we do not know about long-run growth

Last, we must take cognizance of an important fact. We have learned a good deal about the sources of growth in the United States, but we have not really unlocked the secret of the historical trajectory of that growth. In fact, we can now see this trajectory was the result of crosscurrents of many kinds. A rising participation rate, which is a potential sti-

In thinking about technology and growth, it helps to differentiate among scientific knowledge, engineering knowledge, and economic knowledge. The relationship can best be understood if we look at the accompanying figure. Here we assume that knowledge can be arranged along a continuum from the least productive technologies to the most productive. On the extreme left are those techniques we have discarded; for example, water mills or treadmills for the production of energy. Next we come to the range of techniques in use. Here is a "bell curve" of plants, beginning with those that are still in use but almost obsolete—say, old-fashioned utilities—to the newest plant and equipment, perhaps nuclear power plants. Here we reach the *economic frontier,* the limit of knowledge that can be profitably used.

Still further to the right is another frontier—the limit of *engineering knowledge.* For instance, breeder reactors, still in "pilot plant stage" might be located near this point. Then to the far right is the boundary of *scientific knowledge*—for instance, fusion power—where our theoretical knowledge has not yet passed into the stage of engineering feasibility.

DIFFERENT KINDS OF KNOWLEDGE

From an economist's point of view, the level of productivity in an economy depends not only on the location of all these techniques and frontiers, but on the distribution of plants *within* the bell curve. A high-productivity economy will have its curve of plants to the right of a low-productivity economy. Moreover, within that curve, its working equipment will be "bunched" toward the right-hand edge of *best-practice* plants; a low-productivity economy will have the opposite distribution. Incidentally, this is one reason why productivity is very high in industrial nations that have been severely damaged by war but have rebuilt their capital stock. Their factories will tend to incorporate the very newest and best in techniques, whereas an economy that was spared the damages of war will retain in use many older plants that still manage to show a small profit. The rate of growth of productivity depends on how fast the distribution of plants in operation is moving to the right. This depends partly on R&D (research and development), partly on application. For example, someone might invent a train that goes 200 mph, but it could not be used because the roadbeds would not permit trains to go faster than 50 mph. Or social resistances may get in the way: opposition of unions, environmental groups, and others.

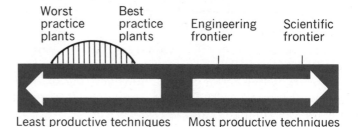

Worst practice plants   Best practice plants   Engineering frontier   Scientific frontier

Least productive techniques   Most productive techniques

mulus to growth, was dampened by a decline in the numbers of hours worked per year. Increases in productivity of labor in manufacturing and agriculture were offset by a shift of labor into the "low productivity" service sector. Figure 5•8 shows the shifting importance of different sources of growth in different periods.

The overall effect of these complex trends is the "steady" rate of 3.5 percent growth evidenced in the United States for many years. We can now see that this steady rate was really the outcome of many contrary trends. Is there any underlying reason why the growth of GNP maintained

such an even pace, or why that pace was 3.5 percent per year?

Not so far as we know. Other nations have different long-run growth rates. and those growth rates are not always as steady as those of the United States, by any means. Furthermore, within the United States, the steadiness of the average rate conceals a great deal of variation in short-run rates, as we have seen. The fact is, then, that we can describe but cannot really explain why our growth has followed the pattern shown in Fig. 5•8. This remains a profound problem for economists and economic historians.

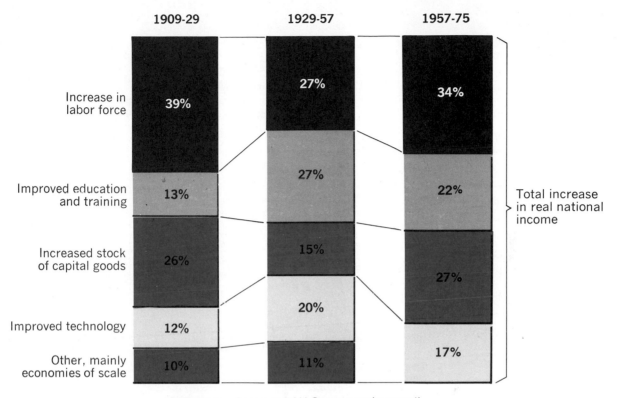

FIG. 5·8 Sources of U.S. economic growth

FOCUS This is a chapter devoted to the subject of growth, a subject that we will be continually referring to in chapters to come. Therefore, you should use this review to fix a few basic ideas firmly in your mind.

At the top of the heap is the matter discussed at the end of our chapter: the "supply" of growth. You must certainly understand how growth can be achieved by increasing the quantity or by improving the quality of the services of the factors of production. You should be able to list the major causes for the increased quality (productivity) of labor and capital.

One way to conceptualize the idea of growth is to draw a production-possibility curve and to see how the efficiency frontier of such a curve moves out as quantities or qualities of inputs rise. At the same time, the *p-p* curve serves a very useful lesson in showing us that there are constraints on the production of combinations of goods that arise from the operation of the law of increasing cost. Because factors are not homogenous, we can produce more and more of one good only by giving up larger and larger quantities of another good. This idea of a "trade-off" gives us a basic insight into the nature of cost as foregone opportunities. Be sure you read the box on p. 63.

WORDS AND CONCEPTS YOU SHOULD KNOW

Production possibility curve, 60–61
Efficiency frontiers, 61
Law of increasing cost, 62–63
Opportunity cost, 62–63 (box)

Participation rate, 64–65
Quantities vs. qualities of inputs, 68–69
Productivity and its sources, 68–71

QUESTIONS

1. Set up a production-possibility curve for an economy producing food and steel. Show how combination of goods cannot be produced, *although a quantity of either good alone is within reach of the economy.*

2. What kind of economy might display constant returns to specialization? Would a very simple, low-technology economy show such a straight-line efficiency frontier if it chose, for example, to hunt or fish? Would this depend on the abundance of game or fish?

3. Explain why an economy might not want to operate on its efficiency frontier.

4. How do you account for the fact there are more people per hundred who want to work today than there were 70 years ago, when the nation was so much poorer? How much does the monetization of labor have to do with this? How much is it a change in life-styles, especially for women? What do you expect for the very long run—say 100 years from now?

5. Why is productivity so essential in achieving growth? What are its main sources? What would you recommend as a long-term program to raise American productivity? Asian productivity?

U.S. standard of living

Americans have traditionally prided themselves on having the world's highest standard of living. But recently we have been passed by a number of oil-rich countries in the Middle East, and we either have been, or are about to be, passed by a number of countries in Europe. Here are the most recent figures:

	Per capita GNP 1975
U.S.A.	$ 7,099
Kuwait	11,094
Qatar	19,819
Switzerland	8,754
Sweden	8,450
Norway	6,944
West Germany	6,842

The oil-rich countries are often dismissed on the grounds that they simply "inherited " wealth, rather than having had to do anything to earn it.* Perhaps this is true, but critics must remember the extent to which U.S. wealth has also been built on inherited resources, including vast quantities of oil, coal, minerals, and the best agricultural land in the world.

Certainly the claim of inherited wealth cannot be applied to the newly-rich nations of Europe. What, then, is the reason for the declining relative position of the U.S. in the world?

If we examine the rates of growth of the U.S. and its new superiors, we discover that the turnabout has not occurred because the United States is doing worse than it used to. Output has been growing in the U.S. at about 3 percent a year (1.9 percent per capita) for over a century. Rather, what has changed dramatically is the performance of other countries. The oil-rich countries have suddenly leaped ahead, owing to the boost in the price of oil after the Arab-Israeli war. The new top GNP countries of Europe and Japan got there because their productivity has been growing twice, even three times as fast as ours for the last decade (see Fig. 5 • 9).

To what do they owe their performance? It used to be popular to explain their rapid growth in terms of "catching up." It was said that Europe and Japan speeded up their economic pace by importing U.S. techniques in place of their old-fashioned ways. If this explanation were true, the new winners would have stopped growing faster than the U.S., once they caught up with us. Instead, they have continued to forge ahead. Evidently it is now they, not we, who are pioneering in the techniques of economic efficiency.

*Their average GNP is so high, of course, because a small number of families have gigantic incomes.

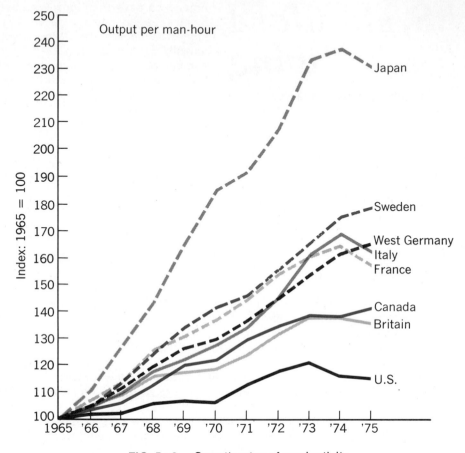

FIG. 5·9   Growth rates of productivity

In what ways are they pioneering? Industrial technology tends to spread around the world fairly rapidly, so that is not likely that Europe or Japan possesses industrial secrets unknown to us. They may, however, have some other secrets. Some of these may have to do with the way in which workers' morale is encouraged, especially in Japan and Sweden. In part, the "secret" may have to do with more effective national planning. In part, it may reflect the fact that Europe and Japan live under an American military umbrella and are not saddled with a cumbersome military sector.

These are only guesses. The fact is that nobody is certain why other nations have learned how to combine the factors of production more efficiently than we have, and no one knows exactly what sorts of changes would be needed in this country if we are to try once more to be Number One in per capita output. Very likely this will be a matter for national discussion over the coming years.

Demand for output

So far, we have talked about GNP from the supply point of view. First we familiarized ourselves with the actual process of production itself—the interaction of the factors of production and the accumulated wealth of the past as they cooperated to bring a flow of output into being. Next we examined the forces that swelled that volume of output over time, mainly the increase in skills and capital equipment and technology that are responsible for our long-term trend of growth.

Now we are going to turn to the other side of the picture, emphasizing the driving forces that generate GNP, rather than the constraining ones that hold it back. To put it differently, we are going to move from a perspective of supply to one of demand.

Before we can go very deeply into the question of demand, we need to understand something about the meaning of demand, as it affects our total output. Hence in this chapter we will not look into the question of growth. Instead, we shall look into the prior question of how the flow of purchasing power is generated in an economy, and how it can be constantly regenerated.

6

Output and Demand

Let us start with a basic question—at once very simple and surprisingly complex. *How do we know that there will be enough demand to buy the amount of output that the factors produce?* Once we understand that, we will be well on the way to unlocking the puzzle of macro-economies.

The question leads us to understand a fundamental linkage between demand and output, for how does output actually come into existence? Anyone in business will give you the answer. The crucial factor in running a business is *demand* or *purchasing power;* that is, the presence of buyers who are willing and able to buy some good or service at a price the seller is willing to accept.

But how does demand or purchasing power come into existence? Any buyer will tell us that dollars come in as part of *income* or cash receipts. But where, in turn, do the dollar receipts or incomes of buyers come from? If we inquire again, most buyers will tell us that they have money in their pockets because in one fashion or another they have contributed to the process of production; that is, because they have helped to make the output that is now being sold.

Thus output is generated by demand—and demand is generated by output! Our quest for the motive force behind the flow of production therefore leads us in a great circle through the market system. Here is the circular flow approached from a macro perspective. We can see this in Fig. 6 • 1.

At the top of the circle we see payments flowing from households to firms or government units (cities, states, federal agencies, etc.), thereby creating the demand that brings forth production. At the bottom of the circle, we see more payments, this time flowing from firms or governments back to households, as busi-

FIG. 6 • 1   The circular flow, view II

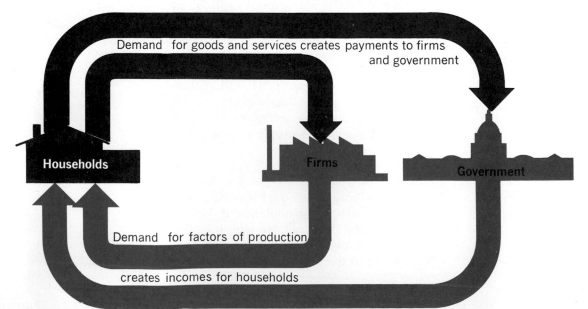

Demand for goods and services creates payments to firms and government

Households

Firms

Government

Demand for factors of production

creates incomes for households

nesses hire the services of the various factors in order to carry out production. *Thus we can see that there is a constant regeneration of demand as money is first spent by the public on the output of firms and governments, and then in turn spent by firms and governments for the services of the public.*

An economic model

Let us begin by examining this chain of payments and receipts as a model of the macro system.

Our model, to begin with, will be a very simple one. We must simplify it, at first, by ruling out some of the very events to which we will later turn as the climax of our study. For instance, we shall ignore changes in *people's tastes,* so that we can assume that everyone will regularly buy the same kinds of goods. We shall ignore differences in the *structure of firms* or *markets,* so that we can forget about differences in competitive pressures. We shall rule out *population growth* and, even more important, *inventive progress,* so that we can deal with a very stable imaginary world. For the time being, we will exclude even *saving* and *net investment* (although of course we must permit replacement investment), so that we can ignore growth. Later, of course, we are to be deeply concerned with just such problems of dynamic change. In order to come to grips with them, we must first understand an economic world as "pure" and changeless as possible.

Cost and output

The very abstract model we have created may seem too far removed from the real world to tell us much about its operation. But if we now go back to the circle of economic activity in which payments to firms, governments, and factors become their incomes, and in turn reappear on the marketplace as demand, our model will enable us to explain a very important problem. *It is how an economy that has produced a given GNP is able to buy it back.*

This is by no means a self-evident matter. Indeed, one of the most common misconceptions about the flow of economic activity is that there will not be enough purchasing power to buy everything we have produced—that somehow we are unable to buy enough to keep up with the output of our factories. So it is well to understand once and for all how an economy can sustain a given level of production through its purchases on the market.

We start, then, with an imaginary economy in full operation. We can, if we wish, imagine ourselves as having collected a year's output, which is now sitting on the economic front doorstep looking for a buyer. What we must now see is whether it will be possible to *sell* this gross national product to the people who have been engaged in producing it. **We must ask whether enough income or receipts have been generated in the process of production to buy back all the products themselves.**

Costs and Incomes

How does production create income? Businesspeople do not think about "incomes" when they assemble the factors of production to meet the demand for their product. They worry about *cost.* All the money they pay out during the production process is paid under the heading of *cost,* whether it be wage or salary cost, cost of materials, depreciation cost, tax cost, or whatever. Thus it seems that the concept of cost may offer us a useful point of entry into the economic chain. *If we can show how all costs become incomes,* we will have taken a major step toward understanding whether our gross national product can in fact be sold to those who produced it.

It may help us if we begin by looking at the kinds of costs incurred by business firms in real life. Since governments also produce goods and services, this hypothetical firm should be taken to represent government agencies as well as business firms. Both incur the same kinds of costs; only the labels differ.

Table 6·1, a hypothetical expense summary of General Output Company, will serve as an example typical of all business firms, large or small, and all government agencies. (If you examine the year-end statements of any business, you will find that costs all fall into one or more of the cost categories shown.)

Table 6·1   General Output Company cost summary

Wages, salaries, and employee benefits	$100,000,000
Rental, interest, and profits payments	5,000,000
Materials, supplies, etc.	60,000,000
Taxes other than income	25,000,000
Depreciation	20,000,000
Total	$210,000,000

Factor costs and national income   Some of these costs we recognize immediately as payments to factors of production. The item for "wages and salaries" is obviously a payment to the factor *labor.* The item "interest" (perhaps not so obviously) is a payment to the factor *capital;* that is, to those who have lent the company money in order to help it carry on its productive operation. The item for rent is, of course, a payment for the rental of *land* or natural resources from their owners.

Note that we have included profits with rent and interest. In actual accounting practice, profits are not shown as an expense. For our purposes, however, it will be quite legitimate and very helpful to regard profits as a special kind of factor cost going to entrepreneurs for their risk-taking function. Later we shall go more thoroughly into the matter of profits.

Two things strike us about these factor costs. First, it is clear that they represent payments that have been made to secure production. In more technical language, they are payments for factor inputs that result in commodity outputs. All the production actually carried on within the company or government agency, all the value it has added to the economy has been compensated by the payments the company or the agency has made to land, labor, and capital. To be sure, there are other costs, for materials and taxes and depreciation, and we shall soon turn to these. But whatever production or assembly or distribution the company or agency has carried out during the course of the year has required the use of land, labor, or capital. Thus *the total of its factor costs represents the value of the total new output that General Output by itself has given to the economy.*

From here it is a simple step to add up *all* the factor costs paid out by *all* the companies and government agencies in the economy, in order to measure the total new *value added* by all productive efforts in the year. This measure is called *national income.* As we can see, it is less than gross national product, for it does not include other costs of output; namely, certain taxes and depreciation.

Factor costs and household incomes

A second fact that strikes us is that *all factor costs are income payments*. The wages, salaries, interest, rents, etc., that were costs to the company or agency were income to its recipients. So are any profits, which will accrue as income to the owners of the business.

Thus, just as it sounds, national income means the total amount of earnings of the factors of production within the nation. If we think of these factors as constituting the households of the economy, we can see that *factor costs result directly in incomes to the household sector*. Thus, if factor costs were the only costs involved in production, the problem of buying back the gross national product would be a very simple one. We should simply be paying out to households, as the cost of production, the very sum needed to buy GNP when we turned around to sell it. A glance at the General Output expense summary shows that this is not the case. There are other costs besides factor costs. How shall we deal with them?

Costs of materials

The next item of the expense summary is puzzling. Called payments for "materials, supplies, etc.," it represents all the money General Output has paid, not to its own factors, but to other companies for other products it has needed. We may even recognize these costs as payments for those *intermediate products* that lose their identity in a later stage of production. How do such payments become part of the income available to buy GNP on the marketplace?

Perhaps the answer is already intuitively clear. When General Output sends its checks to, let us say, U.S. Steel or General Electric or to a local supplier of stationery, each of these recipient firms now uses the proceeds of General Output's checks to pay its own costs. (Actually, of course, they have probably long since paid their own costs and now use General Output's payment only to reimburse themselves. But if we want to picture our model economy in the simplest way, we can imagine U.S. Steel and other firms sending their products to General Output and waiting until checks arrive to pay their own costs.)

And what are those costs? What must U.S. Steel or all the other suppliers now do with their checks? The answer is obvious. They must now reimburse their own factors and then pay any other costs that remain.

Figure 6·2 may make the matter plain. It shows us, looking back down the chain of intermediate payments, that what constitutes material costs to one firm is made up of factor and other costs to another. Indeed, as we unravel the chain from company to company, it is clear that all the contribution to new output must have come from the contribution of factors somewhere down the line, and that *all the costs of new output—all the value added—must ultimately be resolvable into payments to land, labor, and capital.*

Another way of picturing the same thing is to imagine that all firms or agencies in the country were bought up by a single gigantic corporation. The various production units of the new supercorporation would then ship components and semifinished items back and forth to one another, but there would not have to be any payment from one division to another. The only payments that would be necessary would be those required to buy the services of factors—that is, various kinds of labor or the use of property or capital—so that at the end of the year, the supercorporation would show on its expense summary only items for wages

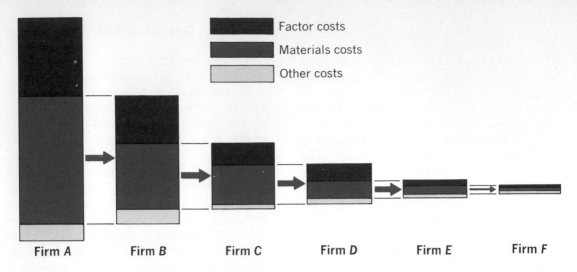

FIG. 6 · 2 How materials costs become other costs

and salaries, rent, and interest (and as we shall see, taxes and depreciation), but it would have no item for materials cost.

We have come a bit further toward seeing how our gross national product can be sold. **To the extent that GNP represents new output made during the course of the year, the income to buy back this output has already been handed out as factor costs, either paid at the last stage of production or "carried along" in the guise of materials costs.**

But a glance at the General Output expense summary shows that entrepreneurs incur two kinds of costs that we have still not taken into account: taxes and depreciation. Here are costs employers have incurred that have not been accounted for on the income side. What can we say about them?

Tax costs   Let us begin by tracing the taxes that General Output pays, just as we have traced its materials payments.* In the first instance, its taxes will go to government

units—federal, state, and local. But we need not stop there. Just as we saw that General Output's checks to supplier firms paid for the suppliers' factor costs and for still further interfirm transactions, so we can see that its checks to government agencies pay for goods and services that these agencies have produced—goods such as roads, buildings, or defense equipment; or services such as teaching, police protection, and the administration of justice. General Output's tax checks are thus used to help pay for factors of production—land, labor, and capital—that are used in the *public sector*.

In many ways, General Output's payments to government units resemble its payments to other firms for raw materials. Indeed, if the government *sold* its services to General Output, charging for the use of the roads, police services, or defense protection it affords the company, there would be *no* difference whatsoever. The reason we differentiate between a company's payment to the public sector and its payments for intermediate products is important, however, and worth looking into.

The first reason is clearly that with few exceptions, the government does *not* sell its output. This is partly because the

*For simplicity, we also show government agencies as taxpayers. In fact, most government units do *not* pay taxes. Yet there will be hidden tax costs in the prices of many materials they buy. No harm is done by treating government agencies like taxpaying firms in this model.

community has decided that certain things the government produces (education, justice, or the use of public parks, for instance) should not be for sale but should be supplied to all citizens without direct charge. In part, it is also because some things the government produces, such as defense or law and order, cannot be equitably charged to individual buyers, since it is impossible to say to what degree anyone benefits from—or even uses— these communal facilities. Hence General Output, like every other producer, is billed, justly or otherwise, for a share of the cost of government.

There is also a second reason why we consider the cost of taxes as a new kind of cost, distinct from factor payments. It is that when business firms have finished paying the factors, they have not yet paid all the sums that employers must lay out. *Some taxes, in other words, are an addition to the cost of production.*

Indirect vs. direct taxes

These taxes—so-called *indirect taxes*—are levied on the productive enterprise itself or on its actual physical output. Taxes on real estate, for instance, or taxes that are levied on each unit of output (such as excise taxes on cigarettes) or taxes levied on goods sold at retail (sales taxes) are all payments that entrepreneurs must make as part of their costs of doing business.

Note that not all taxes collected by the government are costs of production. Many taxes will be paid, not by the entrepreneurs as an expense of doing business, but by the *factors* themselves. These so-called *direct* taxes (such as income taxes) are *not* part of the cost of production. When General Output adds up its total cost of production, it naturally includes the wages and salaries it has paid, but it does not include the taxes its workers or executives have paid out of their incomes. Such direct taxes transfer income from earners to government, but they are not a cost to the company itself.

In the same way, the income taxes on the profits of a company do *not* constitute a cost of production. General Output does not pay income taxes as a regular charge on its operations but waits until a year's production has taken place and then pays income taxes on the profits it makes *after* paying its costs. If it finds that it has lost money over the year, it will not pay any income taxes—although it will have paid other costs, including indirect taxes. *Thus direct taxes are not a cost that is paid out in the course of production and must be recouped, but a payment made by factors (including owners of the business) from the incomes they have earned through the process of production.*

Taxes as cost

Thus we can see two reasons why taxes are handled as a separate item in GNP and are not telescoped into factor costs, the way materials costs are. **One reason is that taxes are a payment to a *sector different* from that of business and thus indicate a separate stream of economic activity.** But the second reason, and the one that interests us more at this moment, is that *certain taxes*—indirect taxes—*are an entirely new kind of cost of production, not previously picked up.* **As an expense paid out by entrepreneurs, over and above factor costs (or materials costs), these tax costs must be part of the total selling price of GNP.**

Will there be enough incomes handed out in the process of production to cover this item of cost? We have seen that there will be. The indirect tax costs paid out by firms will be received by government agencies who will use these tax receipts to pay income to factors working for the government. Any direct taxes (income taxes) paid by General Output or by its factors will also wind up in the hands of a government. Thus all tax payments result in the transfer of purchasing power from the private to the public sector, and when spent by the public sector, they will again become demand on the marketplace.

Depreciation

But there is still one last item of cost. At the end of the year, when the company is totting up its expenses to see if it has made a profit for the period, its accountants do not stop with factor costs, material costs, and indirect taxes. If they did, the company would soon be in serious straits. In producing its goods, General Output has also used up a certain amount of its assets—its buildings and equipment—and a cost must now be charged for this wear and tear if the company is to be able to preserve the value of its physical plant intact. If it did not make this cost allowance, it would have failed to include all the resources that were used up in the process of production, and it would therefore be overstating its profits.

Yet, this cost has something about it clearly different from other costs that General Output has paid. Unlike factor costs or taxes or materials costs, depreciation is not paid for by check. When the company's accountants make an allowance for depreciation, all they do is make an entry on the company's book, stating that plant and equipment are now worth a certain amount less than in the beginning of the year.

At the same time, however, General Output *includes* the amount of depreciation in the price it intends to charge for its goods. As we have seen, part of the resources used up in production was its own capital equipment, and it is certainly entitled to consider the depreciation as a cost. Yet, it has not paid anyone a sum of money equal to this cost! How, then, will there be enough income in the marketplace to buy back its product?

Replacement expenditure

The answer is that in essence it has paid depreciation charges to itself. Depreciation is thus part of its gross income. Together with after-tax profits, these depreciation charges are called a business's *cash flow*.

A business does not *have to* spend its depreciation accruals, but normally it will, *to maintain and replace its capital stock*. To be sure, an individual firm may not replace its worn-out capital exactly on schedule. But when we consider the economy as a whole, with its vast assemblage of firms, that problem tends to disappear. Suppose we have 1,000 firms, each with machines worth $1,000 and each depreciating its machines at $100 per year. Provided that all the machines were bought in different years, this means that in any given year, about 10 percent of the capital stock will wear out and have to be replaced. It's reasonable to assume that among them, the 1,000 firms will spend $100,000 to replace their old equipment over a ten-year span.*

This enables us to see that insofar as there is a steady stream of replacement expenditures going to firms that make capital goods, there will be payments just large enough to balance the addition to costs

---

*What if the machines *were* all bought in one year or over a small number of years? Then replacement expenditures will *not* be evenly distributed over time, and we may indeed have problems. This takes us into the dynamics of prosperity and recession, to which we will turn in due course. For the purpose of our explanatory model, we will stick with our (not too unrealistic) assumption that machines wear out on a steady schedule and that aggregate replacement expenditures therefore also display a steady, relatively unfluctuating pattern.

due to depreciation. As with all other payments to firms, these replacement expenditures will, of course, become incomes to factors, etc., and thus can reappear on the marketplace.

Another view of costs and incomes

Because it is very important to understand the relationship between the "selling price" of GNP and the amount of income available to buy it back, it may help to look at the matter from a different point of view.

This time let us approach it by seeing how the economy arranges things so that consumers and government and business, the three great sectors of final demand, are provided with enough purchasing power to claim the whole of GNP. Suppose, to begin with, that the economy paid out income only to its factors and priced its goods and services accordingly. In that case, consumers could purchase the entire value of the year's output, but business would be unable to purchase any portion of the output to replace its wornout equipment. (Also it raises the awkward question of how we would pay factors working for the government, since government agencies would have very little income.)

That would obviously lead to serious trouble. Hence we must arrange for business to have a claim on output and for government factors to be paid for their services. The latter is simple. By imposing direct (income) taxes on factors, we divert income from the private to the public sector. And by imposing indirect taxes on output, we price output above its factor cost, thus making it impossible for consumers to claim the entire output.

In exactly the same way, business also reserves a claim on output by pricing its products to include a charge for depreciation. By so doing, it again reduces the ability of consumers to buy back the entire output of the economy, while it gives business the purchasing power to claim the output it needs (just as taxes give purchasing power to government). Now, after paying direct and indirect taxes and depreciation, the consumer is finally free to spend all the remainder of his income without danger of encroaching on the output that must be reserved for public activity and for the replacement of capital.

In other words, we can look at taxes and depreciation not merely as "costs" that the consumer has to pay or as "incomes" that accrue to government and business, but also as the means by which the output of the economy is made available to two important claimants besides private households.

The three streams of expenditure

Our analysis is now essentially complete. Item by item, we have traced each element of cost into an income payment, so that we now know there is enough income paid out to buy back our GNP at a price that represents its full cost. Perhaps this was a conclusion we anticipated all along. After all, ours would be an impossibly difficult economy to manage if somewhere along the line purchasing power dropped out of existence, so that we were always faced with a shortage of income to buy back the product we made. But our analysis has also shown us something more unexpected. We are accustomed to thinking that all the purchasing power in the economy is received and spent through the hands of "people"—usually meaning households. Now we can see that this is not true. There is not only one, but there are *three* streams of incomes and costs, all quite distinct from one another (although linked by direct taxes).

1. Factor costs → Households → Consumers goods

          Direct Taxes

2. Indirect taxes → Government agencies → Government goods

          Direct Taxes

3. Depreciation → Business firms → Replacement investment

The one major crossover in the three streams is the direct taxes of households and business firms that go to governments. This flow permits governments to buy more goods and services than could be purchased with indirect taxes alone.

There is a simple way of explaining this seemingly complex triple flow. Each stream indicates the existence of a *final taker* of gross national product: consumers, government, and business itself.* Since output has final claimants other than consumers, we can obviously have a flow of purchasing power that does not enter consumers' or factors' hands.

*We continue to forget about net exports until Chapter 10. We can think of them perfectly satisfactorily as a component of gross private investment.

The Completed Circuit of Demand

The realization that factor owners do not get paid incomes equal to the total gross value of output brings us back to the central question of this chapter: can we be certain that we will be able to sell our GNP at its full cost? Has there surely been generated enough purchasing power to buy back our total output?

We have thus far carefully analyzed and answered half the question. **We know that all costs will become incomes to factors or receipts of government agencies or of firms making replacement items.** To sum up again, factor costs become the incomes of workers, managements, owners

THE THREE FLOWS

To help visualize these three flows, imagine for an instant that our money comes in colors (all of equal value): black, gray, and red. Now suppose that firms always pay their factors in red money, their taxes in gray money, and their replacement expenditures in black money. In point of fact, of course, the colors would soon be mixed. A factor that is paid in red bills will be paying some of his red income for taxes; or a government agency will be paying out gray money as factor incomes; or firms will be using black dollars to pay taxes or factors, and gray or red dollars to pay for replacement capital.

But at least in our mind we could picture the streams being kept separate. A gray tax dollar paid by General Output to the Internal Revenue Service for taxes could go from the government to another firm, let us say in payment for office supplies, and we can think of the office supply firm keeping these gray dollars apart from its other receipts, to pay its taxes with. Such a gray dollar could circulate indefinitely, from government agencies to firms and back again, helping to bring about production but never entering a consumer's pocket! In the same way, a black replacement expenditure dollar going from General Output to, let us say, U.S. Steel could be set aside by U.S. Steel to pay for *its* replacement needs; and the firm that received this black dollar might, in turn, set it aside for its own use as replacement expenditure. We could, that is, imagine a circuit of expenditures in which black dollars went from firm to firm, to pay for replacement investment, and never ended up in a pay envelope or as a tax payment.

of natural resources and of capital; and all these incomes together can be thought of as comprising the receipts of the household sector. Tax costs are paid to government agencies and become receipts of the government sector. Depreciation costs are initially accrued within business firms, and these accruals belong to the business sector. As long as worn-out capital is regularly replaced, these accruals will be matched by equivalent new receipts of firms that make capital goods.

Crucial role of expenditures

What we have not yet established, however, is that these sector receipts will become sector expenditures. That is, we have not demonstrated that all households will now *spend* all their incomes on goods and services, or that government units will necessarily *spend* all their tax receipts on public goods and services, or that all firms will assuredly *spend* their depreciation accruals for new replacement equipment.

What happens if some receipts are not spent? The answer is of key importance in understanding the operation of the economy. A failure of the sectors to spend as much money as they have received means that some of the costs that have been laid out will *not* come back to the original entrepreneurs. As a result, they will suffer losses. If, for instance, our gross national product costs $1 trillion to produce but the various sectors spend only $900 billion in all, then some entrepreneurs will find themselves failing to sell all their output. Inventories of unsold goods will begin piling up, and businessmen will soon be worried about overproducing. The natural thing to do when you can't sell all your output is to stop making so much of it, so that businesses will begin cutting back on production. As they do so, they will also cut back on the number of people they employ. As a result, business costs will go down; but so will factor incomes, for we have seen that costs and incomes are but opposite sides of one coin. As incomes fall, the expenditures of the sectors might very well fall further, bringing about another twist in the spiral of recession.

This is not yet the place to go into the mechanics of such a downward spiral of business. But the point is clear. **A failure of the sectors to bring all their receipts back to the marketplace as demand can initiate profound economic problems. In the contrast between an unshakable equality of costs and incomes on the one hand and the uncertain connection between incomes and expenditures on the other, we have come to grips with one of the most important problems in macroeconomics.**

The closed circuit

We shall have ample opportunity later to observe exactly what happens when incomes are not spent. Now let us be sure that we understand how the great circle of the economic flow is closed when the sectors *do* spend their receipts. Figure 6·3 shows how we can trace our three streams of dollars through the economy and how these flows suffice to buy back GNP for its total cost. For simplicity, we assume that there are no direct taxes.

We can trace the flow from left to right. We begin on the left with the bar representing the total cost of our freshly produced GNP. As we know, this cost consists of all the factor costs of all the firms and government units in the nation, all the indirect tax costs incurred during production, and all the depreciation charges made during production. The bar also shows us the amount of money demand our economy must generate in order to buy back its own output.

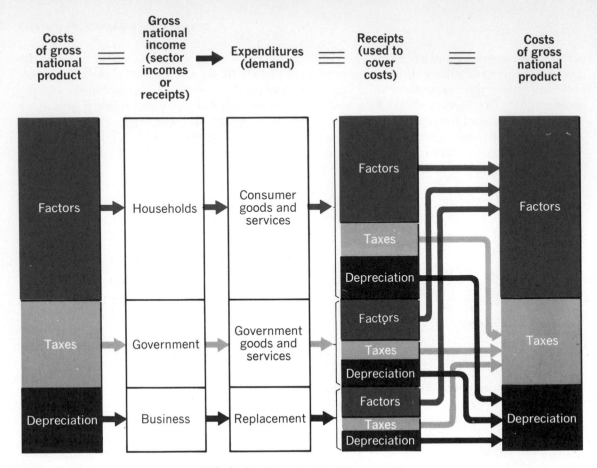

| Costs of gross national product | ≡ | Gross national income (sector incomes or receipts) | → | Expenditures (demand) | ≡ | Receipts (used to cover costs) | ≡ | Costs of gross national product |

FIG. 6·3 The circular flow, view III

From GNP to GNI

The next bars show us the transmutation of costs into sector receipts for householders, government units, and business firms (who retain their own depreciation accruals). This relationship between costs and sector receipts is one of *identity*—all costs *must* be receipts. Hence we use the sign ≡ to indicate that this is a relation of identities—of definitional differences only. If we use GNI to stand for gross national income (the gross incomes of all the sectors), then:

$$GNP \equiv GNI$$

That is an identity to be remembered—and understood.

Incomes and expenditures

Thereafter we notice the crucial link. We assume that each sector dutifully spends all its receipts, as it is supposed to. Our household sector buys the kinds of goods and services householders do in fact buy—consumption goods and services. Our government sector buys government goods and services, and our business sector buys replacement investment. This time we use an arrow (→) because this is emphatically *not* a relationship of identity. Our sectors may not spend all their incomes. Later we will see what happens if they don't.

Now note the next bar. Here we see what happens to these expenditures when they are received by the firms that make consumer goods or by the firms or individuals who make goods and services bought by governments or by the manufacturers of capital equipment. Each of these recipients will use the money he has received to cover factor payments, taxes, and depreciation for his own business. (What we show in our diagram are not these costs for each and every firm but the aggregate costs for all firms selling to each sector.)*

We are almost done. It remains only to aggregate the sector costs; that is, to add up all the factor costs, all the taxes, and all the depreciation accruals of *all* firms and government agencies—to reproduce a bar just like the one we started with. A circle of production has been completed. Firms and government units have received back, on the marketplace, a sum just large enough to cover their initial costs, including their profits for risk. The stage is set for another round of production, similar to the last.

GNP as a Sum of Costs and a Sum of Expenditures

Our bar graph also enables us to examine again the concept of gross national product, for now we can see that GNP can be looked at in one of two ways. **One way is to think of GNP as representing the total costs of a year's final output.** As we know, these are factors costs, indirect tax costs, and depreciation costs. We also know that these costs are identical with the incomes or receipts of sectors. Therefore GNP measures total incomes as well as total costs.

*Recall that for ease of exposition we are treating government agencies like firms and therefore show them as taxpayers.

But we can also look at GNP as a sum of expenditures. For every item of output has been paid for by someone—a household, a government unit, or a business. Even items that have not been sold belong to (and have been paid for) by the business that produced them. Therefore we can look at GNP as the sum of all these expenditures on output—the sum of household or consumption expenditure, government expenditure, and business expenditure, plus a small amount bought by foreigners: net exports.

Two ways of measuring GNP

An illustration may make it easier to grasp this identity of the two ways of measuring GNP. Suppose once again that we picture the economy as a gigantic factory from which the flow of production emerges onto a shipping platform, each item tagged with its selling price. There the items are examined by two clerks. One of them notes down in his book the selling price of each item and then analyzes that price into its cost (as income) components; factor cost (including profit), indirect taxes, and depreciation. The second clerk keeps a similar book in which each item's selling price is also entered, but his job is to note which sector—consumer, government, business investment, or export—is its buyer. Clearly, at the end of the year, the two clerks must show the same value of total output. But whereas the books of the first will show that total value separated into various costs, the books of the second will show it analyzed by its "customers"; that is, by the expenditures of the various sectors.

But wait! Suppose that an item comes onto the shipping platform without an order waiting for it! Would that not make the sum of costs larger than the sum of expenditures?

The answer will give us our final insight into the necessary equality of the two measures of GNP. For what happens to an item that is not bought by one of the sectors? It will be sent by the shipping clerk into inventory *where it will count as part of the business investment of the economy!* Do not forget that increases in inventory are treated as investment because they are a part of output that has not been consumed. In this case it is a very unwelcome kind of investment; and if it continues, it will shortly lead to changes in the production of the firm. Such dynamic changes will soon lie at the very center of our attention. In the meantime, however, *the fact that unbought goods are counted as investment*—as if they were "bought" by the firm that produced but cannot sell them—establishes the absolute identity of GNP measured as a sum of costs or as a sum of expenditures.

GNP and GNI

To express the equality with the conciseness and clarity of mathematics, we can write, as we know:

$$GNP \equiv GNI$$

We already know that:

$$GNP \equiv C + I + G + X$$

and

$$GNI \equiv F + T + D$$

where C, I, G, and X are the familiar categories of expenditure, and F, T, and D stand for factor costs (income to land, capital, and labor), indirect taxes, and depreciation. Therefore, we know that:

$$C + I + G + X \equiv F + T + D$$

It is important to remember that these are all accounting identities, true by definition. The *National Income and Product Accounts*, the official government accounts for the economy, are kept in such a manner as to make them true.* As the name implies, these accounts are kept in two sets of "books," one on the products produced in the economy and one on the costs of production, which we know to be identical with the incomes generated in the economy. Since both sets of accounts are measuring the same output, the two totals must be equal.

NNP and national income

It is now easy to understand the meaning of two other measures of output. One of these is called *net national product* (NNP). As the name indicates, it is exactly equal to the gross national product minus depreciation. GNP is used much more than NNP, since the measures of depreciation are very unreliable. The other measure, national income, we have already met. It is *GNP minus both depreciation and indirect taxes*. This makes it equal to the sum of factor costs only. Figure 6 • 4 should make this relationship clear. The aim of this last measure is to identify the net income that actually reaches the hands of factors of production. Consequently, the measure is sometimes called the *national income at factor cost*. Its abbreviation is Y.

The circular flow

The "self-reproducing" model economy we have now sketched out is obviously still very far from reality. Nevertheless, the particular kind of unreality that we have deliberately constructed serves a highly useful purpose. An economy that regularly and dependably buys back everything it produces gives us a kind of bench mark from which to begin our subsequent inves-

*There is an "Extra word" on these accounts at the end of Chapter 13.

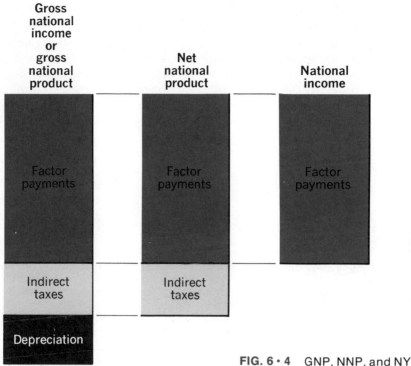

FIG. 6 · 4   GNP, NNP, and NY

tigations. We call such an economy, whose internal relationships we have outlined, an economy in *stationary equilibrium,* and we denote the changeless flow of costs into business receipts, and receipts back into costs, a *circular flow*.

We shall return many times to the model of a circular flow economy for insights into a more complex and dynamic system. Hence it is well that we summarize briefly two of the salient characteristics of such a system.

1. A circular flow economy will never experience a "recession."

Year in and year out, its total output will remain unchanged. Indeed, the very concept of a circular flow is useful in showing us that an economic system can maintain a given level of activity *indefinitely,* so long as all the sectors convert all their receipts into expenditures.

2. A circular flow economy also will never know a "boom."

That is, it will not grow, and its standard of living will remain unchanged. That standard of living may be high or low, for we could have a circular flow economy of poverty or of abundance. But in either state, changelessness will be its essence.

The great puzzle   What   we   have demonstrated in this chapter is an exceedingly important idea. There *can* always be enough purchasing power generated by the process of output to buy back that output.

Yet we all know, from our most casual acquaintance with economics, that in fact there is not always enough purchasing power around, or that on occasions there is too much purchasing power. With too little, we have slumps and recessions; with too much, booms and inflation.

Hence the circular flow sets the stage for the next step in our study of macroeconomics. If there *can be* the right amount of purchasing power generated, why isn't there? Or to put the question more perplexingly: if there *can be* enough purchasing power to buy *any* size output, small or large, what determines how large purchasing power will actually be, and therefore how large output will actually be?

These questions point the way for the next stage of our investigation. We must study the workings of demand much more realistically than heretofore, by removing some of the assumptions that were necessary to create a model of a circular flow system.

FOCUS

This chapter must be given careful study, for it holds the key to understanding how the flow of GNP is generated by demand. The purpose of the chapter is to show that it is possible for an economy to create sufficient demand (purchasing power) to buy all the output that it produces.

This purpose involves us in a step-by-step demonstration that all costs incurred in the process of output become incomes or receipts. First we analyze factor (and materials) costs, then the costs of indirect taxes, and finally those of depreciation. Through this analysis we see that all costs are in fact only one side of a transaction that always creates an equivalent receipt. It is impossible to incur a cost without giving rise to an equivalent income. Thus we trace the three categories of cost—F, T, and D—into the incomes of three sectors: the household sector, the government sector, and the business sector.

Crucial to the analysis is our understanding that this identity of costs and receipts is only half the circular flow. To create enough demand to buy output, all the sectors must spend their incomes. And expenditure is not the other side of the act of receiving an income. If incomes are not all spent by the three sectors, there will not be enough demand to complete the circuit, and GNP will fall. We will study this in greater detail in coming chapters. Now is the time to master the mechanics of a "successful" economy.

We suggest that you carefully answer the questions that follow. If you get them right, you will have no trouble with the essential idea of this chapter. If you cannot answer them correctly, go back through the chapter again and see where you have missed out.

WORDS AND CONCEPTS YOU SHOULD KNOW

Purchasing power, 78
Factor costs, 80–81
Materials costs, 81–82
Direct tax costs, 83–84
Indirect tax costs, 83
Depreciation costs, 84
Costs and Incomes, 79–80, 85

Three streams of expenditure, 85–86, 87
GNP as costs and expenditure, 89–90
GNI $\equiv$ GNP, 90
NNP, 90–91
Y, 90–91
A circular flow economy, 90–91

QUESTIONS

1. How can a model elucidate reality when it is deliberately stripped of the very things that make reality interesting?

2. Why do we need a model to show that an economy can buy back its own production?

3. What are factor costs? What kinds of factor costs are there? To what sector do factor costs go?

4. What are direct taxes? What are indirect taxes? Which are considered part of production costs? Why?

5. To whom are materials costs paid? Why are they not counted separately as part of the sum total of costs in GNP?

6. What is depreciation? Why is it a part of costs? Who receives the payments or accruals made for depreciation purposes?

7. Show in a carefully drawn diagram how costs become income or receipts of the different sectors.

8. Show in a second diagram how the incomes of the various sectors can become expenditures.

9. Why is the link between expenditure and receipt different from that between receipt and expenditure?

10. What is meant by a circular flow economy? Why does such an economy have neither growth nor fluctuation?

11. Explain the two different ways of looking at GNP and write the simple formula for each. Why is GNP the same thing as GNI?

12. Can we have demand without expenditure?

Input-output analysis

Input-output is another means of understanding the production process. It is an analytical procedure developed during the last two decades under the leadership of Wassily Leontieff of Harvard University, who won the Nobel prize for his efforts.

Input-output analysis is an effort to clarify the way the economy literally fits together in terms of the flows of goods from one producer to another or from the last producer to the final buyer. In our normal aggregative way of looking at GNP, we do not see the immensely complex interaction of production flows down the various "stages" of production. All these flows are ignored as we concentrate on *final* production. Input-output analysis concentrates on *all* production, final or intermediate. It thereby gives us a much more detailed understanding of the linkages of output than we can get from normal GNP analysis.

Input-output analysis begins by classifying production into basic inputs or industries. Today the Department of Commerce operates with an input-output table that lists 87 different industries, such as livestock and livestock products, ordnance and accessories, household appliances, amusements. These 87 industries are listed one below the other. Then the output of each industry is placed in a "cell" or "cells" corresponding to the industries to which it is sold. An actual input-output table or *matrix* is too large to be shown here. Instead, Table 6 • 2 gives us a look at a model of such a matrix for an extremely simple hypothetical economy.

Table 6 • 2

	Wheat	Machines	Automobiles	Labor	Total
Wheat (000 bushels)	100	0	0	500	600
Machines (units)	10	5	25	0	40
Automobiles (units)	5	10	3	50	68
Labor (000 man-years)	20	30	60	10	120

What is such a matrix good for? First, let us read across the rows of the table, to trace where output goes. For example, of the total wheat crop of 600 (thousand bushels), 100 are kept back to sow next year's crop, none go to the machine or auto industry, and 500 are used for food (and sold to labor). Machines have a different pattern. Forty machines are produced. Ten are used in harvesting wheat, 5 are used in making more machines (machine tools), 25 go to the auto industry, none are sold to labor. Automobiles are sold to wheat farms (trucks), used by the machinery and auto industry, as trucks or vehicles for salesmen, and sold in large numbers to consumers. Labor is used by all producers, including labor itself (barbers, lawyers, teachers).

This shows us the flow of production "horizontally" through the economy. But we can also use the table to trace its "vertical" distribution. That is, we can see that the production of 600 "units" of wheat (last figure in the top row) required *inputs* (the column under wheat) of 100 units of wheat, 10 machines, 5 automobiles (trucks), and 20 units of labor. To make 40 machines, it takes no wheat, 5 machines, 10 autos, and 30 units of labor. The production of 68 automobiles needs 25 machines, 3 cars, and 60 labor units. To "produce" 120 "units" of labor—to feed and sustain that much labor—takes 500 units of wheat, 50 cars, 10 units of personal services.

Thus our input-output analysis enables us to penetrate deeply into the interstices of the economy. But more than that, it *enables us to calculate production requirements* in a way that far exceeds in accuracy any previously known method. Suppose, for example, that the economy wanted to double its output of autos. Forget for a moment about economies of scale. To begin with, we can see that it will need 25 more machines, 3 additional autos, and 60 more units of labor.

But that is only a list of its *direct demands.* There is also a long series of *indirect demands.* For when the auto industry buys five additional machines, the machine industry will have to increase its output by one-eighth. This means it will need one-eighth more inputs of machines, autos, and labor. But in turn this sets up still further requirements. To "produce" more labor will require more outputs of wheat and cars. To produce more wheat will require still further output of machines and autos. Thus a whole series of secondary, indirect demands spread out through the economy, each generating still further demands.

Input-output analysis uses a technique known as *matrix algebra* to sum up the total effects of any original change. This is not a subject that we will explore here. It is enough to understand how the matrix enables us to calculate production requirements, very much in the manner of an aggregate production function, but in finer detail.

We should note one difficulty with input-output analysis. When we took our example of doubling auto output, we assumed that there would be no changes in the proportions of inputs required to double output and that the input "mixes" for the other industries would be unaffected by increases in their outputs. This assumption of *fixed production coefficients* is not in accord with reality. Increases in output, such as a doubling of auto output, not only usually lead to economies of scale, but may also result from wholly new techniques. Input-output analysis has no way of handling or predicting these kinds of changes. At best it gives us a picture of the production requirements of an economy under the assumption that production methods and products are fixed, although we know they are not.

Nonetheless, no more powerful tool has yet been developed to examine the interactions of the economic system. Input-output analysis is used more and more, not only by government planners or economists, but by large corporations that want to calculate how changes in various sectors of the economy affect demand for their products. Input-output tables enable them to do this because they show the indirect as well as direct demands that economic changes generate.

Saving and investment

Our model of a circular flow economy, continually buying back all the output it has produced, begins to explain the role of demand in determining our gross national product. Yet in one vital particular, our model lacks the illumination we seek. We are ultimately interested in understanding the phenomenon of growth, for we know that in an economy where population and productivity are rising, a failure to grow will result in serious economic difficulties. But our circular flow model, as we have just seen, portrays a stationary economy in which growth (or decline) are never present.

Therefore we must now take a long step toward reality by introducing into our system the key element of growth—the process of saving and investing that is the subject of our chapter.

The meaning of saving

We begin by making sure that we understand a key word in this dynamic analysis—*saving*. We have come across saving many times by now in this book, and so we should be ready for a final mastery of this centrally important economic term. In Chapter 3, "Wealth and Output," we spoke of saving in *real* terms as the act by which society relinquished resources that might have been

7

used for consumption, thereby making them available for the capital-building stream of output. Now we must translate that underlying real meaning of saving into terms corresponding with the buying and selling, paying and receiving discussed in the preceding chapter.

What is saving in these terms? It is very simply *not spending all or part of income for consumption goods or services.** It should be very clear then why saving is such a key term. In our discussion of the circular flow, it became apparent that expenditure was the critical link in the steady operation of the economy. If saving is not-spending, then it would seem that saving could be the cause of just that kind of downward spiral of which we caught a glimpse in our preceding chapter.

And yet this clearly is not the whole story. We also know that the act of investing—of spending money to direct factors into the production of capital goods—requires an act of saving; that is, of not using that same money to direct those factors instead into the production of consumers goods. **Hence, saving is clearly necessary for the process of investment.** Now, how can one and the same act be necessary for economic expansion and a threat to its stability? This is a problem that will occupy us during much of the coming chapters.

Gross vs. net saving

It will help us understand the problem if we again have recourse to the now familiar diagram of the circular flow. But this time we must introduce into it the crucial new fact of net saving. Note *net* saving. Quite unnoticed, we have already encountered saving in our circular flow. In our model economy, when business made expenditures for the replacement of capital, it used money that *could* have been paid in dividends to stockholders or in additional compensation to employees. Before a replacement expenditure was made, someone had to decide not to allocate that money for dividends or bonuses. Thus, there is a flow of saving—that is, of nonconsumption—even in the circular flow.

But this saving is not *net* saving. Like the regular flow investment itself, the flow of saving that finances this replacement serves only to maintain the existing level of capital wealth, not to increase it. Hence, just as with investment, we reserve the term *net saving* for saving that makes possible a rise in the total of our capital assets.

Gross and net saving are thus easy to define. **By gross saving we mean all saving, both for replacement and for expansion of our capital assets, exactly like gross investment. By net saving, we mean any saving that makes possible an increase in the stock of capital, again exactly as in the definition of net investment.**

We have already seen that an economy can maintain a circular flow when it saves only as much as is needed to maintain its capital. But now suppose that it saves more than that, as is shown in Fig. 7 • 1. Here householders save a portion of their incomes, over and above the amount saved by business to insure the maintenance of its assets.*

*Note "for consumption goods or services." Purchasing stocks or bonds or life insurance is also an act of saving, even though you must spend money to acquire these items. What you acquire, however, are assets, not consumption goods and services. Some acts of spending are difficult to classify. Is a college education, for instance, a consumption good or an investment? As we know, it is probably better thought of as an investment, even though in the statistics of GNP it is treated as consumption.

*Figure 7 • 1 represents all net saving as occurring in households, but it should be emphasized that a large fraction of this household savings actually takes place in corporations. We discuss this in the "Extra word" at the end of this chapter.

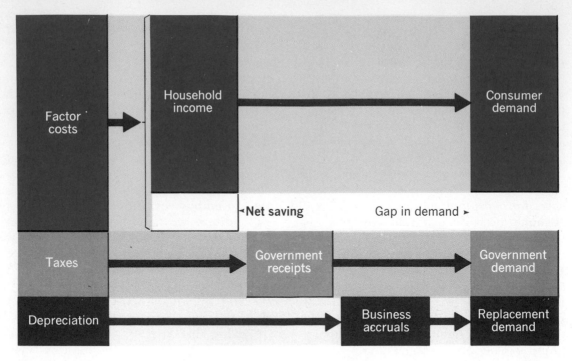

FIG. 7·1   The demand gap

The demand gap

What we see is precisely what we would expect. *There is a gap in demand introduced by the deficiency of consumer spending.* This means that the total receipts of employers who make consumer goods will be less than the total amounts they laid out. It begins to look as if we were approaching the cause of economic recession and unemployment.

Yet, whereas we have introduced net saving, we have forgotten about its counterpart, net investment. Cannot the investment activity of a growing economy in some way close the demand gap?

The dilemma of saving

This is indeed, as we shall soon see, the way out of the dilemma. But before we trace the way investment compensates for saving, let us draw some important conclusions from the analysis we have made up to this point.

1. Any act of saving, in and by itself, creates a gap in demand, a shortage of spending. Unless this gap is closed, there will be trouble in the economic system, for employers will not be getting back as receipts all the sums they laid out

2. If the gap is caused by saving that is implicit in depreciation, it can be closed by replacement expenditures. But if it is caused by net saving, over and above the flow needed to maintain the stock of capital, it will require net investment to be closed.

3. The presence of a demand gap forces us to make a choice. If we want a dynamic, investing economy, we will have to be prepared to cope with the problems that net saving raises. If we want to avoid these problems, we can close the gap by urging consumers or corporations not to save. Then we would have a dependable circular flow, but we would no longer enjoy economic growth.

The Offset to Savings

How, then, shall we manage to make our way out of the dilemma of saving? The previous diagram makes clear what must be done. If a gap in demand is due to the savings of households, then *that gap must be closed by the expanded spending of some other sector*. There are only two other such sectors: government or business. Thus in some fashion or other, the savings of one sector must be "offset" by the increased activity of another.

But how is this offset to take place? How are the resources that are relinquished by consumers to be made available to entrepreneurs in the business sector or to government officials? In a market economy there is only one way that resources or factors not being used in one place can be used in another. Someone must be willing and able to hire them.

Whether or not government and business *are* willing to employ the factors that are not needed in the consumer goods sector is a very critical matter, soon to command much of our attention. But suppose that they are willing. How will they be able to do so? How can they get the necessary funds to expand their activity?

Increasing expenditure   There are six principal methods of accomplishing this essential increase in expenditure.

1. The business sector can increase its expenditures by *borrowing* the savings of the public through the sale of new corporate bonds.

2. The government sector can increase its expenditures by *borrowing* savings from the other sectors through the sale of new government bonds.

3. Both business and government sectors can increase expenditures by *borrowing* additional funds from commercial banks.*

4. The business sector can increase its expenditures by attracting household savings into partnerships, new stock, or other *ownership (or equity)*.

5. The government sector can increase its expenditures by *taxing* the other sectors.

6. Both business and government sectors can increase their expenditures by drawing on *accumulated past savings*, such as unexpended profits or tax receipts from previous years.

Claims   The first four methods above have one attribute that calls them especially to our attention. *They give rise to* claims *that reveal from whom the funds have been obtained and to whom they have been made available, as well as on what terms.* Bonds, corporate or government, show that savings have been borrowed from individuals or banks or firms by business and government units. Shares of stock reveal that savings have been obtained on an equity (ownership) basis, as do new partnership agreements. Borrowing from banks gives rise to loans that also represent the claims of one part of the community against another.

We can note a few additional points about claims, now that we see how many of them arise in the economy. First, many household savings are first put into banks and insurance companies—so-called financial intermediaries—so that the transfer of funds from households to business or government may go through several stages: e.g., from household to insurance company and then from insurance company to corporation.

Second, not *all* claims involve the offsetting of savings of one sector by expendi-

*Actually, they are borrowing from the public through the means of banks. We shall learn about this in Chapter 14.

tures of another. Many claims, once they have arisen, are traded back and forth and bought and sold, as is the case with most stocks and bonds. These purchases and sales involve the *transfer of existing claims*, not the creation of new claims.

Finally, not every claim necessarily involves the creation of an asset. If A borrows $5 from B, bets it on the races, and gives B his note, there has been an increase in claims, but no new asset has been brought into being to match it.

Public and private claims

Now let us look at Fig. 7 • 2. This time we show what happens when savings are made available to the business sector by direct borrowing from households. Note the claim (or equity) that arises.

If the government were doing the borrowing, rather than the business sector, the diagram would look like Fig. 7 • 3. Notice that the claim is now a government bond.

We have not looked at a diagram showing business or government borrowing its funds from the banking system. (This process will be better understood when we take up the problem of money and banking, in Chapter 14.) The basic concept, however, although more complex, is much the same as above.

Completed act of offsetting savings

There remains only a last step, which must now be fully anticipated. We have seen how it is possible to offset the savings in one sector, where they were going to cause an expenditure gap, by increasing the funds available to another sector. It remains only to *spend* those additional funds in the form of additional investment or, in the case of the government, for additional public goods and services. The two completed expenditure circuits now appear in Fig. 7 • 4, p. 102.

While Fig. 7 • 4 is drawn so that the new investment demand or new government demand is exactly equal to net saving, it is important to understand that there is nothing in the economic system guaranteeing that these demands will exactly equal net saving. The desire for new investment or new government goods and services may be either higher or lower than new saving. The need to regulate these new demands so that they will equal net savings is an important objective of *fiscal and monetary policies*, a problem we will study later.

Intersectoral offsets

We shall not investigate further at this point the differences between increased public spending and increased business investment. What we must heed is the crucial point at issue: *if saving in any one sector is to be offset, some other sector (or sectors) must spend more than its income.* A gap in demand due to insufficient expenditure in one sector can be compensated only by an increase in demand—that is, in expenditure—of another.

Once this simple but fundamental point is clearly understood, much of the mystery of macroeconomics disappears, for we can then begin to see that an economy in movement, as contrasted with one in a stationary circular flow, is one in which sectors must *cooperate* to maintain the closed circuit of income and output. In a dynamic economy, we no longer enjoy the steady translation of incomes into expenditure which, as we have seen, is the key to an uninterrupted flow of output. Rather, we are faced with the presence of net saving and the possibility of a gap in final demand. Difficult though the ensuing problems are, let us not forget that net sav-

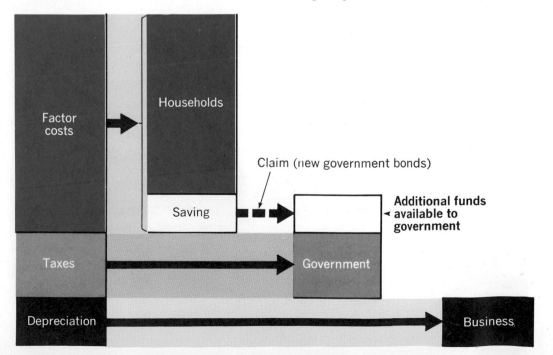

FIG. 7 · 2   "Transfer" of savings to business

FIG. 7 · 3   "Transfer" of savings to government

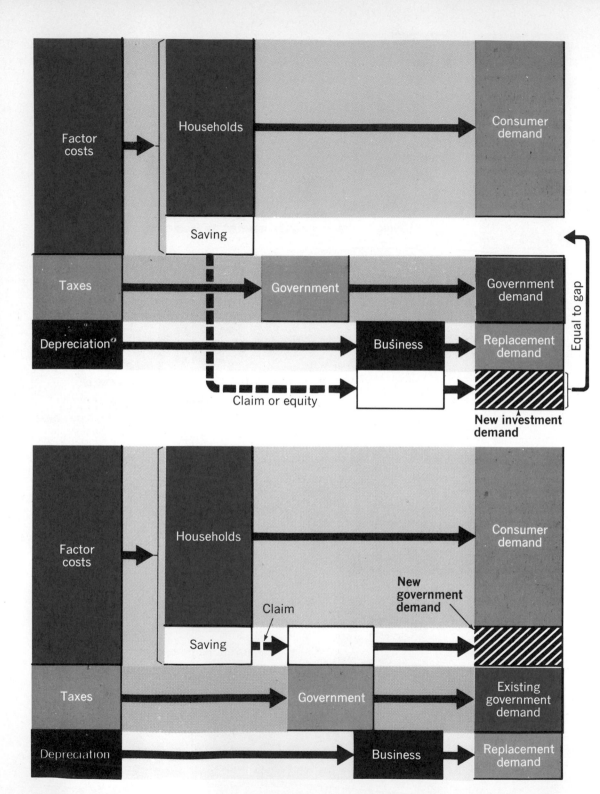

FIG. 7·4 Two ways of closing the demand gap

102

ing is the necessary condition for the accumulation of capital. *The price of economic growth, in other words, is the risk of economic decline.*

Real and money saving

This central importance of saving in a growing economy will become a familiar problem. At this juncture, where we have first encountered the difficulties it can pose, we must be certain that we understand two different aspects that saving assumes.

One aspect, noticed in our initial overview of the economy, is the decision to relinquish *resources* that can be redeployed into capital-building. This is the real significance of saving. But this "real" aspect of saving is not the way we encounter the act of saving in our ordinary lives. We think of saving as a *monetary* phenomenon, not a "real" one. When we save, we are conscious of not using all our incomes for consumption, but we scarcely, if ever, think of releasing resources for alternative employments.

There is a reason for this dichotomy of real and money saving. In our society, with its extraordinary degree of specialization, the individuals or institutions that do the actual saving are not always those that do the actual capital-building. In a simple society, this dichotomy between saving and investing need not, and usually does not, occur. A farmer who decides to build new capital—for example, to build a barn—is very much aware of giving up a consumption activity—the raising of food—in order to carry out his investment. So is an artisan who stops weaving clothing to repair the loom. Where the saver and the investor are one and the same person, there need be no "financial" saving, and the underlying real phenomenon of saving as the diversion of activity from consumption to investment is immediately apparent.

Savers and investors

In the modern world, savers and investors are often the same individual or group—as in the case of a business management that spends profits on new productive capacity rather than on higher executive salaries, or government leaders who use tax revenues to build roads or dams rather than to increase welfare payments.

Frequently, however, savers are not investors. Certainly householders do not personally decide and direct the process of capital formation in the nation. Furthermore, the workers and materials that households voluntarily relinquish by not using all their incomes to buy consumers goods have to be physically transferred to different industries, often to different occupations and locations, in order to carry out their investment tasks. This requires funds in the hands of the investors, so that they can tempt resources from one use to another.

Hence we need an elaborate system for directly or indirectly "transferring" money saving into the hands of those who will be in a position to employ factors for capital construction purposes. Nevertheless, underlying this complex mechanism for transferring purchasing power remains the same simple purpose that we initially witnessed. Resources that have been relinquished from the production of consumption goods or services are now employed in the production of capital goods. Thus, *saving and investing are essentially real phenomena,* even though it may take a great deal of financial manipulation to bring them about.

A final important point. **The fact that the decisions to save and the decisions to invest are lodged in different individuals or groups alerts us to a basic reason why the savings-investment process may not always work smoothly.** Savers may choose to consume less than their total incomes at times when investors have no interest in expanding their capital assets. Alternatively, business firms may wish to form new capital when savers are interested in spending money only on themselves. This separation of decision-making can give rise to situations in which savings are not offset by investment or in which investment plans race out ahead of savings capabilities. In our next chapters we will be investigating what happens in these cases.

Even in the case where savers and investors are the same people, problems arise. A business may wish to save *this* year and invest *next* year. Thus savings and investment decisions may not be coordinated in the shortrun. In our next chapters we will be investigating what happens in these cases.

Transfer Payments and Profits

We have talked about the transfer of purchasing power from savers to investors, but we have not yet mentioned another kind of transfer, also of great importance in the overall operation of the economy. This is the transfer of incomes from sector to sector (and sometimes within sectors).

Transfers . As we already know, income transfers (called *transfer payments*) are a very useful and important means of reallocating purchasing power in society. Through transfer payments, members of the community who do not participate in production are given an opportunity to enjoy incomes that would otherwise not be available to them. Thus Social Security transfer payments make it possible for the old or

the handicapped to be given an "income" of their own (not, to be sure, a currently *earned* income), or unemployment benefits give purchasing power to those who cannot get it through employment.

Not all transfers are in the nature of welfare payments, however. The distribution of money *within* a household is a transfer payment. So is the payment of interest on the national debt.* So is the grant of a subsidy to a private enterprise, such as an airline, or of a scholarship to a college student. Any income payment that is not earned by selling one's productive services on the market falls in the transfer category.

It may help to understand this process if we visualize it in our flow diagram. Figure 7•5 shows two kinds of transfers. The upper one, from government to the household sector, shows a typical transfer of incomes, such as veterans' pensions or Social Security; the transfer below it reflects the flow of income that might be illustrated by a payment to agriculture for crop support. Transfers *within* sectors, such as household allowances, are not shown in the diagram.

One thing we may well note about transfers is that they can only rearrange *the incomes created in the production process; they cannot increase those incomes.* Income, as we learned in the last chapter, is inextricably tied to output—indeed, income is only the financial counterpart of output.

Transfer payments, on the other hand, are a way of arranging individual claims to production in some fashion that strikes the community as fairer or more efficient or more decorous than the way the market

---

*As we know, the payment of interest on corporate debt is not considered a transfer payment, but a payment to a factor of production. Actually, much government interest should also be thought of as a factor payment (for the loan of capital for purposes of public output); but by convention, all government interest is classified as a transfer payment.

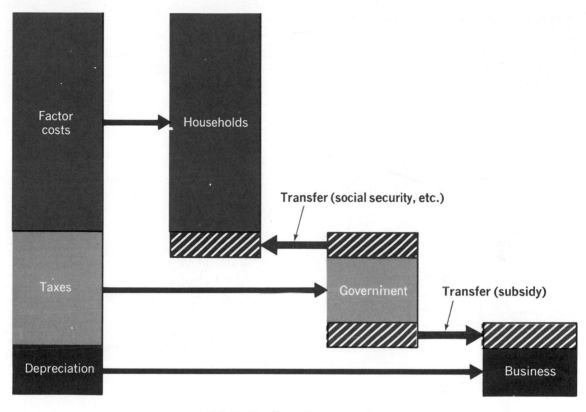

FIG. 7·5   Transfer payments

process allocates them through the production process. As such, transfer payments are an indispensable and often invaluable agency of social policy. But it is important to understand that no amount of transfers can, in themselves, increase the total that is to be shared. That can happen only by raising output itself.

Transfer payments and taxes

We have mentioned, but only in passing, another means of transferring purchasing power from one sector to another: taxation. Heretofore, however, we have often spoken as though all government tax receipts were derived from indirect taxes that were added onto the cost of production.

In fact, this is not the only source of government revenue. Indirect taxes are an important part of state and local revenues, but they are only a minor part of federal tax receipts. Most federal taxes are levied on the incomes of the factors of production or on the profits of businesses after the other factors have been paid.

Once again it is worth remembering that the government taxes consumers (and businesses) because it is in the nature of much government output that it cannot be *sold*. Taxes are the way we are billed for our share—rightly or wrongly figured—of government production that has been collectively decided upon. As we can now see, taxes—both on business and on the household sector—also finance many transfer payments. That is, the government

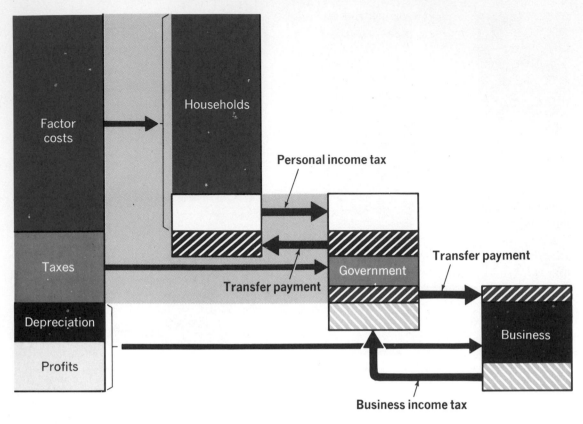

FIG. 7 • 6   Transfers and income taxes

intervenes in the distribution process to make it conform to our politically expressed social purposes, taking away some incomes from certain individuals and groups and providing incomes to others. Figure 7 • 6 shows what this looks like in the flow of GNP. (Note that the business sector is drawn with profits, as our next section will explain.)

As we can see, the exchanges of income between the household and the government sectors can be very complex. Income can flow from households to government units via taxation and return to the household sector via transfer payments; and the same two-way flows can take place between government and business.

Profits and demand

The last diagram has already introduced a new element of reality in our discussion. Taxes on business *income* presuppose that businesses make *profits*. Let us see how these profits fit into the savings-investment process.

During our discussion of the circular flow, we spoke of profits as a special kind of factor cost—a payment to the factor *capital*. Now we can think of profits not merely as a factor cost (although there is always a certain element of risk-remuneration in profits), but as a return to especially efficient or forward-thinking firms who have used the investment process to introduce new products or processes ahead of the run of their industries. We also know that profits accrue to powerful firms who exact a semimonopolistic return from their customers.

What matters in our analysis at this stage is not the precise explanation we give to the origin of profits, but a precise explanation of their role in maintaining a "closed-circuit" economy in which all costs are returned to the marketplace as demand. A commonly heard diagnosis for economic maladies is that profits are at the root of the matter, in that they cause a "withdrawal" of spending power or income from the community. If profits are "hoarded," or kept unspent, this can be true. In fact, however, profits are usually spent in three ways. They may be

1. **Distributed as income to the household sector in the form of dividends or profit shares, to become part of household spending**

2. **Spent by business firms for new plant and equipment**

3. **Taxed by the government and spent in the public sector**

All three methods of offsetting profits appear in Fig. 7 • 7.

Thus, we can see that profits need not constitute a withdrawal from the income stream. Indeed, unless profits are adequate, businesses will very likely not invest enough to offset the savings of the household sector. They may, in fact, even fail to make normal replacement expenditures, aggravating the demand gap still further in this way.

Thus the existence of profits, far from being deflationary—that is, far from causing a fall in income—is, in fact, essential for the maintenance of a given level of income or for an advance to a higher level. Nonetheless, there is a germ of truth in the

FIG. 7 • 7 Profits in the circular flow

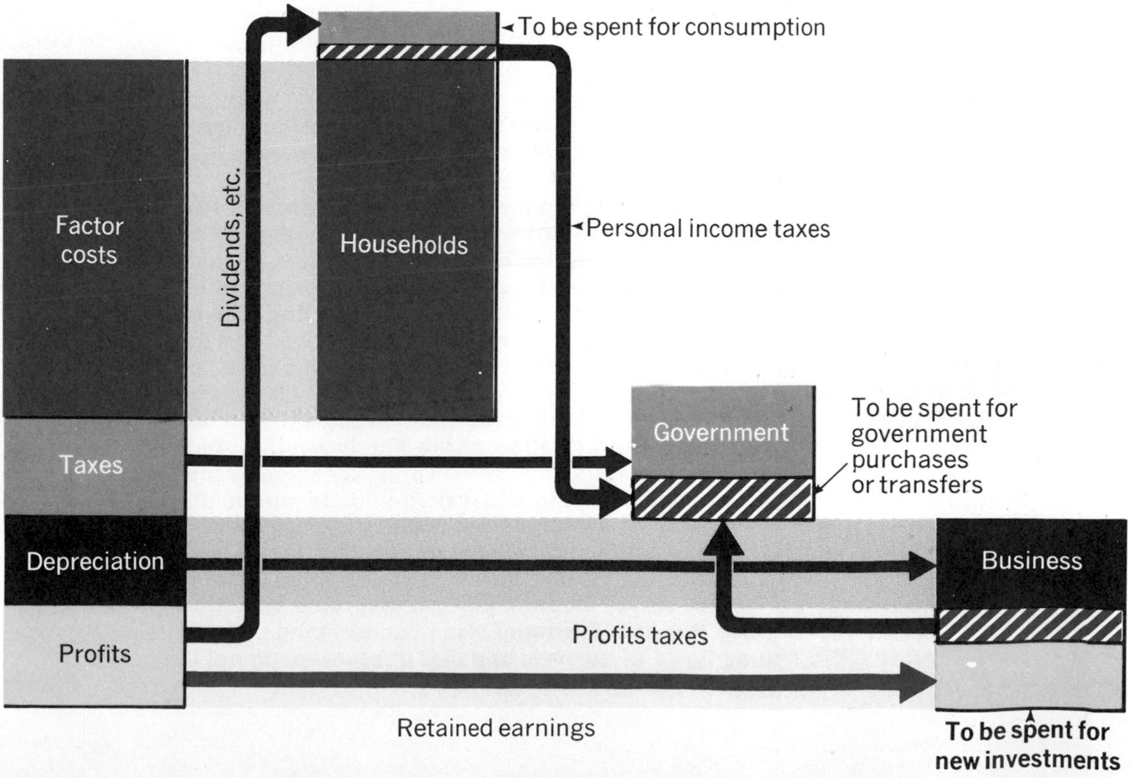

contentions of those who have maintained that profits can cause an insufficiency of purchasing power. For unless profits are returned to the flow of purchasing power as dividends that are spent by their recipients or as new capital expenditures made by business or as taxes that lead to additional public spending, there will be a gap in the community's demand. Thus we can think of profits just as we think of saving—an indispensable source of economic growth or a potential source of economic decline.

Saving, investment, and growth

We are almost ready to leave our analysis of the circle of production and income and to proceed to a much closer study of the individual dynamic elements that create and close demand gaps. Before we do, however, it is well that we take note of one last fact of the greatest importance. In offsetting the savings of any

sector by investment, we have closed the production and income circuit, much as in the stationary circular flow, but there is one crucial difference from the circular flow. Now we have closed the flow by diverting savings into the creation of *additional* capital. Unlike the stationary circular flow where the handing around of incomes did no more than to maintain unchanged the original configuration of the system, in our new dynamic saving-and-investment model *each closing of the circuit results in a quantitative change— the addition of a new "layer" of capital.*

Hence, more and more physical wealth is being added to our system; and thinking back to our first impressions of the interaction of wealth and population, we would expect more and more productiveness from our human factors. With complications that we shall have to deal with in due course, *growth* has entered our economic model.

FOCUS

This lesson continues our exploration of how demand is generated. It takes up the vital question of how saving is accommodated by the system, and the crucial role of saving in making growth possible.

The central idea of the chapter is the interaction among sectors in offsetting demand gaps. Demand gaps arise when any sector fails to spend all its income, so that instead of a completed circular flow, we have a failure to turn all incomes into expenditure. When such a demand gap occurs, the financial savings of that sector must be made available to another sector for investment spending. The transfer of saving is made by borrowing or taxing or creating new equities. The sector that gains savings will often create a claim—a stock or a bond—that shows the transfer of savings to its account.

Once you see how the savings and investment process works, you are well along the way to understanding the operation of the macro system. Probably no single process is as central to the "secret" of growth and recession as the creation of new capital through the process of saving and investment. Be sure to draw all the diagrams in the questions that follow and check them with the originals.

A secondary but by no means unimportant lesson of the chapter is the role of transfer payments and profits in the circular flow. It is important to understand how transfers rearrange but do not create income, and the diagrams on pages 105 and 107 are a good way to grasp this. It is essential also to understand that profits must be returned to GNP, like all flows of income, and that if returned, do not become a "drag" on income, but rather a source of new growth.

WORDS AND CONCEPTS YOU SHOULD KNOW

Real vs. Monetary saving, 96–97
Gross vs. net saving, 97
Demand gap, 98
Claims, 99–100

Intersectoral offsets to saving, 100–102
Transfers, 104
Profits in a circular flow, 106–108
Saving and growth, 108

QUESTIONS

1. What do we mean by a demand gap? Show diagrammatically.

2. How is a demand gap filled by business investment? Show diagrammatically.

3. Why is saving indispensable for growth?

4. Can we have planned business investment without saving? Saving without planned business investment?

5. Draw carefully a diagram that shows how savings can be offset by government spending.

6. How is it possible for a sector to spend more than its income? How does it get the additional money?

7. What is a transfer payment? Draw diagrams of transfers from government to consumers, from government to business. Is charity a transfer? Is a lottery?

8. Diagram the three ways in which profits can be returned to the expenditure flow. What happens if they are not?

9. Why is a problem presented by the fact that those who make the decision to invest may not be the same people who decide to save?

10. In what way is a stationary circular flow economy different from an economy that saves and invests?

Raising the savings rate

One of the sharpest arguments, these days, is whether or not there is a "capital shortage"—an insufficient amount of capital to give us the growth, the new energy, the pollution suppression, the capital-using services we require. In another "Extra word" (p. 144) we will look into some aspects of that problem. But if we assume for the moment that there *is* such a shortage, one important remedy would certainly be to raise the national savings rate. How could we do that?

Let us begin by inquiring into the sources of saving. In our chapter we concentrated almost wholly on the generation of savings in the household sector. But in fact households are by no means the main savers in the economy as we can see:

SOURCES OF SAVINGS, 1976

	$ Billion	%		$ Billion	%
Households	$ 78	34	State and local government	14	6
Businesses	199	86	Federal government	−58	−26

In this table, the household sector shows up as a substantial provider of funds. And so it is. But a very large fraction of those personal savings go into the purchase of homes. If we subtract this flow residential investment, we fine that individuals provide only 4 percent of the funds borrowed by business and government.

Business provides most of its savings through retained earnings—that fraction of its profits, usually about one-third, that is not paid out to shareholders or to government as taxes. And governments save when they use their incomes for capital-building rather than consumption purposes. We are not accustomed to dividing government spending into consumption and investment purposes, but when local, state, or federal governments build roads, schools, hospitals, housing projects, and the like, they are saving-and-investing just as certainly as when corporations use their retained earnings to build plant and equipment. The difference is that the government creates public investment, rather than private investment.

If we were to look for government savings that were available for the use of other sectors of the economy, we would find that state and local governments saved $14 billion over what they invested in 1976, while the federal government absorbed $58 billion in savings from other sectors of the economy. How could the savings rates of these three sectors be increased? Let us begin with the household sector. In Table 7 • 1 we see that high-income families do most of the sector's savings.

Table 7 • 1 Savings rates by income class ($000)

$0–3	$3–6	$6–10	$10–15	$15+
−12%	2%	15%	18%	37%

NOTE: These savings rates are defined as the ratio of change in net assets to current income, rather than the more conventional savings out of current income.

Thus one way of raising household savings would be to reduce income tax rates for upper-income families, who would almost certainly save a large amount of their tax cuts. Opponents of such a proposal argue that a tax cut for the rich would have to be matched by tax increases for the middle and lower groups. They admit that savings might go up and that this would lead to investment and growth. But they object to the pattern of increased inequality that such a policy would bring.

Both the proponents and the opponents of tax cuts for the upper-income groups are right. Tax cuts would create more capital and thus more per capita income; and tax cuts would also increase inequality. The pertinent question is one of magnitudes. How much inequality are we willing to accept to gain additional savings or additional income?

What about raising corporate savings rates? They could be raised by reducing corporate income taxes—with exactly the same arguments pro and con, because corporate stock is largely owned by upper-income individuals, so that a corporate tax cut is equivalent to a personal tax cut for the rich.

Table 7·2 Ownership of stock by income class

Quintile Percent	Lowest 7%	Second 5%	Third 9%	Fourth 9%	Highest 70%

Could governments increase their savings available for other sectors of the economy? One way would be for government to plan budgets that had surpluses—excesses of tax income over expenditures. It could do this by raising taxes or by cutting back on its consumption outlays. The problem here, it need hardly be said, is the political opposition that would be generated by tax increases or by reduced government outlays for consumption purposes, such as schooling, police, health care, recreation, sanitation, and the like.

There are still other ways of raising the savings rate—for example by reducing the ease with which households can get consumer or mortgage credit. If we had a very tough consumer credit policy, households would have to save up *before* they could buy a car or a house, and those savings could be used (via the banking system) to build new industrial capital. The trouble, of course, is that such a policy would deal a terrific blow, in the short run, to the housing or automobile or appliance industry.

Thus there exist many ways of raising the savings rate, but all of them carry social costs. In fact the key thing to note is that all these options require reductions in consumption for some groups. If saving is to go up, someone's consumption must go down. In the case of a tax break for the wealthy, the cut in consumption will be felt by the middle and lower classes whose taxes will rise. A cut in corporation income taxes may induce corporations to save and invest, but that must mean that they pay less taxes. Someone else will have to pay those taxes. And if governments save, as we have seen, this too means less public consumption or higher tax rates.

Thus, if we want to raise the savings rate, someone must pay the cost. Who should that be? This question plunges us into the debate between equity and efficiency that economist Arthur Okun has called "the big trade-off." There is no magic answer to this question. The big trade-off is a value-laden question that forces both proponents and opponents of higher savings rates to declare their preferences for one kind of society or another.

Consumption demand

With a basic understanding of the crucial role of expenditure and of the complex relationship of saving and investment behind us, we are in a position to look more deeply into the question of the determination of gross national product. For what we have discovered heretofore is only the *mechanism* by which a market economy can sustain or fail to sustain a given level of output through a circuit of expenditure and receipt. Now we must try to discover the *forces* that dynamize the system, creating or closing gaps between income and outgo. What causes a demand for the goods and services measured in the GNP? Let us begin to answer that question by examining the flow of demand most familiar to us—consumption.

The Household Sector

8

Largest and in many respects most important of all the sectors in the economy is that of the nation's households—that is, its families and single-dwelling individuals (the two categories together called consumer units) considered as receivers of

112

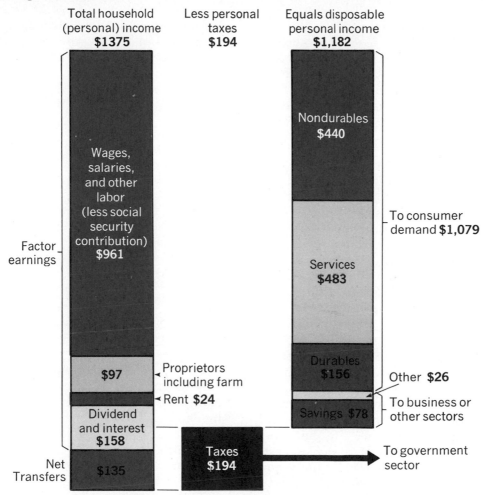

All figures in billions*

Total household (personal) income **$1375**

Less personal taxes **$194**

Equals disposable personal income **$1,182**

Nondurables **$440**

Wages, salaries, and other labor (less social security contribution) **$961**

To consumer demand **$1,079**

Services **$483**

Factor earnings

Durables **$156**

$97 — Proprietors including farm

Other **$26**

◄ Rent **$24**

Dividend and interest **$158**

Savings $78

To business or other sectors

Net Transfers $135

Taxes **$194**

To government sector

* Totals do not always add, owing to rounding

FIG. 8 · 1   Consumption sector 1976

income and transfer payments or as savers and spenders of money for consumption.

How big is this sector? In 1976 it comprised some 57 million families and some 21 million independent individuals who collectively gathered in $1,375 billion in income and spent $1,104 billion.* As Fig.

8 · 1 shows, the great bulk of receipts was from factor earnings, and transfer payments played only a relatively small role. As we can also see, we must subtract per-

*The Department of Commerce has redefined some categories of the national income accounts, and the word *consumption* to-day applies, strictly speaking, only to personal expenditures for goods and services. Included in total consumer spending, however, are sizeable amounts for interest (mainly on installment loans) and for remittances abroad, neither of which sums are included in the amount for goods and services. The proper

nomenclature for the total of consumer spending (goods and services plus interest and remittances) is now *personal outlays*. We shall, however, continue to use the simpler term, *consumption*, although our figures will be those for personal outlays.

Note, also, that the compilation of these figures is a time-consuming process in which earlier estimates are frequently subject to revision. Hence, figures for the components of consumption or, for that matter, for almost all magnitudes in the economic process are apt to vary slightly in successive printed statistics until, eventually, the "final" figures are arrived at.

sonal tax payments from household income (or *personal income* as it is officially designated) before we get *disposable personal income*—income actually available for spending. It is from disposable personal income that the crucial choice is made to spend or save. Much of this chapter will focus on that choice.

Subcomponents of consumption

Finally we note that consumer spending itself divides into three main streams. The largest of these is for *nondurable* goods, such as food and clothing or other items whose economic life is (or is assumed to be) short. Second largest is an assortment of expenditures we call consumer *services*, comprising things such as rent, doctors' or lawyers' or barbers' ministrations, theater or movie admissions, bus or taxi or plane transportation, and other purchases that are not a physical good but work performed by someone or some equipment. Last is a substream of expenditure for consumer *durable* goods, which, as the name suggests, include items such as cars or household appliances whose economic life is considerably greater than that of most nondurables. We can think of these goods as comprising consumers' physical capital.

There are complicated patterns and interrelations among these three major streams of consumer spending. As we would expect, consumer spending for durables is extremely volatile. In bad times, such as 1933, it has sunk to less than 8 percent of all consumer outlays; in the peak of good times in the early 1970s, it came to nearly double that. Meanwhile, outlays for services have been a steadily swelling area for consumer spending in the postwar economy. As a consequence of the growth of consumer buying of durables

and of services, the relative share of the consumer dollar going to "soft goods" has been slowly declining.

Consumption and GNP

The internal dynamics of consumption are of great interest to someone who seeks to project consumer spending patterns into the future—perhaps as an aid to merchandising. But here we are interested in the larger phenomenon of the relationship of consumption as a whole to the flow of gross national product.

Figure 8·2 shows us this historic relationship since 1929. Certain things stand out.

1. **Consumption spending is by far the largest category of spending in GNP.**

Total consumer expenditures—for durable goods such as automobiles or washing machines, for nondurables like food or clothing, and for services such as recreation or medical care—account for approximately two-thirds of all the final buying in the economy.

2. **Consumption is not only the biggest, but the most stable of all the streams of expenditure.**

Consumption, as we have mentioned, is *the* essential economic activity. Even if there is a total breakdown in the social system. households will consume some bare minimum. Further, it is a fact of common experience that even in adverse circumstances, households seek to maintain their accustomed living standards. Thus consumption activities constitute a kind of floor for the level of overall economic activity. Investment and government spending, as we shall see, are capable of

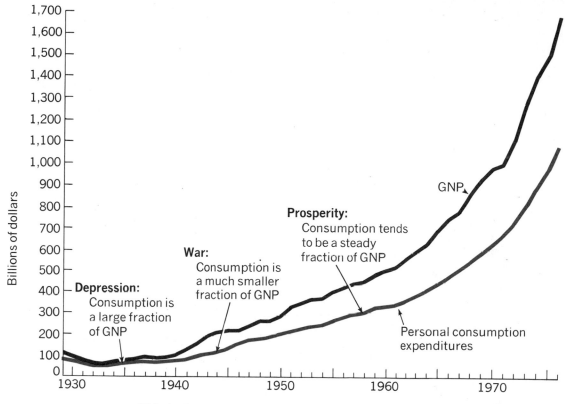

FIG. 8 · 2 Consumption and GNP, current prices

sudden reversals; but the streams of consumer spending tend to display a measure of stability over time.

3. **Consumption is nonetheless capable of considerable fluctuation as a proportion of GNP.**

Remembering our previous diagrams, we can see that this proportionate fluctuation must reflect changes in the relative importance of investment and government spending. And indeed this is the case. As investment spending declined in the Depression, consumption bulked relatively larger in GNP; as government spending increased during the war, consumption bulked relatively smaller.

The changing *relative* size of consumption, in other words, reflects broad changes in *other* sectors rather than sharp changes in consuming habits.

4. **Despite its importance, consumption alone will not "buy back" GNP.**

It is well to recall that consumption, although the largest component of GNP, is still *only* two-thirds of GNP. Government buying and business buying of investment goods are essential if the income-expenditure circuit is to be closed. During our subsequent analysis it will help to remember that consumption expenditure by itself does not provide the only impetus of demand.

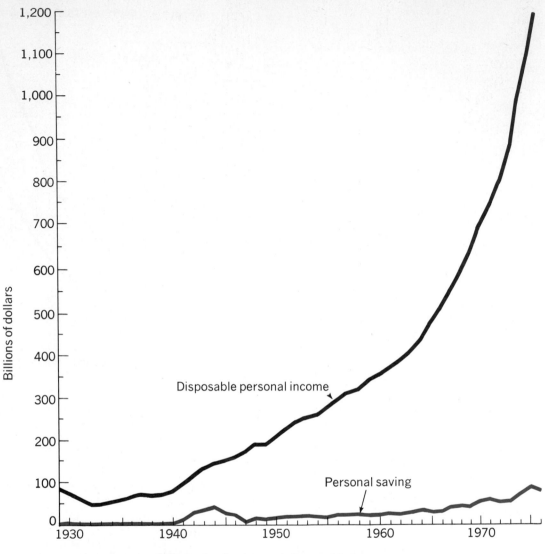

FIG. 8 · 3 Saving and disposable income

Saving in Historic Perspective

This first view of consumption activity sets the stage for our inquiry into the dynamic causes of fluctuations in GNP. We already know that the saving-investment relationship lies at the center of this problem and that much saving arises from the household sector. Hence, let us see what we can learn about the saving process in historic perspective.

We begin with Fig. 8 · 3 showing the relationship of household saving to disposable income—that is, to household sector incomes after the payment of taxes.

What we see here are two interesting facts. First, during the bottom of the Great Depression there were *no* savings in the household sector. In fact, under the duress

116

of unemployment, millions of households were forced to *dissave*—to borrow or to draw on their old savings (hence the negative figure for the sector as a whole). By way of contrast, we notice the immense savings of the peak war years when consumers' goods were rationed and households were urged to save. Clearly, then, the *amount* of saving is capable of great fluctuation, falling to zero or to negative figures in periods of great economic distress and rising to as much as a quarter of income during periods of goods shortages.

In Fig. 8 • 4, we are struck by another fact. However variable the amounts, the savings *ratio* shows a considerable stability in "normal" years. This steadiness is particularly noteworthy in the postwar period. From 1950 to the present, consumption has ranged between roughly 92 to 95 percent of disposable personal income—which is, of course, the same as saying that savings have ranged roughly between 8 percent and 5 percent. If we take the postwar period as a whole, *we can see that in an average year we have consumed a little more than 94 cents of each dollar of income and that this ratio has remained fairly constant even though our incomes have increased markedly.*

Long-run savings behavior

This stability of the long-run savings ratio is an interesting, important phenomenon and something of a puzzling one, for we might easily imagine that the savings ratio would rise over time. Statistical investigations of cross sections of the nation show that rich families tend to save not only larger amounts, but larger *percentages* of their income, than poor families do.* Thus as the entire nation has grown richer and as families have moved from lower income brackets to higher ones, it seems natural to suppose that they would also take on the higher savings characteristics that accompany upper incomes.

Were this so, the economy would face a very serious problem. In order to sustain its higher levels of aggregate income, it would have to invest an ever larger *proportion* of its income to offset its growing ratio of savings to income. As we shall see in our next chapter, investment is always a source of potential trouble because it is so much riskier than any other business function. If we had to keep on making proportionally larger investments each year to keep pace with our proportionally growing

*See Table 7 • 1 on p. 110.

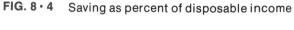

FIG. 8 • 4   Saving as percent of disposable income

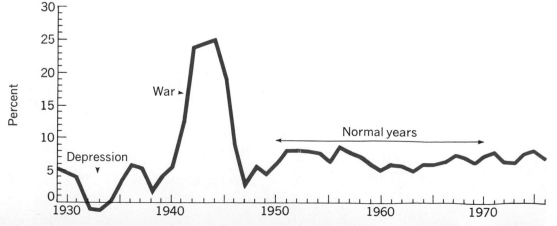

savings, we should live in an exceedingly vulnerable economic environment.

Fortunately, we are rescued from this dangerous situation, because our long-run savings ratio, as we have seen, displays a reassuring steadiness. In fact, there has been no significant upward trend in the savings ratio for the nation's households since the mid-1800s, and there may have been a slight downward trend.*

The Consumption-Income Relationship

What we have heretofore seen are some of the historical and empirical relationships of consumption and personal saving to income. We have taken the trouble to investigate these relationships in some detail, since they are among the most important causes of the gaps that have to be closed by investment. But the statistical facts in

themselves are only a halfway stage in our macroeconomic investigation. Now we want to go beyond the facts to a generalized understanding of the behavior that gives rise to them. Thus our next task is to extract from the facts certain behavioral *relationships* that are sufficiently regular and dependable for us to build into a new dynamic model of the economy.

If we think back over the data we have examined, one primary conclusion comes to mind. This is the indisputable fact that the *amount* of saving generated by the household sector depends in the first instance upon the income enjoyed by the household sector. Despite the stability of the savings ratio, we have seen that the dollar volume of saving in the economy is susceptible to great variation, from negative amounts in the Great Depression to very large amounts in boom times. Now we must see if we can find a systematic connection between the changing size of income and the changing size of saving.

Propensity to consume

There is indeed such a relationship, lying at the heart of macroeconomic analysis. We call it the

*Economists maintain a certain tentativeness in their assertions about long-run trends, since the statistical foundation on which they are based is inevitably subject to some error and uncertainty.

consumption function or, more formally, the propensity to consume, the name invented by John Maynard Keynes, the famous English economist who first formulated it in 1936.* What is this "propensity" to consume? It means that the relationship between consumption behavior and income is sufficiently dependable so that we can actually predict how much consumption (or how much saving) will be associated with a given level of income.

We base such predictions on a schedule that enables us to see the income-consumption relationship over a considerable range of variation. Table 8·1 is such a schedule, a purely hypothetical one, for us to examine.

Table 8·1   A propensity to consume schedule

BILLIONS OF DOLLARS		
Income	Consumption	Savings
$100	$80	$20
110	87	23
120	92	28
130	95	35
140	97	43

One could imagine, of course, innumerable different consumption schedules; in one society a given income might be accompanied by a much higher propensity to consume (or propensity to save) than in another. But the basic hypothesis of Keynes—a hypothesis amply confirmed by research—was that the consumption schedule in all modern industrial societies had a particular basic configuration, despite these variations. The propensity to consume, said Keynes, reflected the fact that on the average, men tended to increase their consumption as

their incomes rose, but not by as much as their income increased. In other words, as the incomes of individuals rose, so did both their consumption and their savings.

Note that Keynes did not say that the proportion of saving rose. We have seen how involved is the dynamic determination of savings ratios. Keynes merely suggested that in the short run, the amount of saving would rise as income rose—or to put it conversely again, that families would not use all their increases in income for consumption purposes alone. It is well to remember that these conclusions hold in going down the schedule as well as up. Keynes' basic "law" implies that when there is a decrease in income, there will be some decrease in the amount of saving, or that a family will not absorb a fall in its income entirely by contracting its consumption.

What does the consumption schedule look like in the United States? We will come to that shortly. First, however, let us fill in our understanding of the terms we will need for our generalized study.

Average propensity to consume   The consumption schedule gives us two ways of measuring the fundamental economic relationship of income and saving. One way is simply to take any given level

Table 8·2   Calculation of the average propensity to consume

BILLIONS OF DOLLARS		Consumption ÷ income (Avg. propensity to consume)
Income	Consumption	
$100	$80	.80
110	87	.79
120	92	.77
130	95	.73
140	97	.69

*More about Keynes in the box on p. 166. Note that his name is pronounced "Kanes," not "Keenes."

of income and to compute the percentage relation of consumption to that income. This gives us the *average propensity to consume*. In Table 8·2, using the same hypothetical schedule as before, we make this computation.

The average propensity to consume, in other words, tells us how a society at any given moment divides its total income between consumption and saving. It it thus a kind of measure of long-run savings behavior, for households divide their incomes between saving and consuming in ratios that reflect established habits and, as we have seen, do not ordinarily change rapidly.

Marginal propensity to consume

But we can also use our schedule to measure another very important aspect of saving behavior: the way households divide *increases* (or decreases) in income between consumption and saving. This *marginal propensity to consume* is quite different from the average propensity to consume, as the figures in Table 8·3 (still from our original hypothetical schedule) demonstrate.

Note carefully that the last column in Table 8·3 is designed to show us something quite different from the last column of the previous table. Take a given income level—say $110 billion. In Table 8·2 the average propensity to consume for that income level is .79, meaning that we will actually spend on consumption 79 percent of our income of $110 billion. But the corresponding figure opposite $110 billion in the marginal propensity to consume table (8·3) is .70. This does *not* mean that out of our $110 billion income we somehow spend only 70 percent, instead of 79 percent, on consumption. It *does* mean that we spend on consumption only 70 percent *of the $10 billion increase* that lifted us from a previous income of $100 billion to the $110 billion level. The rest of that $10 billion increase we saved.

As we know, much of economics, in micro- as well as macroanalysis, is concerned with studying the effects of *changes* in economic life. It is precisely here that marginal concepts take on their importance. When we speak of the average propensity to consume, we relate all consumption and all income from the bottom up, so to speak, and thus we call attention to behavior covering a great variety of situations and conditions. But when we speak of the marginal propensity to consume, we are focusing only on our behavior toward *changes* in our incomes. Thus the marginal approach is invaluable, as we shall see, in dealing with the effects of shortrun fluctuations in GNP.

Table 8·3   Calculation of the marginal propensity to consume

BILLIONS OF DOLLARS				Marginal propensity to consume = Change in consumption ÷ change in income
Income	Consumption	Change in income	Change in consumption	
$100	$80	—	—	—
110	87	$10	$7	.70
120	92	10	5	.50
130	95	10	3	.30
140	97	10	2	.20

A scatter diagram   The essentially simple idea of a systematic, behavioral relationship between income and consumption will play an extremely important part in the model of the economy we shall soon construct. But the relationships we have thus far defined are too vague to be of much use. We want to know if we can extract from the facts of experience not only a general dependence of consumption on income, but a *fairly precise method of determining exactly how much saving will be associated with a given amount of income.*

Here we reach a place where it will help us to use diagrams and simple equations rather than words alone. So let us begin by transferring our conception of a propensity to consume schedule to a new kind of diagram directly showing the interrelation of income and consumption.

The *scatter diagram* (Fig. 8·5) shows precisely that. Along the vertical axis on the left we have marked off intervals to measure total consumer expenditure in billions of dollars; along the horizontal axis on the bottom we measure disposable personal income, also in billions of dollars. The dots tell us, for the years enumerated, how large consumption and income were. For instance, if we take the dot for 1966 and look directly below it to the horizontal axis, we can see that disposable personal income for that year was roughly $510 billion. The same dot measured against the vertical axis tells us that consumption for 1966 was a little more than $475 billion. If we now divide the figure for consumption by that for income, we get a value of 93.1 percent for our propensity to consume. If we subtract that from 100, our propensity to save must have been 6.9 percent.*

*It is difficult to read figures accurately from a graph. The actual values are: disposable income, $512 billion; consumption, $479 billion; average propensity to consume, 93.4 percent.

Returning to the diagram itself, we notice that the black line which "fits" the trend of the dots does not go evenly from corner to corner. If it did, it would mean that each amount of income was matched by an *equal* amount of consumption—in other words, that there was no saving. Instead, the line leans slightly downward, indicating that as income goes higher, consumption also increases, but not by quite as much.

Does the chart also show us marginal propensity to consume? Not really. As we know, our short-run savings propensities are higher than our long-run propensities. This chart shows our "settled" position, from year to year, after the long-run, upward drift of spending has washed out our marginal (short-run) savings behavior.

Nevertheless, if we look at the movement from one dot to the next, we get some notion of the short-run forces at work. During the war years, for instance, as the result of a shortage of many consumer goods and a general exhortation to save, the average propensity to consume was unusually low. That is why the dots during those years form a bulge below the trend line. After the war, we can also see that the marginal propensity to consume must have been very high. As a matter of fact, for a few years consumption actually rose faster than income, as people used their wartime savings to buy things that were unavailable during the war. Between 1946 and 1947, for example, disposable income rose by some $9.8 billion, but personal outlays rose by almost $18 billion! By 1950, however, the consumption-income relationship was back to virtually the same ratio as during the 1930s.

In simple mathematics   There is another way of reducing to shorthand clarity the propensity to consume. For obviously, what we are looking for is a functional rela-

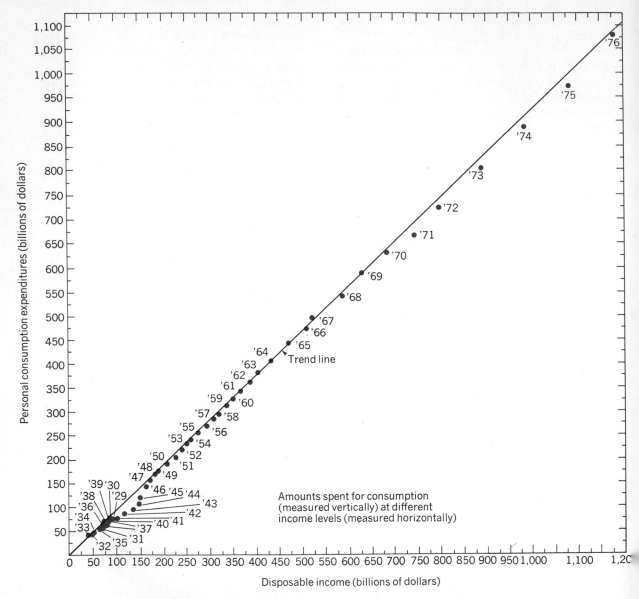

FIG. 8·5   United States' propensity to consume, 1929–1976

tionship between income (Y), the independent variable, and consumption (C), the dependent variable. In the mathematical language now familiar to us, we write

$$C = f(Y)$$

and we want to discover what f looks like.

Highly sophisticated and complex formulas have been tried to "fit" values of C and Y. Their economics and their mathematics both are beyond the scope of this book. But we can at least get a clearer idea of what it means to devise a *consumption function* by trying to make a very simple one ourselves. If we look at Fig. 8·5 we can see that during the Depression years, at very low levels of income, around $50 billion, consumption was just as large as income itself. (In some years it was actually bigger; as we have seen, there was net dissaving in 1933). Hence, we might hypothesize that a consumption function for the United States might have a fixed value representing this "bottom," plus some regular fraction designating the amount of income that would be saved for all income over that amount.

A generalized consumption function

This is a very important hypothesis. It enables us to describe the consumption function as an amount that represents rock-bottom consumption, to which we add additional consumption spending as income rises. If *a* is the "bottom," and subsequent spending out of additional income is $b(Y)$, where *b* represents this spending "propensity," we can now write the consumption function as a whole as:

$$C = a + b(Y)$$

We have seen that *a* is $50 billion, and we know that our actual spending propensity, *b*, is about 94 percent. Therefore, we can get a *very rough* approximation of consumption by taking $50 billion and adding to it 94 percent of our disposable income over $50 billion. In 1973 for example, disposable income was $883 billion. If we add $50 billion and .94 (883 − 50), we get $833. Actual consumption in 1973 was $828 billion.

Let the reader be warned, however, that devising a reliable consumption func-

tion is much more difficult than this simple formula would indicate. The process of translating economics into *econometrics*— that is, of finding ways to represent abstract theoretical relationships in terms of specific empirical relations—is a very difficult one. Nonetheless, even our simple example gives one an idea of what the economist and the econometrician hope to find: a precise way of expressing functional interrelations (like those between consumption and income), so that the relations will be useful in making predictions.

Individual vs. aggregate consumption

Here an important warning is in order. The consumption function should not be taken as a representation of individual consumption patterns. Individual preferences vary enormously, and a wide variety of random factors causes individuals to purchase different commodities at different times. But the task of predicting the consumption expenditures of a large group of people is much easier than the task of predicting the consumption of any individual in the group. The random factors that make individual predictions difficult average out in a large group. Some individuals will spend more than we would predict on the basis of their income, but others will spend less.

Age

In addition to random disturbances, systematic factors other than incomes influence consumption. Age is a critical variable. When individuals marry and establish households of their own they are confronted with the need to acquire many consumer durables. As a result, young families are apt to have low or even negative savings rates—they consume more than they earn by using installment payments. When individuals reach middle age, they have already incurred those expenditures necessary to raise a family and are starting to think about retirement. Their consumption propensities fall, and their savings propensities rise.

If the age distribution of the population were changing rapidly the marginal propensity to consume would not be as stable and constant as it is. Age can be ignored only in the aggregate, since the age distribution of the population does not change rapidly.

Passivity of consumption

Throughout this chapter we have talked of the dynamics of consuming and saving. Now it is important that we recall the main conclusion of our analysis, *the essential passivity of consumption as an economic process.* Consumption spending, we will recall, is a function of income. This means it is a *dependent* variable in the economic process, a factor that is acted *on,* but that does not itself generate spontaneous action.

To be sure, it is well to qualify this assertion. We have earlier paid special attention to the long-term stability of the na-

tional savings ratio and pointed out that one cause of this stability was a general upward tendency of consumption, as families "learned" to spend their rising incomes. This dynamic, although slow-acting, behavioral trend has exerted a strong background force on the trend of the economy. Then, too, there have been occasions, the most famous being the years just following World War II, when consumption seemed to generate its own momentum and—as we have seen—raced out ahead of income. But this was a period when wants were intense, following wartime shortages, and when huge amounts of wartime savings were available to translate those wants into action. During the normal course of things, no matter how intense "wants" may be, consumers ordinarily lack the spendable cash to translate their desires into effective demand. Brief swings in consumption—for example for automobiles—may give rise to short-run fluctuations in saving, but these savings are short-lived and therefore cannot drive the economy upward or downward for any extended period of time.

This highlights an extremely important point. Wants and appetites *alone* do not drive the economy upward; if they did, we should experience a more impelling demand in depressions, when people are hungry, than in booms, when they are well off. Hence the futility of those who urge the cure of depressions by suggesting that consumers should buy more! There is nothing consumers would rather do than buy more, if only they could. Let us not forget, furthermore, that consumers are at all times being cajoled and exhorted to increase their expenditures by the multibillion dollar pressures exerted by the advertising industry.

The trouble is, however, that consumers cannot buy more unless they have more incomes to buy with. It is true,

of course, that for short periods they can borrow or they may temporarily sharply reduce their rate of savings; but each household's borrowing capacity or accumulated savings are limited, so that once these bursts are over, the steady habitual ways of saving and spending are apt to reassert themselves.

Thus it is clear that in considering the consumer sector we study a part of the economy that, however ultimately important, is not in itself the source of major changes in activity. Consumption mirrors and, as we shall see, can magnify disturbances elsewhere in the economy, but it does not initiate the greater part of our economic fortunes or misfortunes.

Focus **The most important thing to remember from this chapter is the very last point: consumption is a passive element in the flow of demand that generates GNP. If you understand the reason for this, all the rest of the chapter will fall in line.**

Consumption is passive (not absolutely passive, since people do go on spending sprees) for two reasons:

1. **We spend for consumption largely out of income; therefore, the amount of consuming we can do depends on how much income we have.**

2. **We are by habit regular savers. Thus as the national income goes up, national consumption goes up, and so does national saving. The percentages remain about the same, in the long run, but the amounts rise.**

This average "propensity" to consume must be carefully distinguished from our *marginal* propensity to consume. The latter is a short-run phenomenon and describes the way we divide increases (or decreases) in income between spending and saving. What we do in the short run is not the same as what we do in the long run, and later we shall see that the marginal propensity to consume is an important behavioral characteristic accounting for fluctuations in GNP.

Be sure to learn the formula $C = a + b(Y)$. Think carefully about what a (the bottom) stands for, and about the meaning of b, the marginal propensity to consume. This is a simple formula that you should not forget. Don't forget, also, that this is not an identity, like $GNP \equiv C + I + G + X$. This new formula describes behavior. It can be tested—and frequently has been.

WORDS AND CONCEPTS YOU SHOULD KNOW

QUESTIONS

1. What are the main components of consumption? Why are some of these components more dynamic than others?

2. "The reason we have depressions is that consumption isn't big enough to buy the output of all our factories." What is wrong with this statement?

3. What do you think accounts for the relative stability of the savings ratio over the long run? Would you expect the savings ratio in the short run to be relatively stable? Why or why not?

4. What is meant by the consumption function? Could we also speak of a savings function? What would be the relation between the two?

5. Suppose that a given family had an income of $8,000 and saved $400. What would be its average propensity to consume? Could you tell from this information what its marginal propensity to consume was?

6. Suppose the same family now increased its income to $9,000 and its saving to $500. What is its new average propensity to consume? Can you figure out the family's marginal propensity to consume?

7. Draw a scatter diagram to show the following:

Family income	Savings
$4,000	$ 0
5,000	50
6,000	150
7,000	300
8,000	500

From the figures above, calculate the average propensity to consume at each level of income. Can you calculate the marginal propensity to consume for each jump in income?

8. How do you read $S = f(Y)$? From what you know of the propensity to consume, how would you describe the relation of S to Y?

9. Why can't we cure depressions by urging people to go out and spend?

Aid in cash or kind

Over the past 15 years there has been a gradual expansion in the public provision of *private* consumption goods—not roads, but actual consumers' goods. For example, food stamps have risen from $.03 billion in 1965 to $5.6 billion in the 1978 budget. Government medical expenditures rose from $7 billion to $26 billion from 1965 to 1975. Why is the government getting increasingly involved in the distribution of private kinds of goods?

Food stamps and medical expenditures can both be viewed as income redistribution measures. Both raise the real incomes of recipients, who are mainly poor. But what arguments can be mustered in favor of giving the poor food or medical aid, rather than cash? Cash, such as welfare payments, could always be used to buy food or medical treatment; and it might yield a much higher real income to the recipient, if he or she did not happen to need food or medical assistance, but something else, such as better housing. Why force the poor to consume things that they may not rank at the top of their lists of needs?

There are two classic arguments in favor of aid-in-kind, rather than aid-in-cash. One is that the poor cannot be trusted to buy what is best for them. They may actually *need* food or medical care, it is said, but if given the money they will spend it on luxuries or liquor. Thus, by "tying" their aid, we are really doing them a favor.

Is this a valid argument? We need hardly point out that it involves value judgments. Indeed, the argument has a patronizing ring about it. To be sure, there probably are people on welfare who *would* spend a cash bonus for luxuries or liquor instead of food or medical help, but the poor are not alone in spending their incomes in ways that maximize short-run pleasures rather than long-run benefits.

The second argument for aid-in-kind is more sophisticated. It revolves around the distinction between luxuries and necessaries. As a society we have quite egalitarian beliefs about how necessaries should be distributed, but we have no such beliefs about luxuries. We look with favor on rationing of a very scarce "necessity," such as a new vaccine, but we easily tolerate a high degree of inequality in the distribution of new Cadillacs. This distinction puts us on the horns of a dilemma. If we distribute welfare through equal amounts of cash, we are helping to bring about a more egalitarian distribution of luxuries, since the poor are free to spend their money on luxuries if they wish. On the other hand, if we distribute cash welfare unequally, we are possibly contributing to the unequal distribution of necessities, where we would like the poor to get a "fair share."

Aid-in-kind is an effort to get around this dilemma. When we distribute medical care equally, we are lending support to the equal sharing of medical care, which we consider a necessity. When we distribute food stamps, we are actually printing a different kind of money, usable only for food, and distributing this money in special ways. Thus aid-in-kind ties egalitarianism to "necessaries."

Does this justify aid-in-kind? Most economists, including ourselves, would prefer to give aid in cash, allowing each recipient to do with it as he or she wished. But to the extent that the preferences of the public are to be taken into account—and the taxpaying public far outnumbers the recipients of aid—the distribution of aid-in-kind may commend itself simply because it seems to accord with the political and social wishes of the public, the supreme arbiter in these matters.

Investment demand

In studying the behavior of the consumption sector, we have begun to understand how the demand for GNP arises. Now we must turn to a second source of demand—investment demand. This requires a shift in our vantage point. As experienced consumers, we know about consumption, but the activity of investing is foreign to most of us. Worse, we are apt to begin by confusing the meaning of investment, as a source of demand for GNP, with "investing" in the sense familiar to most of us when we think about buying stocks or bonds.

Investment: real and financial

We had best begin, then, by making certain that our vocabulary is correct. *Investing, or investment, as the economist uses the term in describing the demand for GNP, is an activity that uses the resources of the community to maintain or add to its stock of physical capital.*

Now this may or may not coincide with the purchase of a security. When we buy an ordinary stock or bond, we usually buy it from someone who has previously owned it, and therefore our personal act of "investment" becomes, in the economic view of things, merely a *transfer* of claims without any direct bearing on the creation of new wealth. A pays B cash and takes his

9

General Output stock; B takes A's cash and doubtless uses it to buy stock from C; but the transactions between A and B and C in no way alter the actual amount of real capital in the economy. Only when we buy *newly issued* shares or bonds, and then only when their proceeds are directly allocated to new equipment or plant, does our act of personal financial investment result in the addition of wealth to the community. In that case, A buys his stock directly (or through an investment banker) from General Output itself, and not from B. A's cash can now be spent by General Output for new capital goods, as presumably it will be.

Thus, much of investment, as economists see it, is a little-known form of activity for the majority of us. This is true not only because real investment is not the same as personal financial investment, but because the real investors of the nation usually act on behalf of an institution other than the familiar one of the household. **The unit of behavior in the world of investment is typically the business firm, just as in the world of consumption it is the household.** Boards of directors, chief executives, or small-business proprietors are the persons who decide whether or not to devote business cash to the construction of new facilities or to the addition of inventory; and this decision, as we shall see, is very different in character and motivation from the decisions familiar to us as members of the household sector.

The Investment Sector in Profile

Before we begin an investigation into the dynamics of investment decisions, however, let us gain a quick acquaintance with the sector as a whole, much as we did with the consumption sector.

Figure 9 • 1 gives a first general impression of the investment sector in a recent year. Note that the main source of gross private domestic investment expenditure is the retained earnings of business; that is, the expenditures come from depreciation accruals or from profits that have been kept in the business. However, as the next bar shows, gross investment *expenditures* are considerably larger than retained earnings. The difference represents funds that business obtains in several ways.

1. It may draw on cash (or securities) accumulated out of retained earnings or depreciation accruals of previous years.
2. It may obtain savings from the household sector by direct borrowing or by sale of new issues of shares of stock or indirectly via insurance companies or savings banks or pension funds, and so on.
3. It may borrow from commercial banks.
4. The difference also represents investment in housing, which is not typically financed by corporate earnings but by consumers, borrowing from banks.

The last two sources of funds we will not fully understand until we reach Chapter 14, when we study the money mechanism. But our chart enables us to see that most gross investment is financed by business itself from its *internal* sources—retained earnings plus depreciation accruals—and that external sources play only a secondary role. In particular, this is true of new stock issues, which, during most of the 1960s and early 1970s, raised only some 3 to 8 percent of the funds spent by the business sector for new plant and equipment.

Categories of investment

From the total funds at its disposal, the business sector now renews its worn-out capital and adds new capital. Let us say a word concerning some of the main categories of investment expenditure.

1. Inventories

At the top of the expenditure bar in Fig. 9•1 we note an item of $14 billion for *additions to inventory*. Note that this figure does not represent total inventories, but only *changes* in inventories, upwards or downwards. If there had been no change in inventory over the year, the item would have been zero, even if existing inventories were huge. Why? Because those huge inventories would have been included in the investment expenditure flow of *previous* years when they were built up.

Additions to inventories are capital, but they need not be additions to capital *goods*. Indeed, they are likely to include farm stocks, consumer goods, and other items of all kinds. Of course, these are goods held by business, and not by consumers. But that is the very point. We count inventory additions as net investment because they are output that has been produced but that has not been consumed. In another year, if these goods pass from the hands of business into consumers' hands, and inventories decline, we will have a negative figure for net inventory investment. This will mean, just as it appears, that we are consuming goods faster than we are producing them— that we are disinvesting.

Inventories are often visualized as completed TV sets sitting in some warehouse. While some inventories are completed goods sitting in storage, most

FIG. 9•1   Business sector 1976

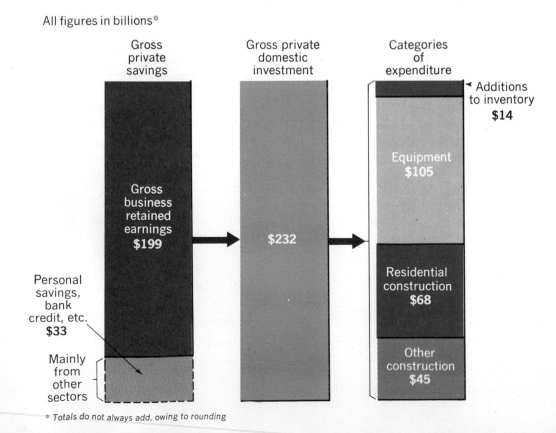

All figures in billions*

* Totals do not always add, owing to rounding

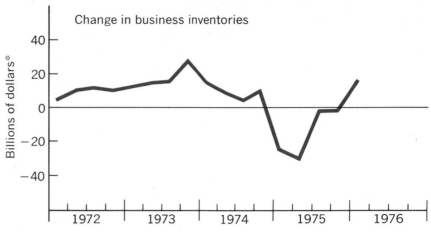

Change in business inventories

FIG. 9 • 2   Inventory swings

*Seasonally adjusted annual rates

are in the form of goods on display in stores, half-finished goods in the process of production, or raw materials to be used in production. When a steel company adds to its stock of iron ore, it is adding to its inventories.

Investments in inventory are particularly significant for one reason. Alone among the investment categories, inventories can be *rapidly* used up as well as increased. A positive figure for one year or even one calendar quarter can quickly turn into a negative figure the next. **This means that expenditures for inventory are usually the most volatile element of any in gross national product.** A glance at Fig. 9 • 2 shows a particularly dramatic instance of how rapidly inventory spending can change. In the fourth quarter of 1973, we were investing in inventories at an annual rate of over $20 billion. Five quarters later, we were working off inventories— *disinvesting* in inventories—by roughly the same amount. Thus, within a span of a year and a half, there was a swing of almost $50 billion in spending. Rapid inventory swings, although not quite of this magnitude, are by no means uncommon.

As we shall see more clearly later, this volatility of investment has much significance for business conditions. Note

that while inventories are being built up, they serve as an offset to saving—that is, some of the resources released from consumption are used by business firms to build up stocks of inventory capital. But when inventories are being "worked off," we are actually making the demand gap bigger. As we would expect, this can give rise to serious economic troubles.

2. Equipment

The next item in the expenditure bar (Fig. 9 • 1) is more familiar: $105 billion for *equipment.* Here we find expenditures for goods of a varied sort—lathes, trucks, generators, computers, office typewriters.* The total includes both *new equipment* and *replacement equipment,* and we need a word of caution here. Exactly what does it mean to "replace" a given item of equipment? Suppose we have a textile loom that cost $100,000 and that is now on its last legs. Is the loom "replaced" by spending another $100,000, regardless of what kind of machine the money will buy? What if loom prices have gone up and $100,000 no longer buys a loom of the same capacity?

*But *not* typewriters bought by consumers. Thus the same good can be classified as a consumption item or an investment item, depending on the use to which it is put.

Or suppose that prices have remained steady but that owing to technological advance, $100,000 now buys a loom of double the old capacity.

From an economic perspective, replacement is the dollar amount that would be necessary to buy the same productive capacity. But this is an amount that is seldom known with great accuracy. It may not be possible to buy new equipment with exactly the same productive capacity as old equipment. Often businesses replace whole factories rather than individual pieces of equipment. These new factories are likely to have very different configurations of equipment as well as different productive capacities. Such problems make the definition of "replacement" an accountant's headache and an economist's nightmare. At the moment there isn't even a generally accepted estimate of replacement investment. We need not involve ourselves deeper in the question, but we should note the complexities introduced into a seemingly simple matter once we leave the changeless world of stationary flow and enter the world of invention and innovation.

3.   Construction—residential

Our next section on the expenditure bar (Fig. 9 · 1) is total *residential construction*. Why do we include this $68 billion in the investment sector when most of it is represented by new houses that householders buy for their own use?

Part of the answer is that most houses are built by business firms, such as contractors and developers, who put up the houses *before* they are sold. Thus the original expenditures involved in building houses typically come from businesses, not from households. Later, when the householder buys a house, it is an existing asset, and his or her expenditure does not pump new incomes into the economy but only repays the contractor who *did* contribute new incomes.

Actually, this is a somewhat arbitrary definition, since, after all, business owns *all* output before consumers buy it. However, another reason for considering residential construction as investment is that, unlike most "consumer goods," houses are typically maintained as if they were capital goods. Thus their durability also enters into their classification as investment goods.

Finally, we class housing as investment because residential purchases "behave" very much like other items of construction. Therefore it simplifies our understanding of the forces at work in the economy if we classify residential construction as an investment expenditure rather than as a consumer expenditure.

4.   Other construction—plant

Last on the bar, $45 billion of *other construction* is largely made up of the "plant" in "plant and equipment"—factories and stores and private office buildings and warehouses. (It does not, however, include public construction such as roads, dams, harbors, or public buildings, all of which are picked up under government purchases.) It is interesting to note that the building of structures, as represented by the total of residential construction plus other private construction, accounts for over half of all investment expenditure, and this total would be further swelled if public construction were included herein. This accords with the dominant role of structures in the panorama of national wealth we first encountered in Table 3 · 1 (p. 42). It tells us, too, that swings in construction expenditure can be a major lever for economic change.

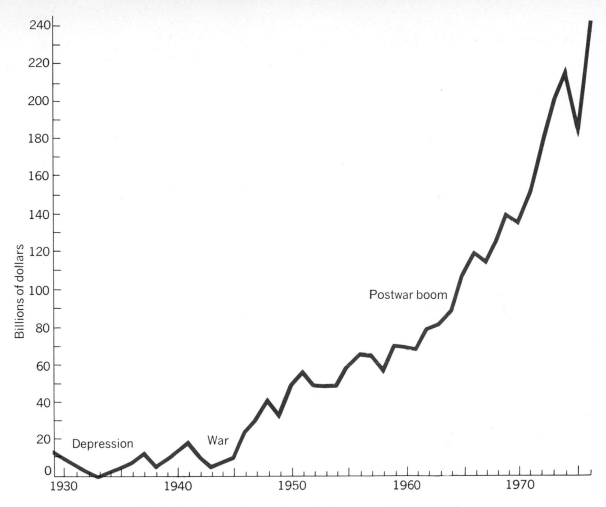

FIG. 9 · 3 Gross private domestic investment, 1929–1976

Investment in Historic Perspective

With this introduction behind us, let us take a look at the flow of investment, not over a single year, but over many years.

In Fig. 9 · 3 several things spring to our notice. Clearly, investment demand is not nearly so smooth and unperturbed a flow of spending as consumption. Note that gross investment in the depths of the Depression virtually disappeared—that we almost failed to *maintain*, much less add to, our stock of wealth. (Net invest-

ment was, in fact, a negative figure for several years.) Note also investment was reduced during the war years as private capital formation was deliberately limited through government allocations.

Three important conclusions emerge from this examination of investment spending:

First, as we have already seen, investment spending contains a component— net additions to inventory—that is capable of drastic, sudden shifts. This accounts for much of the wavelike movement of the total flow of investment expenditure.

Second, investment spending as a whole is capable of more or less total collapses, of a severity and degree that are never to be found in consumption.

Third, unlike household spending, investment can fluctuate independently of income. It may rise when GNP is low, perhaps to usher in a boom. It can fall when GNP is high, perhaps to trigger a recession. It is an independent variable in the determination of demand.

The prime example of such a collapse was, of course, the Great Depression. From 1929 to 1933, while consumption fell by 41 percent, investment fell by *91 percent*, As we can see in Fig. 9 • 3. Similarly, whereas consumption rose by a little more than half from 1933 to 1940, investment in the same period rose by *nine times*.

Importance of investment

This potential for collapse or spectacular boom always makes investment a source of special concern in the economic picture. But even the tendency toward inventory fluctuations, or toward milder declines in other capital expenditures, is sufficient to identify investment as a prime source of economic instability. As we have said before, there is often a tendency among noneconomists to equate all buying in the economy with consumer buying. Let us never lose sight of the fact that the maintenance of, and addition to, capital is also a part of GNP spending and that a considerable part of the labor force depends for its livelihood on the making of investment goods. At the bottom of the Great Depression in 1933, it was estimated that one-third of total unemployment was directly associated with the shrinkage in the capital goods industry.

The Multiplier

In our next chapter we shall look more closely into the reasons for the sensitivity of investment spending. But first a question must surely have occurred to the reader. For all its susceptibility to change, the investment sector is, after all, a fairly small sector. In 1976, total expenditures for gross private domestic investment came to only about one-seventh of GNP, and the normal year-to-year variation in investment spending in the 1960s and 1970s is only about 1 to 2 percent of GNP. To devote so much time to such small fluctuations seems a disproportionate emphasis. How could so small a tail as investment wag so large a dog as GNP?

Snowball effect The answer lies in a relationship of economic activities known as the *multiplier*. The multiplier describes the fact that *additions to spending (or diminutions in spending) have an impact on income that is greater than the original increase or decrease in spending itself.* In other words, even small increments in spending can *multiply* their effects (whence the name).

It is not difficult to understand the general idea of the multiplier. Suppose that we have an island community whose economy is in a perfect circular flow, unchanging from year to year. Next, let us introduce the stimulus of a new investment expenditure in the form of a stranger who arrives from another island (with a supply of acceptable money) and who proceeds to build a house. This immediately increases the islanders' incomes. In our case, we will assume that the stranger spends $1,000 on wages for construction workers, and we will ignore all other expenditures he may make. (We also make the assumption that these workers were previously unemployed, so that the builder is not merely taking them from some other task.)

Now the construction workers, who have had their incomes increased by $1,000, are very unlikely to sit on this money. As we know from our study of the marginal propensity to consume, they are apt to save some of the increase (and they may have to pay some to the government as income taxes), but the rest they will spend on additional consumption goods. Let us suppose that they save 10 percent and pay taxes of 20 percent on the $1,000 they get. They will then have $700 left over to spend for additional consumer goods and services.

But this is not an end to it. The sellers of these goods and services will now have received $700 over and above their former incomes, and they, too, will be certain to spend a considerable amount of their new income. If we assume that their family spending patterns (and their tax brackets) are the same as the construction workers, they will also spend 70 percent of their new incomes, or $490. And now the wheel takes another turn, as still *another* group receives new income and spends a fraction of it—in turn.

Continuing impact of respending

If the newcomer then departed as mysteriously as he came, we would have to describe the economic impact of his investment as constituting a single "bulge" of income that gradually disappeared. The bulge would consist of the original $1,000, the secondary $700, the tertiary $490, and so on. If everyone continued to spend 70 percent of his new income, after ten rounds all that would remain by way of new spending traceable to the original $1,000 would be about $28. Soon, the impact of the new investment on incomes would have virtually disappeared.

But now let us suppose that after our visitor builds his house and leaves, another visitor arrives to build another house. This time, in other words, we assume that the level of investment spending *continues* at the higher level to which it was raised by the first expenditure for a new house. We can see that the second house will set into motion precisely the same repercussive effects as did the first, and that the new series of respendings will be added to the dwindling echoes of the original injection of incomes.

In Fig. 9·4, we can trace this effect. The succession of colored bars at the bot-

---

INTENDED AND UNINTENDED INVENTORY INVESTMENT

Changes in inventories reflect both the desires of firms and their planning errors. *Investment in inventories can therefore be intended or unintended.* If an automobile manufacturer expects to sell 1 million cars and is disappointed in this expectation, actual sales will lag behind expected sales. Since production was planned on the basis of expected sales, it will exceed actual sales until production can be readjusted to the new sales levels. Autos built but not sold will be added to inventories. In this case, inventories go up not because the firm wanted more inventories, but because it made a mistake.

If actual sales exceed expected sales, the reverse will happen. Inventories fall. But again, the firm did not lower inventories because lower inventories were more profitable, but by mistake. Low inventories can be extremely unprofitable. If certain models are not available or in limited supply, the auto maker will find that he is losing potential sales to a competitor that can give the consumer the kind of car he wants at the time he wants it.

These unintended changes in inventories enter into the statistics of GNP, just as do intended changes in inventories. But they obviously have very different significances regarding future economic behavior.

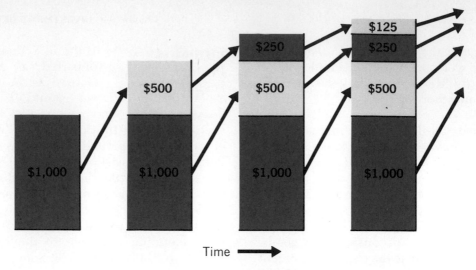

$$\text{Time} \longrightarrow$$

FIG. 9 · 4   The multiplier

tom of the graph stands for the continuing injections of $1,000 as new houses are steadily built. (Note that this means the level of new investment is only being maintained, not that it is rising.) Each of these colored bars now generates a series of secondary, tertiary, etc., bars that represent the respending of income after taxes and savings. In our example we have assumed that the respending fraction is 50 percent.

Let us now examine the effects of investment spending in a generalized fashion, without paying attention to

specific dollar amounts. In Fig. 9 · 5, we see the effects of a single, *once-and-for-all* investment expenditure (the stranger who came and went), contrasted with the effects of a *continuing* stream of investment.

Our diagrams show us two important things:

1. A single burst of investment creates a bulge of incomes larger than the initial expenditure, but a bulge that disappears.

2. A continuing flow of investment creates a new steady level of income, higher than the investment expenditures themselves.

FIG. 9 · 5   Once-over and continuing effects of investment

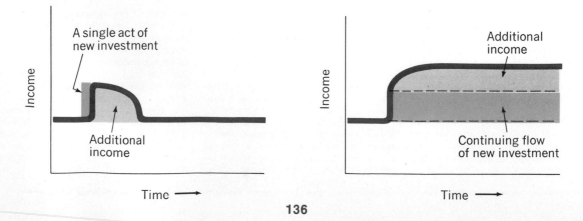

Marginal propensity to save

We can understand now that *the multiplier is the numerical relation between the initial new investment and the total increase in income.* If the initial investment is $1,000 and the total addition to income due to the respending of that $1,000 is $3,000, we have a multiplier of 3; if the total addition is $2,000, the multiplier is 2.

What determines how large the multiplier will be? The answer depends entirely on our marginal consumption (or, if you will, our marginal saving) habits— that is, on how much we consume (or save) out of each dollar of additional income that comes to us. Let us follow two cases below. In the first, we will assume that each recipient spends only one-half of any new income that comes to him, saving the rest. In the second case, he spends three-quarters of it and saves one-quarter.

It is very clear that the amount of income that will be passed along from one receiver to the next will be much larger where the marginal propensity to consume

is higher. In fact, we can see that the total amount of new incomes (total amount of boxes below) must be mathematically related to the proportion that is spent each time.

What is this relationship? The arithmetic is easier to figure if we use not the consumption fraction, but the *saving fraction* (the two are, of course, as intimately related as the first slice of cake and the remaining cake). **If we use the saving fraction, the sum of new incomes is obtained by taking the reciprocal of (i.e., inverting, or turning upside down) the fraction we save.** Thus, if we save ½ our income, the total amount of new incomes generated by respending will be ½ inverted, or 2 (twice the original increase in income). If we save ¼, it will be the reciprocal of ¼, or 4 times the original change.

Basic multiplier formula

We call the fraction of new income that is saved the *marginal propensity to save* (often abbreviated as mps). As we have just seen, this fraction is

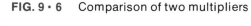

FIG. 9 · 6   Comparison of two multipliers

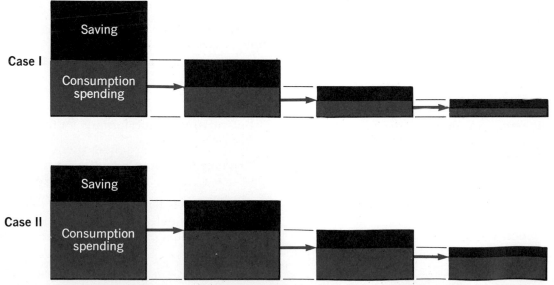

How do we know that the multiplier will be 4, if the marginal propensity to save is ¼? Most of us "intuitively" see that the sum of respending hinges on the savings fraction, and we take on faith the simple formula that tells us how to calculate that sum by taking the reciprocal of the mps and multiplying it by the change in spending.

But some students may want to go beyond faith, to understanding. Here is a simple mathematical demonstration that the multiplier formula is "really" true.

What we are trying to get at, with the multiplier formula, is the *sum of a series,* in which an initial term is multiplied again and again by some number that is less than 1 (and greater than 0). Suppose the initial term is $10 and the number-less-than-one is .8. Then we want to know the sum of the following problem:

$$10 + .8(10) + .8[.8(10)]\ldots.$$

This is the same as if we wrote:

$$10 + .8(10) + .8^2(10) + .8^3(10)\ldots$$
$$+\ldots.8^n(10)$$

If we think of .8 as designating the marginal propensity to consume, we are looking for the sum of an initial new expenditure of $10, of which $8 will be spent in the first round (.8 × $10); $6.40 (.8² × $10) in the second round; $5.12 (.8³ × $10) in the third, and so on. From the textbook, we "know" that this sum is found by taking the mps, which is .2, or 1/5, and multiplying the original expenditure by its reciprocal. Thus, $10 × 5 = $50. Now let's prove it.

We can restate our multiplier series in simple algebra by calling the initial term *a* and the number-less-than-one (.8 above) *b*. Then the series looks like this:

$$a + b \cdot a + b^2 \cdot a \ldots + \ldots b^n \cdot a$$

where b^n stands for the fraction spent on the last (nth) round.

Suppose we call the sum of this series *S*. Now we are going to perform a truly magical (but perfectly legitimate) mathematical trick. We will first write the formula we have just described, and below it we will write the same formula, after we have multiplied both sides of the equation by *b*.

$$S = a + b \cdot a + b2 \cdot a \ldots + \ldots b^n a$$

$$b \cdot S = b \cdot a + b2 \cdot a \ldots + \ldots b^{n+1} \cdot a$$

We have strung out the second equation so that terms such as $b \cdot a$ lie underneath their counterparts in the first equation.

Now we subtract the second equation from the first. All the terms that are under one another just disappear. This leaves us:

$$S - b \cdot S = a - b^{n+1} \cdot a$$

Next we factor out *S* on the left side, giving us $S(1 - b)$, and divide both sides by $(1 - b)$. The result:

$$S = a - b^{n+1} \cdot a/(1 - b)$$

We are almost at the end. Now we examine what happens as the exponent *n* approaches infinity. Remember that by definition *b* is a number less than 1, so that with each successive increase in the exponent, *b* becomes *smaller.* Thus we can assume that the final term approaches zero, .as its exponent approaches infinity. That is to say, it "vanishes." This is very convenient because it leaves us with the much simpler formula:

$$S = a/(1 - b)$$

Do you see the connection with the multiplier? The term *b* was the fraction (.8) by which we constantly multiplied the initial sum ($10). *Thus this fraction was exactly like the marginal propensity to consume!* Therefore, $1 - b$ must be the difference between 1 and the mpc (or .2).

We know this is the mps. Therefore we can write mps in place of $1 - b$; and while we are about it, we can write $10, or ΔI, or any other number in place of *a*.

Hence our formula becomes translated into economic terms and looks like this:

$$S = \Delta I / mps$$

The term *S* stood for the sum of the series. An economist will call it ΔY since this is the sum of the additional incomes generated by each round of spending.

ΔY is therefore $10 ÷ .2 (or $50). And that is why the formula is true.

---

the complement of an already familiar one, the marginal propensity to consume. If our marginal propensity to consume is 80 percent, our marginal propensity to save must be 20 percent; if our mpc is three-quarters, our mps must be one-quarter. In brief, mps + mp ≡ 1.

Understanding the relationship between the marginal propensity to save and the size of the resulting respending fractions allows us to state a very simple (but very important) formula for the multiplier:

change in income = multiplier × change in investment

Since we have just learned that the multiplier is determined by the reciprocal of the marginal propensity to save, we can write:

$$\text{multiplier} = \frac{1}{\text{mps}}$$

If we now use the symbols we are familiar with, plus a Greek letter Δ, delta, that means "change in," we can write the important economic relationship above as follows:

$$\Delta Y = (\frac{1}{\text{mps}}) \times \Delta I$$

Thus, if our mps is 1/4 (meaning, let us not forget, that we save a quarter of increases in income and spend the rest), then an increase in investment of $1 billion will lead to a total increase in incomes of $4 billion

$$(\$4 \text{ billion} = 1/(\tfrac{1}{\tfrac14}) \times \$1 \text{ billion}$$

Note that the multiplier is a complex or *double* fraction:

it is 1/(1/4) and *not* 1/4.

If the mps is 1/10, $1 billion gives rise to incomes of $10 billion; if the mps is 50 percent, the billion will multiply to $2 billion. And if mps is 1? This means that the entire increase in income is unspent, that our island construction workers tuck away (or find taxed away) their entire newly earned pay. In that case, the multiplier will be 1 also, and the impact of the new investment on the island economy will be no more than the $1,000 earned by the construction workers in the first place.

Leakages

The importance of the size of the marginal savings ratio in determining the effect that additional investment will have on income is thus apparent. Now, however, we must pass from the simple example of our island economy to the more complex behavioral patterns and institutional arrangements of real life. The average propensity to save (the ratio of saving to disposable income) runs around 6 to 7 percent. In recent years, the *marginal* propensity to save (the ratio of additional saving to increases in income) figured over the period of a year has not departed very much from this figure. If this is the case, then, following our analysis, the multiplier would be very high. If mps were even as much as 10 percent of income, a change in investment of $1 billion would bring a $10 billion change in income. If mps were nearer 6 percent—the approximate level of the average propensity to save—a change of $1 billion would bring a swing of over $16 billion. Were this the case, the economy would be subject to the most violent disturbances whenever the level of spending shifted. For example, the $50 billion swing in inventory investment from late 1973 to early 1975 would have produced a sixteenfold fall in GNP—a fall of $800 billion!

In fact, however, the impact of the multiplier is greatly reduced because the successive rounds of spending are dampened by factors other than personal saving. One of them we have already introduced in our imaginary island economy. This is the tendency of *taxation* to "mop up" a fraction of income as it passes from hand to hand. This mopping-up effect of taxation is in actuality much larger than that of saving. For every dollar of change in income, federal taxes will take about 30 cents, and state and local taxes another 6 cents.

Another dampener is the tendency of respending to swell *business savings* as well as personal incomes. Of each dollar of new spending, perhaps 10 cents goes into business profits, and this sum is typically saved, at least for a time, rather than immediately respent.

Still another source of dampening is the tendency of consumers and businesses to increase purchases from abroad as their incomes rise. These rising *imports* divert 3 to 4 percent of new spending to foreign nations and accordingly reduce the successive impact of each round of expenditure.

All these withdrawals from the respending cycle are called *leakages,* and the total effect of all leakages together (personal savings, business savings, taxes, and imports) is to reduce the overall impact of the multiplier from an impossibly large figure to a very manageable one. In dealing with the multiplier equation ($\Delta Y = 1/\text{mps} \times \Delta I$), we usually interpret mps to mean the total withdrawal from spending due to all leakages. The combined effect of all leakages brings the actual multiplier in the United States in the 1970s to a little more than 2 over a period of 2 years.*

To be sure—and this is very important—all these leakages *can* return to the income stream. Household saving can be turned into capital formation; business profits can be invested; tax receipts can be disbursed in government spending programs; and purchases from foreign sellers can be returned as purchases *by* foreigners. What is at stake here is the regularity and reliability with which these circuits will be closed. In the case of ordinary income going to a household, we can count with considerable assurance on a "return expenditure" of consumption. In the case of the other recipients of funds, the assurance is much less; hence we count their receipts as money that has leaked out of the expenditure flow, for the time being.

*It is interesting to note that the leakages all tend to increase somewhat in boom times and to decline in recessions, which results in a multiplier slightly larger in bad times than in good.

The downward multiplier

The multiplier, with its important magnifying action, rests at the very center of our understanding of economic fluctuations. Not only does it explain how relatively small stimuli can exert considerable upward pushes, but it also makes much clearer than before how the failure to offset a small savings gap can snowball into a serious fall in income and employment.

For just as additional income is respent to create still further new income, a loss in income will not stop with the affected households. On the contrary, as families lose income, they cut down on their spending, although the behavior pattern of the propensity to consume schedule suggests that they will not cut their consumption by as much as their loss in income. Yet each reduction in consumption, large or small, lessens to that extent the income or receipts of some other household or firm.

We have already noted that personal savings alone do not determine the full impact of the multiplier. This is even more fortunate on the way down than on the way up. If the size of the multiplier were solely dependent on the marginal propensity to save, an original fall in spending would result in a catastrophic contraction of consumption through the economy. But the leakages that cushion the upward pressure of the multiplier also cushion its downward effect. As spending falls, business savings (profits) fall, tax receipts dwindle, and the flow of imports declines. We shall discuss this cushioning effect when we look into the government sector.

All of these leakages now work in the direction of mitigating the repercussions of the original fall in spending. The fall in business profits means that less will be saved by business and thus less withdrawn from responding; the decline in taxes means that more money will be left to consumers; and the drop in imports similarly releases additional spending power for the domestic market. Thus, just as the various leakages pulled money away from consumption on the way up, on the way down they lessen their siphoning effect and in this way restore purchasing power to consumers' hands. As a result, in the downward direction as in the upward, the actual impact of the multiplier is about 2, so that a fall in investment of, say, $5 billion will lower GNP by $10 billion.

Even with a reduced figure, we can now understand how a relatively small change in investment can magnify its impact on GNP. If the typical year-to-year change in investment is around $10 billion to $20 billion, a multiplier of 2 will produce a change in GNP of $20 billion to $40 billion, by no means a negligible figure. In addition, as we shall shortly see, the multiplier may set up repercussions that feed back onto investment. But more of that momentarily. First let us make three final points in regard to the multiplier.

1. Other multipliers

We have talked of the multiplier in connection with changes in investment spending. But we must also realize that any original change in any spending has a multiplier effect. We have used investment as the "trigger" for the multiplier because it is, in fact, a component of spending that is likely to evidence *large* and *sudden* changes. But an increase in foreigners' purchases of our exports has a multiplier effect, as does an increase in government spending or a decrease in taxes, or a spontaneous increase in consumption itself due to, say, a drop in the propensity to save.

Any stimulus to the economy is thus not confined to its original impact, but gives a series of successive pushes to the system until it has finally been absorbed in leakages. We shall come back to this important fact in our next chapter.

2. Idle resources

Finally, there is a very important proviso to recognize, although we will not study its full significance until Chapter 15. This is the important difference between an economy with idle resources—unemployed labor or unused machines or land—and one without them.

For it is only when we have idle resources that the respending impetus of the multiplier is useful. Then each round of new expenditure can bring idle resources into use, creating not only new money incomes but *new production and employment*. The situation is considerably different when there are no, or few, idle men or machines. Then the expenditure rounds of the multiplier bring higher money incomes, but these are not matched by increased real output.

In both cases, the multiplier exerts its leverage, bringing about an increase in total expenditure larger than the original injection of new spending. In the case without idle resources, however, the results are solely *inflationary*, as the increased spending results in higher incomes and higher prices, but not in higher output. In the case where idle resources exist, we can avoid this mere "money" multiplication and enjoy a rise in output as a result of our increased spending. Indeed, we can even speak of the *employment multiplier* in situations where there is considerable unemployment, meaning by this the total increase in employment brought about by a given increase in spending. We shall return in subsequent chapters to a fuller scrutiny of the difference between the case of idle and of fully employed resources, but we must bear the distinction in mind henceforth.

3. The importance of time lags

Last we must distinguish between the multiplier as a mathematical relationship and the multiplier in real life.

In equations, the multiplier is "instantaneous." If investment rises by $10 billions and the multiplier is 2, we "instantly" have a $20 billion rise in output. **In actuality, the successive "rounds" of spending display very important time lags.** Investment expenditures of $10 billion will first show up as increased sales of businesses. Businesses usually will draw down on inventories rather than immediately increasing production (and factor incomes), to hedge

against the possibility that the increase is only temporary. This leads to a smaller increase in incomes, other than profits, than might be expected. And for the same hedging reason, businesses are unlikely at first to use their additional profits to pay higher incomes or to finance new investment.

Moreover, incomes that do go to consumers are also not instantaneously spent. One recent study has shown that families spent only 66 cents out of each dollar of new income in the first three months during which they received that income. Only gradually did their spending propensities build up to "normal." And even when they *did* spend their additional incomes, the businesses that enjoyed larger sales were again likely to display the cautious hedging attitudes we have described. That is another reason why the multiplier, 2 years after an investment increase, is in fact only about 2.

FOCUS   There are two central ideas in this chapter, one of which is easy to learn; the other demands some time and thought. The easy but absolutely central idea is that investment is a flow of demand capable of deep, sudden shifts. Unlike changes in consumption, which reflect prior changes in income, investment can go "against" the trend of income, rising in bad times, perhaps to lead the way to recovery; falling in good times, perhaps to set off a recession. This idea is very important to grasp. It also calls attention to the role of inventory change, as the most volatile component of a volatile flow.

The second main idea is the multiplier. The multiplier is important because it explains why changes in spending—investment or government or export or whatever—can lift or lower the economy by more than the original change itself. This multiplying effect is the consequence of the marginal propensity to consume— the fact that we respend large fractions of increases on our income, thereby creating incomes for others. (Look at question 4.) The very high respending fraction of the marginal propensity to consume is greatly reduced by leakages into business profits, taxes and imports, reducing the effect of the multiplier to about 2, over 2 years.

It should be needless to say—but it is critical to see—the effect of the multiplier will be useful going "up" when we have unemployed resources, but not when we do not. We shall come back to that critical difference later on when we study inflation.

WORDS AND CONCEPTS YOU SHOULD KNOW

Real vs. financial investment, 128–29
Four types of investment, 130, 131, 132
The multiplier, 134–136
Marginal propensity to save, 137
$\Delta Y = 1/mps \times \Delta I$, 139

Four kinds of leakage, 139–140
The downward multiplier, 140
The multiplier and idle resources, 141–42
The multiplier and time, 140

QUESTIONS

1. If you buy a share of stock on the New York Stock Exchange, does that always create new capital? Why, or why not?

2. Why are additions to inventory so much more liable to rapid fluctuation than are other kinds of investment?

3. Why do we face the possibility of a total collapse of investment, but not of consumption?

4. Draw a diagram of boxes showing the multiplier effect of a $1,000 expenditure when the marginal propensity to save is one-tenth. Draw a second diagram, showing the effect when the marginal propensity to consume is nine-tenths?

5. Compare two multiplier diagrams: one where the marginal propensity to save is one-quarter; the other where it is one-third. The *larger* the saving ratio, the larger or smaller the multiplier?

6. Calculate the impact on income if investment rises by $10 billion and the multiplier is 2. If the multiplier is 3. If it is 1.

7. Income is $500 billion; investment is $50 billion. The multiplier is 2. If inventories decline by $10 billion, what happens to income?

8. Draw a diagram showing what happens to $1 billion of new investment given the following leakages: mps 10 percent; marginal taxation 20 percent; marginal propensity to import 5 percent; marginal addition to business saving 15 percent. What will be the size of the second round of spending? the third? the final total?

9. If the marginal propensity to consume is three-quarters, what is the size of the marginal propensity to save? If it is five-sixths? If it is 70 percent?

10. What is the formula for the multiplier?

A capital shortage

Many businessmen and some economists argue that there will be a "capital shortage" in the 1980s. They point to the rising needs for capital equipment for such new purposes as pollution control or energy, and they warn that the demand for capital will grow much faster than in the past. This will mean that capital will become scarce relative to other goods, and that its price—the rate of interest—will rise.

It is difficult to know, yet, exactly how large the demand for capital will be over the next decade. But we can at least clarify some issues in the capital shortage argument. The first is that it would be incorrect to calculate the degree of "shortage" simply by adding prospective expenditures on pollution or energy investment to the normal expectations of investment. To do so ignores the shifts in demands that will take place as a consequence of these very additional expenditures. Goods that are "pollution-intensive" or "energy-intensive" will cost more, relative to other goods. They will thereby probably absorb more of our spending. Thus, as the sales of other goods fall behind, less capital will be required to keep their production abreast of national demand.

In other words, the extra capital needed in some branches will be offset to some degree by less capital needed in others. Statisticians estimate the net effect on total capital may raise the demand for it by ½ to 1 percent of GNP at current interest rates. Is this a large number? In actual dollar amounts, it comes to something like $250 billion over the next decade. On the other hand, total GNP over the same period, assuming present rates of growth and inflation, comes to a staggering $31 trillion. Thus the additional capital sums, although large, are not likely to distort the traditional patterns of GNP significantly.

The second main issue is how to raise the added new capital. We have already looked into the problem of trying to raise saving rates, and we have seen that there is a real social cost in trying to do so. So suppose that we do nothing. Then the new capital demands will certainly raise interest rates. In turn this will exert an effect—and a very uneven effect—across the economy. As we shall see later on (see page 244), a credit squeeze most hurts small business, residential construction, and state and local government. It means more business failures for small enterprise, fewer homes, less urban services.

This puts a different light on the question of raising the savings rate. For the course of leaving things alone will also impose costs—perhaps more severe costs than in trying to raise the flow of savings. These costs will, however, be borne by different groups. Which policy is best? The policy that lessens the costs on those groups whose well-being you happen to prefer. It would be nice if there were a more "scientific" answer, but there is not.

Motivation of investment

The inherent instability of investment, and the multiplier repercussions that arise from changes in investment, begin to give us an understanding of the special importance of the business sector in determining the demand for GNP. In our next chapter we shall look into equally special characteristics of government demand before assembling the demand functions of all the sectors, to match them against the supply of GNP.

But before we proceed to that goal, we must learn something further about the nature of investment demand—in particular, about the motivations that give rise to it—for if we compare the underlying behavioral drives that impel consumption and investment, we can see a fundamental difference of the greatest significance.

Utility vs. profit Consumption demand, we remember, is essentially directed at the satisfaction of the individual—at providing him with the "utilities" of the goods and services he buys. An increasingly affluent society may not be able to say that consumer expenditure is any longer solely geared to necessity, but at least it obeys the fairly constant promptings of the cultural and social environment, with the result that

145

10

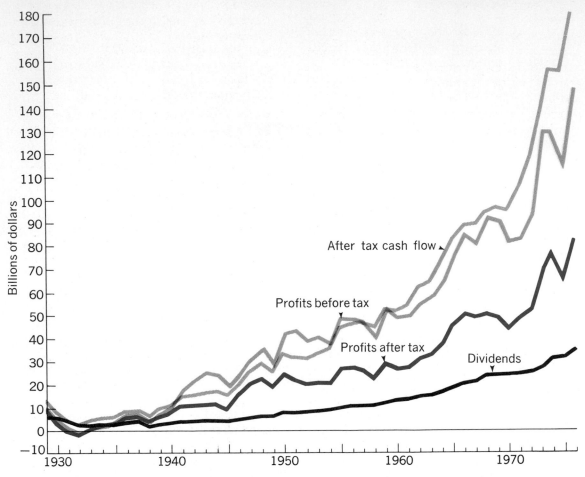

FIG. 10 · 1 Profits, taxes, and dividends

consumer spending, in the aggregate, fluctuates relatively little, except as income fluctuates.

A quite different set of motivations drives the investment impulse. Whether the investment is for replacement of old capital or for the installation of new capital, the ruling consideration is not apt to be the personal use or satisfaction that the investment yields to the owners of the firm. Instead, the touchstone of investment decisions is *profit*.

Figure 10 · 1 shows corporate profits since 1929 and their division into retained earnings, dividends, and taxes. What is strikingly apparent, of course, is the extreme fluctuation of profits between prosperity and recession. Note that corporations as a whole lost money in the depths of the Depression years, but that even in the lush postwar period, the swings from year to year have been considerable (compare 1958 and 1959).

Expectations The chart shows us how corporate profits looked to business when the books were tallied at the end of each year. But the results of last year's operation, although very important, is not the main thing that motivates business to invest. Primarily, it is interested in the profits expected from *next year's* operations. The view is never backward, but always forward.

Note the important stress on *expectations*. One firm may be enjoying large profits on its existing plant and equipment at the moment; but if it anticipates no profits from the sale of goods that an *additional* investment would make possible, the firm will make no additions to capital. Another firm may be suffering current losses; but if it anticipates a large profit from the production of a new good, it may launch a considerable capital expenditure.

There is a sound reason for this anticipatory quality of investment decisions. Typically, the capital goods bought by investment expenditures are expected to last for years and to pay for themselves only slowly. In addition, they are often highly specialized. If capital expenditures could be recouped in a few weeks or months, or even in a matter of a year or two, or if capital goods were easily transferred from one use to another, they would not be so risky and their dependence on expectations not so great. But it is characteristic of most capital goods that they *are* durable, with life expectancies of ten or more years, and that they tend to be limited in their alternative uses, or to have no alternative uses at all. You cannot spin cloth in a steel mill or make steel in a cotton mill.

The decision to invest is thus always forward-looking. Even when the stimulus to build is felt in the present, the calculations that determine whether or not an investment will be made necessarily concern the flow of income to the firm in the future. These expectations are inherently much more volatile than the current drives and desires that guide the consumer. Expectations, whether based on guesses or forecasts, are capable of sudden and sharp reversals of a sort rare in consumption spending. Thus in its orientation to the future we find a main cause for the volatility of investment expenditures.

Induced and Autonomous Investment

One kind of profit expectation, and the investment that stems from it, derives from *an observed rise in current consumption spending*, as a result of higher incomes.

Many business firms decide to invest because they must expand their capacity to maintain a given share of a growing market. Real estate developers who build to accommodate an already visible suburban exodus, or supermarkets that build to serve a booming metropolis, or gas stations that must be built to serve a new highway, or additions to manufacturing ca-

---

HAVE CORPORATE PROFITS CHANGED?

Have corporate profits changed as a percent of GNP? This question is not easy to answer for a number of reasons. Corporate profits are very sensitive to the business cycle (rising and falling much faster than output). Averages will be very misleading if they cover different phases of the business cycle. Depreciation charges must also be subtracted from gross corporate earnings before profits can be estimated. But no one knows exactly how fast equipment wears out or becomes technologically obsolete.

In addition, worn out equipment is almost never replaced by exactly the same equipment, because technical advances lead to new configurations. What new configuration is equivalent to what old configuration?

If we compare the periods from 1947 through 1953 and the period from 1965 through 1972, we have two periods with both a war and a mild recession. Corporate gross cash flow was 15.4 percent of the GNP in the first period and 14.2 percent of the GNP in the second. Thus there was a slight decline between the two periods; but in the recessionary period from 1973 through 1976, corporate gross cash flow was also 14.2 percent of the GNP. The fact that there was no decline in corporate profits (as a share of GNP) during a very severe recession indicates a shift toward corporate profits that may have eliminated, or more than eliminated, the previous decline.

pacity that must be made because existing facilities cannot keep up with demand—these are all examples of what we call *induced investment*.

The acceleration principle

When rising incomes and consumption lead to induced investment, the relationship is called the *acceleration principle* or the *accelerator*. The name springs from the fact that the amount of induced investment depends upon the rate of growth of the economy. An economy that is not growing has no induced investment. Also, an economy that has unutilized capacity will not have induced investment.

Table 10·1 is a model that explains this phenomenon. It shows us an industry whose sales rise for six years, then level off, and finally decline. We assume it has no unused equipment and that its equipment wears out every ten years. Also, we will make the assumption that it requires a capital investment of $2 to produce a flow of output of $1.

Now let us see the accelerator at work.

In our first view of the industry, we find it in equilibrium with sales of, let us say, 100 units, capital equipment valued at 200 units, and regular replacement demand of 20 units, or 10 percent of its stock of equipment. Now we assume that its sales rise to 120 units. To produce 120 units of goods, the firm will need (according to our assumptions) 240 units of capital. This is 40 units more than it has, so it must order them. Note that its demand for capital goods now shoots from 20 units to 60 units: 20 units for replacement as before, and 40 new ones. Thus investment expenditures *triple*, even though sales have risen but 20 percent!

Now assume that in the next year sales rise further, to 130 units. How large will our firm's investment demand be? Its replacement demand will not be larger, since its new capital will not wear out for ten years. And the amount of new capital needed to handle its new sales will be only 20 units, not 40 as before. Its total investment demand has *fallen* from 60 units to 40.

What is the surprising fact here? It is that *we can have an actual fall in induced investment, though sales are still rising!* In fact, as soon as the *rate of increase* of consumption begins to fall, *the absolute amount* of induced investment declines. Thus a slowdown in the rate of improve-

Table 10·1   A model of the accelerator

Year	Sales	Existing capital	Needed capital (2 × sales)	Replacement investment	Induced new investment (2 × addition to sales)	Total investment
1	$100	$200	$200	$20	—	$20
2	120	200	240	20	$40	60
3	130	240	260	20	20	40
4	135	260	270	20	10	30
5	138	270	276	20	6	26
6	140	276	280	20	4	24
7	140	280	280	20	—	20
8	130	280	260	—	—	0
9	130	260	260	20	—	20

ment in sales can cause an absolute decline in the orders sent to capital goods makers. This helps us to explain how weakness can appear in some branches of the economy while prosperity seems still to be reigning in the market at large. It will play a role when we come to explain the phenomenon of the business cycle.

Now look at what happens to our model in the eighth year, when we assume that sales slip back to 130. Our existing capital (280 units) will be greater by 20 units than our needed capital. That year the industry will have no new orders for capital goods and may not even make any replacements, because it can produce all it needs with its old machines. Its orders to capital goods makers will fall to zero, even though its level of sales is 30 percent higher than at the beginning. The next year, however, if sales remain steady, it will again have to replace one of its old machines. Its replacement demand again jumps to 20. No wonder capital goods industries traditionally experience feast or famine years!

There is, in addition, an extremely important point to bear in mind. **The accelerator's upward leverage usually takes**

effect only when an industry is operating at or near capacity. When an industry is not near capacity, it is relatively simple for it to satisfy a larger demand for its goods by raising output on its underutilized equipment. Thus, unlike the multiplier, which yields its effects on output only when we have unemployed resources, the accelerator yields its effects only when we do *not* have unemployed capital.

Autonomous investment

Not all investment is induced by prior rises in consumption. A very important category of investment is that undertaken in the expectation of a profit to be derived from a *new* good or a *new* way of making a good. This type of investment is usually called *autonomous* investment.

In autonomous investment decisions, prior trends in consumption have little or nothing to do with the decision to invest. This is particularly the case when new technologies provide the stimulus for investment. Then the question in the minds of the managers of the firm is whether the new product will create *new* demand for itself.

Technological advance is not, however, the only cause for autonomous investment, and therefore we cannot statistically separate autonomous from induced investment. With some economic stimuli, such as the opening of a new territory or shifts in population or population growth, the motivations of both autonomous and induced investment are undoubtedly present. Yet there is a meaningful distinction between the two, insofar as induced investment is sensitive and responsive to sales, whereas autonomous investment is not. This means that induced investment, by its nature, is more foreseeable than autonomous investment.

At the same time, both spontaneous and induced investments are powerfully affected by the overall investment "climate"—not alone the economic climate of confidence, the level and direction of the stock market, etc., but the political scene, international developments, and so on. Hence it is not surprising that investment is often an unpredictable component of GNP, and thus a key "independent" variable in any model of GNP.

The Determinants of Investment

As we have seen, profit expectations that guide investment decisions are largely unpredictable. But there exists one influence on investment decisions that seems to offer a more determinable guide. This is the influence of the *rate of interest* on the investment decisions of business firms.

Interest costs   The rate of interest should offer two guides to the investing firm. If the business must borrow capital, a higher rate of interest makes it more expensive to undertake an investment. For huge firms that target a return of 15 to 20 percent on their investment projects, a change in the interest rate from 7 to 8 percent may be negligible. But for certain kinds of investment—notably utilities and home construction—interest rates constitute an important component of the cost of investment funds. To these firms, the lower the cost of borrowed capital, the more stimulus for investment. The difference in *interest costs* for $1 million borrowed for 20 years at 7 percent (instead of 8 percent) is $200,000, by no means a negligible sum. Since construction is the largest single component of investment, the interest rate therefore becomes an important influence on the value of total capital formation.

A second guide is offered to business not directly seeking to borrow money for investment but debating whether to invest the savings (retained earnings) of the firms. This problem of deciding on investments introduces us to an important idea: the discounting of future income.

Discounting the future   Suppose that someone gave you an iron-clad promise to pay you $100 a year hence. Would you pay him $100 *now* to get back the same sum 365 days in the future? Certainly not, for in parting with the money you are suffering an *opportunity cost* or a cost that can be measured in terms of the opportunities that your action (to pay $100 now) has foreclosed for you. Had the going rate of interest been 5 percent, for example, you could have loaned your $100 at 5 percent and had $105 at the end of the year. Hence, friendship aside, you are unlikely to lend your money unless you are paid something to compensate you for the opportunities you must give up while you are waiting for your money to return. Another way of saying exactly the same thing is that we arrive at the *present value* of a specified sum in the future by discounting it by some percentage. If the discount rate is 5 percent, the present value of $100 one year in the future is $100 ÷ 1.05, or approximately $95.24.

This brings us back to the business that is considering whether or not to make an investment. Suppose it is considering investing $100,000 in a machine that is expected to earn $25,000 a year for 5 years, over and above all expenses, after which it will be worthless. Does this mean that the expected profit on the machine is therefore $25,000—the $125,000 of expected earnings less the $100,000 of original cost? No, it does not, for the expected earnings will have to be discounted by some appropriate percentage to find their present value. Thus the first $25,000 to be earned by the machine must be reduced by some discount rate; and the second $25,000 must be discounted *twice* (just as $100 to be repaid in *two* year's time will have to yield the equivalent of *two* years' worth of interest); the third $25,000, three times, etc.*

Clearly, this process of discounting will cause the present value of the expected future returns of the machine to be less than the sum of the undiscounted returns. If, for example, its returns are discounted at a rate of 10 percent, the business will find that the present value of a five-year flow of $25,000 per annum comes not to $125,000 but to only $94,700. This is *less* than the actual expenditure for the machine ($100,000). Hence, at a discount rate

*The formula for calculating the present value of a flow of future income that does not change from year to year is:

$$\text{Present value} = \frac{R}{(1+i)} + \frac{R}{(1+i)^2} + \ldots + \frac{R}{(1+i)^n}$$

where R is the annual flow of income, i is the interest rate, and n is the number of years over which the flow will last.

of 10 percent, the business would not undertake the venture.

On the other hand, if it used a discount rate of 5 percent, the present value of the same future flow would be worth (in round numbers) $109,000. In that case, the machine *would* be a worthwhile investment.

Interest rates and investment

What rate should our business use to discount future earnings? Here is where the rate of interest enters the picture. Looking out at the economy, the business manager sees that there is a whole spectrum of interest rates, ranging from very low rates on bonds (usually government bonds) where the element of risk is very small, to high rates on securities of the same maturity (that is, coming due in the same number of years) where the risk is much greater, such as "low-grade" corporate bonds or mortgages. Among this spectrum of rates, there will be a rate at which he or she can borrow—high or low, depending on each one's credit worthiness in the eyes of the banking community. By applying that rate the manager can discover whether the estimated future earning from the venture, properly discounted, is actually profitable or not.

We can see the expected effect of interest rates on investment in Fig. 10 • 2. Suppose that a businessman has a choice among different investment projects from which he anticipates different returns. The technical name for these returns is the *marginal efficiency of investment*. Suppose he ranks those projects, as we have in Fig. 10 • 2, starting with the most profitable (*A*) and proceeding to the least profitable (*G*). How far down the list should he go? The rate of interest gives the answer. Let us say that the rate (for projects of comparable risk) is shown by *OX*. Then all his

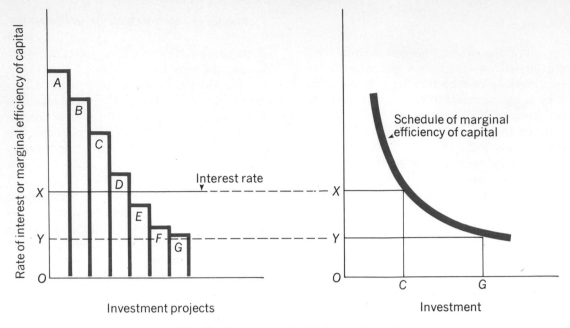

FIG. 10 · 2   Marginal efficiency of capital

investment projects whose marginal efficiency is higher than OX (investments A through D) will be profitable, and all those whose marginal efficiency falls below OX (E through G) will be discarded or at least postponed.

Note that if the interest rate falls, more investments will be worthwhile; and that if it rises, fewer will be. As the figure on the right shows in generalized form, a fall in the rate of interest (e.g., from OX to OY) induces a rise in the quantity of investment (from OC to OG).

Increases in autonomous investment or induced investment can be represented as the marginal efficiency of capital schedule shifting to the right. New opportunities, either arising from the development of new goods and services or because of increasing sales of old goods, mean that a given amount of capital can earn a higher rate of return or that more investment will occur at any given rate of interest. Draw in a new marginal efficiency curve in Fig. 10 · 2 and prove this to yourself.

DISCOUNTING GOVERNMENT AND INDIVIDUAL INVESTMENT

Does the process of discounting earnings and comparing them with costs apply to public investment or to individuals investing in, say, education?

It may. A government contemplating an investment in roads, parks, or police stations does not expect to show a financial profit, but it does expect a flow of benefits—a kind of *social profit*. These benefits can often be roughly measured in terms of their financial worth, and the public institution can then compare the discounted value of these expected benefits against their costs.

In similar fashion, an individual contemplating a personal investment, such as acquiring a new skill, may make a similar calculation. He estimates the future increase in earnings that he expects from his training, discounts this sum, and compares it with

the cost of undertaking the investment. Of course, individuals do not always act with the precision of "economic man." Nonetheless, the idea of discounting future returns helps give analytic clarity to the reason why a 20-year-old person will willingly accept the cost of becoming a doctor or an engineer, whereas a 55-year-old will not. For the younger person, the investment is expected to pay off (quite aside from the pleasures of the increased skills themselves). For the older person, it is not. An older person may go to school for pleasure, but not for profit.

Thus, whether we figure interest as a cost or as a guideline against which we measure the expected returns of a capital investment, we reach the important conclusion that *low interest rates should encourage investment spending*—or in more formal language, that *investment should be inversely related to the rate of interest.* To be sure, the fact that a given investment, such as project *B* above, has a marginal efficiency higher than the interest rate is no guarantee that a business actually will undertake it. Other considerations—perhaps political, perhaps psychological—may deter management, despite its encouraging calculations. But assuredly a business will not carry out a project that yields less than the interest rate, because it can make more profit by lending the money, at the same degree of risk, than by investing it.*

The Export Sector

Before we go on to the problem of public demand, we must mention, if only in passing, a sector we have so far largely overlooked. This is the foreign sector, or more properly the sector of net exports.

If we lived in Europe, South America, or Asia, we could not be so casual in our treatment of foreign trade, for this sector constitutes the very lifeline of many, perhaps even most, countries. Our own highly self-sustained economy in which foreign trade plays only a small quantitative (although a much more important qualitative) role in generating total output

is very much the exception rather than the rule.*

In part, it is the relatively marginal role played by foreign trade in the American economy that allows us to treat it so cavalierly. But there is also another problem. The forces that enter into the flows of international trade are much more complex than any we have heretofore discussed. Not alone the reactions of American consumers and firms, but those of foreign consumers and firms must be taken into account. Thus comparisons between international price levels, the availability of foreign or domestic goods, credit and monetary controls, exchange rates—a whole host of other such considerations—lie at the very heart of foreign trade. To begin to unravel these interrelationships, one must study international trade as a subject in itself, and that we will defer until Chapter 19. Nevertheless, we should try to understand the main impact of foreign trade on the demand for GNP, even if we cannot yet investigate the forces and institutions of foreign trade as thoroughly as we might like.

Impact of foreign trade We must begin by repeating that our initial overview of the economic system, with its twin streams of consumption and investment, was actually incomplete. It portrayed what we call a "closed" system, an economy with no flows of goods or services from within its borders to other nations or from other nations to itself.

Yet such flows must, of course, be taken into account in computing our national output. Let us therefore look at a chart that shows us the main streams of

---

*The relation between the interest rate and housing investment or investment in utilities is as we have described it. The matter is more complicated with regard to manufacturing investment. See "An extra word" at the end of this chapter for details.

*In Chapter 20 we shall see, however, that international currency problems can play a very important role in our economic affairs.

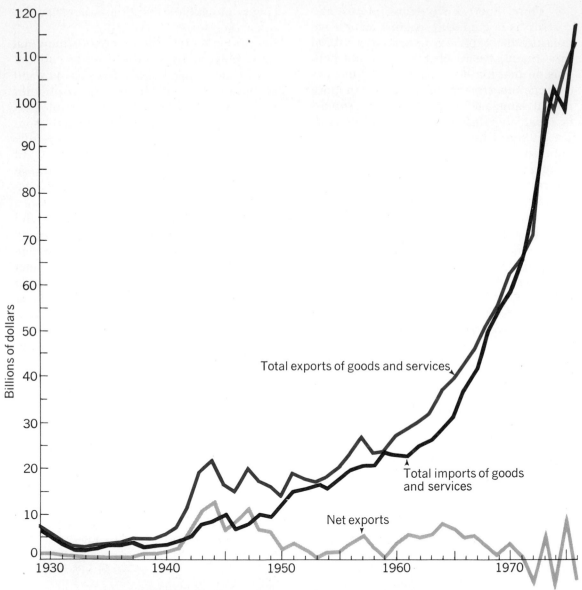

FIG. 10 · 3 Exports, imports, and net exports

goods and services that cross our borders, as well as a table of the magnitudes in our benchmark years (see Fig. 10 · 3).

First a word of explanation. Exports show the total value of all goods and services we sold to foreigners. Imports show the total value of all goods and services we bought from foreigners. Our bottom line shows the net difference between exports and imports, or the difference between the value of the goods we sold abroad and the value we bought from abroad. This difference is called *net exports*, and it constitutes the net contribution of foreign trade to the demand for GNP.

If we think of it in terms of expenditures, it is not difficult to see what the net contribution is. When exports are sold to foreigners, their expenditures add to American incomes. Imports, on the contrary, are expenditures that we make to other countries (and hence that we do not make at home). If we add the foreign expenditures made here and subtract the domestic expenditures made abroad, we will have left a net figure that will show the contribution (if any) made by foreigners to GNP.

The export multiplier

What is the impact of this net expenditure on GNP? It is much the same as net private domestic investment. If we have a rising net export balance, we will have a net increase in spending in the economy.

Conversely, if our net foreign trade balance falls, our demand for GNP will decline, exactly as if the demand for domestic investment fell. Thus, even though we must defer for a while a study of the actual forces at work in international trade, we can quickly include the effects of foreign trade on the level of GNP by considering the net trade balance as a part of our investment demand for output.

One point in particular should be noted. If there is a rise in the net demand generated by foreigners, this will have a *multiplier effect*, exactly as an increase in investment will have. Here is, in fact, the parable of an individual visiting an island (p. 134) come to life. Additional net foreign spending will generate new incomes which will generate new buying; and decreased net foreign spending will diminish incomes, with a similar train of secondary and tertiary effects. We will look into this problem again when we study the foreign trade difficulties of the United States in Chapter 21.

FOCUS This chapter continues the exploration and explanation of investment as a source of the demand for GNP. The reason that we take two chapters to do so is that investment opens the way to many other subjects, such as the multiplier analysis of our last chapter. Here we concentrate on a complementary aspect of the investment flow, the accelerator. Together with the multiplier, the accelerator helps us explain the phenomenon of economic instability. The multiplier tells us how relatively small changes in spending can give rise to larger changes in income. The acceleration principle tells us how relatively small changes in consumption spending can give rise to bigger changes in investment. That is a key thing to learn.

Investment, unlike consumption, looks to expected profit for its motivation. Whether investment is induced or autonomous, it is always hoped-for profit that lies behind the decision to invest. Thus investment is not simply a function of current GNP.

But the interest rate also plays a role in establishing the level of investment, especially in certain industries such as housing. Interest rates affect the actual cost of investment and also help to establish the profitability of investment. That's a second main idea of this chapter.

We conclude with a brief glance at the export sector, to which we will return when we study foreign trade in depth.

WORDS AND CONCEPTS YOU SHOULD KNOW

Utility vs. expected profit, 145–46
Induced investment, 147–149
Acceleration principle (accelerator), 148–49
Autonomous investment, 149–150
Interest costs, 150

Discounting the future, 150–51
Interest rates and investment, 151–53
Export sector, 153–55
Marginal efficiency of investment, 151–53
The export multiplier, 155

QUESTIONS

1. Discuss the difference in the motivation of a consumer buying a car for pleasure and the same person buying a car for business.

2. Which of the following are induced and which autonomous investment decisions: a developer builds homes in a growing community; a city enlarges its water supply after a period of water shortage; a firm builds a laboratory for basic research; an entrepreneur invests in a new gadget.

3. What is the basic idea of the acceleration principle? Describe carefully how the acceleration principle helps explain the instability of investment.

4. What is meant by "discounting" the value of an expected return? If the rate of interest were 10 percent, what would be the *present value* of $100 due a year hence? What would be its present value two years hence? (HINT: the first year's discounted value has to be discounted a *second* time.)

5. Assume that it costs 7 percent to borrow from a bank. What is the minimum profit that must be expected from an investment before it becomes worthwhile? Could we write that $I = f(r)$ where r stands for the rate of interest? What would be the relation between a change in r and I? Would $I = f(r)$ be a complete description of the motivation for investment? Why should future costs as well as profits be discounted?

6. Why doesn't the accelerator work when there is idle equipment? What significance does this have for the flow of investment as the economy moves from a position of underutilization to one of high utilization?

7. Explain how exports stimulate income. Does this mean that imports are bad? Are savings bad?

The elusive investment function

We are familiar with the consumption function that relates income to consumption. If our analysis in this chapter is valid, there should also be an *investment function* relating investment to the rate of interest. That is, we should be able to specify that for each percentage point fall in interest, investment rises by such-and-such a percent. We would expect the function to show a curve like the hypothetical one in Fig. 10 • 4.

In fact, when econometricians first began to inquire into the interest-investment relationship, they found exactly this kind of relation between interest rates and residential construction. As they expected, when it became cheaper to borrow or take out a mortgage, home-building increased. But to their consternation, when they investigated the relation between interest rates and plant and equipment investment, no such relationship appeared. Worse, the data seemed to show a "wrong" relationship: when interest rates went up, plant and equipment investment also went up! Figure 10 • 5 shows the kind of relation that research established between plant and equipment investment (shown as a proportion of GNP) and interest rates, *i*.

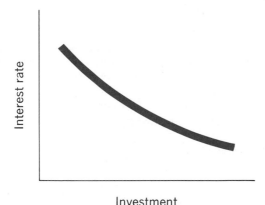

FIG. 10 • 4 The hypothetical interest-investment function

Investment

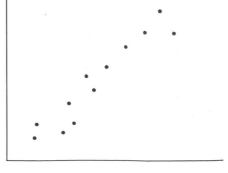

i

FIG. 10 • 5 The econometric interest-investment function

Plant and equipment (% of GNP)

Does this mean that our theory is wrong in some fundamental sense? Econometricians have tried a number of ways to make it come out right. One method was to correct the money rate of interest to the *real rate of interest.* The real rate of interest is the money rate reduced by the rate of inflation. If you get 5 percent on a savings bank deposit, but prices rise by 5 percent, your real interest return is zero. So, too, if businessmen could borrow at 8 percent, but prices rose by 5 percent, their real interest cost was only 3 percent. Unhappily, when money interest rates were corrected for inflation, the expected investment functions still did not appear.

Numerous other attempts have also been made to "specify" an investment function that would reconcile the observed phenomenon of investment perversely rising with interest rates. Econometricians have struggled to incorporate after-tax profit rates and many other possible influences into their investment function term, but all to no avail. No testable interest rate—manufacturing investment function has yet been devised!

Is there no way, then, of explaining a phenomenon that seems to fly in the face of common sense as well as theory? One plausible explanation has been advanced. Historically, interest rates rise during periods of rapid growth. This happens for two reasons. During these periods, the demand curve for *induced* investment shifts to the right. Therefore, even if higher interest rates tend to discourage autonomous investment, this effect may be overridden by the accelerator taking hold elsewhere.

Second, periods of rapid growth push economies toward full employment. Governments thereupon deliberately raise interest rates through the money mechanism to try to cool off the economy. In this complex of cross currents we can have the curious parallel of higher interest rates and higher investment in plant and equipment, but we can see that the influence of interest rates alone is difficult—even impossible—to isolate. Therefore we continue to assume that *if* we could isolate those effects, they would show the negatively sloped investment function we use in economic theory. We make this assumption because it is logical, and because we believe we can explain away the seeming disconfirmation of our theory in real life. Nevertheless, the interest rate—investment relationship remains something of a puzzle and a source of discomfiture to economists.

Government
demand

We turn now to the last of the main sources of demand for GNP—the government. As before, we should begin by familiarizing ourselves with its long historical profile. Figure 11 • 1 at once shows the signal fact that will underlie the discussion in this chapter. It is that up to 1940 the government was almost insignificant as a source of economic demand. More important, the New Deal (1933–1940) and the postwar era marked a turning point in the *philosophy* of government, from a passive to an active force in macroeconomic affairs. In Europe, government has played a substantial economic role for a longer period; but in Europe as well as America, the deliberate *public management* of demand is a modern phenomenon on which this chapter will focus.

Government in the Expenditure Flow

Before we begin our analysis, let us take a closer look at a recent year, to help us fit the government sector into the flow of national expenditure. Figure 11 • 2 has the fa-

11

159

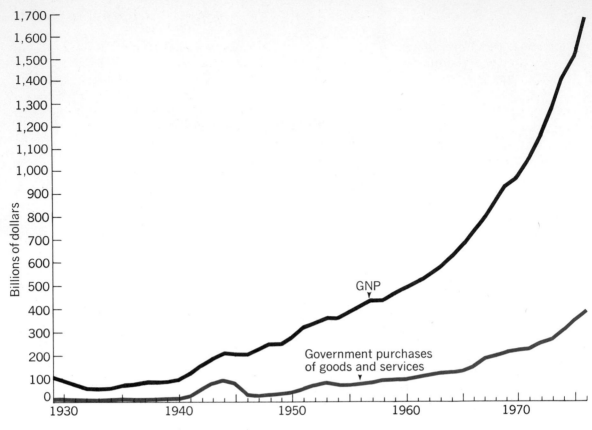

FIG. 11·1   GNP and the government sector

miliar bars of our flow diagram. Note that indirect taxes, totaling some $150 billion in 1976, amounted to almost 10 percent of the value of GNP. As can be seen, however, income taxes on households and businesses are much more important than indirect taxes in providing total government revenues. (What the diagram does not show is that about two-thirds of the indirect taxes are state and local in origin: property taxes, excise taxes, motor vehicle and gasoline taxes, and others. Income taxes and Social Security contributions constitute about nine-tenths of the income of the federal government.)

On the expenditure side, we see once again that state and local purchases of goods and services are more important than federal purchases in providing public demand; however, since two-thirds of all transfer payments are federal in origin, total federal *expenditures* (as contrasted with purchases of goods and services) run about one-fifth higher than all state and local expenditures.

Purchases vs. transfers   Finally, it is worth reminding ourselves of the different significance and impact of public purchases and transfers. *Public purchases of goods and services, whether they originate with local or federal government, require the use of land, labor and capital. They thus contribute to GNP. Transfer payments, on the other hand, do not increase output. They are simply a reallocation of income, from factors to various groups of the community in the business sector or the household sector.*

Transfers, therefore, do not require new production and therefore do not add to GNP.

Government sector in historical perspective

How large does the public sector bulk in the total flow of GNP? Let us again try to put a perspective into our answer by observing the trend of government purchases over the years.

We have already pointed out the striking change from prewar to postwar years. The government sector, taken as a whole, has changed from a very small sector to a very large one. In 1929, total government purchases of goods and services were only half of total private investment spending; in 1976 total government purchases were almost 50 percent *larger* than private investment. In terms of its contributions to

GNP, government is now second only to consumption.

Thus, the public sector, whose operation we will have to examine closely, has become a major factor in the economy as a whole. Let us begin by learning to distinguish carefully among various aspects of what we call "government spending." As we shall see, it is very easy to get confused between "expenditures" and "purchases of goods and services"; between federal spending and total government spending (which includes the states and localities); and between war and nonwar spending.[3]

1. **Government expenditures vs. purchases of goods and services**

When we speak of government spending, we must take care to specify whether we mean total *expenditures of the govern-*

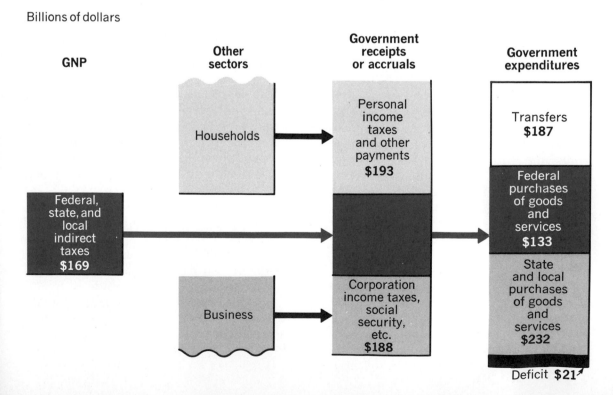

FIG. 11·2   Government sector, 1976

ment, which include transfer payments, or *purchases of goods and services by the government,* which represent only actual economic activity performed for, and bought by, the government. In the latter category we include all "production" that owes its existence to public demand, whether from federal, state, or local agencies; in the former we include activities performed for the government *plus* transfer payments made by government, at all levels, as part of the redistribution of income. Thus, under "purchases" we include items such as arms and education and police and roads; under "expenditures" we count all these plus Social Security; interest on the debts of localities, states, and the federal government; welfare and other such transfers.

The distinction is important in terms of the relative bulk of what we call government spending. The purchases of goods and services by all government agencies amounted in 1976 to about $365 billion (of which, as Fig. 11•2 shows, the federal government accounted for $133 billion). *The term "G" in our GNP equation stands for these total purchases.* The larger "expenditure" category came to $531 billion. Thus government purchases were the direct cause of the production of about 22 percent of GNP itself, whereas government expenditures amounted in all to not quite one-third of GNP. Remember that a rise in transfers does not increase GNP, so that you must be careful not to use "expenditures" and "purchases" indiscriminately.

2. Federal vs. state and local spending

In dealing with the public sector we must also be careful to distinguish between expenditures or purchases that originate with the federal government and those that stem from state and local agencies. As we noted in Figure 11•2, state and local spending for goods and services is *larger* than federal purchasing. This is the consequence of the rise of an urbanized, motorized, education-minded society that has imposed vast new burdens on state and local authorities: the supervision of vehicular traffic alone requires the employment of roughly one out of every ten state and local employees, and the support of education now runs to $100 billion a year. These services have been increasing during the last decade, and now, annual state and local spending for such goods and services runs about 75 percent ahead of federal purchases.

On the other hand, federal expenditures, *including transfers,* make *total* federal spending larger than total state-and-local spending. In 1976, for example, federal expenditures, including transfers such as Social Security, interest on the debt, various subsidies, grants to the states, etc., brought total federal outlays of all kinds to more than double the amount it spent for goods and services alone.

3. Welfare vs. warfare

Most of the rise in federal purchases of goods and services is the result of our swollen armaments economy. Defense spending in 1976 amounted to almost 30 percent of our federal expenditures of all kinds including transfers, and to a much larger fraction—about two-thirds—of federal purchases of goods and services. In contrast, Table 11•1 shows that federal purchases of nonwar goods and services as a percent of GNP are actually smaller than in the prewar days and have shown only a slight rise during the last decade.

Meanwhile, social welfare expenditures of all kinds and of all government agencies (federal, state, and local), including such payments as Social Security,

Table 11·1   Federal nondefense purchases

Selected years	1929	1933	1940	1960–65	1966	1967	1968	1969	1970	1971	1972	1973	1974	1975	1976
Percent of GNP	1.0*	3.0*	4.0	2.1	2.2	2.3	2.5	2.5	2.4	2.5	2.6	2.6	2.4	2.6	2.7

*Estimated.

health and medical programs, public education, public housing, welfare assistance, etc., have risen from about 10 percent of GNP in the mid-1930s to about 19 percent today. This is not a large percentage by international standards. In recent years at least 4 other nations spent a higher proportion of their GNP on education than we did. Other social welfare spending (excluding education) amounted to about 13 percent of our GNP, compared with an average of more than 15 percent among the industrialized nations of Europe. It is noteworthy that in 1975 the average monthly Social Security check per married couple came to just over $340. In Scandinavian countries the payments, compared to average earnings, were roughly twice as generous as ours.

The Main Tasks of Government

The forms and functions of government spending are so complex that it may help us if we now step back and simplify the picture. Basically the federal government has three major economic functions. Measured in terms of expenditures, its largest responsibility lies in the conduct of *international affairs.* Here we find expenditures for defense, foreign aid, veterans' expenditures, military research including space exploration. In 1975 this was 33 percent of all federal spending.

Second, the federal government writes checks in the form of *transfer payments* and *interest payments* to individuals and businesses. Here are the farm

---

PUBLIC AND PRIVATE BUYING

It is important to realize that government buying can be divided into consumption and investment expenditures, just as private expenditures are. In 1975 for example, governments—federal, state, and local—spent $66 billion for structures and durable goods such as roads, schools, parks, sewage disposal plants and the like, as well as $97 billion on manpower training programs and education to upgrade human skills. These are all *public investment* programs.

Governments also spend large sums on *public consumption;* that is, on providing goods that are enjoyable or necessary for the public at large. Streets are swept, zoos operated, bombers flown, criminals caught.

Why do we separate government consumption and investment from private consumption and investment?

The immediate answer is that the money is spent by some government agency rather than by a household or a firm. But there is a deeper reason behind this. It is that a *political decision* has been made to put certain types of expenditures into the hands of the public authorities.

This decision varies from nation to nation. Some countries, like the U.S., have private airlines. Others, such as most of the nations of Europe, have public airlines. In the old days, roads were private; today roads are public, although occasionally one finds a privately owned road. (Note, by the way, that we could not utilize our

private consumption of automobile travel unless we simultaneously "consumed" the public road on which we travel.) All nations provide public defense, justice, administration; most provide some public health; a few provide public entertainment. Ideology draws the line, not only between socialist and capitalist governments, but within socialist and capitalist governments: there is a large private agricultural sector in Yugoslavia, a very small one in Russia; many municipally owned power stations in Europe; far fewer here.

What is important to realize is that government expenditure is not a form of economic activity different from consumption or investment. It is the same kind of economic activity, undertaken collectively, through a public agency, rather than privately.

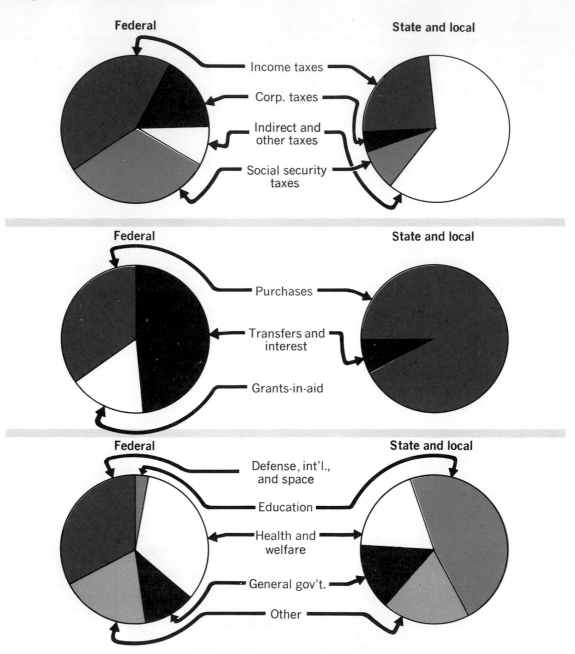

FIG. 11·3   Federal, state, and local finances

subsidies, subsidies for the merchant marine, and the very large outflow for Social Security and other welfare. In all, this adds up to another 41 percent of federal expenditure.

Third, the federal government writes checks, in the form of *grants-in-aid* to states and local governments. This accounts for 15 percent of federal outlays. The remainder of federal spending—11 percent—represents direct federal government operating costs and various miscellaneous functions.

It will help us review the main outlines of government spending if we look at Fig. 11·3. The first chart shows us the strikingly different *sources of funds* that flow to the federal and to state and local governments. Note the much heavier reliance of the federal government on income taxes, and the corresponding dependence of state and local governments on indirect taxes. The middle chart shows us the difference in the division of activity between federal and other governments by kinds of payments. But this table obscures a still more basic division, which we see in the third chart. Here we contrast the functions of federal and state and local governments. Now the importance of the three main functions of the federal government clearly emerges.

Economics of the Public Sector

So far we have been mainly concerned with problems of a definitional kind—in finding out what the government does. Now we want to examine the public sector from a different angle; namely, its unique *economic* character. And here the appropriate place to begin seems to be in the difference in *motivations* that guide public, as contrasted with private, spending.

We recall that the motivations for the household sector and the business sector are lodged in the free decisions of their respective units. Householders decide to spend or save their incomes as they wish, and we are able to construct a propensity to consume schedule only because there seem to be spending and saving patterns that emerge spontaneously from the householders themselves. Similarly, business firms exercise their own judgments on their capital expenditures, and as a result we have seen the inherent variability of investment decisions.

But when we turn to the expenditures of the public sector, we enter an entirely new area of motivation. It is no longer fixed habit or profit that determines the rate of spending, but *political decision*— that is, the collective will of the people as it is formulated and expressed through their local, state, and federal legislatures and executives.

As we shall soon see, this does not mean that government is therefore an entirely unpredictable economic force. There are regularities and patterns in the government's economic behavior, as there are in other sectors. Yet the presence of an explicit political will that can direct the income or outgo of the sector *as a whole* (especially its federal component) gives to the public sector a special significance. *This is the only sector whose expenditures and receipts are open to deliberate control.* We can exert (through public action) very important influences on the behavior of households and firms. But we cannot directly alter their economic activity in the manner that is open to us with the public sector.

JOHN MAYNARD KEYNES

Few economists have left so deep a mark on their own times as John Maynard Keynes, and few have roused such passions, pro and con. It is difficult now, when (as a famous conservative economist has said) ''We are all Keynesians,'' to recall the impact of Keynes's seminal book, *The General Theory of Employment, Interest and Money,* when it appeared in 1936. Yet there were debates in the halls of academe in which voices shook and faces became empurpled over questions such as whether or not savings and investment were equal, as Keynes *defined* them to be! (We shall come to that question shortly.)

What made Keynes so controversial? Partly it was the economic philosophy that lay half explicit, half implicit in his great book—a philosophy of active government intervention. In a period when the reigning philosophy in many circles was still laissez faire, this was reason enough for Keynes's disturbing impact.

But perhaps another reason was Keynes's personality. Inordinately gifted, he was successful at a dozen things: a brilliant mathematician, a major diplomat, a great collector of modern French art, a dazzlingly skillful investor and speculator—here was one theoretical economist who *did* make a lot of money—a fascinating speaker, a consummate stylist. Keynes was not one to wear these talents modestly, and his wit was savage. Sir Harry Goshen, chairman of a Scottish bank, once deplored a Keynesian proposal and urged that things should be allowed to take ''their natural course.'' ''Is it more appropriate to smile or rage at these artless sentiments?'' Keynes asked. ''Best perhaps to let Sir Harry take *his* natural course.''

Fiscal policy

The deliberate use of the government sector as an active economic force is a relatively new conception in economics. Much of the apparatus of macroeconomic analysis stems essentially from the work of John Maynard Keynes during the Great Depression. At that time his proposals were regarded as extremely daring, but they have become increasingly accepted by both major political parties. Although the bold use of the economic powers of the public sector is far from commanding unanimous assent in the United States today, there is a steadily growing consensus in the use of fiscal policy—that is, the deliberate utilization of the government's taxing and spending powers—to help insure the stability and growth of the national economy.

The basic idea behind modern fiscal policy is simple enough. We have seen that economic recessions have their roots in a failure of the business sector to offset the savings of the economy through sufficient investment. If savings or leakages are larger than intended investment, there will be a gap in the circuit of incomes and expenditures that can cumulate downward, at first by the effect of the multiplier, thereafter, and even more seriously, by further decreases in investment brought about by falling sales and gloomy expectations.

But if a falling GNP is caused by an inadequacy of expenditures in one sector, our analysis suggests an answer. Could not the insufficiency of spending in the business sector be offset by higher spending in another sector, the public sector? Could not the public sector serve as a supplementary avenue for the "transfer" of savings into expenditure?

As Fig. 11·4 shows, a demand gap can indeed be closed by "transferring" savings to the public sector and spending them. The diagram shows savings in the household sector partly offset by business investment and partly by government spending. It makes clear that at least so far as the mechanics of the economic flow are concerned, the public sector can serve to offset savings or other leakages equally as well as the private sector.

How is the "transfer" accomplished? It can be done much as business does it, by offering bonds that individuals or institutions may buy with their savings. Unlike business, the government cannot offer stock, for it is not run as a profit-making enterprise. However, government has a source of funds quite different from business; namely, *taxes. In effect, government can "commandeer" purchasing power in a way that business cannot.*

Taxes, expenditures, and GNP

We shall look more carefully into the question of how the government can serve as a kind of counterbalance for the private economy. But first we must discover something about the normal behavior of the public sector; for despite the importance of political decisions in determining the action of the public sector, and despite the multiplicity of government units and activities, *we can nonetheless discern "propensities" in government spending and receiving*—propensities that play their compensating role in the economy quite independently of any direct political intervention.

The reason for these propensities is that both government income and government outgo are closely tied to private activity. Government receipts are derived in the main from taxes, and taxes—direct or indirect—tend to reflect the trend of business and personal income. In fact, we can generalize about tax payments in much the same fashion as we can about consumption, describing them as a predictable function of GNP. To be sure,

FIG. 11·4 Public expenditure and the demand gap

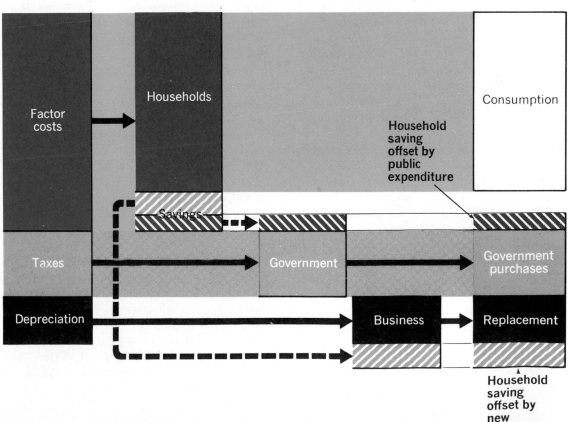

this assumes that tax *rates* do not change. But since rates change only infrequently, we can draw up a general schedule that relates tax receipts and the level of GNP. The schedule will show not only that taxes rise as GNP rises, but that they rise *faster* than GNP.

Why faster? Largely because of the progressive structure of the federal income tax. As household and business incomes rise to higher levels, the percentage "bite" of income taxes increases. Thus as incomes rise, tax liabilities rise even more. Conversely, the tax bite works downward in the opposite way. As incomes fall, taxes fall even faster, since households or businesses with lowered incomes find themselves in less steep tax brackets.

Government expenditures also show certain "propensities," which is to say, *some government spending is also functionally related to the level of GNP.* A number of government programs are directly correlated to the level of economic activity in such a way that spending *decreases* as GNP *increases*, and vice versa. For instance, unemployment benefits are naturally higher when GNP is low or falling. Many payments such as food stamps, aid to dependent children, or various welfare programs are highly sensitive to unemployment: in 1976, for example, when unemployment neared 9 percent, such outlays were $20 billion higher than if unemployment had been 5 percent. So, too, disbursements to farmers under various agricultural programs also vary inversely with GNP.

| *Automatic* | All these automatic |
| *stabilizers* | effects taken together |

are called the *automatic stabilizers* or the *built-in stabilizers* of the economy. What they add up to is an

automatic government counterbalance to the private sector. As GNP falls because private spending is insufficient, taxes decline even faster and public expenditures grow, thereby automatically causing the government sector to offset the private sector to some extent. In similar fashion, as GNP rises, taxes tend to rise even faster and public expenditures decline, thereby causing the government sector to act as a brake.

The public sector therefore acts as an automatic compensator, even without direct action to alter tax or expenditure levels, pumping out more public demand when private demand is slowing, and curbing public demand when private demand is brisk.

How effective are the built-in stabilizers? It is estimated that the increase in transfer payments plus the reduction in taxes offset about 35¢ of each dollar of original decline in spending. Here is how this works. Suppose that private investment were to fall by $10 billion. If there were no stabilizers, household spending might fall by another $10 billion (the multiplier effect), causing a total decline of $20 billion in incomes.

The action of the stabilizers, however, will prevent the full force of this fall. First, the reduction in incomes of both households and firms will lower their tax liabilities. Since taxes take about 35¢ from each dollar, the initial drop of $10 billion in incomes will reduce tax liabilities by about $3.5 billion. Most of this—let us say $3 billion—is likely to be spent. Meanwhile some public expenditures for unemployment insurance and farm payments will rise, pumping out perhaps $1 billion into the consumption sector, all of which we assume to be spent by its recipients.

Thus, the incomes of firms and households, having originally fallen by

$10 billion, will be offset by roughly $4 billion—$1 billion in additional transfer incomes and $3 billion in income spent by households because their taxes are lower. As a result, the decline in expenditure will be reduced from $10 billion to about $6 billion (actually $6.5 billion, according to the calculations of the Council of Economic Advisers).

This is certainly an improvement over a situation with no stabilizers. Yet if the drop in investment is not to bring about some fall in GNP, it will have to be *fully* compensated by an equivalent increase in government spending or by a fall in taxes large enough to induce an equivalent amount of private spending. This will require public action more vigorous than that brought about automatically. Indeed, it requires that the government take on a task very different from any we have heretofore studied, the task of "demand management," or acting as the *deliberate* balancing mechanism of the economy.

Demand management

How does the government manage demand? It has three basic alternatives. It can

1. increase or decrease expenditures
2. raise or lower taxes
3. alter its monetary policy

We have already looked into the mechanics of the first option in Fig. 11·4, where we showed that government expenditure fills a demand gap exactly like private expenditure. It follows that a decrease in government spending will also create a decrease in final demand, just as a drop in the spending of any other sector.

Our diagram did not show the direct effect of tax changes, simply because it is difficult to draw such a diagram clearly.

But it is not difficult to understand the effect of a tax change. When the government lowers taxes it diminishes the transfer of income from households or firms into the public sector. Households and firms therefore have more income to spend. Contrariwise, in raising taxes, a government withdraws spending power from households and firms. As a result, we can expect that private spending will fall.

Full employment budgets

The direct effects of expenditures and taxes are thus easy to picture, and the rule for demand management should be simple: establish a government budget that will have an expansionary influence when GNP is too low and a restraining influence when it is too high; and balance the budget when GNP is at desired levels.

But this seemingly obvious guideline is not as simple as it looks. Suppose that we are suffering from mild unemployment and the President's advisers accordingly recommend a level of expenditure that, combined with existing tax rates, would produce a small deficit. Isn't this following the proper guide?

The answer is: not necessarily. For if we calculate the flow of tax receipts that the government would be receiving *if we were operating at full employment*, the planned level of expenditure may in fact be so small that it would not even produce a neutral budget, but a deflationary one at the *desired* level of GNP! A glance at Fig. 11·5 shows that this can indeed be the case. In 1974, for example the actual budget was in substantial deficit, as the colored line shows. But if we calculate the budget *at full employment levels* of tax receipts, we find that our flow of expenditure was far too short of the levels needed

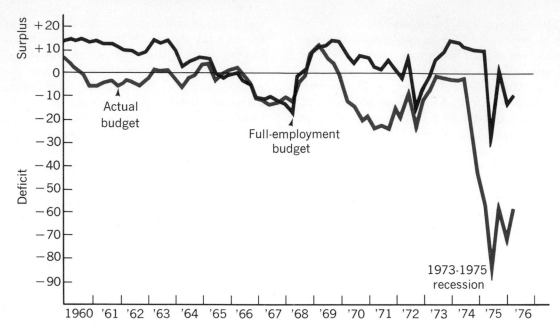

FIG. 11·5   Full-employment and actual budget deficits

to spend our receipts *at that level.* As the black line shows, our flows of taxes and expenditures would have given us a surplus at full employment! Therefore the $12 billion deficit was too little to give us the stimulus we needed to reach full employment. A true full-employment budget would have raised expenditures (or cut taxes) to bring the economy up to a high level of operation.

Paradoxically, although this would have required more expenditures or a lower tax rate, the effect at full employment might have been a government budget that was balanced, rather than one in deficit. That would have depended on how the other sectors behaved. If the flow of investment spending was strong, the net budget contribution of the government at full employment might well have been zero. If investment was weak, the government might—and should—plan to run a

deficit at full employment *to bring us there.*

Time lags

Second, there is a long delay between the adoption of a new tax or expenditure policy and the realization of its effects.* Increased expenditures or new tax proposals have to move through Congress, often a time-consuming process. In addition, if expenditures require capital construction, it may take months, even years, before spending really gets rolling. Thus by the time the new expenditures begin to give their boosting effect, the economic situation may have changed in a

*The other side of the same coin is the lag before a changed economic condition is *recognized.* How do we know when a recession begins? When unemployment goes up? By the time that statistics are in, it is already too late—the recession isn't beginning, it's begun. When the stock market dips? That may be a false alarm. The very great difficulties of knowing what is going on directly under our own noses is a major reason why demand management is inherently difficult.

way that makes those expenditures unwelcome. So, too, with expenditure cuts. It takes a long time to turn off most government programs. By the time the spending ceases, we may wish it were still with us!

Some economists have therefore suggested that we should have "stockpiles" of approved expenditure projects and "standby" authority to permit the President to raise or lower tax rates, within stated limits, in order to speed up the process of demand management. Other countries have successfully used such expenditure "stockpiles" as a means of accelerating the demand management process, and the last several U.S. administrations have sought—so far in vain—for executive power to adjust tax rates. Most economists would probably favor both proposals, but neither is yet an actuality. As a result, *very long time lags must be taken into account in the normal process of demand management.*

Tax cuts vs. expenditures

Which of these two methods of managing demand—taxes or spending—is preferable? The question basically asks us which we need more: public goods or private goods. But there are a number of technical economic criteria that we must also bear in mind.

First, tax cuts and expenditures tend to favor different groups. Tax cuts benefit those who pay taxes, and expenditures benefit those who receive them. This simple fact reveals a good deal about the political and economic pros and cons of each method. Tax cuts help well-to-do families and are of little direct benefit to poor families whose incomes are so low that they pay little or no income taxes. Expenditure programs *can* benefit these disadvantaged groups or areas—for example, by slum clearance in specific cities, training programs, or simply higher welfare payments. Expenditure programs can also help special groups, such as military or road contractors, or middle-income families who usually benefit from housing programs.

The difference, then, is that tax programs have a widespread impact, whereas expenditure programs tend to have a concentrated impact: *tax cuts or increases are diffused across the economy, exerting their influences on different income strata, whereas expenditure programs are often concentrated geographically or occupationally.* (Some expenditure programs, such as Social Security or medical aid, can have a broad "horizontal effect" as well.)

Second, expenditure programs tend to be more reliable as a means of increasing demand, whereas tax programs tend to be effective in decreasing demand. The reason is clear enough. If the government wishes to increase final demand and chooses to lower taxes, it makes possible a higher level of private spending, but there is no guarantee that firms or households will in fact spend all their tax savings. Indeed, the marginal propensity to consume leads us to be quite certain that firms and households will not spend all their tax reductions, at least for a time. Thus if the government wants to increase demand by say $7 billion, it may have to cut taxes by about $10 billion.

On the other hand, tax increases are a very reliable method of decreasing demand. Individuals or firms *can* "defy" tax increases and maintain their former level of spending by going out and borrowing money or by spending their savings, but it is unlikely they will do so. If the government tries to hold back total demand by cutting its own expenditure programs, however, there is the chance that firms and individuals will undo the government's effort to cut demand by borrowing and spending more themselves.

There is no magic formula that will enable us to declare once and for all what policy is best for demand management. It is often impossible to raise taxes for political reasons, in which case a decrease in expenditures is certainly the next best way to keep total demand from rising too fast. So too, it may be impossible to push through a program of public expenditure because public opinion or congressional tempers are opposed to spending. In that case, a tax cut is certainly the best available way to keep demand up if the nation is threatened with a recession.*

Fiscal drag

Thus the management of demand is fraught with difficulties. One of these is the problem known as *fiscal drag*, a problem that arises from the same mechanism that gives rise to the automatic stabilizers. We have seen that most taxes depend on the level of income and that the federal government tends to increase its tax collections faster than income grows. At present tax rates, federal revenues rise about 1.2 percent for every 1 percent of GNP growth, while federal outlays rise by only 0.8 percent. As a result, if the government maintains a more or less "do nothing" policy, there will be a tendency toward a chronic, rising surplus in the federal budget. In macroeconomic terms, this means the government is taking income away from the household and business sectors and failing to spend it. Such a surplus could seriously hold back the economy from attaining its maximum output. Thus the government would have to declare a "fiscal dividend" by cutting taxes or increasing expenditures, if it is to prevent a slowdown. It is the pressure of fiscal drag that lies behind the idea of a full-employment budget.

Grants-in-aid vs. revenue sharing

A different kind of demand management problem relates to the fiscal aid that the federal government gives to the states. As we have seen, this is a major function of our federal sector. Traditionally it has been accomplished through grants-in-aid—cash transfers, some of which are tied to specific purposes, others of which are available for whatever purposes the recipient states wish. These grants-in-aid have risen from $12.7 billion in 1966 to $60.2 in 1976.

During the Nixon administration, however, many of these grants were replaced by a system of *revenue sharing*, under which the states were automatically given a percentage of federal tax revenues. Proponents of this plan stress two advantages. One is that the federal government is a much more effective tax gatherer than the states or cities. By agreeing to share its revenues with states and localities it will give them spending abilities they could not otherwise enjoy. Second, the plan accords with the general philosophy of those who would like to see economic power deconcentrated and brought back toward local government.

Opponents of the plan fear that the more-or-less unrestricted granting of funds may lead to state and local tax cuts instead of to additional state and local spending. These cuts may occur because states tend

---

*We should also note that different kinds of private and public spending programs may have different multipliers if they go to different spending groups. A government public works program that uses unskilled labor is apt to have a larger initial repercussion on GNP than a private investment project in computers. Additional transfer expenditures may also have initial multiplier effects different from direct purchases of goods and services. And finally, different tax structures will cause changes in GNP to affect private spending differently.

to compete with one another for new industry, each state trying to keep its taxes lower than its neighbors. When all states do this, no one gains a competitive advantage, but the result is too little spending for domestic purposes. The danger is that the assurance of federal aid will take the pressure off states and localities, who will use their revenue shares to cut down on local taxation, thereby cutting down as well on local programs. Proponents of revenue sharing reply that the share of revenue going to each state can be determined by formulas that will reward states for making a strong local tax effort. Opponents then charge that this will benefit rich states that can afford higher taxes and penalize poor ones that cannot.

These complex considerations force us to confront the difficult question of what level of government should make various expenditure and tax decisions. There is disagreement over which functions are best "reserved" for the federal government (e.g., highways?); over how much intervention the federal government should have in economic activities traditionally reserved for the states (education?); and over what sorts of strictly local programs should be aided by categorical grants (such as local police forces). These are matters for political determination, but their effects on the level and distribution of public demand can be very considerable. We shall come back to these questions in Chapters 16 and 17.

Responsibility of public demand

All these considerations point out how difficult it is to conduct demand management as smoothly in practice as in textbooks. There was a time, not too long ago, when economists talked rather glibly of "fine-tuning" the economy. That was in the first flush of triumph of the *idea* of managed demand, before the hard realities of full-employment budgets and fiscal drag and other problems had been fully faced. Economists are a good deal more modest in their claims these days.

Nevertheless, the basic idea of using the government as a balancing mechanism for the economy remains valid, however difficult it may be to realize the perfect balance in fact. It is valid because the federal sector is the only sector whose operations we can collectively control. There is no way for business to determine how much it should spend as a sector, no way for consumers to concert their activity. More important, even if there were such a way, business and consumer actions might not accord with the needs of the macroeconomy. Only the public sector can act consciously on behalf of the public interest; only the public sector can attempt to reconcile the needs of all groups. However exasperating or inefficient or clumsy public demand management may be, it remains a major accomplishment, both in theory and fact, of twentieth-century economics.

FOCUS   The central idea of this chapter should by now be very easy to grasp: the government is an economic sector whose expenditures are subject to public (political) control. This places a special responsibility on government for the management of demand; that is, for the adoption of fiscal and monetary policies that will compensate for deficiencies or offset excesses in the expenditures of the private sectors. We have seen how this can be done by government taxing and borrowing (and in our next chapter we shall look into the associated problem of the federal budget).

The issue of demand management is simple to state but surrounded with thorny side issues. Some of these have to do with the operation of the automatic stabilizers—the propensity for taxes to rise, and for certain welfare expenditures to fall, when GNP rises, and vice versa. Other issues concern the choice of tax cuts or expenditures to boost or restrain the economy, the pressures of fiscal drag, the choice between helping states through grants-in-aid or general revenue sharing, and the very important need to plan the government contribution at full-employment rates of flow.

There are no "answers" to these issues. Your purpose in learning them is to acquaint you with the complexity of the real business of managing demand. You should bring away from this chapter a clear picture of the big role of government in the economy and a keen understanding of how hard it is to go from general purposes to specific policy decisions.

WORDS AND CONCEPTS YOU SHOULD KNOW

Government purchases vs. transfers, 160–61
Government purchases vs. expenditures, 161–62
Federal vs. state and local spending, 162
Tasks vs. revenues of federal and state & local government, 163–65
Fiscal policy, 166

Automatic stabilizers, 168–69
Demand management, 169
Full employment budgets, 169
Tax cuts vs. expenditures, 171–72
Fiscal drag, 172
Revenue sharing, 172–73
Grants-in-aid, 172–73

QUESTIONS

1. What are the main differences between the public and the private sectors? Are these differences economic or political?

2. Show in a diagram how increased government expenditure can offset a demand gap. Show also how decreased government taxation can do the same.

3. What is meant by the automatic stabilizers? Give an example of how they might work if we had an increase in investment of $20 billion and the multiplier were 2; and if the increase in taxes and the decrease in public expenditure associated with the boom in investment were $3 billion and $1 billion, respectively.

4. What do you consider a better way of combating a mild recession—tax cuts or higher expenditures? Why? Suppose we had a deep recession, then what would you do?

5. In what sorts of economic conditions should the government run a surplus? Explain the idea of a full-employment budget.

6. Suppose the government cuts taxes by $10 billion and also cuts its expenditures by the same amount. Will this stimulate the economy? Suppose it raises its expenditures and also raises taxes? Would this be a good antirecession policy?

State and local finances

State and local finances are very sensitive to the condition of the economy. When national output goes down, state and local revenues (in real terms) also decline. Occasionally a state goes up against the national trend, but usually a national slowdown pulls down all state and local revenues. As household incomes fall, state and local income taxes decline. As household spending weakens, sales tax receipts fall. As employment worsens, revenues from payroll taxes fall off. All this results in pressure to cut back state and local budgets. And this, in turn, adds its undertow to the national picture, giving the recession additional force.

One suggested remedy for this built-in weakness of state and local finance is *countercyclical revenue sharing.* This remedy would automatically authorize federal grants-in-aid to state and local governments, when times were bad. Such grants would be sufficiently large to maintain state and local spending at the levels they would have reached if the recession had not occurred. This would allow state and local governments to make long-range plans without having to worry about short-run fluctuations in their revenues, and it would also prevent these governments from inadvertently worsening a national recession by cutting back on their own expenditures.

A difficulty in countercyclical revenue sharing lies in different regional growth rates. Incomes and output have been growing faster in the West and South, for example, than in the Midwest or Northeast. This uneven pace has been going on for some years, but has recently been exaggerated by high energy prices. The slower-growing Northeast and Midwest have to use expensive oil, whereas the faster-growing South and West have available to them the relatively cheaper energy source of regulated natural gas.

As a result, the lucky states in high-growth regions may show budget surpluses when the unlucky states in slow-growth regions show deficits. Countercyclical revenue sharing would then have to make the difficult choice of whether or not to seek to equalize differences or to ignore them.

There is a natural tendency to say "Ignore them," because such differences hardly seem a matter of federal concern. But a second look shows us that the matter is not as simple as this. For the federal government itself is a partial cause of some of these very differences! When we look at federal individual income taxes received and grants-in-aid paid out in different areas, it is clear that the federal government is taking net spending power out of the slow-growing Northeast and Midwest and injecting it in the fast-growing South and West.

**Table 11·2 Ratio of federal expenditures to
federal tax collections, 1975**

Northeast	.86
Midwest	.76
South	1.14
West	1.20

Source: *National Journal,* June 26, 1976, p. 881.

Thus the federal government is contributing to the differences in growth rates, although we should stress that this is only one cause of the differences, and certainly not the main one.

What should the federal government do? Beginning with Franklin Roosevelt, it has followed a deliberate policy of trying to equalize regional differentials. TVA is probably the most well-known effort to aid one particular region, but actually nearly all federal programs are structured to give more help to low-income states than to high-income ones. If the South, for example, has been, and still is, favored in federal policy it is because, despite its rapid growth, its average family income remains below that of the Northeast, $12,236 compared to $14,481 in 1975.

Most people favor this federal equalizing role. The question today is whether, and to what degree, the policy should now be extended within states to localities. New York City, for example, lies in the middle of one of the richest regions in the nation, but it is a pocket of serious poverty. (In our next "Extra word" we shall look into the financial plight of New York.) If the federal government decides that it wants to help low-income localities, as well as low-income states, how should this be done? By federalizing welfare? By relieving localities of hospital expenses through federal health insurance? By giving federal aid to primary education in low-income cities? These are some of the suggestions that have been put forth. None of them is without problems. But at issue is the basic question whether we want the federal government to play the same role with localities that it has long played with regions. Once that issue is clarified, the problems will begin to take care of themselves.

Deficit
spending

Up to this moment, we have been analyzing the public sector in terms of its effect on the demand for GNP. Now we are going to take a brief but necessary respite from our systematic examination of the various sources of demand for output. The use of the public sector as a source of deliberate demand management poses a question that we must understand before we can comfortably resume our inquiry. This is the question of the government debt.

Any government that uses its budget as a stabilizing device must be prepared to spend more than it takes in in taxes. On occasion it must purposefully plan a budget in which outgo exceeds income, leaving a negative figure called a *deficit*.

That raises a problem that alarms and perplexes many people. Like a business or consumer, the government cannot spend money it does not have. Therefore it must *borrow* the needed funds from individuals, firms, or banks in order to cover its deficit. Deficit spending, in other words, means the spending of borrowed money, money derived from the sale of government bonds.

12

Deficits and losses

Can the government safely run up a deficit? Let us begin to unravel this important but perplexing question by asking another: can a private business afford to run up a deficit?

There is one kind of deficit that a private business *cannot* afford: a deficit that comes from spending more money on current production than it will realize from its sale. This kind of deficit is called a *business loss;* and if losses are severe enough, a business firm will be forced to discontinue its operations.

But there is another kind of deficit, although it is not called by that name, in the operations of a private firm. This is an excess of expenditures over receipts brought about by spending money on *capital assets*. When the American Telephone and Telegraph Company or the Exxon Corporation uses its own savings or those of the public to build a new plant and new equipment, it does not show a "loss" on its annual statement to stockholders, even though its total expenditures on current costs and on capital may have been greater than sales. Instead, expenditures are divided into two kinds, one relating current costs to current income, and the other relegating expenditures on capital goods to an entirely separate "capital account." Instead of calling the excess of expenditures a deficit, they call it investment.*

Debts and assets

Can A.T.&T. or Exxon afford to run deficits of the latter kind indefinitely? We can answer the question by imagining

*Investment does not *require* a "deficit," since it can be financed out of current profits. But many expanding companies do spend more money on current and capital account than they take in through sales, and thereby incur a "deficit" for at least a part of their investment.

ourselves in an economic landscape with no disturbing changes in technology or in consumers' tastes, so that entrepreneurs can plan ahead with great safety. Now let us assume that in this comfortable economy, Exxon decides to build a new refinery, perhaps to take care of the growing population. To finance the plant, it issues new bonds, so that its new asset is matched by a new debt.

Now what about this debt? How long can Exxon afford to have its bonds outstanding?

The answer is—forever!

Remember that we have assumed an economy remaining changeless in tastes and techniques, so that each year the new refinery can turn out a quota of output, perfectly confident that it will be sold; and each year it can set aside a reserve for wear and tear, perfectly confident that the refinery is being properly depreciated. As a result, each year the debt must be as good as the year before—no better and no worse. The bondholder is sure of getting his interest, steadily earned, and he knows that the underlying asset is being fully maintained.

Admittedly, after a certain number of years the new factory will be worn out. But if our imaginary economy remains unchanged and if depreciation accruals have been properly set aside, when the old plant gives out, an identical new one will be built from these depreciation reserves. Meanwhile, the old debt, like the old plant, will also come to an end, for debts usually run for a fixed term of years. The Exxon Corporation must now pay back its debtholders in full. But how? The firm has accumulated a reserve to buy a new plant, but it has not accumulated a second reserve to repay its bondholders.

Nevertheless, the answer is simple enough. When the bonds come due in our

Table 12·1   Corporate net long-term debt*

Year	1929	1933	1940	1950	1960	1970	1971	1972	1973	1974	1975	1976
Billions of dollars	47	48	44	60	231	360	402	447	484	524	574	616

*Maturity over one year.

imaginary situation, the Exxon Corporation issues *new* bonds equal in value to the old ones. It then sells the new bonds and uses the new money it raises to pay off the old bondholders. When the transaction is done, a whole cycle is complete: both a new refinery and a new issue of bonds exist in place of the old. Everything is exactly as it was in the first place. Furthermore, as long as this cycle can be repeated, such a debt could safely exist in perpetuity! And why not? Its underlying asset also exists, eternally renewed, in perpetuity.

Real corporate debts

To be sure, not many businesses are run this way, for the obvious reason that tastes and techniques in the real world are anything but changeless. Indeed, there is every reason to believe that when a factory wears out it will *not* be replaced by another costing exactly as much and producing just the same commodity. Yet, highly stable businesses such as the Exxon Corporation or A.T.&T. do, in fact, continuously "refund" their bond issues, paying off old bonds with new ones, and never "paying back" their indebtedness as a whole. A.T.&T., for instance, actually increased its total indebtedness from $1.1 billion in 1929 to $31.8 billion in 1975. Exxon ran up its debt from $170.1 million in 1929 to $3.5 billion in 1975. And the credit rating of both companies today is as good as, or better than, it was in 1929.

Thus some individual enterprises that face conditions of stability similar to our imaginary situations do actually issue bonds "in perpetuity," paying back each issue when it is due, only to replace it with another (and, as we have seen, *bigger*) issue.

Total business debts

Most strong individual businesses can carry their debts indefinitely, and the business sector *as a whole* can easily do so. For although individual businesses may seek to retire their debts, as we look over the whole economy we can see that as one business extinguishes its debt, another is borrowing an even larger sum. Why larger? Because the *assets* of the total business sector are also steadily rising.

Table 12·1 shows this trend in the growth of corporate debt.*

Note that from 1929 through 1940, corporate debt *declined*. The shrinkage coincided with the years of depression and slow recovery, when additions to capital plant were small. But beginning with the onset of the postwar period, we see a very rapid increase in business indebtedness, an increase that continues down to our present day.

*We do not show the parallel rise in new equities (shares of stock), since changes in stock market prices play so large a role here. We might, however, add a mental note to the effect that business issues new stock each year, as well as new bonds. During the 1960s and early 1970s, net new stock issues have ranged from about $2 to $9 billion per annum.

If we think of this creation of debt (and equity) as part of the savings-investment process, the relationship between debts and assets should be clear. Debts are claims, and we remember how claims can arise as the financial counterpart of the process of real capital formation. Thus, rising debts on capital account are a sign that assets are also increasing. It is important to emphasize the *capital account*. Debts incurred to buy capital assets are very different from those incurred to pay current expenses. The latter have very little close connection with rising wealth, whereas when we see that debts on corporate capital account are rising, we can take for granted that assets are probably rising as well. The same is true, incidentally, for the ever-rising total of consumer debts that mirror a corresponding increase in consumers' assets. As our stock of houses grows, so does our total mortgage debt; as our personal inventories of cars, washing machines, and other appliances grow, so does our outstanding consumer indebtedness.

Government deficits

Can government, like business, borrow "indefinitely"? The question is important enough to warrant a careful answer. Hence, let us begin by comparing government borrowing and business borrowing.

One difference that springs quickly to mind is that businesses borrow in order to acquire productive assets. That is, matching the new claims on the business sector is additional real wealth that will provide for larger output. From this additional wealth, business will also receive the income to pay interest on its debt or dividends on its stock. But what of the government? Where are its productive assets?

We have already noted that the government budget includes dams, roads, housing projects, and many other items that might be classified as assets. During the 1960s, federal expenditures for such civil construction projects averaged about $5 billion a year. Thus the total addition to the gross public debt during the 1960s (it rose from roughly $239 billion in 1960 to $619 billion in 1976) could be construed as merely the financial counterpart of the creation of public assets.

Why is it not so considered? Mainly because, as we have seen, the peculiar character of public expenditures leads us to lump together all public spending, regardless of kind. In many European countries, however, public capital expenditures are sharply differentiated from public current expenditures. If we had such a system, the government's deficit on capital account could then be viewed as the public equivalent of business's deficit on capital account. Such a change might considerably improve the rationality of much discussion concerning the government's deficit.

Sales vs. taxes

But there is still a difference. Private capital enhances the earning capacity of a private business, whereas most public capital, save for such assets as toll roads, does not "make money" for the public sector. Does this constitute a meaningful distinction?

We can understand, of course, why an individual business insists that its investment must be profitable. The actual money that the business will pay out in the course of making an investment will almost surely not return to the business that spent it. A shirt manufacturer, for instance, who invests in a new factory cannot hope that the builders of that factory will spend all their wages on the firm's shirts. The manufacturer knows that the money spent through investment will soon be dissipated throughout the economy and that it can be recaptured only through strenuous selling efforts.

Not quite so with a national government, however. Its income does not come from sales but from taxes, and those taxes reflect the general level of income of the country. Thus any and all that government lays out, just because it enters the general stream of incomes, redounds to the taxing capacity or, we might say, the "earning capacity" of government.

How much will come back to the government in taxes? That depends on two main factors: the impact of government spending on income via the multipler, and the incidence and progressivity of the tax structure. Under today's normal conditions, the government will recover about half or a little more of its expenditure.* But in any event, note that the government does not "lose" its money in the way that a business does. Whatever goes into the income stream is always *available* to the government as a source of taxes; but whatever goes into the income stream is not necessarily available to any single business as a source of sales.

This reasoning helps us understand why federal finance is different from state and local government finance. An expenditure made by New York City or New York State is apt to be respent in many other areas of the country. Thus taxable incomes in New York will not, in all probability, rise to match local spending. As a result, *state and local governments must look on their finances much as an individual business does.* The power of full fiscal recapture belongs solely to the federal government.

*We can make a rough estimate of the multiplier effect of additional public expenditure as 2 and of the share of an additional dollar of GNP going to federal taxes as about ⅓ (see p. 139). Thus $1 of public spending will create $2 of GNP, of which 65¢ will go back to the federal government.

The National Debt

Internal and external debts
This difference between the limited powers of recoupment of a single firm and the relatively limitless powers of a national government lies at the heart of the basic difference between business and government deficit spending. It helps us understand why the government has a capacity for financial operation that is inherently of a far higher order of magnitude than that of business. We can sum up this fundamental difference in the contrast between the *externality of business debts* and the *internality of national government debts.*

What do we mean by the externality of business debts? We simply mean that business firms owe their debts to someone distinct from themselves—someone over whom they have no control—whether this be bondholders or the bank from which they borrowed. Thus, to service or to pay back its debts, business must transfer funds from its own possession into the possession of outsiders. If this transfer cannot be made, if a business does not have the funds to pay its bondholders or its bank, it will go bankrupt.

The government is in a radically different position. Its bondholders, banks, and other people or institutions to whom it owes its debts belong to the same community as that whence it extracts its receipts. In other words, the government does not have to transfer its funds to an "outside" group to pay its bonds. It transfers them, instead, from some members of the national community over which it has legal powers (taxpayers) to other members of the *same* community (bondholders). The contrast is much the same as that between a family that owes a debt to another family, and a family in which the husband has borrowed money from his wife; or again between a firm that owes money to another, and a firm in which one branch has borrowed money from another. **Internal debts do not drain the resources of one community into another, but merely redistribute the claims among members of the same community.**

To help bring home the point, imagine that you and your roommate exchange $1000 IOUs. Each of you now has a $1,000 asset (an IOU from the other person) but each of you also has a $1,000 liability (the IOU each owes the other). The total debt of the room is now $2,000. But is your room richer or poorer, or is any individual in the room richer or poorer? The answer is obviously no. No one is better or worse off than before. And what happens if you now each pay off your IOUs? Once again no one is richer or poorer than before. The same thing is true at the national level. The national debt makes us neither richer nor poorer, since we (as taxpayers) owe it to ourselves (as bondholders).

Problems of a national debt

A government cannot always borrow without trouble, however. Important and difficult problems of money management are inseparable from a large debt. More important, the people or institutions from whom taxes are collected are not always exactly the same people and institutions to whom interest is paid, so that servicing a government debt often poses problems of *redistribution of income*. For instance, if all government bonds were owned by rich people and if all government taxation were regressive (i.e., proportionately heavier on low incomes), then servicing a government debt would mean transferring income from the poor to the rich. Considerations of equity aside, this would also probably involve distributing income from spenders to savers and would thereby intensify the problem of closing the savings gap.

In addition, a debt that a government owes to foreign citizens is *not* an internal debt. It is exactly like a debt that a corporation owes to an "outside" public, and it can involve payments that can cripple a nation. Do not forget that the internality of debts applies only to *national* debts held as bonds by members of the same community of people whose incomes contribute to government revenues.

Perpetual public debts

Can a national government therefore have a perpetual debt? We have seen that it can. To be sure, the debt must be constantly refunded, much as business refunds its debts, with new issues of bonds replacing the old. But like the business sector, we can expect the government debt in this way to be maintained indefinitely.

Will our public debt grow forever? That depends largely on what happens to our business debts and equities. If business debts and equities grow fast enough—that is, if we are creating enough assets through investment—there is no reason why government debts should grow. Government deficits, after all, are designed as *supplements* to private deficits. The rationale behind public borrowing is that it will be used only when the private sector is not providing enough expenditure to give us a large enough GNP to provide reasonably full employment.

Nonetheless, the prospect of a rising national debt bothers many people. Some day, they say, it will have to be repaid. Is this true? It may aid us to think about the problem if we try to answer the following questions:

1. Can we afford to pay interest on a rising debt?

The capacity to expand debts, both public and private, depends largely on the willingness of people to lend money, and this willingness in turn reflects their confidence that they will be paid interest regularly and will have their principal returned to them when their bonds are due.

We have seen how refunding can take care of the repayment problem. But what about interest? With a private firm, this requires that interest costs be kept to a modest fraction of sales, so that they can easily be covered. With government, similar financial prudence requires that interest costs stay well within the taxable capacity of government. The figures in Table 12·2 give us some perspective on this problem today.

It can be seen that interest is a much higher percentage of federal revenues than of corporate revenues. But there is a reason for this. Corporations are supposed to maximize their revenues; the government is not supposed to maximize its tax income. Hence we must also judge the size of the federal interest cost in comparison with the size of GNP, the total tax base from which the government can draw. Finally, we should know that interest as a percentage of all federal receipts has remained very steady in recent years, and it is actually much lower than in the 1920s, when interest costs amounted to about 20 to 30 percent of the federal budget.

2. Can we afford the burden of a rising debt?

What is the "burden" of a debt? For a firm, the question is easy to answer. It is the *interest cost* that must be borne by those who owe the debt. Here, of course, we are back to the externality of debts. **The burden of a debt is the obligation it imposes to pay funds from one firm or community to another.**

But we have seen that there is no such cost for an internal debt, such as that of a nation. The *cost* of the debt—that is, the taxes that must be levied to pay interest— becomes *income* to the very same community, as checks sent to bondholders for their interest income. Every penny that the debt costs our economy in taxes returns to our economy as income.

The same is also true of the principal of the debt. The debts we owe inside the nation we also *own* inside the nation—just as the case of the IOUs, or, again, just as an amount borrowed by Branch A of a multibranch firm is owed to Branch B of the same firm.

There is a further point here. Internal debts are debts that are considered as financial *assets* within the "family." Nobody within A.T.&T. considers its debts to be part of the assets of the firm, but many

Table 12·2　Debt and interest costs

	Net interest ($ billions)	Interest as proportionate cost
Nonfinancial corporations (1976)	$36	3.7 percent of gross corporate revenues
Federal government (1976)	28	{ 8.4 percent of receipts { 1.7 percent of GNP

thousands of people in the U.S. consider the country's debts to be their assets. Indeed, everyone who owns a government bond considers it an asset. Thus in contrast to external debts, paying back an internal debt does not "lift a burden" from a community, because no burden existed in the first place! When a corporation pays off a debt to a bank, it is rid of an obligation to an outside claimant on its property. But when a husband pays his wife, the *family* is no richer, any more than the *firm* is better off if one branch reimburses another. So, too, with a nation. If a national debt is repaid, the national economy is not rid of an obligation to an outside claimant. We would be rid only of obligations owed to one another.

Real burdens

This is not to say—and the point is important—that *government spending is costless.* Consider for a moment the main cause of government spending over the past fifty years: the prosecution of three wars. There was surely a terrific cost in lives, health, and (in economic terms) in the use of factors of production to produce guns instead of butter. But note also that all of this cost is irrevocably and unbudgeably situated in the past. The cost of all wars is borne during the years when the wars are fought and must be measured in the destruction that was then caused and the opportunities for creating real wealth that were then missed. The debt inherited from these wars is no longer a "cost." Today it is only an instrument for the transfer of incomes within the American community.

So, too, with debts incurred to fight unemployment. The cost of unemployment is also borne once and for all at the time it occurs, and the benefits of the government spending to combat unemployment will be enjoyed (or if the spending is ill-advised, the wastes of spending will be suffered) when that spending takes place. Afterward, the debt persists as a continuing means of transferring incomes, but the debt no longer has any connection to the "cost" for which it was incurred.

Costs, in other words, are *missed opportunities*, potential well-being not achieved. Debts, on the other hand (when they are held within a country) only transfer purchasing power and do not involve the nation in giving up its output to anyone else.

Indirect effects

Does this mean that there are no disadvantages whatsoever in a large national debt?

We have talked of one possible disadvantage, that of transferring incomes from spenders to savers, or possibly of transferring purchasing power from productive groups to unproductive groups. But we must pay heed to one other problem. This is the problem a rising debt may cause indirectly, but nonetheless painfully, *if it discourages private investment.*

This could be a very serious, real cost of government debts, were such a reaction to be widespread and long-lasting. It may well be (we are not sure) that the long drawn-out and never entirely successful recovery from the Great Depression was caused, to a considerable extent, by the adverse psychological impact of government deficit spending on business investment intentions. Business did not understand deficit spending and interpreted it either as the entering wedge of socialism (instead of a crash program to save capitalism) or as a wastrel and a harebrained economic scheme. To make matters worse, the amount of the government deficit (at its peak $4 billion), while large enough to

In view of the fact that our national debt today figures out to approximately $2,880 for every man, woman, and child, it is not surprising that we frequently hear appeals to "common sense," telling us how much better we would be without this debt, and how our grandchildren will groan under its weight.

Is this true? We have already discussed the fact that internal debts are different from external debts, but let us press the point home from a different vantage point. Suppose we decided that we would "pay off" the debt. This would mean that our government bonds would be redeemed for cash. To get the cash,

PERSONAL DEBTS AND PUBLIC DEBTS

we would have to tax ourselves (unless we wanted to roll the printing presses), so that what we would really be doing would be transferring money from taxpayers to bondholders.

Would that be a net gain for the nation? Consider the typical holder of a government bond—a family, a bank, or a corporation. It now holds the world's safest and most readily-sold paper asset from which a regular income is obtained. After our debt is

redeemed, our families, banks, and corporations will have two choices: (1) they can hold cash and get *no* income, or (2) they can invest in other securities that are slightly *less* safe. Are these investors better off? As for our grandchildren, it is true that if we pay off the debt they will not have to "carry" its weight. But to offset that, neither will they be carried by the comfortable government bonds they would otherwise have inherited. They will also be relieved from paying taxes to meet the interest on the debt. Alas, they will be relieved as well of the pleasure of depositing the green Treasury checks for interest payments that used to arrive twice a year.

frighten the business community, was not big enough to begin to exert an effective leverage on total demand, particularly under conditions of widespread unemployment and financial catastrophe.

Today, however, it is much less likely that deficit spending would be attended by a drop in private spending. A great deal that was new and frightening in thought and practice in the 1930s is today well-understood and tested. World War II was, after all, an immense laboratory demonstration of what public spending could do for GNP. The experience of recent years gives good reason to believe that deficit spending in the future will not cause a significant slowdown in private investment expenditure.

A modern version of this old fear is that the large demands for funds needed to finance and refinance the federal budget will "crowd out" private borrowers or force up interest rates to levels that will interfere with private expansion. The pros and cons of this argument need not delay us here. So far, there has been no demonstrated crowding-out of private borrowing.

The public sector again in perspective

We have spent enough time on the question of the debt. Now we must ask what is it that close examination of the problems of government finance reveals, making them look so different from what we expect. The answer is largely that we think of the government as if it were a firm or a household, when it is actually something else. *The government is a sector;* and if we want to think clearly about it, we must compare it, not to the maxims and activities of a household or a firm, but to those of the entire consumer sector or the entire business sector.

Then we can see that the government sector plays a role not too dissimilar from that of the business sector. We have seen how businesses, through their individual decisions to add to plant and equipment, act in concert to offset the savings of consumers. The government, we now see, acts in precisely the same way, except that its decisions, rather than reflecting the behavior of innumerable entrepreneurs in a search for profit, reflect the deliberate political will of the community itself.

Persons who do not understand the intersectoral relationships of the economy like to say that business must "live within its income" and that government acts irresponsibly in failing to do so. These critics fail to see that business does *not* live within its income, but borrows the savings of other sectors and thus typically and normally spends more than it takes in from its sales alone. By doing so, of course, it serves the invaluable function of providing an offset for saving that would otherwise create a demand gap and thereby precipitate a downward movement in economic activity.

Once this offsetting function is understood, it is not difficult to see that government, as well as business, can serve as a "spender" to offset savings, and that in the course of doing so, both government and business typically create new assets for the community.

Public and private assets

Finally, we have seen something else that gives us a last insight into government spending. We have seen that the creation of earning assets is indispensable for business, because each asset constitutes the means by which an individual business seeks to recoup its own investment spending. But with the government, the definition of an "earning asset" can properly be much larger than with a business firm. The government does not need its assets to make money for itself directly, for the government's economic capability arises from its capacity to tax *all* incomes. So far as government is concerned, then, all that matters is that savings be turned into expenditures, and thereby into taxable incomes.

As a result, government can and should be motivated—even in a self-interested way—by a much wider view of the economic process than would be possible or proper for a single firm. Whereas a firm's assets are largely its capital goods, the assets of a nation are not only capital wealth but the whole productive capacity of its people. Thus government expenditures that redound to the health or well-being or education of its citizens are just as properly considered asset-building expenditures as are its expenditures on dams and roads.

FOCUS   The object of this lesson must be very plain. It is to reveal that most of the fears with regard to government "deficits" and "unbalanced budgets" are unfounded. People do not understand how government can safely go into debt, although households often cannot. The answer, of course, lies in the fact that the government is a sector and a household is not. The government can command revenues through taxation; no household can demand that society pay it an income. Moreover, a government debt is owed by some members of the national community to others; a household debt is owed to individuals or institutions who are outside the household. Of course these same arguments apply to the difference between national government and business debts or between federal and state debts.

This is not to say that national debts, even when internally held, are costless. They involve flows of income from taxpayers to interest receivers. The taxpayers may be households of modest means; the bondholders may be wealthy individuals or banks. Thus financing the debt may worsen income distribution or cause political friction. Moreover, even though government debts do not pose a burden on the nation as a whole, government spending is certainly not costless or burdenless.

These central ideas should be carefully mastered, for they recur constantly in the press or in political discussion. The best way to master the argument is to explain to yourself exactly how government debts resemble and differ from business debts. The questions will help you do this.

WORDS AND CONCEPTS YOU SHOULD KNOW

Deficits vs. losses, 178
Debts and assets, 178
Refunding a debt, 178–79
Business debts, 179–80

Government deficits, 180–81
Internal vs. external debts, 181–82
Perpetual public debts, 182–84
Problems of a national debt, 182–85

QUESTIONS

1. In what ways is a government deficit comparable to business spending for investment purposes? In what ways is it not?

2. If the government is going to go into debt, does it matter if it spends money for roads or for relief? For education or for weapons? Is there any connection between the use to which government spending is put and *the economic analysis of deficit spending*? Think hard about this; suppose you could show that some spending increased the productivity of the country and that other spending didn't. Would that influence your answer?

3. What is meant by the internality of debts? Is the debt of New York State internal? The debt of a country like Israel?

4. What relation do debts generally have to assets? Can business debts increase indefinitely? Can a family's? Can the debt of all consumers?

5. What are the real burdens of a national debt?

6. Trace out carefully all the consequences of paying back the national debt.

7. How would you explain to someone who is adamantly opposed to socialism that government deficit spending was (a) safe and (b) not necessarily "socialistic"? Or do you think it is not safe and that it is socialistic?

The New York City debt crisis

New York City's 1976 debt crisis was a vivid illustration of how even very large and seemingly rich government institutions *that are not national in scope* have limits to the amount of deficit finance they can safely undertake. Because any resident can leave New York, all the city's debt is potentially "external" to it.

As Table 11·3 shows, New York City's debt has been building up for a long period. But over most of these years its bonds were rated very highly by various companies, such as Standard and Poor's, that give ratings (risk designations) to private and public bonds. We can also see that the debt build-up accelerated after 1970, partly the consequence of financially imprudent actions on the part of New York City officials, partly the result of the 1974–1975 recession that hit many northeastern cities hard.

Table 11·3   New York City's debt ($ billions)

1950	$ 3
1960	6
1970	8
1974	14

To pay its bills, the city had to borrow larger and larger sums at the very time that the federal government had created a very tight situation in the money markets—a "credit crunch"—as part of its efforts to curb inflation. In a tight-money period, everyone has trouble borrowing, and banks and other lenders reexamine their credit applicants to determine who should be first in line and who should be last.

In this reexamination, New York City fared very badly. Its bond ratings suddenly fell. Overnight it became apparent to everyone that its debt and deficit had reached levels that could not be sustained in the long run. As a result, New York suddenly found itself unable to borrow. Not only was no one willing to lend funds to cover its current deficit, which had reached a staggering $700 million for the year 1974, but banks or other lenders would not even lend the city money to finance its outstanding debt. That is, the normal process of "rolling over" the debt, by replacing bonds that had become due with new bonds, was impossible.

What were the city's options at this point? All were unpleasant. One was to slash expenditures to the point at which the deficit would be eliminated, and revenues would cover debt repayments. This would have required so drastic a cut in expenditures (something on the order of 25 percent) that city officials feared the city could not be safely operated—too few police, firemen, sanitation workers, teachers.

Another option was to raise taxes by the amount needed to cover debt repayment. There were two problems here. First, the course would have required additional taxing powers for the city, which the state legislature was loathe to hand over. Second, city taxes, already among the highest in the nation, would have soared to such astronomical levels that many taxpayers would have voted with their feet, by moving out of the city to the suburbs or to neighboring states.

A third option was to default on debt repayments—simply not to honor the old bonds that came due. Here the difficulties were obvious. A default would still have left the city short of funds to cover its current deficit. And, of course, a default would have terribly damaged its prospects for selling bonds in the future. Once burned, twice shy in the bond market. Then, too, many worried lest a default in New York's bonds might not set off a series of defaults in other municipal bonds, giving rise to a serious panic in the capital markets.

Last was the hope that the federal government would save the situation, and city officials pled with the Ford administration to add a federal guarantee to city bonds, thereby assuring their salability, or for outright federal loans or grants to cover the deficit. But the Ford administration was not eager to rescue the city on easy terms. It felt that the city was itself responsible for much of its financial plight and that a rescue operation for New York could lead to requests from many other hard-pressed cities.

What happened in the end? All options were used to some extent. The city did cut its services. City taxes were raised. Default was technically avoided, but holders of city bonds were forced to exchange their securities for long-term bonds that carried lower interest rates. And the federal government made some necessary loans.

As part of the rescue operation, city finances were placed under the scrutiny of a committee of state, federal, and private representatives, who will monitor its union contracts and other expenditures, its taxes, and its budgets. If all goes well, the city should be back in the black by 1980. In all likelihood, however, by then the burden of local finance for other cities as well as New York will have been lightened through some kind of federalization of welfare payments, some kind of health insurance, and perhaps by still other revenue-sharing procedures. Short of such basic remedies, it is unlikely that New York or any other major municipality can enjoy fiscal health in the decades ahead.

The determination of GNP

We have reached the destination toward which we have been traveling for many chapters. We are finally in a position to understand how the forces of supply and demand determine the actual level of GNP that confronts us in daily life—"the state of the economy" that affects our employment prospects, our immediate well-being, our satisfaction or dissatisfaction with the way things are going.

Supply and Demand in Macro

13

As we have begun to see, the short-run level of GNP is determined by the outcome of two opposing tendencies of supply and demand, just as the level of prices and quantities in a marketplace is "set" by the counterplay of these forces. In fact, the opposition of supply and demand play just as central a role in macroeconomics as in microeconomics. **The crucial difference is that in macroeconomics we talk of supply and demand in relation to GNP, whereas** in microeconomics we speak of them mainly in relation to price.

Short-run fixed supply

Here we come to an interesting analog with microeconomics. Perhaps we remember (and those who have not had microeconomics will easily understand) that in the short run we often take the supply curve in a given market as fixed. It may, for example, represent the catch of fish that a fishing fleet has brought back. The crucial thing is that this short-run supply of goods is unalterable, so that the only "active" force in determining price is the position and movement of the demand curve. Of course this does not mean that the supply curve plays no role in the price-determining process, for without supply there would be no market in the first place. But demand is where the action lies.

Exactly the same situation confronts us in considering the short-run determination of GNP. In the long run, of course, the supply of GNP expands as our production possibilities curve moves outward, as we saw in Chapter 5, "Supply of Output." **But in the short run we take the p-p curve as given, and we are interested only in determining how much of our potential GNP will in fact be produced.** Just to create a sharp image in your mind, you might think of the supply of GNP in the short run as the range of possibilities before an economy suffering a total general strike that brought its production down to zero, and that same economy using every resource at its command to bring production up to its limits.

Demand curve for GNP

What do the demand and supply curves for GNP look like? We will begin with the demand curve, for we are already very familiar with the forces that give rise to it. **The demand curve will show us the amount of spending (demand for output) that will be generated by the community, as output rises from zero (the general strike) to the full utilization of existing resources.**

Of course such a curve will slope upward. In Fig. 13 • 1 we see why this is so. The total spending on output, as we know, will consist of the sum of the spending for consumer goods, investment goods (we'll lump exports in here for convenience sake), and government goods. Panel I shows the spending for consumer goods (on the vertical axis). Even if output is zero, consumers will still spend money out of past savings to buy necessaries; and as production grows, pumping incomes into households, consumer spending will rise. Consumer demand is therefore a graphic representation of our familiar consumption function, $a + b(Y)$.

It is not so simple to draw an accurate investment or government demand function. Once again we assume that in the event of zero production (our general strike), both business and government would wish to make certain expenditures. As output rises, their expenditures would also increase because their incomes will rise, although we know that the relation between investment and government outlays and incomes is by no means so passive as is the case with household. Therefore we have drawn their respective demand functions with only a small upward slope, to emphasize the independent nature of these components of demand.

Panel IV shows that total demand is obtained by summing the demand of consumption, investment, and government. *It shows that total spending will rise as output rises: here is our upward sloping demand curve.*

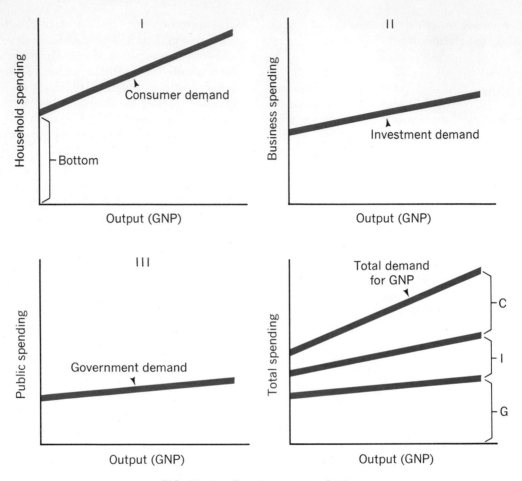

FIG. 13 · 1   The demand for GNP

Short-run supply curve   Now what about the short-run supply curve? *It will show us how much income—not spending—will rise as we "relax" the general strike and allow production to expand. Here we make use of an identity that we learned in Chapter 6. Incomes and output are always the same. The amount of income made available to the community must rise, dollar for dollar, with the amount of production, because every dollar going*

into production must become income to some individual or institution.

Our supply curve must show this identity, and Fig. 13·2 makes clear that the resulting curve will be a 45° line. Notice that $OX = OY$, $OX' = OY'$, and so on. Notice also that this supply curve is fixed, in that the relation between incomes (GNI) and output (GNP) is always the same—identical. In our demand curve, the relation between demand (or spending) and output was not identical.

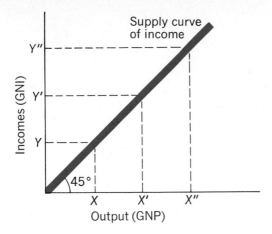

FIG. 13·2   Supply curve of income

This equilibrium shows us the money value of GNP brought about by the flow of demand against supply. It might, for example, indicate that this equilibrium value of GNP was $1.5 trillion. It does *not* tell us whether $1.5 trillion is a *good* size for GNP, any more than an equilibrium price of $20 for a commodity tells us whether that is a good or bad price from the viewpoint of buyers, producers, or the economy at large. We shall return to this critical point at the end of our chapter.

Equilibrium

It now remains only to put the demand and supply curves together, as in Fig. 13·3

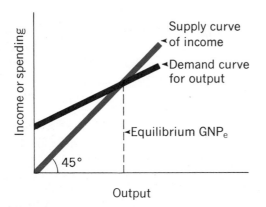

FIG. 13·3   Supply and demand for GNP

The circular flow

First, however, we must be sure we understand the nature of the GNP-establishing process, just as we must understand how a market works before we can get into issues of social policy connected with a market. Let us therefore take another step and connect our supply-demand equilibrium for GNP with our previous discussion of the circular flow. In Fig. 13·4 let us take out a thin slice of output at equilibrium and examine it under a magnifying glass.

As always, GNP can be analyzed into its component factor, indirect tax, and depreciation costs $(F + T + D)$ and into its

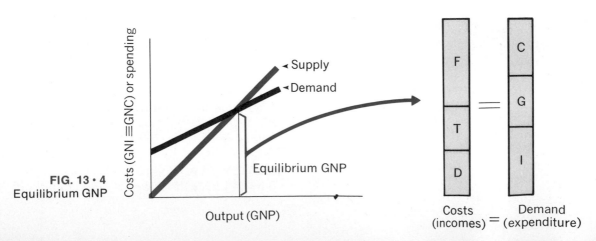

FIG. 13·4
Equilibrium GNP

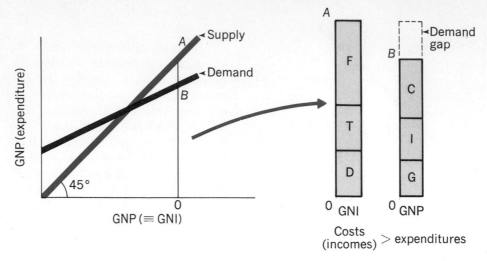

FIG. 13·5   Analysis of equilibrium GNP

component expenditures or demands ($C + G + I$). From our earlier discussion we recall that *all costs become incomes.* Therefore we could relabel the GNI axis Gross National Cost. What we see in our diagram is that at equilibrium, total demand for GNP equals total cost for GNP, much like our circular flow (p. 88).*

The demand gap

Now let us examine another slice of GNP that is above equilibrium, as in Fig. 13·5.

Here the cost of GNP is represented by OA, composed of $F + T + D$. But now the demand for GNP, OB, is less than OA. The difference consists of the demand gap, with which we are familiar.

If we had taken a slice below equilibrium, what would have been the situation? Now the demand curve lies above the supply curve. That is, total expenditures would have been larger than total costs. **We would have had a demand surplus, rather than a demand gap.** You might try

drawing such a slice and seeing what the relation of $F + T + D$ would be to $C + G + I$.

Movement to equilibrium

Now let us trace the forces that would push GNP toward the position of equilibrium. At the level of GNP that lies above equilibrium, entrepreneurs and public agencies would have paid out larger sums as costs ($\equiv$ incomes) than they would receive back as sales ($\equiv$ demand). Sales would be below the level of expectations that led to the employment of the factors in the first place. The first result would be a piling up of unsold inventories. Quickly, however, production plans would be revised downward. Fewer factors would be employed. With the fall in employment, incomes would fall; and as incomes fell, so would demand.

The analysis is exactly reversed if GNP is below equilibrium. Now demand ($C + G + I$) is greater than costs or incomes ($F + T + D$). Entrepreneurs will meet this extra demand out of inventories, and they will begin to plan for higher output, hiring more factors, and embarking

---

*But not *exactly* like our circular flow. We are now dealing with an economy that has saving and investing, profits and losses. Therefore we must think of the cost category "depreciation" (D) as including profits, and the expenditure category "investment" (I) as including net investment as well as replacement. We also continue to forget about exports, for simplicity.

on investment programs, thereby raising costs and incomes.

Note that in both cases, demand does **not change as rapidly as income.** In the first case it does not fall as fast as income; in the second it rises more slowly than income. This is mainly the result of the marginal propensity to consume, which, as we have seen, reflects the unwillingness of households to raise or lower their consumption spending as much as any change in their incomes.

Assuming for the moment that G and I remain unchanged, we can see that as the employment of factors increases because we have a demand surplus, or decreases because we have a gap, total demand must come closer to total costs or incomes. **If there is a demand gap, employment will be reduced, but income will fall more rapidly than spending, and the gap will close. If there is a demand surplus, employment will rise, but income will rise faster than spending and the surplus will gradually disappear.** In both cases, the economy will move toward equilibrium.

Movement of equilibrium

If we now introduce changes in G and I, we can see that *the equilibrium point itself may move.* As the economy enters a downward spiral, investment spending may fall, outbalancing the supportive action of the automatic stabilizers. If this is the case, then the equilibrium level of GNP will move leftward, and the recession may not halt until we reach a very low level of GNP. This is, in fact, exactly what happens when a severe recession causes investment to fall, and the economy does not "bottom out" until GNP has fallen substantially, bringing with it considerable unemployment. Figure 13·6 shows us this process schematically.

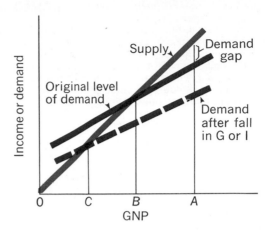

FIG. 13·6   A change in equilibrium GNP

Let us begin at a level of GNP indicated by output OA. A demand gap exists, and the level of output begins to fall toward OB, which is an equilibrium level at the *original level of demand.* But now the fall in GNP adversely affects I as well as C, so that the demand schedule for output shifts downward to the dotted line. Hence the economy will not settle at output OB but will continue downward until OC, where once again the demand for output equals the supply of output.

The expansion process

Just the opposite course of events helps us explain an upward movement. Suppose our economy "began" in equilibrium at output OC, following a severe recession. Now let us suppose that a rise in demand takes place. This could be the consequence of a burst of autonomous investment or simply the result of brighter expectations or the consequence of more government spending or any combination. If you will extend the line at OC up to the new demand curve (the upper line, this time), you can see that demand for output $(C + I + G)$ is now larger than the costs of output $(F + T + D)$.

As a result, entrepreneurs will find their receipts rising. They will add factors, rehiring labor that has been let go during the recession and adding to their stock of inventories or equipment. The economy will begin to move toward the equilibrium depicted by output *OB*.

Once again, however, we must be careful not to imagine that the equilibrium point is fixed. As the economy moves, so will autonomous investment and government spending and taxing. Hence the final equilibrium level may be less than, equal to, or greater than *OC*, depending on further shifts in the demand curve. But the *process* by which an equilibrium level of GNP is reached is always indicated by the relationship between the supply curve of GNI and the demand curve for GNP.

Another View of Equilibrium

Saving and investment

Equilibrium is always a complicated subject to master, so let us fix the matter in our minds by going over the problem once more. Suppose that, by means of a questionnaire, we are going to predict the level of GNP for an island community. To simplify our task, we will ignore government and exports, so that we can concentrate solely on consumption, saving, and investment.

We begin by interrogating the island's business community about their intentions for next year's investment. Now we know that some investment will be induced and that, therefore, investment will partly be a result of the island's level of income; but again for simplification, we assume that businesses have laid their plans for next year. They tell us they intend to spend $30 million for new housing, plant, equipment, and other capital goods.

Next, our team of pollsters approaches a carefully selected sample of the island's householders and asks them what their consumption and savings plans are for the coming year. Here the answer will be a bit disconcerting. Reflecting on their past experience, our householders will reply: "We can't say for sure. We'd *like* to spend such-and-such an amount and save the rest, but really it depends on what our incomes will be." Our poll, in other words, will have to make inquiries about different possibilities that reflect the island's propensity to consume.

Now we tabulate our results, and find that we have the schedule in Table 13 • 1

Table 13 • 1

Income	Consumption	**Saving**	**Investment**
	(In millions)		
$100	$75	$25	$30
110	80	30	30
120	85	35	30

Interplay of saving and investment

If we look at the last two columns, those for saving and investment, we can see a powerful cross play that will characterize our model economy at different levels of income, for the forces of investment and saving will not be in balance at all levels. At some levels, the propensity to save will outrun the act of purposeful investment; at others, the motivations to save will be less than the investment expenditures made by business firms. In fact, our island model shows that at only one level of income—$110 million—will the saving and investment schedules coincide.

What does it mean when intended savings are greater than the flow of intended investment? It means that people are *trying* to save out of their given incomes a larger amount than businesses are willing to invest. Now if we think back to the exposition of the economy in equilibrium, it will be clear what the result must be. The economy cannot maintain a closed circuit of income and expenditure if savings are larger than investment. This will simply give rise to a demand gap, the repercussions of which we have already explored.

But a similar lack of equilibrium results if intended savings are less than intended investment expenditure (or if in-vestment spending is greater than the propensity to save). Now business will be pumping out more than enough to offset the savings gap. The additional expenditures, over and above those that compensate for saving, will flow into the economy to create new incomes—and out of those new incomes, new savings.

Income and output will be stable, in other words, only when the flow of intended investment just compensates for the flow of intended saving. Investment and saving thus conduct a tug of war around this pivot point, driving the economy upward when intended investment exceeds the flow of intended saving; downward when it fails to offset saving. In Fig. 13·7 we show this crosscurrent in schematic form. Note that as incomes fall very low, householders will *dissave*.

Injections vs. leakages

We can easily make our graph more realistic by adding taxes (*T*) and imports (*M*) to savings, and exports (*X*) and government spending to investment. The vertical axis in Fig. 13·8 now shows all *leakages and injections*.

We recall that leakages are any acts, such as savings, increased taxes, profits or imports, that reduce spending. Similarly, injections are any acts, such as investment

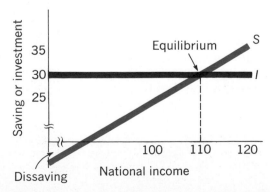

FIG. 13·7 Saving and investment

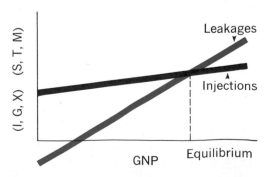

FIG. 13·8 Leakages and injections

or higher government spending or rising exports or even a spontaneous jump in consumption, that lead to higher spending. And just to introduce another feature of the real world, we will tilt the injection line upward, on the assumption that induced investment will be an important constituent of total investment. The leakages curve will not be exactly the same shape as the savings curve, but it will reflect the general tendency of savings and imports and taxes to rise with income.

Intended and unintended S and I

The careful reader may have noted that we speak of *intended* savings and *intended* investment as the critical forces in establishing equilibrium. This is because there is a formal balance between *all* saving and investment (or all leakages and all injections) at every moment in the economy.

This sounds very strange. Are there not demand gaps, when saving is not offset by investment? Have we not just shown a schedule in which *S* was not equal to *I* at every level of income? How then can saving and investment be identities?

The answer is unexpectedly simple. **Both saving and investment are made up of *intended* and *unintended* flows.** I may intend to save a great deal, but if my income falls, my actual savings may be very small. As an entrepreneur, I may intend to invest nothing this year; but if sales are poor, I may end up with an unintended investment in unsold inventories. Thus, through fluctuations in incomes, profits, and inventories, people are constantly saving and investing more or less than they intended. These unintended changes make *total* savings equal to (identical with) *total* investment, whereas obviously the intended portions of saving or investment may be unequal.

Ex post and ex ante

Economists speak of the difference between intended and unintended activities as *ex ante* and *ex post*. *Ex ante* means "looking forward;" *ex post* means "looking backward." Ex ante savings and investment (or leakages and injections) are usually not equal. But at each and every moment, ex post savings and investment *will* be equal because someone will have been stuck with higher or lower inventories or greater or lesser saving than he intended ex ante.*

The strict balance between the formal accounting meanings of saving and investment and the tug-of-war between the active forces of *intended* saving and investment are sources of much confusion to students who ask why the terms are defined in this difficult way. In part we owe the answer to Keynes, who first defined *S* and *I* as identities. Since then the usage has become solidified because it is useful for purposes of national accounting.

For our purposes, we must learn to distinguish between the formal, ex post identity between total saving and investment (or between all leakages and all injections) and the active, ex ante difference between *intended* savings and investment (or *intended* saving, *intended* imports, *intended* business saving, etc., and *intended* additional expenditures of all kinds).

What matters in the determination of GNP are the *actions* people are taking—actions that lead them to try to save or to invest or that make them struggle to get rid of unintended inventories or to build up desired inventories. These are the kinds of activities that will be moving the economy up and down in the never-ending "quest"

---

*In the same way, purchases in any market must exactly equal sales at each and every moment, but that does not mean the market is in equilibrium at all times.

for its equilibrium point. The fact that at each moment ex post savings and investment are identical from the viewpoint of the economy's balance sheet is important only insofar as we are economic accountants. As analysts of the course of future GNP, we concentrate on the inequality of ex ante, intended actions.

The paradox of thrift

The fact that income must always move toward the level where the flows of intended saving and investment are equal leads to one of the most startling—and important—paradoxes of economics. This is the so-called paradox of thrift, a paradox that tells us that the *attempt to increase intended saving* may, under certain circumstances, lead to a *fall in actual saving.*

The paradox is not difficult for us to understand at this stage. An attempt to save, *when it is not matched with an equal willingness to invest or to increase government expenditure,* will cause a gap in demand. This means that business will not be getting back enough money to cover costs. Hence, production will be curtailed or costs will be slashed, with the result that incomes will fall. As incomes fall, savings will also fall, because the ability to save will be reduced. Thus, by a chain of activities working their influence on income and output, the effort to *increase* savings may end up with an actual *reduction* of savings.

This frustration of individual desires is perhaps the most striking instance of a common situation in economic life, the incompatibility between some kinds of individual behavior and some collective results. An individual farmer, for instance, may produce a larger crop in order to enjoy a bigger income; but if all farmers produce bigger crops, farm prices are apt to fall so heavily that farmers end up with less income. So too, a single family may wish to save a very large fraction of its income for reasons of financial prudence; but if all families seek to save a great deal of their incomes, the result—unless investment also rises—will be a fall in expenditure and a common failure to realize savings objectives. The paradox of thrift, in other words, teaches us that the freedom of behavior available to a few individuals cannot always be generalized to all individuals.*

The Multiplier

There remains only one part of the jigsaw puzzle to put into place. This is the integration of the *multiplier* into our analysis of the determination of GNP.

We remember that the essential point about the multiplier was that changes in investment, government spending, or exports resulted in larger changes in GNP because the additions to income were respent, creating still more new incomes. Further, we remember that the size of the multiplier effect depended on the marginal propensity to consume, the marginal propensity to tax, and the marginal propensity to buy imports as GNP rises. Now it remains only to show how this basic analytic concept enters into the determination of equilibrium GNP.

*The paradox of thrift is actually only a subtle instance of that type of faulty reasoning called the fallacy of composition. The fallacy consists of assuming that what is true of the individual case must also be true of all cases combined. The flaw in reasoning lies in our tendency to overlook "side effects" of individual actions (such as the decrease in spending associated with an individual's attempt to save more, or the increase in supply when a farmer markets his larger crop) which may be negligible in isolation but which are very important in the aggregate.

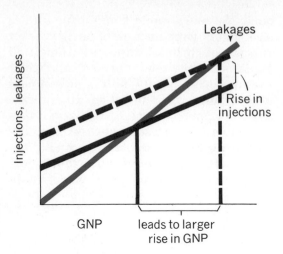

FIG. 13 · 9   Multiplier in graphic form

Let us begin with the diagram that shows injections and leakages, and let us now draw a new line showing an increase in injections (Fig. 13 · 9). Notice that the increase in GNP is larger than the increase in injections. *This is the multiplier itself in graphic form.*

We can see exactly the same result in our diagram of the supply and demand for GNP. Notice how a rise in the demand for GNP (a rise in injections) leads to a larger rise in the output of GNP (see Fig. 13 · 10).

FIG. 13 · 10   Multiplier and GNP

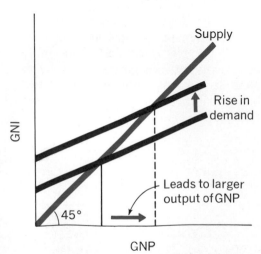

Slope of the leakage curve

Both diagrams also show that the relation between the original increase in injections and the resulting increase in GNP depends on the *slope* of the leakage line. Figure 13 · 11 shows us two different injection-GNP relationships that arise from differing slopes.

Notice how the *same* increase in spending (from *OA* to *OB* on the injections axis) leads to a much smaller increase in panel I GNP (from *OX* to *OY*), where the leakage slope is high, than in panel II (from *OX'* to *OY'*), where the slope is more gradual.

Why is the increase greater when the slope is more gradual? The answer should be obvious. The slope represents the marginal propensity to save, to tax, to import—in short, all the marginal propensities that give rise to leakages. If these propensities are high—if there are high leakages—then the slope of the leakage curve will be high. If it is low, the leakage curve will be flat.

A last look at equilibrium

Thus we finally understand how GNP reaches an equilibrium position after a change in demand. Here it is well to reiterate, however, that the word "equilibrium" does not imply a static, motionless state. Nor does it mean a desired state. We use the word only to denote the fact that *given* certain behavior patterns, there will be a determinate point to which their interaction will push the level of income; and *so long as the underlying patterns of injections and leakages remain unchanged, the forces they exert will keep income at this level.*

In fact, of course, the flows of spending and saving are continually changing, so that the equilibrium level of the economy is constantly shifting, like a Ping-Pong ball suspended in a rising jet of water. Equilibrium

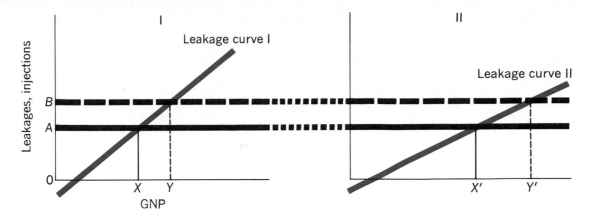

I

Leakage curve I

II

Leakage curve II

Leakages, injections

B

A

0

X   Y

GNP

X'   Y'

FIG. 13 · 11   Two multipliers

can thus be regarded as a target toward which the economy is constantly propelled by the push-pull between leakages and injections. The target may be attained but momentarily before the economy is again impelled to seek a new point of rest. What our diagrams and the underlying analysis explain for us, then, is not a single determinate point at which our economy will in fact settle down, but the *direction* it will go in quest of a resting place, as the dynamic forces of the system exert their pressures.

Equilibrium and full employment

Like the market for any single good or service, the market for all goods and services will find its equilibrium where the total quantity of goods demanded equals that supplied. But now we must note something of paramount importance. While the economy will automatically move to this equilibrium point, the point need not bring about the full employment of the factors of production, particularly labor. In Fig. 13 · 12, the economy at equilibrium produces a GNP indicated by GNP_e, but as our diagram indicates this may be well short of the volume of production needed to bring about full employment (GNP_f). Equilibrium can thus occur at any level of capacity utilization. All we can say about it—exactly as in the market

for goods and services—is that it is the level toward which the system will move, and from which it will not budge unless the demand curve shifts. It is certainly not necessarily the "right" level in any sense, and it may indeed be a very poor or unsatisfactory level, as during the Great Depression.

The aim of macroeconomic policy making is therefore to raise or lower the demand curve for GNP so that it crosses the supply curve at, or near, full employment or some other desired level of output. As we have already seen, this is an objective that is exceedingly difficult to accomplish; but at least we possess, in the body of macroeconomics itself, the basic intellectual tools needed to understand the nature of the task.

FIG. 13 · 12   Supply and demand for GNP

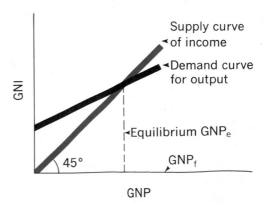

Supply curve of income

Demand curve for output

GNI

Equilibrium GNP_e

GNP_f

45°

GNP

You can see the relation between our multiplier analysis and our graphical analysis by thinking about the following two examples.

1. Suppose that the leakage fraction is 1; in other words, that we absorb *all* increases in income in additional savings, taxes, imports. What will the multiplier be? We know that the multiplier is 1/*mps*. If *mps* = 1,

THE MULTIPLIER ONCE AGAIN

then the multiplier fraction will be 1, and the increase in income will be 1 times the injection. In graphical terms, this looks like the figure on the left, below.

The leakage curve shows that each dollar of additional GNP leads to

another dollar of leakage. Hence the increase in GNP arising from an increase in injections is exactly equal to the original increase in injections. The multiplier is unity.

2. Now suppose that the leakage fraction is .5. The multiplier, once again, is 1/.5 or 2. In the figure on the right, we show the same relationship in graphical terms.

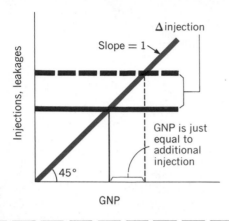

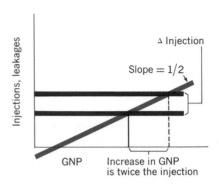

FOCUS

There is one big idea to master in this lesson—how the level of GNP is determined by the outcome of two forces, supply and demand. We have now spent a number of chapters on the components of demand, so that it should not be difficult to grasp the idea of the demand curve. We see that it slopes upward because we are relating the volume of spending with the short-run level of "utilization" of output.

The supply curve is less self-evident. It is not a curve showing the growth of GNP over time, such as we might draw from a study of history. The supply curve shows us the amount of income that will be made available to households, firms, and government agencies at various levels of utilization of the economy. Keep in mind the parable of a functioning economy shut down by a general strike and then going back into full blast production. As we go from zero to full production, income payments will rise exactly as rapidly as the value of production. This is because, as we know, incomes are an identity with costs. Demand (spending) will rise more slowly than production, because demand will not fall to zero, even if production comes to a full stop.

Thus the supply curve becomes a fixed 45° slope, showing the income-cost identity; and against it we match the force of demand, represented by our upward sloping demand curve.

After this basic and essential idea, you must master the idea of a shift in demand. This will happen every time the flow of spending of any sector—usually business or government—suddenly changes.* With the shift in demand will come a new equilibrium, which will be determined by the amount of the shift in demand times the multiplier. You should be able to show that diagrammatically.

Finally, keep in mind that equilibrium is only a technical term. At equilibrium, savings and investment are equal. Costs and expenditures are also equal: $F + T + D = C + G + I$. There is no meaning to equilibrium other than that it is a stable level of GNP. That level may, however, be far below the point of full employment or optimum social benefit. The task of fiscal and monetary policy will then be to change the demand curve so that a socially satisfactory equilibrium is reached.

*As in microeconomics, a change in demand means a shift in the position of the demand curve, not a movement along it.

WORDS AND CONCEPTS YOU SHOULD KNOW

Demand for GNP, 191–92
Supply curve of GNP ≡ GNI, 191, 193
Equilibrium of GNP, 193–94
Changing equilibrium, 195
Saving and investment and GNP
   equilibrium, 196–97
Leakages and injections, 197–98

Intended and unintended S and I, 198
Ex post vs. ex ante, 198–99
Paradox of thrift, 199
Multiplier and slope of leakage curve,
   199–200
Equilibrium and full employment, 201–202

QUESTIONS

1. Explain equilibrium in terms of the demand and supply for output. Why does the supply curve begin at the origin? Why doesn't the demand curve?

2. Draw an equilibrium diagram and indicate the volume of GNP it implies. Can you tell from the diagram if this is a full-employment GNP? What information would you need to draw in the various ranges of employment on the GNP axis?

3. Why is GNP an identity with GNI? Why does the "curve" of an identity always have a 45° slope? Demonstrate this by plotting a curve that relates the number of bachelors (horizontal axis) with the number of unmarried men (vertical axis).

4. Describe the "scenario" by which GNP is "pushed" from a point above equilibrium back to equilibrium. Do the same for a GNP below equilibrium.

5. Can you show why there is no demand gap at equilibrium?

6. Now show how a shift in the demand curve will bring about a new equilibrium point. What is the difference between this and the scenario in Question 4?

7. Show the interplay in the simplest form between savings and investment. Enlarge the saving/investment diagram to a leakage/injection diagram.

8. Show how the multiplier affects the size of changes in GNP, according to the slope of the leakage curve. What does this slope represent? Relate the slope to the *mps*.

9. What is the paradox of thrift? Can you turn it upside down? Suppose no one wanted to save, and everyone tried to spend all his income. What would happen to total income? What would probably happen to saving?

10. Suppose that an economy turns out to have the following consumption and saving schedule (in billions):

Income	Saving	Consumption
$400	$50	$350
450	55	395
500	60	440
550	70	480
600	85	515

Now suppose that firms intend to make investments of $60 billion during the year. What will be the level of income for the economy? If investment rises to $85 billion, then what will be its income? What would be the multiplier in this case?

National income and product accounts

The computation of GNP—requires a vast array of statistics. But behind the numbers lie very important concepts about what the statistics are supposed to represent. Every July issue of the *Survey of Current Business* (a publication of the U.S. Department of Commerce) contains a detailed set of National Accounts for the previous year. Here are a few of the basic tables, indispensable for anyone who wants to become a practicing economist in business or government.

As we now know, there are two ways of viewing the economy's output. One can add up all the costs of the outputs that the economy produces, or one can add up the expenditures of the groups in society who buy this output. Because every item of output is bought by someone, the sum of all costs must be identical with the sum of all expenditures.

Table 13 • 2 presents the official breakdown of these two ways of viewing total output. To avoid the confusion of calling the same total by two different names—GNP and GNI—the official National Income and Product Accounts refer to the sum of both columns as gross national product.

Table 13 • 2 National income and product accounts: 1976

Expenditures on output		Income (costs)	
Personal consumption expenditures	1078	**1.** Compensation of employees	1028
Durable goods	156	**2.** Proprietors income	97
Nondurable goods	440	**3.** Rental income	24
Services	482	**4.** Corporate profits and	
Gross private domestic investment	241	inventory valuation	
Nonresidential structures and		adjustment	119
equipment	160	**5.** Net interest	82
Residential structures	68	**6.** National income	1349
Change in inventories	13	**7.** Indirect business taxes	
Net exports of goods and services	7	and nontax liability	150
Exports	162	**8.** Business transfer payments	7
Imports	155	**9.** Statistical discrepancy	8
Government purchases	366	**10.** Minus: subsidies less current	
Federal	133	surplus of government	
defense	88	enterprises	1
nondefense	45	**11.** Net national product	1512
State and local	232	**12.** Capital consumption allowances	180
Gross national product	1692	**13.** Gross national (income) product	1692

A BREAKDOWN OF THE ACCOUNTS

Many of the terms in the table are now familiar to us. But let us examine a few that need special attention.

First, note (on the output side) that *change in inventories,* not inventories, enters the GNP. Since GNP measures goods and services produced during a given year, it takes into account goods that have been made and put into inventory only during that year. Goods held over in inventory from last year do not count.

What happens, then, if we sell goods out of last year's inventory and do not replace them? From the point of view of overall output, this is exactly the same as if a business firm did not replace its worn-out capital. By convention, we count this diminution in the level of our capital stock as a fall in the total value of output. Hence, the item "change in inventories" is the only item on the product side of GNP that can have a negative value. We cannot produce less than zero consumers goods or government output, but we can produce less goods for inventories than we need to maintain their levels.

The first strange term on the income side is the *inventory valuation adjustment* (no. 4 on the list). Remember than the GNP accounts attempt to measure incomes that are produced this year. If a corporation made a good last year but did not sell it, it will add that good to its inventories. If the good is actually sold this year when prices and costs have risen, measured corporate profits will be higher than they would have been if the good had been produced in the year in which it was sold. The good is sold for this year's higher prices, but the cost of making it is last year's lower cost. As a result, measured profits are higher because of production undertaken in the past. If we are trying to measure the profits that are produced this year, we must subtract these extra profits; and that is what the "valuation adjustment" attempts to do. (If prices and costs were falling, we would make a similar adjustment to increase this year's true profits.)

Indirect business taxes (no. 7) are already known to us. They are the sales and excise taxes (gas taxes, liquor taxes, etc.) that are assessed on the value of some products. Nontax *liabilities* (no. 7) refer to the public fees (licenses, etc.) that are collected from businesses. *Business transfer payments* (no. 8) are corporate gifts to nonprofit institutions, consumer bad debts, and a few other minor payments.

DISCREPANCIES AND SUBSIDIES

Now for the *statistical discrepancy* (no. 9). As we have seen, theoretically the gross national product must equal the gross national income. In practice, however, if you gave one group of statisticians the task of estimating the gross national product and another the task of estimating the gross national income, they would not come up with identical numbers. Why? Each side of the accounts is subject to measurement errors, and there is no reason why the errors should be identical. The statistical discrepancy is an estimate of these errors. Since the GNP and the GNI must be equal, we add a term (positive or negative) to the income side of the accounts to make them equal. The statistical discrepancy is simply the number that will make the final sum of both sides of the accounts the same.

Let's move on to *subsidies less current surplus of government enterprises* (no. 10). This entry refers to the profits and losses of TVA, state liquor stores, and other such government businesses. When the government loses money on one of its enterprises, these losses must be subtracted from the other income flows, because a loss means that incomes have been paid out, but no corresponding product has been produced.* If the losses were not subtracted, the gross national product would not equal the gross national income.

This loss is an example of a true but misleading number. The loss occurs because some activities that the ordinary individual would not consider a business are counted as a business. The agriculture support programs of the federal government are such a "business." When the government pays the farmer $2.00 for a bushel of corn and then sells it for $1.50, it incurs a loss. The purpose is to raise farm incomes through subsidies, but this shows up in the GNP accounts as though it were an accidental loss. Most government businesses that are designed to make money do in fact make money.

Subtracting subsidies less surpluses is just a convention. One could just as easily add surpluses less subsidies. In the former case you are subtracting a positive number; in the latter case you are adding a negative number.

NET VS. GROSS NATIONAL PRODUCT

In theory, the net national product (no. 11) is a more useful number than the gross national product. NNP measures the output of the economy that can be used for consumption or net investment after capital consumption allowances (no. 12)—funds that have been set aside to replace the capital equipment that has worn out in the process of production.

In fact, however, most analysts use the gross national product, GNP. There are three major reasons for this. First, it is very difficult to estimate how much capital equipment has in fact worn out during the year. As a result, the gross national product is a more accurate figure than the net national product. Second, the gross national product shows the value of all goods and services that are actually available for different uses. If we wished to use it all for consumption, we could. Third, old capital equipment is almost never replaced with identical equipment. We replace it instead

---

*If a private business loses money, this shows up in negative corporate profits or proprietor's income. Thus, this is really a government counterpart to these private income categories.

with the latest available equipment. Thus "replacement" investment actually becomes a source of economic growth. As a result, the net national product is much less useful than might be supposed from simply looking at definitions. Recent revisions of GNP accounts have attempted to make the figures for NNP more accurate by adjusting depreciation to reflect replacement prices. We will have to wait and see if this leads to a greater use of NNP as a measure of output.

PRODUCTION OF GNP

We have examined only the most basic table of GNP; and as we have said, there are dozens more. One of them is worth looking at. It shows who *produces* GNP, rather than who buys it or who earns it.

Table 13 · 3   Production of GNP, 1976

Private gross national product	1692.4
Business	1428.4
Farm	50.8
Nonfarm	1377.6
Households and institutions	55.9
Rest of the world	13.3
Gross government product	194.8

NOTE: Institutions are nonprofit private institutions such as universities and hospitals. They are added together with households, since neither attempts to earn profits. The *household* production of GNP includes the paid services of domestic servants and others.

Notice also that in this table, consumption and investment disappear, since all sectors—farms, households, governments, etc.—both consume and invest.

Many other tables are to be found in the Department of Commerce publications, including tables that show in much finer detail the large figures that appear on these tables. For anyone doing research on the activity of the economy, the annual July issue of the *Survey of Current Business* is indispensable. But before using these tables, one must understand the problems and pitfalls we have discussed in this introduction to the U.S. Income and Product Accounts.

Money

We have almost completed our analysis of the major elements of macroeconomics, and soon we can bring our analysis to bear on some major problems of the economy. But first there is a matter that we must integrate into our discussion. This is the role that money plays in fixing or changing the level of GNP, along with the other forces that we have come to know.

Actually, we have been talking about money throughout our exposition. After all, one cannot discuss expenditure without assuming the existence of money. But now we must look behind this unexamined assumption and find out exactly what we mean when we speak of money. This will entail two tasks. In this chapter we shall investigate the question of what money *is*, for money is surely one of the most perplexing inventions of human society. Then in our next chapter, once we have come to understand what currency and gold and bank deposits are and how they come into being, we will look into the effect that money has on our economic operations.

14

The Supply of Money

Let us begin by asking "What is money?" Coin and currency are certainly money. But are checks money? Are the deposits from which we draw checks money? Are savings accounts money? Government bonds?

The answer is somewhat arbitrary. Basically, money is anything we can use to make purchases with. But there exists a spectrum of financial instruments that serve this purpose—a continuum that varies in liquidity, or the ease with which it can be used for purchasing. By law, coin and currency are money because they are defined by law as "legal tender": a seller *must* accept them as payment. Checks do not have to be accepted (we have all seen signs in restaurants saying, "WE DO NOT ACCEPT CHECKS"), although in fact checks are overwhelmingly the most prevalent means of payment. In some states checks can be written on savings accounts as well as on checking accounts. On occasion, government bonds are accepted as a means of payment.

Thus, a variety of things can be counted as money. Most economists, however, agree that what we mean by "money" is cash in the hands of the public plus checking accounts, and they call this sum M_1. Some economists prefer to include savings accounts, along with cash and checking accounts, and call this M_2. And some definitions of money go as high as M_8. (If savings banks expand their new accounts on which checks can be drawn, there will no longer be any difference between M_1 and M_2.)

Currency

Money, then, is mainly currency and checking accounts. In 1976 for example, our total money supply was $312 billion, of which $81 billion was currency in the hands of the public, and $231 billion was the total of checking accounts (or demand deposits, as they are also called).

Of the two kinds of "money," currency is the form most familiar to us. Yet there is a considerable mystery even about currency. Who determines how much currency there is? How is the supply of coins or bills regulated?

We often assume that the supply of currency is "set" by the government that "issues" it. Yet when we think about it, we realize that the government does not just

---

Money serves as a mechanism for storing potential purchasing power and for actually purchasing goods and services. Since cash and personal checks are the principal means for making these purchases, money has come to be defined as cash outside banks plus checking accounts. But what about credit cards. Shouldn't they be considered money?

Credit cards clearly can be used to make purchases, so that they appear on the surface to have a vital attribute of money. But a moment's reflection shows that in fact they *substitute* for cash or checks in which payment is finally made. The moment you pay your credit card bill, or the

CREDIT CARDS

moment the credit card company pays the local merchant, the credit card is replaced by standard money. *Thus credit cards play the role of money only to the extent that credit bills are unpaid!*

In this role credit cards are not unique. Any unpaid bill or charge account is like money, in that you are able to purchase goods and services in exchange for your personal IOU. In a sense, each person is able to "print" money to the extent that he can persuade people to accept his IOUs. For most of us, that extent is very limited.

From an economist's point of view, the value of all outstanding trade credit (unpaid bills, unpaid charge accounts, or credit cards) *should* be considered money. It is not included in the official statistics for two reasons. First, it is difficult or impossible to figure how much trade credit is outstanding at any moment. Second, fluctuations in trade credit do not have a big impact on the economy. Ordinarily, the value of trade credit does not vary much, and therefore trade credit does not give rise to substantial changes in the effective money supply.

hand out money, and certainly not coins or bills. When the government pays people, it is nearly always by check.

Then who does fix the amount of currency in circulation? You can answer the question by asking how you yourself determine how much currency you will carry. If you think about it, the answer is that you "cash" a check when you need more currency than you have, and you put the currency back into your checking account when you have more than you need.

What you do, everyone does. The amount of cash that the public holds at any time is no more and no less than the amount that it *wants* to hold. When it needs more—at Christmas, for instance—the public draws currency by cashing checks on its own checking accounts; and when Christmas is past, shopkeepers (who have received the public's currency) return it to their checking accounts.

Thus the amount of currency we have bears an obvious, important relation to the size of our bank accounts, for we can't write checks for cash if our accounts will not cover them.

Does this mean, then, that the banks have as much currency in their vaults as the total of our checking accounts? No, it does not. But to understand that, let us follow the course of some currency that we deposit in our banks for credit to our accounts.

Bookkeeping money

When you put money into a commercial bank,* the bank does not hold that money for you as a pile of specially earmarked bills or as a bundle of checks made out to you from some payer. The bank takes notice of your deposit simply by crediting your "account," a

bookkeeping page recording your present "balance." After the amount of the currency or check has been credited to you, the currency is put away with the bank's general store of vault cash and the checks are sent to the banks from which they came, where they will be charged against the accounts of the people who wrote them.

There is probably no misconception in economics harder to dispel than the idea that banks are warehouses stuffed with money. In point of fact, however, you might search as hard as you pleased in your bank, but you would find no money that was yours other than a bookkeeping account in your name. This seems like a very unreal form of money; and yet, the fact that you can present a check at the teller's window and convert your bookkeeping account into cash proves that your account must nonetheless be "real."

But suppose that you and all the other depositors tried to convert your accounts into cash on the same day. You would then find something shocking. There would not be nearly enough cash in the bank's till to cover the total withdrawals. In 1976 for instance, total demand deposits in the United States amounted to about $231 billion. But the total amount of coin currency held by the banks was only $9 billion!

At first blush, this seems like a highly dangerous state of affairs. But second thoughts are more reassuring. After all, most of us put money into a bank because we do *not* need it immediately, or because making payments in cash is a nuisance compared with making them by check. Yet, there is always the chance—more than that, the certainty—that some depositors *will* want their money in currency. How much currency will the banks need then? What will be a proper reserve for them to hold?

---

*A commercial bank is a bank that is empowered by law to offer checking services. It may also have savings accounts.

Federal reserve system

For many years, the banks themselves decided what reserve ratio constituted a safe proportion of currency to hold against their demand deposits (the technical name for checking accounts). Today, however, most large banks are members of the Federal Reserve, a central banking system established in 1913 to strengthen the banking activities of the nation. Under the Federal Reserve System, the nation is divided into twelve districts, each with a Federal Reserve Bank owned (but not really controlled) by the member banks of its district. In turn, the twelve Reserve Banks are themselves coordinated by a seven-member Federal Reserve Board in Washington. Since the President, with the advice and consent of the Senate, appoints members of the board for fourteen-year terms, they constitute a body that has been purposely established as an independent nonpolitical monetary authority.*

One of the most important functions of the Federal Reserve Board is to establish reserve ratios for different categories of banks, within limits set by Congress. Historically these reserve ratios have ranged between 13 and 26 percent of demand deposits for city banks, with a somewhat smaller reserve ratio for country banks. Today, reserve ratios are determined by size, and they vary between 16 percent for the largest banks and 7 percent for the smallest. The Federal Reserve Board also sets reserve requirements for "time" deposits (the technical term for savings deposits). These range from 1 to 6 percent, depending on the ease of withdrawal.

The banks' bank

Yet here is something odd! We noticed that in 1976 the total amount of deposits was $231 billion and that banks' holdings of coin and currency were only $9 billion. This is much less than the 18 percent—or even 8 percent—reserve against deposits established by the Federal Reserve Board. How can this be?

The answer is that cash is not the only reserve a bank holds against deposits. Claims on other banks are also held as its reserve.

What are these claims? Suppose, in your account in Bank A, you deposit a check from someone who has an account in Bank B. Bank A credits your account and then presents the check to Bank B for "payment." By "payment" Bank A does not mean coin and currency, however. Instead, Bank A and Bank B settle their transaction at still *another* bank where both Bank A and Bank B have their own accounts. These accounts are with the twelve Federal Reserve Banks of the country, where all banks who are members of the Federal Reserve System (and this accounts for banks holding most of the deposits in our banking system) *must* open accounts. Thus at the Federal Reserve Bank, Bank A's account will be credited, and Bank B's account will be debited, in this way moving reserves from one bank to the other.†

The Federal Reserve Banks serve their member banks in exactly the same way as the member banks serve the public. Member banks automatically deposit in their Federal Reserve accounts all checks they get from other banks. As a result, banks are constantly "clearing" their checks with one another through the Federal Reserve System, because their depositors are constantly writing checks on their own banks payable to someone who

†When money is put into a bank account, the account is credited; when money is taken out, the account is debited.

banks elsewhere. Meanwhile, the balance that each bank maintains at the Federal Reserve—that is, the claim it has on other banks—counts, as much as any currency, as part of its reserve against deposits.

In 1976, therefore, when demand deposits were $231 billion and cash in the banks only $9 billion, we would expect the member banks to have had heavy accounts with the Federal Reserve banks. And so they did—$26 billion in all. Thus, total reserves of the banks were $35 billion ($9 billion in cash plus $26 billion in Federal Reserve accounts), enough to satisfy the legal requirements of the Fed.

Fractional reserves

Thus we see that our banks operate on what is called a *fractional reserve system*. That is, a certain specified fraction of all demand deposits must be kept "on hand" at all times in cash or at the Fed. The size of the minimum fraction is determined by the Federal Reserve, for reasons of control that we shall shortly learn about. It is *not* determined, as we might be tempted to think, to provide a "safe" backing for our bank deposits. For under *any* fractional system, if *all* depositors decided to draw out their accounts in currency and coin from all banks at the same time, the banks would be unable to meet the demand for cash and would have to close. We call this a "run" on the banking system. Needless to say, runs can be terrifying and destructive economic phenomena.*

Why, then, do we court the risk of runs, however small this risk may be? What is the benefit of a fractional banking system? To answer that, let us look into our bank again.

*A "run" on the banking system is no longer so much of a threat as in the past, because the Federal Reserve could supply its members with vast amounts of cash. We shall learn how, later in this chapter.

Loans and investments

Suppose its customers have given our bank $1 million in deposits and that the Federal Reserve Board requirements are 20 percent, a simpler figure to work with than the actual one. Then we know that our bank must at all times keep $200,000, either in currency in its own till or in its demand deposit at the Federal Reserve Bank.

But having taken care of that requirement, what does the bank do with the remaining deposits? If it simply lets them sit, either as vault cash or as a deposit at the Federal Reserve, our bank will be very "liquid," but it will have no way of making an income. Unless it charges a very high fee for its checking services, it will have to go out of business.

And yet there is an obvious way for the bank to make an income, while performing a valuable service. The bank can use all the cash and check claims it does not need for its reserve to make *loans* to businesses or families or to make financial *investments* in corporate or government bonds. It will thereby not only earn an income, but it will assist the process of business investment and government borrowing. Thus the mechanics of the banking system lead us back to the concerns at the very center of our previous analysis.

Inside the Banking System

Fractional reserves allow banks to lend, or to invest in securities, part of the funds that have been deposited with them. But that is not the only usefulness of the fractional reserve system. It works as well to help enlarge or diminish the supply of

ext begin.

ORIGINAL BANK

Assets	Liabilities
$1,000,000 (cash and checks)	$1,000,000 (money owed to depositors)
Total $1,000,000	Total $1,000,000

investible or loanable funds, as the occasion demands. Let us follow how this process works. To make the mechanics of banking clear, we are going to look at the actual books of the bank—in simplified form, of course—so that we can see how the process of lending and investing appears to the banker himself.

Assets and liabilities

We begin by introducing two basic elements of business accounting: *assets* and *liabilities*. Every student at some time or another has seen the balance sheet of a firm, and many have wondered how total assets always equal total liabilities. The reason is very simple. Assets are all the things or claims a business owns. Liabilities are claims against those assets—some of them the claims of creditors, some the claims of owners (called the Net Worth of the business). Since assets show everything that a business owns, and since liabilities show how claims against these self-same things are divided between creditors and owners, it is obvious that the two sides of the balance sheet must always come to exactly the same total. The total of assets and the total of liabilities are an identity.

T accounts

Businesses show their financial condition on a *balance sheet* on which all items on the left side represent assets and all those on the right side represent liabilities. By using a simple two-column balance sheet (called a "T account" because it looks like a T), we can follow very clearly what happens to our bank as we deposit money in it or as it makes loans or investments. (See T account above.)

We start off with the example we have just used, in which we open a brand new bank with $1 million in cash and checks on other banks. Accordingly, our first entry in the T account shows the two sides of this transaction. Notice that our bank has gained an asset of $1 million, the cash and checks it now owns, and that it has simultaneously gained $1 million in liabilities, the deposits it *owes* to its depositors (who can withdraw their money).

As we know, however, our bank will not keep all its newly-gained cash and checks in the till. It may hang on to some of the cash, but it will send all the checks it has received, plus any currency that it feels it does not need, to the Fed for deposit in its account there. As a result, its T account will now look like this:

ORIGINAL BANK

Assets		Liabilities	
Vault Cash	$100,000	Deposits	$1,000,000
Deposit at Fed	900,000		
Total	$1,000,000*	Total	$1,000,000

*If you will examine some bank balance sheets, you will see these items listed as "Cash and due from banks." This means, of course, cash in their own vaults plus their balance at the Fed.

Excess reserves   Now we recall from our previous discussion that our bank does not want to remain in this very liquid, but very unprofitable, position. According to the law, it must retain only a certain percentage of its deposits in cash or at the Federal Reserve—20 percent in our hypothetical example. All the rest it is free to lend or invest. As things now stand, however, it has $1 million in reserves—$800,000 more than it needs. Hence, let us suppose that it decides to put these *excess reserves* to work by lending that amount to a sound business risk. (Note that banks do not lend the excess reserves themselves. These reserves, cash and deposits at the Fed, remain right where they are. Their function is to tell the banks how much they may loan or invest.)

Making a loan   Assume now that the Smith Corporation, a well-known firm, comes in for a loan of $800,000. Our bank is happy to lend them that amount. But "making a loan" does not mean that the bank now pays the company in cash out of its vaults. Rather, *it makes a loan by opening a new checking account for the firm* and by crediting that account with $800,000. (Of if, as is likely, the Smith firm already has an account with the bank, it will simply credit the proceeds of the loan to that account.)

Now our T account shows some interesting changes.

There are several things to note about this transaction. First, our bank's reserves (its cash and deposit at the Fed) have not yet changed. The $1 million in reserves are still there.

Second, notice that the Smith Corporation loan counts as a new asset for the bank because the bank now has a legal claim against the company for that amount. (The interest on the loan is not shown in the balance sheet; but when it is paid, it will show up as an addition to the bank's cash.)

Third, deposits have increased by $800,000. Note, however, that this $800,000 was not paid to the Smith firm out of anyone else's account in the bank. It is a new checking account, one that did not exist before. As a result, the supply of money is also up! More about this shortly.

The loan is spent   Was it safe to open this new account for the company? Well, we might see whether our reserves are now sufficient to cover the Smith Corporation's account as well as the original deposit accounts. A glance reveals that all is well. We still have $1 million in reserves against $1.8 million in deposits. Our reserve ratio is much higher than the 20 percent required by law.

It is so much higher, in fact, that we might be tempted to make another loan to the next customer who requests one, and in that way further increase our earning capacity. But an experienced banker shakes

ORIGINAL BANK

Assets		Liabilities	
Cash and at Fed	$1,000,000	Original deposits	$1,000,000
Loan (Smith Corp.)	800,000	New deposit (Smith Corp.)	800,000
Total	**$1,800,000**	**Total**	**$1,800,000**

his head. "The Smith Corporation did not take out a loan and agree to pay interest on it just for the pleasure of letting that money sit with you," he explains. "Very shortly, the company will be writing checks on its balance to pay for goods or services; and when it does, you will need every penny of the reserve you now have."

That, indeed, is the case. Within a few days we find that our bank's account at the Federal Reserve Bank has been charged with a check for $800,000 written by the Smith Corporation in favor of the Jones Corporation, which carries its account at another bank. Now we find that our T account has changed dramatically to look like this:

Now if we refigure our reserves we find that they are just right. We are required to have $200,000 in vault cash or in our Federal Reserve account against our $1 million in deposits. That is exactly the amount we have left. Our bank is now fully "loaned up."

Expanding the money supply

But the banking *system* is not yet fully loaned up. So far, we have traced what happened to only our bank when the Smith Corporation spent the money in its deposit account. Now we must trace the effect of this action on the deposits and reserves of other banks.

We begin with the bank in which the

ORIGINAL BANK

Assets		Liabilities	
Cash and at Fed	$ 200,000	Original deposits	$1,000,000
Loan (Smith Corp.)	800,000	Smith Corp. deposits	0
Total	$1,000,000	Total	$1,000,000

SECOND BANK

Assets		Liabilities	
Cash and at Fed	$800,000	Deposit (Jones Corp.)	$800,000
Total	$800,000	Total	$800,000

Let us see exactly what has happened. First, the Smith Corporation's check has been charged against our account at the Fed and has reduced it from $900,000 to $100,000. Together with the $100,000 cash in our vault, this gives us $200,000 in reserves.

Second, the Smith Corporation's deposit is entirely gone, although its loan agreement remains with us as an asset.

Jones Corporation deposits the check it has just received from the Smith Corporation. As the above T account shows, the Jones Corporation's bank now finds itself in exactly the same position as our bank was when we opened it with $1 million in new deposits, except that the addition to this "second generation" bank is smaller than the addition to the "first generation" bank.

SECOND BANK
(after Brown Co. spends the proceeds of its loan)

Assets		Liabilities	
Cash and at Fed	$160,000	Deposits (Jones Corp.)	$800,000
Loan (to Brown Co.)	640,000	Deposits (Brown Co.)	0
Total	**$800,000**	**Total**	**$800,000**

THIRD BANK
(after Black Co. gets the check of Brown Co.)

Assets		Liabilities	
Cash and at Fed	$640,000	Deposit (Black Co.)	$640,000
Total	**$640,000**	**Total**	**$640,000**

As we can see, our second generation bank has gained $800,000 in cash and in deposits. Since it needs only 20 percent of this for required reserves, it finds itself with $640,000 excess reserves, which it is now free to use to make loans as investments. Suppose that it extends a loan to the Brown Company and that the Brown Company shortly thereafter spends the proceeds of that loan at the Black Company, which banks at yet a third bank. The two T accounts above show how the total deposits will now be affected.

As Fig. 14 • 1 makes clear, the process will not stop here but can continue from one bank to the next as long as any lending power remains. Notice, however, that this lending power gets smaller and smaller and will eventually reach zero.

Expansion of the Money Supply

If we now look at the bottom of Fig. 14 • 1 we will see something very important.

Every time any bank in this chain of transactions has opened an account for a new borrower, *the supply of money has increased.* Remember that the supply of money is the sum of currency outside the banking system (i.e., in our own pockets) plus the total of demand deposits. As our chain of banks kept opening new accounts, it was simultaneously expanding the total check-writing capacity of the economy. Thus, money has materialized, seemingly out of thin air.

Now how can this be? If we tell any banker in the chain that he has "created" money, he will protest vehemently. The loans he made, he will insist, were backed at the time he made them by excess reserves as large as the loan itself. Just as we had $800,000 in excess reserves when we made our initial loan to the Smith Corporation, so every subsequent loan was always backed 100 percent by unused reserves when it was made.

Our bankers are perfectly correct when they tell us that they never, never lend a penny more than they have. Money is not created in the lending process be-

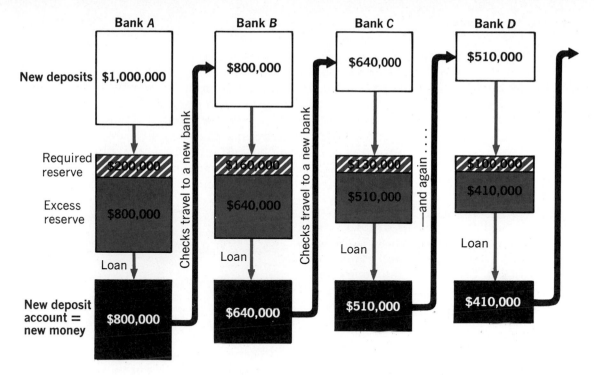

FIG. 14·1   Expansion of the money supply

cause a banker lends money he doesn't have. **Money is created because you and I generally pay each other by checks that give us claims against each other's bank.** If we constantly cashed the checks we exchanged, no new money would be created. But we do not. We deposit each other's checks in our own bank accounts; and in doing so, we give our banks more reserves than they need against the deposits we have just made. These new excess reserves make it possible for our banks to lend or invest, and thereby to open still more deposit accounts, which in turn lead to new reserves.

Limits on the expansion

This all sounds a little frightening. Does it mean that the money supply can go on expanding indefinitely from a single new deposit? Wouldn't that be extremely dangerous?

It would of course be very dangerous, but there is no possibility that it can happen. For having understood how the supply of money can expand from an original

---

MONEY AND DEBT

All this gives us a fresh insight into the question of what money is. We said before that it is whatever we use to make payments. But what do we use? The answer is a surprising one. We use *debts*—specifically, the debts of commercial banks. Deposits are, after all, nothing but the liabilities that banks owe their customers. Furthermore, we can see that one purpose of

the banking system is to buy debts from other units in the economy, such as businesses or governments, in exchange for its own debts (which are money). For when a bank opens an account for a business to which it has granted a loan or when it buys a government bond, what else is it doing

but accepting a debt that is *not* usable as money, in exchange for its deposit liabilities that *are* usable as money. And why is it that banks create money when they make loans, but you or I do not, when we lend money? Because we all accept bank liabilities (deposits) as money, but we do not accept personal or business IOUs to make payments with.

increase in deposits, we may now understand equally well what keeps an expansion within bounds.

1. **Not every loan generates an increase in bank deposits.**

If our bank had opened a loan account for the Smith Corporation at the same time that another firm had paid off a similar loan, there would have been no original expansion in bank deposits. In that case, the addition of $800,000 to the Smith account would have been exactly balanced by a decline of $800,000 in someone else's account. Even if that decline would have taken place in a different bank, it would still mean that the nation's total of bank deposits would not have risen, and therefore no new money would have been created. **Thus, only net additions to loans have an expansionary effect.** We will shortly see how such net additions arise in the first place.

2. **There is a limit to the rise in money supply from a single increase in deposits.**

As Fig. 14•1 shows, in the chain of deposit expansion each successive bank has a smaller increase in deposits, because each bank has to keep some of its newly gained cash or checks as reserve. Hence the amount of *excess* reserves, against which loans can be made, steadily falls.

Further, we can see that the amount of the total monetary expansion from an original net increase in deposits is governed by the size of the fraction that has to be kept aside each time as reserve. **In fact, we can see that just as with the multiplier, the cumulative effect of an increase in deposits will be determined by the reciprocal of the reserve fraction.** If each bank must keep one-fifth of its increased deposits as reserves, then the

cumulative effect of an original increase in deposits, when it has expanded through the system, is five times the original increase. If reserves are one-fourth, the expansion is limited to four times the original increase, and so on.

If M is the money supply, D is net new deposits, and r is the reserve ratio, it follows that:

$$\Delta M = 1/r \times \Delta D$$

Notice that this formula is exactly the same as that for the multiplier.*

3. **The monetary expansion process can work in reverse.**

Suppose that the banking system as a whole suffers a net loss of deposits. Instead of putting $1 million into a bank, the public takes it out in cash. The bank will now have too few reserves, and it will have to cut down its loans or sell its investments to gain the reserves it needs. In turn, as borrowers pay off their loans, or as bond buyers pay for their securities, cash will drain from other banks who will now find *their* reserves too small in relation to their deposits. In turn, they will therefore have to sell more investments or curtail still other loans, and this again will squeeze still other banks and reduce their reserves, with the same consequences.

Thus, just as an original expansion in deposits can lead to a multiple expansion, so an original contraction in deposits can lead to a multiple contraction. The size of this contraction is also limited by the reciprocal of the reserve fraction. If banks have to hold a 25 percent reserve, then an original fall of $100,000 in deposits will lead to a total fall of $400,000, assuming

---

*Why is ΔM determined by multiplying ΔD by $1/r$? Same reason as the multiplier. See box on p. 138.

that the system was fully "loaned up" to begin with. If they had to hold a 20 percent reserve, a fall of $100,000 could pyramid to $500,000.

4. The expansion process may not be fully carried through.

We have assumed that each bank in the chain always lends out an amount equal to its excess reserve, but this may not be the case. The third or fifth bank along the way may have trouble finding a credit-worthy customer and may decide—for the moment, anyway—to sit on its excess reserves. Or borrowers along the chain may take out cash from some of their new deposits and thereby reduce the banks' reserves and their lending powers. Thus the potential expansion may be only partially realized.

5. The expansion process takes time.

Like the multiplier process, the expansion of the money supply encounters many "frictions" in real life. Banks do not instantly expand loans when their reserves rise; bank customers do not instantly spend the proceeds of bank loans. The time lags in banking are too variable to enable us to make an estimate of how long it takes for an initial increase in new deposits to work its way through the system, but the time period is surely a matter of months for two or three "rounds."

Why banks must work together   There is an interesting problem concealed behind this crisscrossing of deposits that leads to a slowly rising level of the money supply. Suppose that an imaginary island economy was served by a single bank (and let us forget about all complications of international trade, etc.), and this bank, which

worked on a 20 percent reserve ratio, was suddenly presented with an extra one million dollars worth of reserves—let us say newly mined pure gold. Our bank could, of course, increase its loans to customers. By how much? *By five million dollars!*

In other words, our island bank, all by itself, could use an increase in its reserves to create a much larger increase in the money supply. It is not difficult to understand why. Any borrower of the new five million, no matter where he spent his money on the island, would only be giving his checks to someone who also banked at the single, solitary bank. The whole five million, in other words, would stay *within* the bank as its deposits, although the identity of those depositors would, of course, shift. Indeed, there is no reason why such a bank should limit its expansion of the money supply to five million. As long as the "soundness" of the currency was unquestioned, such a bank could create as much money as it wanted through new deposits, since all of those deposits would remain in its own keeping.

The imaginary bank makes it plain why ordinary commercial banks *cannot* expand deposits beyond their excess reserves. Unlike the monopoly bank, they must expect to *lose* their deposits to other banks when their borrowers write checks on their new accounts. As a result they will also lose their reserves, and this can lead to trouble.

Overlending   This situation is important enough to warrant taking a moment to examine. Suppose that in our previous example we had decided to lend the Smith Corporation not $800,000 but $900,000, and suppose as before that the Smith Corporation used the proceeds of that loan to pay the Jones Cor-

Original Bank

Assets		Liabilities	
Cash and at Fed	$ 100,000	Original deposits	$1,000,000
Loan (Smith Corp.)	900,000	Smith Corp. deposit	0
Total	**$1,000,000**	**Total**	**$1,000,000**

poration. Now look at the condition of our bank after the Smith payment has cleared.

Our reserves would now have dropped to 10 percent! Indeed, if we had loaned the company $1,000,000 we would be in danger of insolvency.

Banks are, in fact, very careful not to overlend. If they find that they have inadvertently exceeded their legal reserve requirements, they quickly take remedial action. One way that a bank may repair the situation is by borrowing reserves for a short period (paying interest on them, of course) from another bank that may have a temporary surplus at the Fed; this is called borrowing *federal funds*. Or a bank may quickly sell some of its government bonds •and add the proceeds to its reserve account at the Fed. Or again, it may add to its reserves the proceeds of any loans that have come due and deliberately fail to replace these expired loans with new loans. Finally, a bank may borrow reserves directly from its Federal Reserve Bank and pay interest for the loan. We shall shortly look into this method when we talk about the role of the Federal Reserve in regulating the quantity of money.

The main point is clear. A bank is safe in lending only an amount that it can afford to lose to another bank. But of course one bank's loss is another's gain. That is why, by the exchange of checks, the banking system can accomplish the same result as the island monopoly bank, whereas no individual bank can hope to do so.

Investments and interest

If a bank uses its excess reserves to buy securities, does that lead to the same multiplication effect as a bank loan?

It can. When a bank buys government securities, it usually does so from a securities dealer, a professional trader in bonds.* Its check (for $800,000 in our example) drawn on its account at the Federal Reserve will be made out to a dealer, who will deposit it in his bank. As a result, the dealer's bank suddenly finds itself with an $800,000 new deposit. It must keep 20 percent of this as required reserve, but the remainder is excess reserve against which it can make loans or investments as it wishes.

Is there a new deposit, corresponding to that of the borrower? There is: the new deposit of the securities dealer. Note that in his case, as in the case of the borrower, the new deposit on the books of the bank has not been put there by the transfer of money from some other commercial bank. The $800,000 deposit has come into being through the deposit of a check of the Federal Reserve Bank, which is not a commercial bank. Thus it represents a new addition to the deposits of the private banking system.

Let us see this in the T accounts. After our first bank has bought its $800,000 in

---

*The dealer may be only a middleman, who will in turn buy from, or sell to, corporations or individuals. This doesn't change our analysis, however.

bonds (paying for them with its Federal Reserve checking account) its T account looks like this.

than a 4 percent return ($40 is only 3.6 percent of $1,100). If the price should fall to $900, the $40 return will be more than 4

Original Bank

Assets		Liabilities	
Cash at Fed	$ 200,000	Deposits	$1,000,000
Government bonds	800,000		
Total	$1,000,000	Total	$1,000,000

As we can see, there are no excess reserves here. But look at the bank in which the seller of the government bond has deposited the check he has just received from our bank. Here there are excess reserves of $640,000 with which additional investments can be made. It is possible for such new deposits, albeit diminishing each time, to remain in the financial circuit for some time, moving from bank to bank as an active business is done in buying government bonds.

percent ($40 is 4.4 percent of $900). Thus the *yield* of a bond varies inversely—in the other direction—from its market price.

When the price of government bonds changes, all bond prices tend to change in the same direction. This is because all bonds are competing for investors' funds. If the yield on "governments" falls, investors will switch from governments to other, higher yielding bonds. But as they bid for these other bonds, the prices of these bonds will rise—and their yields will fall,

Second Bank

Assets		Liabilities	
Cash	$800,000	New deposit of bond seller	$800,000
Total	$800,000	Total	$800,000

Yields

Meanwhile, however, the very activity in bidding for government bonds is likely to raise their price and thereby lower their rate of interest.

This is a situation that you will probably be faced with in your personal life, so you should understand it. A bond has a *fixed* rate of return and a stated face value. If it is a 4 percent, $1,000 bond, this means it will pay $40 interest yearly. If the bond now sells on the marketplace for $1,100, the $40 yearly interest will be less

too!

In this way, a change in yields spreads from one group of bonds to another. A lower rate of interest or a lower yield on government securities is quickly reflected in lower rates or yields for other kinds of bonds. In turn, a lower rate of interest on bonds makes loans to business look more attractive. Thus, sooner or later, excess reserves are apt to be channeled to new loans as well as new investments. Thereafter the deposit-building process follows its familiar course.

Controlling the Money Supply

We have now seen how a banking system can create money through the successive creation of excess reserves. But the key to the process is the creation of the *original* excess reserves, for without them the cumulative process will not be set in motion. We remember, for example, that a loan will not result in an increase in the money supply if it is offset by a decline in lending somewhere else in the banking system; neither will the purchase of a bond by one commercial bank if it is only buying a security sold by another. **To get a net addition to loans or investments, however, a banking system—assuming that it is fully loaned up—needs an increase in its reserves.** Where do these extra reserves come from? That is the question we must turn to next.

Role of the Federal Reserve

In our example we have already met one source of changes in reserves. When the public needs less currency, and it deposits its extra holdings in the banks, reserves rise, as we have seen. Contrariwise, when the public wants more currency, it depletes the banks' holdings of currency and thereby lowers their reserves. In the latter case, the banks may find that they have insufficient reserves behind their deposits. To get more currency or claims on other banks, they will have to sell securities or reduce their loans. This might put a very severe crimp in the economy. Hence, to allow bank reserves to be regulated by the public's fluctuating demand for cash would seem to be an impossible way to run our monetary system.

But we remember that bank reserves are not mainly currency; in fact, currency is a relatively minor item. Most reserves are the accounts that member banks hold at the Federal Reserve. Hence, if these accounts could somehow be increased or decreased, we could regulate the amount of reserves—and thus the permissible total of deposits—without regard to the public's changing need for cash.

This is precisely what the Federal Reserve System is designed to do. Essentially, the system is set up to regulate the supply of money by raising or lowering the reserves of its member banks. When these reserves are raised, member banks find themselves with excess reserves and are thus in a position to make loans and investments by which the supply of money will increase further. Conversely, when the Federal Reserve lowers the reserves of its member banks, they will no longer be able to make loans and investments, or they may even have to reduce loans or get rid of investments, thereby extinguishing deposit accounts and contracting the supply of money.

Monetary control mechanisms

How does the Federal Reserve operate? There are three ways.

1. Changing reserve requirements

It was the Federal Reserve itself, we will remember, that originally determined how much in reserves its member banks should hold against their deposits. Hence by changing that reserve requirement for a given level of deposits, it can give its member banks excess reserves or can create a shortage of reserves.

In our imaginary bank we have assumed that reserves were set at 20 percent of deposits. Suppose now that the Federal Reserve determined to lower reserve requirements to 15 percent. It would thereby automatically create extra lending or investing power for our *existing* reserves. Our bank with $1 million in deposits and $200,000 in reserves could now lend or invest an additional $50,000 without any new funds coming in from depositors. On the other hand, if requirements were raised to, say, 30 percent, we would find that our original $200,000 reserve was $100,000 short of requirements, and we would have to curtail lending or investing until we were again in line with requirements.

Do not forget that these new reserve requirements affect *all* banks. **Therefore, changing reserve ratios is a very effective way of freeing or contracting bank credit on a large scale. But it is an instrument that sweeps across the entire banking system in an undiscriminating fashion. It is therefore used only rarely, when the Federal Reserve Board feels that the supply of money is seriously short or dangerously excessive and needs remedy on a countrywide basis.** For instance, in early 1973, the board raised reserve requirements one-half percent for all banks, partly to mop up excess reserves and partly to sound a general warning against what it considered to be a potentially dangerous inflationary state of affairs.

2. Changing discount rates

A second means of control uses interest rates as the money-controlling device. Recall that member banks that are short on reserves have a special privilege, if they wish to exercise it. They can *borrow* reserve balances from the Federal Reserve Bank itself and add them to their regular reserve account at the bank.

The Federal Reserve Bank, of course, charges interest for lending reserves, and this interest is called the *discount rate.* By raising or lowering this rate, the Federal Reserve can make it attractive or unattractive for member banks to borrow to augment reserves. Thus in contrast with changing the reserve ratio itself, changing the discount rate is a mild device that allows each bank to decide for itself whether it wishes to increase its reserves. In addition, changes in the discount rate tend to influence the whole structure of interest rates, either tightening or loosening money.*

Although changes in the discount rate can be used as a major means of controlling the money supply and are used to control it in some countries, they are not used for this purpose in the U. S. The Federal Reserve Board does not allow banks to borrow whatever they would like at the current discount rate. The discount "window" is a place where a bank can borrow small amounts of money to cover a small deficiency in its reserves, but it is not a place where banks can borrow major amounts of money to expand their lending portfolios. As a result, the discount rate serves more as a signal of what the Federal Reserve would like to see happen than as an active force in determining the total borrowings of banks.

3. Open-market operations

Most frequently used, however, is a third technique called open-market operations. This technique permits the Federal Reserve Banks to change the supply of reserves by buying or selling U.S. government bonds on the open market.

How does this work? Let us suppose that the Federal Reserve authorities wish to increase the reserves of member banks. They will begin to buy government securities from dealers in the bond market, and

*When interest rates are high, money is called tight. This means not only that borrowers have to pay higher rates, but that banks are stricter and more selective in judging the credit worthiness of business applications for loans. Conversely, when interest rates decline, money is called easy, meaning that it is not only cheaper but literally easier to borrow.

they will pay these dealers with Federal Reserve checks.

Notice something about these checks: *they are not drawn on any commercial bank!* They are drawn on the Federal Reserve Bank itself. The security dealer who sells the bond will, of course, deposit the Fed's check, as if it were any other check, in his own commercial bank; and his bank will send the Fed's check through for credit to its own account, as if it were any other check. *As a result, the dealer's bank will have gained reserves, although* *no other commercial bank has lost reserves.* On balance, then, the system has more lending and investing capacity than it had before. In fact, it now has *excess* reserves, and these, as we have seen, will spread out through the system. **Thus by buying bonds, the Federal Reserve has, in fact, deposited money in the accounts of its members, thereby giving them the extra reserves that it set out to create** (see box).

Conversely, if the authorities decide that member banks' reserves are too large, they will sell securities. Now the process

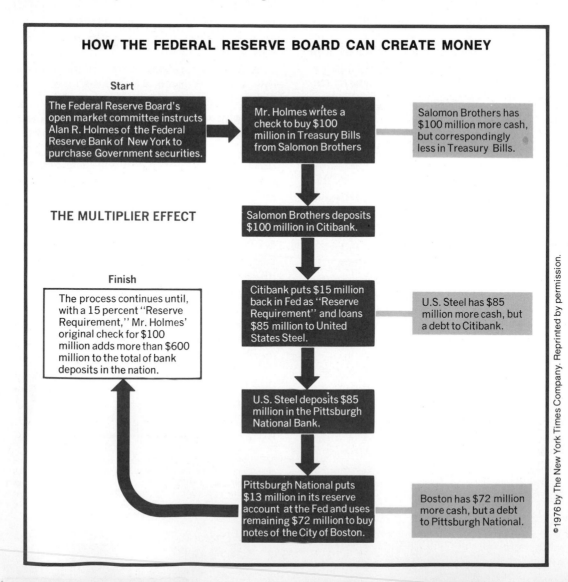

HOW THE FEDERAL RESERVE BOARD CAN CREATE MONEY

Start

The Federal Reserve Board's open market committee instructs Alan R. Holmes of the Federal Reserve Bank of New York to purchase Government securities.

Mr. Holmes writes a check to buy $100 million in Treasury Bills from Salomon Brothers

Salomon Brothers has $100 million more cash, but correspondingly less in Treasury Bills.

THE MULTIPLIER EFFECT

Salomon Brothers deposits $100 million in Citibank.

Finish

The process continues until, with a 15 percent "Reserve Requirement," Mr. Holmes' original check for $100 million adds more than $600 million to the total of bank deposits in the nation.

Citibank puts $15 million back in Fed as "Reserve Requirement" and loans $85 million to United States Steel.

U.S. Steel has $85 million more cash, but a debt to Citibank.

U.S. Steel deposits $85 million in the Pittsburgh National Bank.

Pittsburgh National puts $13 million in its reserve account at the Fed and uses remaining $72 million to buy notes of the City of Boston.

Boston has $72 million more cash, but a debt to Pittsburgh National.

works in reverse. Security dealers or other buyers of bonds will send their own checks on their own regular commercial banks to the Federal Reserve in payment for these bonds. This time the Fed will take the checks of its member banks and charge their accounts, thereby reducing their reserves. **Since these checks will not find their way to another commercial bank, the system as a whole will have suffered a diminution of its reserves.** By selling securities, in other words, the Federal Reserve authorities lower the Federal Reserve accounts of member banks, thereby diminishing their reserves.*

Asymmetric control

How effective are all these powers over the money supply? The Federal Reserve Board's capacity to control money is often compared to our ability to manipulate a string. If the Federal Reserve Board wishes to *reduce* the money supply, it can increase the discount rate or sell bonds. Sooner or later, this tends to be effective. If banks have free or excess reserves, they will not immediately have to reduce their lending portfolios; but eventually, by pulling on the string hard enough, the Fed can force a reduction in bank loans and the money supply.

The Federal Reserve Board's capacity to increase the money supply is not equally great. It can reduce reserve rates and buy bonds, but it cannot *force* banks to make loans if they do not wish to do so. Banks can, if they wish, simply increase their excess reserves. Normally, banks wish to make loans and earn profits; but if risks are high, they may not wish to do so. Such a situation occurred in the Great Depression. Banks piled up vast reserves rather than make loans, since the risks of defaults were too high to make most loans an attractive economic gamble. In terms of our analogy, the Federal Reserve Board can pull, but it cannot push on its string of controls.

Sticky prices

We are almost ready to look into the dynamics of money, in our next chapter, but we must examine a question that we have heretofore passed over in silence. We have taken for granted that we need a larger supply of money in order to expand output. But why should we? Why could we not grow just as well if the supply of money were fixed?

Theoretically we could. If we cut prices as we increased output, a given amount of money (or a given amount of expenditure) could cover an indefinitely large real output. Furthermore, as prices fell, workers would be content not to ask for higher wages (or would even accept lower wages), since in real terms they would be just as well or better off.

It is not difficult to spot the flaw in this argument. In the real world, prices of many goods cannot be cut easily. If the price of steel rose and fell as quickly and easily as prices on the stock exchange or if wages went down without a murmur of resistance or if rents and other contractual items could be quickly adjusted, then

---

*Isn't this, you might ask, really the same thing as raising or lowering the reserve ratio? If the Fed is really just putting money into member bank accounts when it buys bonds and taking money out when it sells them, why does it bother to go through the open market? Why not just tell the member banks that their reserves are larger or smaller?

Analytically, you are entirely right. There are however cogent reasons for working through the bond market. The open-market technique allows banks to *compete* for their share of the excess reserves that are being made available or taken away. Banks that are good at attracting depositors will thereby get extra benefit from an increase in the money supply. Thus, rather than assigning excess reserves by executive fiat, the Fed uses the open market as an allocation device.

In addition, open-market operations allow the Fed to make very small changes in the money supply, whereas changes in reserve requirements would be difficult to adjust in very fine amounts.

prices would be flexible and we would not require any enlargement of our money supply to cover a growing real output.

In fact, as we know, prices are extremely "sticky" in the downward direction. Union leaders do not look with approval on wage cuts, even when living costs fall. Contractual prices cannot be quickly adjusted. Many big firms administer their prices and carefully avoid price competition: note, for example, that the prices of many customer items are printed on the package months before the item will be sold.

Thus we can see that a fixed supply of money would put the economy into something of a straitjacket. As output tended to increase, business would need more money to finance production, and consumers would need more money to make their larger expenditures. If business could get more money from the banks, all would be well. But suppose it could not. Then the only way it could get a larger supply of cash would be to persuade someone to lend the money, and persuasion would be in the form of a higher rate of interest. But this rising interest rate would discourage other businesses from going ahead with their plans. Hence the would-be-boom would be stopped dead in its tracks by a sheer shortage of spending power.

A flexible money supply obviates this economic suffocation. The fact that banks can create money (provided that they have excess reserves) enables them to take care of businesses that wish to make additional expenditures. The expenditures themselves put additional money into the hands of consumers. And the spending of consumers in turn sends the enlarged volume of purchasing power back to business firms to complete the great flow of expenditures and receipt.

Paper Money and Gold

Finally, let us clear up one last mystery of the monetary system—the mystery of where currency (coin and bills) actually comes from and where it goes. If we examine most of our paper currency, we will find that it has "Federal Reserve Note" on it: that is, it is paper money issued by the Federal Reserve System. We understand, by now, how the public gets these notes: it simply draws them from its checking accounts. When it does so, the commercial banks, finding their supplies of vault cash low, ask their Federal Reserve district banks to ship them as much new cash as they need.

And what does the Federal Reserve Bank do? It takes packets of bills ($1 and $5 and $10) out of its vaults, *where these stacks of printed paper have no monetary significance at all,* charges the requisite amount against its member banks' balances, and ships the cash out by armored truck. So long as these new stacks of bills remain in the member banks' possession, they are still not money! But soon they will pass out to the public, where they will be money. Do not forget, of course, that as a result, the public will have that much *less* money left in its checking accounts.

Could this currency-issuing process go on forever? Could the Federal Reserve ship out as much money as it wanted to? Suppose that the authorities at the Fed decided to order a trillion dollars worth of bills from the Treasury mints. What would happen when those bills arrived at the Federal Reserve Banks? The answer is that they would simply gather dust in their vaults. There would be no way for the Fed to "issue" its money unless the public wanted cash. And the amount of cash the

GOLDFINGER AT WORK

Some years ago a patriotic women's organization, alarmed lest the Communists had tunneled under the Atlantic, forced an inspection of the gold stock buried at Fort Knox. It proved to be all there. An interesting question arises as to the repercussions, had they found the great vault to be bare. Perhaps we might have followed the famous anthropo-logical example of the island of Yap in the South Seas, where heavy stone cartwheels are the symbol of wealth for the leading families. One such family was particularly remarkable insofar as its cartwheel lay at the bottom of a lagoon, where it had fallen from a canoe. Although it was absolutely irretrievable and even invisible, the family's wealth was considered unimpaired, since everyone knew the stone was there. If the Kentucky depository had been empty, a patriotic declaration by the ladies that the gold really was in Fort Knox might have saved the day for the United States.

public could want is always limited by the amount of money it has in its checking accounts.

The gold cover Are there no limitations on this note-issuing or reserve-creating process? Until 1967 there *were* limitations imposed by Congress, requiring the Federal Reserve to hold gold certificates equal in value to at least 25 percent of all outstanding notes. (Gold certificates are a special kind of paper money issued by the U.S. Treasury and backed 100 percent by gold bullion in Fort Knox.) Prior to 1964 there was a further requirement that the amount of gold certificates also be sufficient to give a 25 percent backing as well to the total amount of member bank deposits held by the Fed. Thus the legal obligation not to go beyond this 25 percent gold cover provided a strict ceiling on the amount of member bank reserves the Federal Reserve system could create or on the amount of notes it could ship at the request of its member banks.

All this presented no problem in, say, 1940, when the total of member bank reserves plus Federal Reserve notes came to only $20 billion, against which we held gold certificates worth almost $22 billion. Trouble began to develop, however, in the 1960s when a soaring GNP was accompanied by a steadily rising volume of both member bank reserves and Federal Reserve notes. By 1964, for example, member bank reserves had grown to $22 billion, and outstanding Reserve notes to nearly $35 billion. At the same time, for reasons that we shall learn more about in Chapter 21, our gold stock had declined to just over $15 billion. With $57 billion in liabilities ($22 billion in member bank reserves plus $35 billion in notes) and only $15 billion in gold certificates, the 25 percent cover requirement was clearly imperiled.

Congress thereupon removed the cover requirement from member bank reserves, leaving all our gold certificates available as "backing" for our Federal Reserve notes. But even that did not solve the problem. Currency in circulation continued to rise with a record GNP until it exceeded $40 billion in 1967. Our gold stock meanwhile continued to decline to $12 billion in that year and threatened to fall further. The handwriting on the wall indicated that the 25 percent cover could not long be maintained.

There were basically two ways out. One would have been to change the gold cover requirements from 25 percent to, say, 10 percent. That would have made our gold stock more than adequate to "back" our paper money (and our member bank deposits, too).*

The second way was much simpler: *eliminate the gold cover entirely.* With very little fuss, this is what Congress did in 1967.

Gold and money

Does the presence or absence of a gold cover make any difference? From the economist's point of view it does not. Gold is a metal with a long and rich history of hypnotic influence, so there is undeniably a psychological usefulness in having gold "behind" a currency. But unless that currency is 100 percent convertible into gold, *any* money demands an act of faith on the part of its users. If that faith is destroyed, the money becomes valueless; so long as it is unquestioned, the money is "as good as gold."

Thus the presence or absence of a gold backing for currency is purely a psychological problem, so far as the value of a domestic currency is concerned. In Chapter 21 we will look into its international significance. But the point is worth pursuing a little further. Suppose our currency *were* 100 percent convertible into gold—suppose, in fact, that we used only gold coins as currency. Would that improve the operation of our economy?

A moment's reflection should reveal that it would not. We would still have to cope with a very difficult problem that our bank deposit money handles rather easily. This is the problem of how we could increase the supply of money or diminish it, as the needs of the economy changed. With gold coins as money, we would either have a frozen stock of money (with

consequences that we shall trace in the next chapter), or our supply of money would be at the mercy of our luck in gold-mining or the currents of international trade that funneled gold into our hands or took it away. And incidentally, a gold currency would not obviate inflation, as many countries have discovered when the vagaries of international trade or a fortuitous discovery of gold mines increased their holdings of gold faster than their actual output.

Money and belief

As we cautioned at the outset, money is a highly sophisticated and curious invention. At one time or another nearly everything imaginable has served as the magic symbol of money: whales' teeth, shells, feathers, bark, furs, blankets, butter, tobacco, leather, copper, silver, gold, and (in the most advanced nations) pieces of paper with pictures on them or simply numbers on a computer printout. In fact, anything is usable as money, provided that there is a natural or enforceable scarcity of it, so that men can usually come into its possession only through carefully designated ways. Behind all the symbols, however, rests the central requirement of faith. Money serves its indispensable purposes as long as we believe in it. It ceases to function the moment we do not. Money has well been called "the promises men live by."

But the creation of money and the control over its supply is still only half the question. We have yet to trace how our money supply influences the flow of output itself—or to put it differently, how the elaborate institutions through which men promise to honor one another's work and property affect the amount of work they do and the amount of new wealth they accumulate. This is the subject to which our next chapter will be devoted.

---

*Actually as we shall see in the box on the gold standard on p. 329—the gold never really backed our currency, since no American was legally permitted to buy gold bullion.

FOCUS   This is the first time we have had a chance to investigate the "mystery" of money. Your central purpose should be to dispel whatever shrouds of mystery still cling to the idea of money.

Money is mysterious because it is not simply gold coins; it is a *symbol* of wealth. For that matter, gold coins are also symbols of wealth which, in the last analysis, is production. Therefore, we have to understand how the symbolic pieces of paper we use, both currency and checks, come into being. We should also see that "money" can be defined to include other symbols of wealth, such as savings accounts or even government bonds.

Most money consists of checking accounts owned by individuals or firms or government agencies at banks. Money "circulates" when owners of deposits draw checks on these accounts. Money can also take the form of currency whenever the public exchanges its deposits for coins or bills. But most money is "in" the bank, where it is nothing more than a bookkeeping entry showing the size of your account.

Each commercial bank must keep a certain fraction of its demand deposits in cash or as a deposit at its Federal Reserve Bank. This fraction is set by the Fed. The remaining "excess reserves" indicate the amount that a bank can lend or invest, in order to make money. When a loan or investment is made, a bank opens a new account in the name of the borrower or bond seller. When these new accounts are subsequently used, they become new deposits for other banks, and in this way the money supply can be expanded (or contracted if the first bank curtails a loan or sells a bond). You should study the diagram on p. 217 and the series of T accounts, to be sure you understand this process. Better yet, using T accounts, work your way through questions 4 to 8.

The second main point to learn is how the Federal Reserve System controls the money supply. We have seen that the reserve ratio is established by the Fed. This is not to "safeguard" deposits. In the case of a real panic only 100 percent reserves would be a safeguard (and the Fed could easily print up and ship out trillions of dollars of Federal Reserve Notes if the public had a mass, panicky urge to get into cash.) The Fed sets reserve ratios as one of its ways of controlling the supply of money. The other ways are to change the discount rate and to buy or sell U.S. government bonds—"open market" operations. Be sure that you understand these three methods: they are crucial to understanding how our money mechanism works. Questions 11, 12, and 13 should help you here.

Any mysteries left?

WORDS AND CONCEPTS YOU SHOULD KNOW

QUESTIONS

1. Why do we not count cash in the tills of commercial banks in the money supply? When you deposit currency in a commercial bank, what happens to it? Can you ask for your particular bills again? If you demanded to see "your" account, what would it be?

2. What determines how much vault cash a bank must hold against its deposits? Would you expect this proportion to change in some seasons, such as Christmas? Do you think it would be the same in worried times as in placid times? In new countries as in old ones?

3. Is currency the main reserve of a bank? Do reserves ensure the safety of a currency? What function do they have?

4. What are excess reserves? Suppose a bank has $500,000 in deposits and that there is a reserve ratio of 30 percent imposed by law. What is its required reserve? Suppose it happens to hold $200,000 in vault cash or at its account at the Fed. What, if any, is its excess reserve?

5. If the bank above wanted to make loans or investments, how much would it be entitled to lend or invest?

6. Suppose its deposits increased by another $50,000. Could it lend or invest this entire amount? Any of it? How much?

7. If a bank lends money, it opens an account in the name of the borrower. Now suppose the borrower draws down his new account. What happens to the reserves of the lending bank? Show this in a T account.

8. Suppose the borrower sends his check for $1,000 to someone who banks at another bank. Describe what happens to the deposits of the second bank. If the reserve ratio is 20 percent, how much new lending or investing can it do?

9. If the reserve ratio is 20 percent, and the original addition to reserves is $1,000, what will be the total potential amount of new money that can be created by the banking system? If the ratio is 25 percent?

10. What is the difference between a banking system and a single competitive bank? Can a single bank create new money? Can it create more new money than an amount equal to its excess reserves? Can a banking system create more money than its excess reserves?

11. Suppose that a bank has $1 million in deposits, $100,000 in reserves, and is fully loaned up. Now suppose the Federal Reserve System lowers reserve requirements from 10 percent to 8 percent. What happens to the lending capacity of the bank?

12. The Federal Reserve Banks buy $100 million in U.S. Treasury notes. How do they pay for these notes? What happens to the checks? Do they affect the reserves of member banks? Will buying bonds increase or decrease the money supply?

13. Now explain what happens when the Fed sells Treasury notes. Who buys them? How do they pay for them? Where do the checks go? How does payment affect the accounts of the member banks at the Federal Reserve Banks?

14. Why do you think gold has held such a place of prestige in the minds of men?

Independence of the Fed

The Federal Reserve Board is run by 7 governors, each appointed to a 14-year term by the President with the approval of Congress. The governors of the Federal Reserve System cannot be removed during their terms of office except for wrongdoing. Thus, although fiscal policy is located in the executive and legislative branches of the government, monetary policy is vested in an independent board.

There were two initial justifications for this institutional arrangement. The first was that monetary policies were necessarily subject to quick changes. Second, it was felt that monetary policies ought to be insulated from the political process.

Are these reasons still valid? Some economists think so; others, including ourselves, think not. To take the first argument, it is true that Congress cannot be expected to operate an efficient open-market system on a daily basis. But this is not an argument for divorcing the responsibility for such operations from the *executive* branch. In most of the world's governments, Central Banks (the equivalent of the Fed) are located within the executive establishment, usually as a part of the Treasury or Finance ministries or departments. These banks have no trouble making quick decisions. Moreover, even if Congress could not be expected to approve of every jiggle in monetary measures, there is no reason why it could not endorse or direct the major thrust of monetary strategy toward an expansionary or a contractive general objective.

The argument about "insulation" depends on one's view of democracy, where values once again reign supreme. There is a curious inconsistency, however, in trying to insulate only monetary policies, not fiscal policies. Why should we trust the democratic mechanism to establish expenditures and taxes, but not the supply of money?

As in most institutional debates, dramatic changes are unlikely to happen, although we seem to be moving in a more "democratic" direction in our monetary management. Congress now expects to be briefed every quarter on the Fed's monetary targets for the following year. There are also bills pending in Congress to integrate the Fed more fully by altering the tenure of the Chairman to be concomitant with that of the President; or to require the Fed to issue an economic report directly after the President's Economic Report, stating what differences, if any, lie between them, and justifying the Fed's course of action if it differs from that of the Administration.

Meanwhile, a high degree of integration exists in fact, although not in law. More and more, the Fed bows to public pressure or to pressure from the Administration. This is hardly surprising. As we shall see in our next chapter, we live at a time when the importance of money in the economy is more highly regarded than it used to be. The idea of an "independent" Fed does not sit so well in an era when we think of the Fed as bearing a prime responsibility for our economic well-being. Having created the Federal Reserve Board in the first place, Congress can alter it, as it wishes; and it undoubtedly would alter it, were the Fed to risk a direct confrontation with congressional or presidential economic objectives. The more important money management becomes, the more powerful are the pressures to place it within, not outside of, the main political mechanisms of the nation.

Money
and the
macro system

In our preceding chapter, we found out something about what money is and how it comes into being. Now we must turn to the much more complicated question of how money works—the level of output. What happens when the banks create or destroy deposits? Can we directly raise or lower incomes by altering the quantity of money? Can we control inflation or recession by using the monetary management powers of the Federal Reserve System? These extremely important questions will be the focus of discussion in this chapter.

The Quantity Theory of Money

Quantity equation

One relation between money and economic activity must have occurred to us. It is that the quantity of money must have something to do with *prices*. Does it not stand to reason that if we increase the supply of money, prices will go up, and that if we decrease the amount of money, prices will fall?

Something very much like this belief lies behind one of the most famous equations (really identities) in economics. The equation looks like this:

15

232

$$MV \equiv PT$$

where

M = *quantity of money* (currency outside banks plus demand deposits)

V = *velocity of circulation,* or the number of times per period or per year that an average dollar changes hands

P = *the general level of prices,* or a price index

T = *the number of transactions made in the economy* in a year, or a measure of *physical output*

If we think about this equation, its meaning is not hard to grasp. What the quantity equation says is that the amount of *expenditure* (M times V, or the quantity of money times the frequency of its use) equals the amount of *receipts* (P times T, or the price of an average sale times the number of sales). Naturally, this is an identity. In fact, it is our old familiar circular flow. What all factors of production receive (PT) must equal what all factors of production spend (MV).

Just as our GNP identities are true at every moment, so are the quantity theory of money identities true at every instant. They merely look at the circular flow from a different vantage point. And just as our GNP identities yielded useful economic insights when we began to inquire into the functional relationships within those identities, so the quantity theory can also shed light on economic activity if we can find functional relationships concealed within its self-evident "truth."

Assumptions of the quantity theory

To move from tautologies to operationally useful relationships, we need to make assumptions that lend themselves to investigation and evidence. In the case of the GNP $\equiv C + G + I + X$ identity, for instance, we made a critical assumption about the propensity to consume, which led to the multiplier and to predictive statements about the influence of injections on GNP. In the case of $MV \equiv PT$, we need another assumption. What will it be?

The crucial assumptions made by the economists who first formulated the quantity theory were two: (1) the velocity of money—the number of times an average dollar was used per year—*was constant*; and (2) transactions (sales) *were always at a full-employment level.* If these assumptions were true, it followed that the price level was a simple function of the supply of money:

$$P = \frac{V}{T} \cdot M$$

$$P = kM$$

where k was a constant defined by V/T.

If the money supply went up, prices went up; if the quantity of money went down, prices went down. Since the government controlled the money supply, it could easily regulate the price level.

Testing the quantity theory

Is this causal relation true? Can we directly manipulate the price level by changing the size of our stock of money?

The original inventors of the quantity equation, over half a century ago, thought this was indeed the case. And of course it *would* be the case if everything else in the equation held steady while we moved the quantity of money up or down. In other words, if the velocity of circulation, V, and the number of transactions, T, were fixed, changes in M would have to operate directly on P.

Can we test the validity of this assumption? There is an easy way to do so. Figure 15 • 1 shows us changes in the supply of money compared with changes in the level of prices.

A glance at Fig. 15·1 answers our question. Between 1929 and 1973, the supply of money in the United States increased over eightfold, while prices rose only a little more than twofold. Clearly, something *must* have happened to V or to T to prevent the eightfold increase in M from bringing about a similar increase in P. Let us see what those changes were.

Changes in V

Figure 15·2 gives us a first clue as to what is wrong with a purely mechanical interpretation of the quantity theory. In it we show how many times an average dollar was used to help pay for each year's output.* We derive this number by dividing the total expenditure for each year's output (which is, of course, the familiar figure for GNP) by the actual supply of money—currency plus checking accounts—for each year. As the chart shows, the velocity of money fell by 50 percent between 1929 and 1946, only to rise again to the 1929 level over the postwar years.

We shall return later to an inquiry into why people spend money less or more quickly, but it is clear beyond question that they do. This has two important implications for our study of money. First, it gives a very cogent reason why we cannot apply the quantity theory in a mechanical way, asserting that an increase in the supply of money will *always* raise prices. For if people choose to spend the increased quantity of money more slowly, its impact on the quantity of goods may not change at all; whereas if they spend the same

quantity of money more rapidly, prices can rise without any change in M.

Second and more clearly than we have seen, the variability of V reveals that money itself can be a destabilizing force—destabilizing because it enables us to do two things that would be impossible in a pure barter economy. We can:

1. **delay between receiving and expending our rewards for economic effort**
2. **spend more or less than our receipts by drawing on, or adding to, our cash balances**

Classical economists used to speak of money as a "veil," implying that it did not itself play an active role in influencing the behavior of the economic players. But we can see that the ability of those players to vary the rate of their expenditure—to hang onto their money longer or to get rid of it more rapidly than usual—makes money much more than a veil. Money (or rather, people's wish to hold or to spend money) becomes an independent source of change in a complex economic society. To put it differently, the use of money introduces an independent element of uncertainty into the circular flow.*

Changes in T

Now we must turn to a last and perhaps most important reason why we cannot relate the supply of money to the price level in a mechanical fashion. This reason lies in the role played by T; that is, by the volume of output.

Just as the early quantity theorists thought of V as essentially unvarying, so they thought of T as a relatively fixed term in the quantity equation. In the minds of nearly all economic theorists before the Depression, output was always assumed to

---

*Note that final output is not quite the same as T, which embraces *all* transactions, including those for intermediate goods. But if we define T so that it includes only *transactions that enter into final output*, PT becomes a measure of gross national product. In the same way, we can count only those expenditures that enter into GNP when we calculate MV. It does no violence to the idea of the quantity theory to apply it only to final output, and it makes statistical computation far simpler.

*Technically, the standard economic definition of money is that it is both a means of exchange and a store of value. It is the latter characteristic that makes money a potentially disturbing influence.

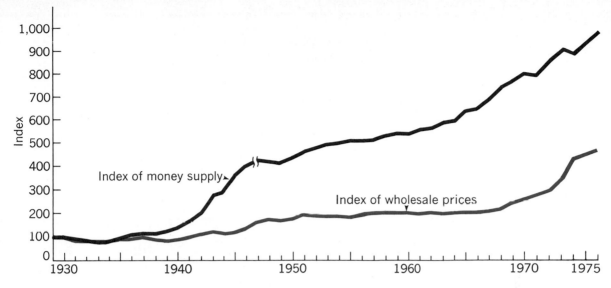

FIG. 15 · 1 Money supply and prices

be as large as the available resources and the willingness of the factors of production would permit. While everyone was aware that there might be minor variations from this state of full output, virtually no one thought they would be of sufficient importance to matter. Hence the quantity theory implicitly assumed full employment or full output as the normal condition of the economy. With such an assumption, it was easy to picture T as an unimportant term in the equation and to focus the full effect of changes in money on P.

The trauma of the Great Depression effectively removed the comfortable assumption that the economy "naturally" tended to full employment and output. At the bottom of the Depression, real output had fallen by 25 percent. Aside from what the Depression taught us in other ways, it made unmistakably clear that changes in the volume of output (and employment) were of crucial importance in the overall economic picture, and that the economy does not "naturally" graduate to full employment levels.

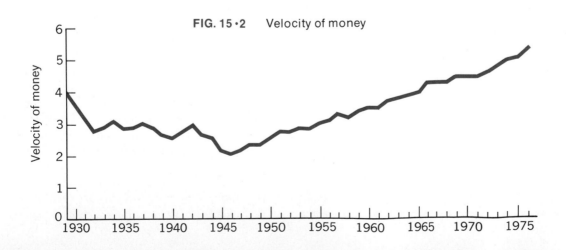

FIG. 15 · 2 Velocity of money

Output and prices

How does our modern emphasis on the variability of output and employment fit into the overall question of money and prices? The answer is very simple, but very important. **We have come to see that the effect of more money on prices cannot be determined unless we also take into account the effect of spending on the volume of transactions or output.**

It is not difficult to grasp the point. Let us picture an increase in spending, perhaps initiated by a business launching a new investment program or by the government inaugurating a new public works project. These new expenditures will be received by many other entrepreneurs, as the multiplier mechanism spreads the new spending through the economy. But now we come to the key question. What will entrepreneurs do as their receipts increase?

It is at this point that the question of output enters. For if factories or stores are operating *at less than full capacity,* and if there is an *employable supply of labor available,* the result of their new receipts is almost certain to be an increase in output. That is, employers will take advantage of the rise in demand, to produce and sell more goods and services. They may also try to raise prices and increase their profits further; but *if their industries are reasonably competitive,* it is doubtful that prices can be raised very much. Other firms with idle plants will simply undercut them and take their business away. An example is provided by the period 1934 through 1940, when output increased by 50 percent while prices rose by less than 5 percent. The reason, of course, lay in the great amount of unemployed resources, making it easy to expand output without price increases.

Prices and employment

Thus we reach a general conclusion of the greatest importance. *An increase in spending of any kind tends to result in more output and employment, with or without price increases, whenever there are considerable amounts of unemployed resources.* But this is no longer true when we reach a level of high employment or very full plant utilization. **Now an increase in spending *cannot* quickly lead to an increase in output, simply because the resources for more production are lacking.** The result, instead, can only be a rise in prices, for no firm can lose business to competitors when competitors are unable to fill additional orders. Thus the corollary of our general conclusion is that *additional spending from any source is inflationary when it is difficult to raise output.*

Full employment vs. under-employment

It is impossible to overstress the importance of this finding for macroeconomic policy. Policies that make sense when we are fully employed may make no sense when we are badly underemployed, and vice versa.

To spend more in the public or in the private sector is clearly good for an economy that is suffering from underutilized resources, but equally clearly inflationary and bad for an economy that is bumping up against the ceiling of output. Similarly, to balance budgets or run budget surpluses makes little sense when people are looking for work and business is looking for orders, but it is the course of wisdom when there are no idle resources to absorb the additional expenditure.

One of the main differences between contemporary economic thought and that of the past is precisely this sharp division between policies that make sense in full employment and those that make sense in conditions of underemployment. It was not that the economists of the past did not recognize the tragedy of unemployment or did not wish to remedy it. It was rather that they did not see how an economy could be in *equilibrium* even though there was heavy unemployment.

The dragging years of the Great Depression taught us not only that output could fall far below the levels of full utilization, but—perhaps this was its most intellectually unsettling feature—that an economy could be plagued with unemployed men and machines for almost a decade and yet not spontaneously generate the momentum to reabsorb them. Today we understand this condition of unemployment equilibrium, and we have devised various remedial measures to raise the equilibrium point to a satisfactory level, including, not least, additional public expenditure. But this new understanding must be balanced with a keen appreciation of its relevance to the underlying situation of employment. Remedies for an underemployed economy can be ills for a fully employed one.

Inflation and public finance

We can see that the conclusion we have reached puts a capstone on our previous analysis of deficit spending. It is now possible to add a major criterion to the question of whether or not to use the public sector as a supplement to the private sector. That criterion is whether or not substantially "full" employment has been reached.

If the economy is operating at or near the point of full employment, additional net public spending will only add more MV to a situation in which T is already at capacity and where, therefore, P will rise.

MAXIMUM VS. FULL EMPLOYMENT

What is "full" employment? Presumably government spending is guided by the objectives of the Employment Act of 1946, which declares the attainment of "maximum employment" to be a central economic objective of the government.

But what is "maximum" employment? Does it mean zero unemployment? This would mean that no one could quit his job even to look for a better one. Or consider the problem of inflation. Zero unemployment would probably mean extremely high rates of inflation, for reasons we will look into more carefully later. Hence no one claims that "full" employment is maximum employment in the sense of an absence of *any* unemployment whatsoever.

But this opens the question of how much *unemployment* is accepted as consistent with "maximum" employment. Under Presidents Kennedy and Johnson, the permissible unemployment rate was 4 percent. Under Presidents Nixon and Ford the permissible unemployment rate rose to a range of 4.5 to 5 or even 6 percent, largely because inflation had worsened. Hence the meaning of "full employment" is open to the discretion of the economic authorities, and their policies may vary from one period to another.

But note that this conclusion attaches to more than additional *public* spending. When full employment is reached, additional spending of any kind—public or private, consumption or investment—will increase MV and, given the ceiling on T, affect P.

A different conclusion is reached when there is large-scale unemployment. Now additional public (or private) spending will result not in higher prices, but in larger output and higher employment. Thus we cannot say that public spending in itself is "inflationary." Rather, we must see that *any kind of additional spending can be inflationary in a fully employed economy.*

Money and Expenditure

We have almost lost sight of our subject, which is not really inflation (we will come back to that in Chapter 16), but how money affects GNP. And here there is an important point. How does an increased supply of money get "into" GNP? People who have not studied economics often discuss changes in the money supply as if the government "put" money into circulation, mailing out dollar bills to taxpayers. The actual connection between an increase in M and an increase in MV is much more complex. Let us look into it.

Interest rates and the transactions demand for money

From our previous chapter, we know the immediate results of an increased supply of money, whether brought about by open-market operations or a change in reserve ratios. *The effect in both cases is a rise in the lendable or investible reserves of banks.* Ceteris paribus, this will lead to a fall in interest rates as banks compete with one another in lending their additional unused reserves to firms or individuals.

As interest rates decline, some firms and individuals will be tempted to increase their borrowings. It becomes cheaper to take out a mortgage, to buy a car on an installment loan, to finance inventories. Thus, as we would expect, the demand curve for "spending money," like that for most commodities, slopes downward. As money gets cheaper, people want to "buy" (borrow) more of it. To put it differently, the lower the price of money, the larger the quantity demanded. We speak of this demand curve for money to be used for expenditure as the *transactions demand for money.*

Financial demand

But there is also another, quite separate source of the demand for money. This is the demand for money for *financial purposes,* to be held by individuals or corporations as part of their assets.

What happens to the demand for money for financial purposes as its price goes down? Financial demand also increases, although for different reasons. When interest rates are high, individuals and firms tend to keep their wealth as fully invested as possible, in order to earn the high return that is available. But when interest rates fall, the opportunity cost of keeping money idle is much less. If you are an investor with a portfolio of $10,000, and the rate of interest is 7 percent, you give up $700 a year if you are very "liquid" (i.e., all in cash); whereas if the interest rate is only 3 percent, your opportunity cost for liquidity falls to $300.

Liquidity preference

Economists call this increased willingness to be in cash as interest rates fall *liquidity preference*. The motives behind liquidity preferences are complex—partly speculative, partly precautionary. With low opportunity costs for holding money, we can afford to hold cash for any good investment or consumption opportunity that happens to come along. Similarly, it is cheaper to hold more money to protect ourselves against any unexpected emergencies.

In this way, both the speculative and precautionary motives make us more and more willing or eager to be in cash when interest rates are low, and less and less willing when rates are higher. Thus the financial demand for cash, like the transactions demand, is a downward sloping demand curve.

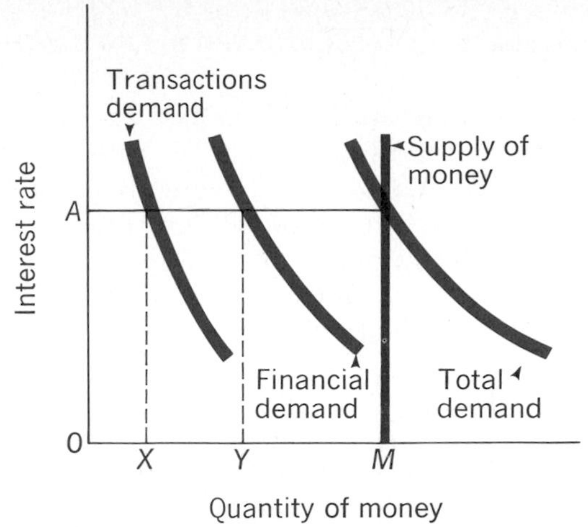

FIG. 15·3   Transactions and financial demands for money

Demand curve for money

We can now put together the two demand curves for money and add the supply curve of money—the actual stock of money available. The result looks like Fig. 15 · 3.

PRECAUTIONARY AND SPECULATIVE DEMAND

Both the precautionary and the speculative demand for money can be illustrated in the problem of buying or selling bonds. Most bonds are a promise to pay a certain stated amount of interest and to repay the principal at some fixed date. To simplify things, forget the repayment for a moment and focus on the interest. Suppose that you paid $1,000 for a perpetual bond that had a "coupon"—an interest return—of $100 per year with no date of repayment. And suppose that you wanted to sell that bond. What would it be worth?

The answer depends wholly on the current market rate of interest for bonds of equal risk. Suppose that this rate of interest were 10 percent. Your bond would then still be worth $1,000, because the coupon would yield the buyer of the bond 10 percent on his money. But suppose that interest rates had risen to 20 percent. You would now find that your bond was only worth $500. A buyer can go into the market and purchase other bonds that will give him a 20 percent yield on his money. Therefore he will pay you only $500 for your bond, because your $100

coupon is 20 percent of $500. If you want to sell your bond, that is the price you will have to accept.

On the other hand, if interest rates have fallen to 5 percent, you can get $2,000 for your bond, for you can show the buyer that your $100 coupon will give him the going market return of 5 percent at a price of $2,000. (If you were to buy a *new* $1,000 bond at the going 5 percent interest rates, it would carry a coupon of only $50.)

As these numbers indicate, enormous capital gains or losses can be made as market rates of interest change. Your $1,000 bond can fluctuate from $500 to $2,000 if interest rates rise to 20 percent and then drop to 5 percent.

These calculations also show that it can be very profitable at times to hold money. When interest rates are rising, bond prices are falling. Therefore, the longer you wait before

you buy, the bigger will be your chances for a capital gain if interest rates turn around and go the other way. This means that we tend to get "liquid" whenever we think that interest rates are below "normal" levels and bonds are too high; and that we tend to get out of money and into bonds whenever we think that interest rates are above normal levels, and therefore bonds are cheap. The trick, of course, is being right about the course of interest rates before everyone else.

Actual operations in the bond market are complicated, because we must take into account not only interest rates but the time left until a bond becomes "mature" (i.e., is repaid). The closer it is to maturity, the less its price will depart from its face value or principal. Nonetheless, very great gains and losses can be made in bonds that have some years to go before maturity. Even the most "conservative" bonds, such as government bonds, will swing in price as our speculative and precautionary impulses incline us now toward liquidity, now towards a fully-invested position.

Our diagram shows us that at interest rate OA, there will be OX amount of money demanded for transactions purposes and OY amount demanded for liquidity purposes. The total demand for money will be OM (= OX + OY), which is just equal to the total supply.

Changing the supply of money

Now let us suppose that the monetary authorities reduce the supply of money. We show this in Fig. 15 • 4. Now we have a curious situation. The supply of money has declined from OM to OM'. But notice that the demand curve for money shows that firms and individuals want to hold OM, at the given rate of interest OA. *Yet they cannot hold amount* OM, *because the monetary authorities have cut the supply to* OM'. What will happen?

The answer is very neat. As bank reserves fall, banks will "tighten" money—raise lending rates and screen loan applications more carefully. Therefore individuals and firms will be competing for a reduced supply of loans and will bid more for them. At the same

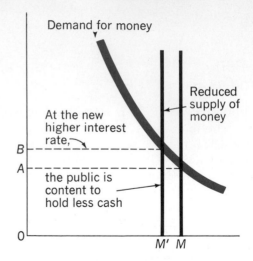

FIG. 15 • 5   Determination of new equilibrium

time, individuals and firms will feel the pinch of reduced supplies of cash and will try to get more money to fulfill their liquidity desires. The easiest way to get more money is to sell securities, to get out of bonds and into cash. Note, however, that selling securities does not create a single additional dollar of money. It simply transfers money from one holder to another. But it does change the rate of interest. As bonds are sold, their price falls; and as the price of bonds falls, the interest yield on bonds rises (see p. 221).

Our next diagram (Fig. 15 • 5) shows what happens. As interest rates rise, the public is content to hold a smaller quantity of money. Hence a new interest rate, OB, will emerge, at which the public is *willing* to hold the money that there *is to hold*. The attempt to become more liquid ceases, and a new equilibrium interest rate prevails.

Suppose the authorities had increased the supply of money. In that case, individuals and firms would be holding more money than they wanted at the going rate of interest. They would try to get out of money, into bonds, sending bond prices up and yields down. Simultaneously, banks would find themselves with extra

FIG. 15 • 4   Reducing the supply of money

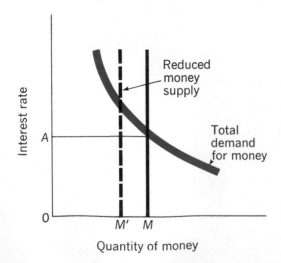

Quantity of money

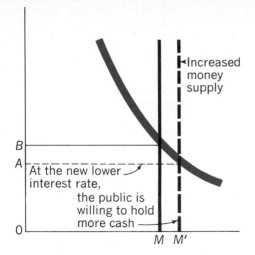

FIG. 15·6   Increasing the supply of money

reserves and would compete with one another for loans, also driving interest rates down. As interest rates fell, firms and individuals would be content to hold more money either for transactions or liquidity purposes, until a new equilibrium was again established. Fig. 15·6 shows the process at work.

Determination of interest rates

This gives us the final link in our argument. We have seen that interest rates determine whether we wish to hold larger or smaller balances, either for transactions or financial (liquidity) purposes. But what determines the interest rate itself? We can now see that the *answer is the interplay of our demand for money and the supply of money.*

Our demand for money is made up of our transactions demand curve and our financial (liquidity) demand curve. The supply of money is given to us by the monetary authorities. The price of money—interest—is therefore determined by the demand for, and supply of, money, exactly as the price of any commodity is determined by the demand and supply for it.

Money and expenditure

What our analysis enables us to see, however, is that once the interest rate is determined, it will affect the use to which we put a given supply of money. Now we begin to understand the full answer to the question of how changes in the supply of money affect GNP (and prices). Let us review the argument one last time.

1. Suppose that the monetary authorities want to increase the supply of money. They will lower reserve ratios or buy government bonds on the open market.

2. Banks will find that they have larger reserves. They will compete with one another and lower lending rates.

3. Individuals and firms will also find that they have larger cash balances than they want at the going rate of interest. They will try to get rid of their extra cash by buying bonds, thereby sending bond yields down.

4. As interest rates fall, both as a result of bank competition and rising bond prices, the new, larger supply of money will find its way into use. *Part of it will be used for additional transactions purposes, as individuals and firms take advantage of cheaper money and increase their borrowings. Part of it will be used for larger financial balances, as the public's desire for liquidity grows with falling interest rates.*

The process in diagram

We can see the process very clearly in Fig. 15·7. We begin with *OM* money supply and a rate of interest *OA*. As we can see, *OL* amount of money is held for liquidity purposes, and *OY* for transactions purposes. Now the stock of money is increased to *OM'*. The interest rate falls, for the reasons we now understand, until it reaches *OB*. At the

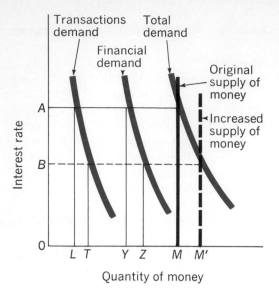

Transactions demand

Financial demand

Total demand

Original supply of money

Increased supply of money

A

B

Interest rate

0

L T   Y Z   M M'

Quantity of money

FIG. 15 · 7   Using money for two purposes

new interest rate, liquidity balances have increased to *OT*, and transactions balances to *OZ*.

Exactly the same process would take place in reverse if the stock of money were decreased from *OM'* to *OM*. Can you see that the decreased supply of money will result partly in smaller transactions balances and partly in smaller liquidity balances? Do you understand that it is the higher rate of interest that causes the public to hold these smaller balances?

Monetarism

We have traced the circuitous manner in which a change in *M* "gets into" GNP. But there is yet another route that bypasses the rate of interest entirely. The "monetarist" school suggests that increases in *M* directly affect our spending habits, *even though interest rates remain unchanged.*

The monetarists suggest that changes in the supply of money directly affect our spending propensities because changes in the money supply alter our portfolios. A portfolio describes the way in which we hold our assets—in cash, savings accounts, checking accounts, various kinds of bonds,

stocks, real estate, etc. When the money supply is altered, for example through open-market operations, the government is tempting the public to shift its portfolios into cash. But there is no reason to believe that the public wants this much cash. If it *had* wanted it, it would not have held the bonds (at their going rate of interest) in the first place. Therefore the public will seek to reduce its undesired cash holdings by buying real assets—cars, homes, inventories, and other things.

Most economists are willing to add this *liquidity effect* to the *interest rate effect*, so that monetary policy is believed to affect the economy both through its impact on the price of money and also directly through its impact on our portfolio preferences. What remains in doubt is the degree of influence that should be attributed to interest or to liquidity.

Modern quantity theory

We are now in a position to reformulate the quantity theory. Modern proponents of the theory recognize that economies do not always operate at full employment and that the velocity of money changes (we can see that liquidity preferences must be closely related to velocity). Hence they do not argue that an increase in the quantity of money is mechanically reflected in a proportionate rise in prices.

Instead, they contend that the demands for money for transaction purposes and liquidity purposes are *calculable functions*, just as consumption is a calculable function of income. The variables on which the demand for money depend are very complex—too complex to warrant explanation here. What is important is the idea that the relation between an increase in money supply and in transactions and financial demand can be estimated, much as the propensity to consume is estimated.

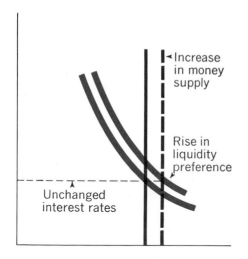

Increase
in money
supply

Rise in
liquidity
preference

Unchanged
interest rates

FIG. 15 · 8　A shift in liquidity preference

The Art of Money Management

We finally have all the pieces of the puzzle. We understand the curiously complex way in which changes in the supply of money affect changes in the expenditures of the public. It remains only to consider one aspect of the problem: the art of managing the supply of money so that the *right* increases in the supply of money will be forthcoming at the right time.

Why "art"? Is not the task of the monetary authority very clear? By increasing the supply of money, it pushes down interest rates and encourages expenditure. Hence all it has to do is to regulate the quantity of money to maintain a level of spending that will keep us at a high, but not too high, level of employment.

We have already seen some of the reasons why things are not that simple. The effect of interest rates on investment expenditure, as we previously learned, is obscure. So is the effect of liquidity on expenditure. We know that unwanted liquidity will encourage spending, but

there is a time lag involved, and this lag may vary considerably at different phases of the business cycle. To add to the problem, the Federal Reserve Board can control the money supply with an eye on interest rates, or it can control it with an eye on liquidity effects, but it cannot do both at the same time. As a result, sometimes the board seems to focus entirely on the "price effect" of interest rates, and at other times on the liquidity effect of money supply. When two policies clash and there is no scientific means of judging between them, we trust to good sense or to a "feel" of the economy. Hence the need for an "art" of money management.

Shifting liquidity preferences　Still another difficulty enforces the need for artful control. Suppose, for example, that the Federal Reserve creates excess reserves, in the expectation that interest rates will go down and that new loans will be pumped into investment. But suppose that at the same time, the public's "liquidity preferences" are rising because investors feel nervous and want to be more liquid. Then the shift in the quantity of money, as shown in Fig. 15 · 8, will be offset by a shift in liquidity preferences, and the rate of interest will not change at all! The new money will simply wind up in larger financial cash holdings, and none will be available for more transactions.

In other words, an attempt by the monetary authorities to drive down the rate of interest in order to encourage expenditure may be frustrated if the public uses all the additional funds for liquidity. At the bottom of the Great Depression, for example, banks had huge excess reserves because business would not risk expenditure for new capital projects. People had an insatiable desire for liquidity, and no attempted reductions of the rate of interest could persuade them to spend the money they held for security.

In the same way, an attempt to raise interest rates and to halt price inflation by making credit tight may come to naught if the public reacts to higher interest rates by giving up its liquidity, thereby making funds available to others to finance increased transactions expenditure. Or take another instance: if the Fed tries to lower interest rates by increasing M, the effort may result in a general expectation of inflation and a movement out of bonds into stocks. In that case, interest rates, instead of falling, will go up! This actually happened in 1968.

Credit crunches

Still another difficulty of monetary management lies in *credit crunches*. These occur whenever the monetary authorities attempt to brake the economy quickly, as they did in 1974. Such braking periods are called crunches, since curtailments in the growth of the money supply do not evenly affect all sectors of the economy. Interest rates go up rapidly, but lending institutions also "ration" credit. Mortgage loans, for example, were almost unattainable at any rate of interest during the late fall of 1974. Banks also had to reduce their lending, and they directed their available funds toward large regular customers rather than small or less regular customers.

The uneven reduction in lending was very marked in the crunch of 1974. While residential and state and municipal lending declined by 24 percent, corporate lending rose by 114 percent. Even these figures understate the differences among sectors of the economy. Large corporations were not only able to gain more domestic loans than small business or local governments, but they also had access to international money markets. Thus to some extent they were exempt from the control of domestic monetary authorities. Many large firms, for instance, borrowed in West Germany to make investments in the United States.

But even large corporations can run into trouble during credit crunches. In the 1968 crunch the Chrysler Corporation, one of the largest industrial enterprises in the nation, almost collapsed. And the Penn Central did collapse. Such disasters, together with the uneven effects of a crunch, place a limit on monetary policies. Very stringent restraints seem both institutionally and politically impossible. After the 1969–1970 credit crunch, efforts were made to develop financial intermediaries that would lend to the sectors most severely hurt and thus spread the effects of monetary policies more evenly across the economy. During the 1974 recession, however, these intermediaries proved to be ineffective. A painful credit crunch occurred despite these new institutions, and it will likely reoccur whenever monetary policies shift sharply toward restriction

Monetary and fiscal policy

All these problems of monetary management help us understand why economists are generally reluctant to entrust the overall regulation of the economy to monetary policy alone. There is too much slippage between changes in the money supply and changes in expenditure; too little reliability as to the effects of changes in M on desired changes in MV.

Thus we look for our overall controls to both monetary policies and fiscal policies. Few economists today would rely solely on the money mechanism to move the general economy. Instead, they seek a combination of monetary and fiscal policies—easy money and more government spending (or tax cuts), or tight money and a public budgetary surplus.

Focus

The purpose of this lesson is to learn how monetary policy works—that is, how changes in the supply of money affect the economy. Therefore, we begin with a consideration of the quantity theory, one of the first attempts to explain the effects of a change in M.

The quantity theory erred because it believed that *V* and *T* were constants. We know now that they are not, especially *T* (the level of output). Hence, we must look for a better explanation of how changes in M will affect P or PT, the value of output (GNP). The critical link is through the rate of interest.

The monetary authorities cannot themselves decree that all interest rates must change. They can only alter the stock of money. But they know that changes in money must affect bank reserves. In turn, changes in bank reserves will usually lead banks to increase or decrease loans and investments. As a result, the public will be more or less liquid than before the change. If it is more liquid, it will try to get rid of its unwanted cash by buying bonds. This will send bond prices up and bond yields (interest rates) down. At lower interest rates, the public will hold its new larger cash balances. And at lower interest rates it will also be tempted to spend more.

This sequence of events or its reverse is not easy to understand immediately. The best way to master it is to trace very carefully, step by step, the effects of both an increase in money stock and a decrease. In imagination you can put yourself in the position of an entrepreneur and picture the effect of changing interest rates on your propensity to spend. You can also try to imagine how an investor would rearrange his or her holdings between a checking account and a portfolio of stocks and bonds if interest rates changed from 5 percent to 12 percent. Working through question 6 will help you here.

The purpose of learning this intricate web of connections must always be kept uppermost in your mind. We want to discover how the central bank can affect the level of GNP. This forces us to trace the elaborate chain of cause and effect from changes in bank reserves to the ultimate changes in spending.

Finally, as with fiscal policy, it is plain that monetary management is an art, not a mechanical procedure. Nonetheless, it is an art based on a scientific theory of behavior. It is this theory that you want to master in this chapter.

WORDS AND CONCEPTS YOU SHOULD KNOW

QUESTIONS

1. Why is the quantity equation a truism? Why is the interpretation of the quantity equation that *M* affects *P* not a truism?

2. The basic reason why the original quantity theorists thought that *M* affected *P* was their belief that *V* and *T* were fixed. Discuss the validity of these beliefs.

3. Why is the level of employment a critical determinant of fiscal policy?

4. If employment is "full," what will be the effects of an increase in private investment on prices and output, supposing that everything else stays the same?

5. In what way can an increase in excess reserves affect *V* or *T*? Is there any certainty that an increase in reserves will lead to an increase in *V* or *T*?

6. Suppose that you had $1,000 in the bank. Would you be more willing to invest it if you could earn 2 percent or 5 percent? What factors could make you change your mind about investing all or any part at, say, 5 percent? Could you imagine conditions that would make you unwilling to invest even at 10 percent? Other conditions that would lead you to invest your whole cash balance at, say, 3 percent?

7. Suppose that the going rate of interest is 7 percent and that the monetary authorities want to curb expenditures and act to lower the quantity of money. What will the effect be in terms of the public's feeling of liquidity? What will the public do if it feels short of cash? Will it buy or sell securities? What would this do to their price? What would thereupon happen to the rate of interest? To investment expenditures?

8. Suppose that the monetary and fiscal authorities want to encourage economic expansion. What are the general measures that each should take? What problems might changing liquidity preference interpose?

9. Do you unconsciously keep a "liquidity balance" among your assets? Suppose that your cash balance rose. Would you be tempted to spend more?

10. Show in a diagram how a decrease in the supply of money will be reflected in lower transactions balances and in lower financial balances. What is the mechanism that changes these balances?

11. Do you understand (a) how the rate of interest is determined; (b) how it affects our willingness to hold cash? Is this in any way different from the mechanism by which the price of shoes is determined or the way in which the price of shoes affects our willingness to buy them?

Monetarism

Monetarism is a theory that has had a great vogue during the past few years. In its purest form it is associated with the name of Milton Friedman, an eminent economist and staunch philosophic conservative. Monetarism has two basic tenets. First, it claims that *only* monetary policies affect the long-run level of economic activity. In the slogan of the day, only money "matters"; fiscal policies don't count. Second, within the area of monetary policy proper, monetarists hold that central banks should concern themselves only with the supply of money (which should grow at a steady rate), and not with the level of interest rates. In other words, only the quantity of money counts, not its price!

Why do the monetarists take these seemingly extreme positions? Basically their argument rests on the assumption that any increase in government expenditures will lead to an equal and offsetting decrease in private expenditures (investment or consumption), unless the money supply rises to accommodate the larger public spending. The reasoning is that the government will have to gather the funds for additional spending either by taxing, which will dry up private spending, or by borrowing, which will cause interest rates to rise. Higher interest costs and less credit availability for the public sector will lead to a fall in investment or consumption spending. Thus what the government gains, the private sector loses.

Is this argument valid? Some economists believe that increased public expenditures do crowd out private expenditures. Others think that the "crowding out" is only a partial, not an entire, phenomenon. Still others stress that the "crowding out" is a long-run process and that the government can still effectively use short-run, antibusiness cycle spending, even if the long-run effect of higher spending is nil.

It will take more empirical investigation before we know how valid the first monetarist contention is. Meanwhile, there is an interesting implication in the monetarist position, quite in opposition to the conservative, generally antigovernment spending position of Professor Friedman and his followers. For if only money matters, it follows that inflations are wholly and solely monetary problems. That is, they must be caused by the monetary authorities, not by government fiscal policies. It follows, then, that the government can run a very large deficit with impunity, because its policies will exert no lasting effect on the economy! Curiously, what starts out as a conservative argument against the usefulness of government spending ends up as an argument that can justify rapidly rising government spending, because no monetarist can argue that it is inflationary unless financed by expanding the money supply!

Now what about central bank policy? Here the monetarist position also hinges on an empirical question: namely, is spending affected, in the long term, by the price of money or by its sheer availability, regardless of price? Once again, we do not have enough facts to give us an answer. Therefore, the Fed carries on its day-by-day activities with one eye on interest rates and one on the money supply. In times of accelerating inflation, it tends to lay more emphasis on credit availability; and by braking the expansion of credit, it brings about those crunches we have talked about. In periods of low inflation, the Fed pays more heed to interest rates. This mixed policy implies that credit availability is a more powerful deterrent to spending than are high interest rates, but that low interest rates are a more powerful stimulus for spending than easy money is, by itself.

Because business conditions can change rapidly, and because the monetary authorities necessarily rely on facts that are already "old" to determine policy for the future, monetary policies tend to move rapidly from expansionary to contractionary operations—the Fed buying bonds in the open market one week and selling them the next. The monetarists believe that these attempts to use money as a "fine tuning" device are bound to fail. They would like to hitch the growth in the supply of money to long-term steady factors, such as the growth in productivity. By expanding the money supply by a fixed amount—say, 0.3 percent—each month, the monetarists believe they would be introducing a powerful force for stability into the economy. Whether they are right depends on whether only the supply of money "matters." And that, as we have seen, we just don't know.

For all the uncertainty that surrounds its more extreme beliefs, monetarism has had a strong influence on modern economic thought. This is because many economists during the 1950s and 1960s tended to overlook the importance of money. Just as generals are said always to be prepared to fight the last war, so economists are ready to solve yesterday's problems. Brought up in the traumatic memory of the Great Depression, economists were inclined to place heavy emphasis on the power of spending to prevent this kind of collapse from recurring. But their emphasis on the power of spending and their disregard of the power of money were less relevant for an age dominated by inflation. It is almost certainly not true that *only* money matters. But there is no question that money does matter, and economists are grateful to Milton Friedman for calling to their attention this forgotten truth.

The problem of inflation

In Chapter 1 we looked at inflation, the problem Americans worry about most. Now we are finally in a position to examine that problem more thoroughly. This does not mean we will discover answers to questions we earlier described as ill-understood. Inflation remains something of an economic puzzle. But now we can do what was impossible before we had mastered a good deal of economics. We can divide inflation into its ABC, which we *do* understand, and its XYZ, which we don't.

The ABC of the Inflationary Process

What do we know about inflation? A good way to start is by refreshing our memories of how an individual price rises. As we have seen, prices go up when demand curves shift to the right or when supply curves shift to the left. This happens all the time in innumerable markets. Are these price rises "inflationary"?

16

249

Supply and demand once again

The question begins to sharpen our understanding of what we mean by inflation. In the first place, *inflation means that individual prices must be going up in all or nearly all markets at the same time.* Price rises in some markets, offset by price declines in others, are not an inflationary situation.

Second, *inflation means that the shift of supply and demand curves does not result in a new stable equilibrium.* In an inflationary economy there is no stable price level. Prices rise—and then rise higher. Inflation is a process, not a once-for-all shift.

Supply and demand curves

Our supply and demand apparatus can help us go deeper into the question, for we can see that an inflationary process must be characterized by two elements in the supply/demand picture. **First, demand curves must be moving outwards, to the right. Second, supply curves must be upward sloping.** That describes ratner than explains things, but it also tells us where to look for explanations.

Changes in total demand

Part of the explanation we already understand. **The continuing rightward shift in demand curves is the result of *a continuous rise in the volume of expenditure.*** More and more dollars are earned and spent. This in turn means that the supply of money must be increasing, or that the velocity of circulation must be constantly increasing, or both. *MV* must be rising if the national price level is rising. You cannot have inflation unless demand curves in most markets are shifting to the right, and this in

turn cannot occur unless money incomes and expenditures are rising in the economy.

The supply constraint: bottlenecks

But this is only half the picture. There is also the question of supply. A rightward shift of a demand curve will not cause prices to rise in a market if the supply curve shifts outward to meet it or if the industry is producing under conditions of constant or decreasing cost. Thus, **corresponding to the rightward shift in total demand must come an upward tilt in supply curves, as Fig. 16·1 shows.**

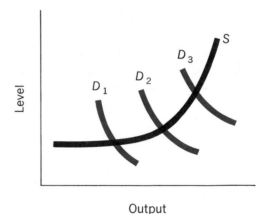

FIG. 16·1   The bottleneck supply curve

As demand moves from D_1 to D_2, prices hardly rise at all. But the shift from D_2 to D_3 brings a sharp increase because we run into *bottlenecks* where output cannot be further increased except at much higher cost. These bottlenecks, moreover, may begin to exert their constricting influence before the economy as a whole can be considered in a condition of overall full employment. Thus as demand curves for various goods and services move outward, we will experience price rises in some industries, even though there is unused capacity in others or even though considerable unemployment exists. If these industries bulk large in the pattern of production or in consumer budgets—for example, if we hit bottlenecks in steel or food output—the general price level will begin to rise.

Demand pull vs. cost push

Economists sometimes talk about the two processes that enter into inflation as *demand pull* or *cost push*. Demand pull focuses attention on forces that are causing thousands of demand curves to move to the right—for example, policies of easy money or expansionary fiscal policy. Cost push emphasizes the supply side, with cost curves moving to the left or becoming more vertical.

Cost-push analyses often concentrate on the wage level as a prime causative agency for inflation. Of course, rising wages can be a source of higher costs. But it is important to distinguish between increases in *wage costs per hour* and increases in *wage costs per unit*. Wages may rise; but if *labor productivity keeps pace, cost per unit will not rise* (see box on p. 8).

Corresponding to cost push from rising wage costs per unit, there is cost push from higher profits, an argument frequently put forward by labor. Again we must distinguish between higher profits for the company and higher profits per unit. The latter may occur if the increase in demand outruns the increase in productive capacity, strengthening the market power of large companies.

No doubt there are periods in which the immediate inflationary pressure seems to come from more spending or when it comes from a jump in costs, but it is wrong to separate the two entirely. *More spend-*

ing without higher unit costs will give us more output at the same price, and this is certainly not inflationary. Higher unit costs will lead to inflation only if they occur across the economy. Otherwise, higher unit costs in one area will simply cause people to rearrange their expenditure patterns, moderating the overall inflationary effect.

The Phillips curve

To determine the inflationary pressure in thousands of markets, each with a different configuration of supply and demand curves, would be an impossible task. Hence, the English economist A. W. Phillips has suggested that we show the general relationship between higher wages and/or profits per unit and the degree of capacity utilization. As industries move toward higher rates of utilization, their costs per unit begin to mount more steeply. This is because they are operating in ever tighter markets, especially for labor. Hence Phillips has drawn a curve showing the overall relationship between unemployment, a good indicator

FIG. 16·2   The Phillips curve

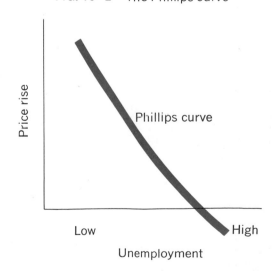

of capacity utilization, and the rise in prices. As Fig. 16·2 shows, the lower unemployment falls, the higher is the tendency toward inflation.

Phillips curves are often interpreted as if they implied a causal relationship between employment and inflation, but that is not what the curves actually show. All that we can deduce from the Phillips curve is that there seems to be a statistical relation between high employment rates and high inflation rates. *That is not the same thing as saying that high employment is the cause of high inflation.* It may well be that both high employment and rapid inflation are the consequences of another element not shown on the chart; for example, rising aggregate demand or aggressive monetary expansion.

The trade-off dilemma   The Phillips curve does more than point out a general empirical relationship between employment and price rises. To the extent that the Phillips curve represents reality (a subject that we shall investigate later in this chapter), it also points up a fundamental dilemma. The dilemma is that we cannot choose one target for unemployment and another target for the price level, *independent of each other*. We cannot, for example, "decide" to have 2 percent inflation and 2 percent unemployment, because we do not know how to reconcile low unemployment and low inflation rates. *We have to trade off unemployment against price stability.* The dilemma thus imposes a cruel choice. Governments must choose between alternatives, *both* of which are painful and costly. Before we investigate the means by which they seek to bring about whatever choice they finally make, let us inquire into the costs of these alternatives.

Economic Costs of Unemployment

Suppose the government decides to lessen inflation by increasing the rate of unemployment. What does this cost?

The unemployment option   We can begin with a fairly straightforward estimate of the losses that result from unemployment. For each percentage point of increase in the official unemployment figures, United States' gross national product falls by about 3 percent, or roughly $51 billion. The percentage reduction in GNP is much larger than the percentage increase in officially measured unemployment because (as we shall see on page 268), the labor force and the hours worked per week both shrink as employment opportunities shrink.

Is this, then, the cost of choosing the unemployment "option"? Not quite. For the losses of output and income are by no means equally distributed. If increasing the unemployment rate from 4.5 to 5.5 percent meant that each person found himself unemployed for 14 instead of only 11 out of 250 working days, the income losses would be evenly shared among the labor force. On the other hand, if the additional one percent of unemployment meant that one percent of the working force was permanently unemployed all year, then the costs of unemployment would be entirely concentrated on this group.

If most people were asked which of the two ways of bearing the costs of unemployment were more equitable, they would probably choose the first. But in fact, the way unemployment is actually shared is closer to the second. Joblessness tends to concentrate in certain groups, especially in cyclical downswings. For instance, when the white unemployment rate rises by 1 percentage point, black unemployment rises by 2 percentage points. So, too, in 1976 when the average rate of unemployment among married men was only 4.2 percent, among young workers (16 to 19 years old) it was more than 19 percent. For white workers as a whole it was 7.0 percent; for black workers, 13.1 percent; among black teenagers it was 39 percent. To repeat a fact from Chapter 1: in 1975, 15 percent of the unemployed—over 1.3 million people—had been without work for over half a year.

To be sure, these costs are partly—but only partly—offset by unemployment insurance, as we shall see in our next chapter. But there is no doubt that the costs, psychic as well as economic, are very heavy. And they are not confined solely to workers without jobs. Capitalists also bear some of the loss of unemployment. When aggregate demand falls, output declines. As a result, profits fall; and because management is reluctant to fire overhead office staff, profits often fall more rapidly than output. As in the case of the labor force, the losses borne by firms are not evenly shared. Some industries, such as durable goods, tend to bear more than their share. Others, such as household staples, are relatively depression-proof.

Economic Costs of Inflation

As we have seen, the costs of unemployment tend to be concentrated among certain groups or industries, rather than diffusely shared by all. Now, what of the costs of inflation? Are they also concentrated? Do they resemble the costs of unemployment?

Inflation and income

Let us begin to answer this very important question by reviewing an important, familiar fact. It is our old identity between gross national product and gross national income. We recall that all costs of GNP must become the incomes of the factors of production. This gives us the knowledge that whenever the monetary value of GNP goes up, so must the monetary value of gross national income. This is true whether the increase in GNP results from increased output or higher prices, for in either case the factors of production must receive the monetary value of the output they have produced.

This provides a very important point of departure in comparing unemployment and inflation. **For the nation as a whole, inflation cannot decrease the total of incomes.** Here it differs sharply from unemployment. Whenever unemployment increases, there is a loss in potential GNP. But whatever the price at which GNP is sold, the real output of the nation remains the same—at least up to the point at which hyperinflation threatens to destroy the system itself.

A zero sum game

Discussions of inflation tend to overlook this fact. They often speak of the losses that inflation brings to this or that group. Of course inflation *can* lower an individual's standard of living by raising the prices he or she must pay. **But since the total GNI is equal to GNP, one person's loss must be transferred as a gain to another.** This in no way lessens the importance or even the dangers of inflations. But it makes clear that unlike unemployment, in which there are losers but no gainers, in inflation every loss is offset by an equal gain. We call this a *zero sum game*. What is important, then, is to try to weigh the benefits that inflation gives to some, against the losses it inflicts on others.

Who gains by inflation? Who loses?

Winners and losers

Speculators are one group of winners. During an inflation everything does not rise by the same amount or at the same rate. Some items will shoot up, others lag behind, just as in a booming stock market not all stocks share alike in the rise. Speculators are those lucky or skillful individuals who have bought goods that enjoy the sharpest rises. This may be land, gold, or (in hyperinflations) food. Indeed, one of the reasons that hyperinflations result in a collapse of GNP is that more and more persons are *forced* to become speculators, seeking to sell or trade possessions for basic necessities. As individuals spend more and more time trading or scrounging, they begin to spend less and less time at their regular jobs. Thus output begins to fall, and we have the strange coexistence of an economic collapse and soaring prices.

Fixed-income receivers

By definition, anyone who lives on a fixed income, such as an annuity, must be a loser in inflation. Therefore retirees, as a group, seem certain to be badly penalized when prices continually rise. Curiously, they are not. Undoubtedly, there exist the much advertised widows and orphans living off small pensions, but they are probably a very small group. Most retirees live on (or depend largely on) Social Security, and this is quite another story. Social Security benefits have been periodically hiked up by Congress, so that a typical recipient in 1973 was well ahead of the game in terms of the purchasing power of benefits he received. Moreover, in 1973, Congress added to Social Security a cost-of-living escalator clause that automatically adjusted Social Security payments to compensate for cost-of-living increases. Welfare recipients have also had their benefits periodically increased, and they too, have not come out behind in the race since 1950.

Labor and capital

What about labor and capital? Table 16·1 gives us a breakdown of the income shares of strategic groups as a percentage of GNP for the last 25 years.

Table 16·1   Pretax income shares as percentage of GNP*

Year	Capital income Cash flow (corp. profits + depreciation) and interest income	Labor income (wages and other income)	Proprietors' income	Rental income	Income redistribution Transfer income
1950	29.0%	54.1%	13.4%	3.5%	5.3%
1960	28.9	58.3	9.3	3.5	5.7
1970	28.8	62.0	6.6	2.6	8.1
1976	30.8	60.8	6.0	2.4	11.3

*Totals add to more than 100 percent because of transfers.

We must be cautious in reading this table, as we shall see, but it shows some important results. First, let us compare 1950 and 1975. Capital income as a percentage of GNP has barely changed during the last twenty-plus years. Many factors besides inflation influence corporate profits, but it is clear that inflation by itself has not been enough to increase profits.

Second, over the 25-year period, labor income has increased as a share of GNP. Here again a caution is needed: note the decline in proprietors' income in the third column. Much of that decline is the result of proprietors' giving up independent establishments to work for large enterprises. Their proprietors' income has become "wages." But if we add labor income and proprietors' income, we find that their combined share was just under 67.5 percent in 1950 and 66.8 percent in 1976 a trifling change. Landlords' income (rental income) has evidently fallen considerably as a share of GNP, as we would expect, since rents always lag behind rising prices. And transferees, as we have already seen, were strong gainers.

Changes in recent years

These are long-term trends. But what about the period from 1970 to 1975, when we had a combination of rapid inflation and high unemployment? As the table also shows, the shares of various sectors of the economy did not show any dramatic change.

Of course, just as in the case of unemployment, the impact of inflation is not evenly spread across all groups. Some unions made better settlements than others; some landlords may have made profits while others had losses. But this jockeying for position is a normal state of affairs, and there is no evidence to show that inflation has systematically biased the outcome of the race for real income in comparison with noninflationary times.

We buttress this conclusion if we examine the statistics for the distribution of income among families during the years of high inflation and mounting unemployment. Table 16 • 2 shows the shares of income going to various income groups in the nation in 1970 and 1975. Again, we see little or no evidence that inflation has brought about any substantial change.

Table 16 • 2 Shares of income by family, 1970 and 1975

	1970	1975
The poor (bottom 20 percent)	5.4	5.4
Working class (next 40 percent)	29.8	29.4
Middle class (next 35 percent)	49.2	49.7
Upper class (top 5 percent)	15.6	15.5

Why is inflation such a problem?

The figures raise an important question. Over the long run, there has been very little change in relative shares as a result of inflation. Moreover, even with inflation, real incomes are way up. *Why, then, the fuss about inflation?* Why is it not a popular economic process?

There are several plausible reasons. One is that *the losing groups, such as small proprietors and landlords, are politically influential and articulate and complain about their losses more loudly than the winners (labor or transferees) announce their gains.*

A second reason is that inflation is worrisome just because it affects everyone to some degree. Unlike the concentrated loss of unemployment, the diffuse gains-and-losses of inflation touch us all. *They give rise to the fear that the economy is*

HYPERINFLATIONS

Hyperinflations are among the most destructive economic experiences that a modern economic society can undergo. In the German hyperinflation of the 1920s, for example, prices rose so rapidly that hotels and restaurants with foreign guests would not reveal the price of a meal until the diner had finished; then they would determine the "going" value of marks at that moment. Inflation mounted until a common postage stamp cost 9 billion marks, and a worker's weekly wage came to 120 trillion marks. Newspapers and magazines of the period showed people bringing home their weekly pay in wheelbarrows—billions and billions of marks literally worth less than the paper they were printed on.

Hyperinflations have also occurred in Hungary in 1923 and in China after World War II. They are in large part psychological—even pathological—phenomena, rather than strictly economic ones. That is, they signal a collapse of faith in the vitality and viability of the economy. Farmers typically hoard foodstuffs, rather than accept payment in currencies that they fear will be only so much wallpaper in a matter of weeks.

Merchants and manufacturers are unable to make contracts, since suppliers ask for enormous prices in anticipation of price rises to follow. Shopkeepers are reluctant to sell to customers because this means giving up the true wealth of goods for the spurious wealth of paper money that no one trusts. Thus there is flight from all paper currency and a scramble to get into goods or into commodities such as gold, in which people retain faith. Meanwhile, governments find their expenses skyrocketing and are forced to turn to the printing presses as the only way to collect the revenues they require. Finally, people find that they must *barter* goods, as in primitive economic societies.

The only cure for a hyperinflation is the abandonment of the currency in which everyone has lost faith, and the institution of a new currency that people can be once again induced to believe will serve as a reasonably stable "store of value." For example, in 1958 General de Gaulle stopped an incipient runaway French inflation when he simply announced that there would be a new franc worth one hundred of the old, deteriorating francs. Because of de Gaulle's extraordinary prestige, Frenchmen willingly changed their old 100-franc notes for new one-franc coins and then stopped trying to get "out" of money and into goods. The same magic feat was performed in the 1920s in Germany when the government announced that there would be a new mark "backed" by land. People believed that, and hyperinflation stopped.

There is a curious aspect of hyperinflation that we might stop to notice. Why do workers trundle their wages home in wheelbarrows? Why doesn't the government simply print trillion-mark notes, so that a man's wage would fit into his pocketbook? The answer is purely bureaucratic. The printing presses are busy turning out notes in denominations that would have been suitable for the price level of, say, six months earlier. No one dares give orders for denominations that might meet needs when the notes will actually be issued. Why? Because an order to print, say, trillion-mark notes instead of billion-mark notes would be construed as *inflationary!*

"*out of control*"—*which indeed, to a certain extent, it is.*

Third *is the lurking fear that moderate inflation may give way to a galloping inflation.* The vision of a hyperinflation is a specter that chills everyone, and not one to be lightly dismissed. There is always the chance, albeit a small one, that a panic wave may seize the country and that prices may skyrocket while the production of goods declines. Fortunately, hyperinflations are rare. Nations have inflated as much as 200 or 300 percent per year without experiencing the breakdown and disorganization of a real runaway inflation.

Fourth, *the effect of inflation on incomes is not always mirrored in its effects on assets.* Some assets, such as land, typically rise markedly during inflation because they are fixed in supply and because people, forgetting about the land booms and crashes of the past, want to get into something that has "solid value." But many middle-class families have their assets in savings banks or in government bonds, and they watch with dismay as the value of their savings declines. For as interest rates rise, bond prices fall, and stock prices do not typically stay abreast of the price level, although most people think they do. For instance, in late 1968 there was a stock market fall that brought stocks below their levels of 1966–67; and again in early 1973, stock prices fell by a fifth, while consumer prices rose at record rates. Between 1968 and 1976, the cost of living rose by more than 60 percent, but the average of stock prices was basically unchanged.

Inflation vs.
unemploy-
ment again

Can we now compare the costs of unemployment and inflation? Two points stand out from our analysis.

1. From the point of view of the economy as a whole, unemployment is more costly than moderate inflation. That is because unemployment results in less production, whereas inflation does not. From the point of view of winners and losers, unemployment is also more costly than inflation; for unlike inflation, unemployment is not a zero sum game. The losers in unemployment—the direct unemployed and the hidden unemployed—are not matched by winners who benefit from unemployment.

2. The psychological impact of moderate inflation is probably much greater than that of moderate unemployment. This is because we all feel affected by the inflationary process, whereas few of us worry too much about the unemployed—unless they happen to be ourselves.

Thus, there is a kind of myopia that inflation produces. We blame inflation for reducing our real incomes by raising prices, but we do not give it credit for raising our incomes to pay those higher prices. That is, for 364 days in the year we are painfully aware of price rises as part of the inflationary process, but we do not connect the income increase we receive on the 365th day (if we get a yearly hike in pay) as being part of that selfsame process. Or to put the last point differently: on the one day of the year that we get a raise and feel ahead of the game, our gain in pleasure is less than our 364 days of displeasure in which that gain is eroded by rising prices. In the end, we may still be ahead of the game, but it no longer *feels* that way.

Can we conclude from this that a nation should prefer inflation to unemployment—that a wise and humane policy would deliberately trade off a quite high degree of inflation in exchange for a low rate of unemployment? Some economists might recommend such a course, but it is doubtful that the nation as a whole would vote for it. Rightly or wrongly, most citizens feel that inflation is at least as great a danger as moderate unemployment, and they are not likely to support policies that reduce the joblessness of others in exchange for higher prices (or even higher prices and higher incomes!) for themselves.

The XYZ of Inflation

Until this point we have largely been concerned with conveying knowledge—what we know about inflation. Now we must change our track. The rest of this chapter is mainly concerned with conveying ignorance. There is a great deal that we do not know about inflation, and a student should be as aware of our ignorance as of our knowledge.

The elusive
Phillips curve

Let us begin with the Phillips curve. Consider Fig. 16 • 3. The colored line shows that there is perhaps a *general* tendency of inflation to be inversely correlated with unemployment. When unemployment is *very* high, inflation is low, and vice versa, although there are exceptions: look at 1975! But now examine the scatter of dots within the tinted band representing the range from 3.5 to 6 percent unemployment. Compare 1964 and 1974, for instance. In 1964 an

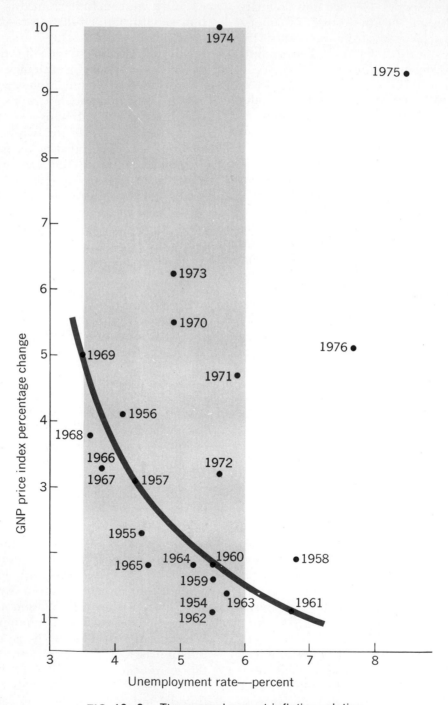

FIG. 16·3   The unemployment-inflation relation

unemployment rate of just over 5 percent was associated with a rate of inflation of less than 2 percent. In 1974 an unemployment rate of 5.6 percent was associated with an inflation of almost 10 percent.

What we have, in other words, is a relationship that is subject to such wide variations that economists have not been able to establish a function that enables them to *predict* what rate of unemployment will actually accompany a given inflation rate. This means that we cannot "target" a mix of inflation and unemployment, as our schematic diagram on p. 251 suggested, *because we do not know where the Phillips curve will be located.*

Indeed, given the lack of empirical evidence, we can even ask why the idea of a Phillips "curve" survives. The answer is that we continue to believe in the existence of an inflation-unemployment trade-off at extreme ranges. If we were willing to run the economy at Depression rates of 25 percent unemployment, few doubt that inflation would halt or even go into reverse. Conversely, if we were to strive for World War II rates of unemployment, when only 1 percent or 2 percent of the labor force was idle, there is little doubt that we would have to expect rampant inflation. The problem lies in the middle range—say between an unemployment rate of 3 percent and 7 percent. Here our knowledge is inadequate. We simply do not know what rate of inflation to associate with any given level of unemployment in this range.

The quantity theory

What about money? Is there not a clear theory of inflation in the quantity theory of money, especially in its new-fangled guise that we studied in our preceding chapter?

As with the relation between unemployment and inflation, no one denies the inflationary impact of increases in the supply of money, or the anti-inflationary effects of reductions in the supply of money, *at the extremes.* If the Fed were to go on an open-market buying spree, there isn't any question that spending would rise with inflationary consequences; or if the Fed were to put on the brakes hard, it would certainly bring about a credit crunch that would stop the economy (and the inflation) dead in its tracks.

The trouble once again lies in the middle range. And here the problem with the quantity theory is that it also has no predictive value. In our preceding chapter we saw how difficult it was for the Fed to know in advance whether an increase in money would lead to more transactions or simply to more liquidity. Add to that the fact that even "monetarists" admit that there is a lag of up to 9 months between the injection of new money by the Fed and a rise in prices, and we can see that for all practical purposes, the quantity theory, like the Phillips curve, fades away as a guide to policy. Just as we do not know what level of inflation will be associated with a given level of unemployment, so we do not know what effect a given change in the money supply will have on prices.

The problem of expectations

At the root of our problem is the question of expectations. As economist James Tobin has written:

To predict the rate of inflation next quarter or year, the most valuable single piece of information is the rate of inflation in the period immediately preceding. . . .The trend of prices is solidly built into the economy, with a powerful and persistent momentum.

Inflations thus perpetuate themselves, in part, because they breed expectations that lead to inflation-producing actions. Labor union leaders expect prices to rise, and they take that into account in setting wage goals. Business does likewise.

Not only do expectations help perpetuate inflation, but they also play hob with theory, for it is very difficult to predict the effects of pronouncements or news on expectations themselves. Will an announcement that the cost-of-living index is up over last month send people on a buying spree, in anticipation of next month's expected increase? Or will it result in a tightening of budgets for the very same reason?

Thus, our inability to predict the course of inflation stems in large part from uncertainties about expectations. Until we learn to anticipate expectations or to influence expectations, the movements of the marketplace—and of that gigantic marketplace called the economy—are likely to take us by surprise.

Controlling Inflation

Can we stop inflation? Of course—at a price. For example, wage and price controls with terrific penalties for noncompliance would surely dampen inflation. So would a decision not to increase the money supply at all. The trouble is that no one is willing to pay so great a price—the price of a police state in the first case, or of massive unemployment in the second. Therefore, we seek to control inflation with *politically acceptable* measures, and these have not been too successful.

Since World War II every major government has tried to keep the lid on inflation, but with scant results. In the United States, the Kennedy administration inaugurated the idea of "wage-price guidelines" that were intended to serve as an official index of productivity, to which it was hoped labor leaders would conform their demands. But the wage-price guidelines allowed for increases of only about 3.4 percent per year and were not very effective. Some unions whose productivity had gone up more rapidly than 3.4 percent claimed that they had the *right* to higher wages; other unions simply ignored the guidelines; and most companies tried only halfheartedly to stick by them in wage bargaining sessions, because they counted on inflation itself to help them pass along any cost increases in higher prices.

Another tactic used by subsequent administrations was called "jawboning." This was simply the use of public pressure, usually through presidential statements, to get companies (or less frequently unions) to scale down price increases. For instance in 1971 Bethlehem Steel suddenly announced that it was about to raise steel prices by 12 percent. Angry comments from the White House, coupled with stories carefully leaked to the newspapers about the possibility of relaxing steel import quotas, brought the welcome response of a much smaller (6 percent) increase from Bethlehem's main competitors. In the end, Bethlehem had to back down to the 6 percent mark.

Wage and price controls   Still, 6 percent is a stiff price increase. Hence more and more pressure built up for the imposition of direct controls over wages and prices, which were finally instituted by the Nixon administration in 1971.

The problem with controls is that they are administratively clumsy, hard to enforce, and almost invariably evaded in one way or another. A wage and price freeze always catches someone at a disadvantage: a union that was just about to sign an advantageous but perhaps deserved contract, a store whose prices were at "sale" levels on the day that the freeze is announced, a business whose costs increase as a result of a rise in the prices of imported goods. Thus price controls lead to endless adjustment and adjudication. Moreover, unless there is a general sentiment of patriotic "pulling together" (as during World War II or the Korean war, when controls were fairly successful in repressing inflation), controls tend to lead to black or gray markets or to downgrading the quality of the "same" goods that are sold at fixed prices.

Not surprisingly, efforts to control wages tend to be more successful than efforts to control prices. This is because the government has an ally to help it enforce its wage regulations; namely, employers. Employers know what their employees make and have an interest in keeping wages within the legal limits. Consumers, on the other hand, usually do not know what products cost and cannot demand that stores refrain from marking up items. Renters are perhaps in the best position as consumers to enforce price controls on rents, but even they are in a weak position when they look for vacant apartments.

As a result, when controls are imposed, they tend to work fairly well for a short period of time on the wage side, while prices continue to creep upward. After a certain point, consumer resentment explodes in the form of demands from workers that their wage restraints be loosened. In nation after nation, this process has been repeated.

The Recession Approach

The Ford administration abandoned efforts to impose controls and substituted a policy of severe economic restraint. The administration, determined to hold federal spending as low as possible, encouraged the Fed to rein in the growth of the money supply. This does not mean that government spending or the money supply fell. It meant, rather, that the federal budget did not expand as rapidly as it would have under a different-minded administration and that the increase in the money supply was much slower than under past administrations.

The upshot of the new policies was a considerable rise in unemployment—indeed, a recession of severe magnitude. Grimly the administration clung to its policies of restriction while unemployment mounted at one point to almost 10 percent of the labor force. Meanwhile, each month the movement of prices was anxiously scanned. Was the restraining policy finally "paying off"? At the end of 1974 inflation had reached an annual rate of 13 percent. By early 1976 it had been brought down to 3.9 percent, although it again moved back to 5 and 6 percent.

Did the policy "work"? The answer is yes and no. Inflation certainly fell from its frightening levels of late 1974, probably (although not certainly) because of this deflationary policy. But a terrible price was exacted in joblessness and in public programs that were postponed or shelved. Whether the overall policy should be deemed a success therefore depends very much on the weight we place on unemployment as a social cost. There is no scientific way of declaring whether this cost is "justified." Our judgments, as we have so often said, reflect our values.

Stop-go   As a result of these partly economic, partly political difficulties, anti-inflationary policies here and abroad take on an aspect of "stop-go." When prices begin to rise too fast, remedial measures are put into effect. The money supply is tightened to curb spending. Governments trim their budgets. Taxes may be increased somewhat. Wage and price controls are put into effect.

For a time, these "stop" measures succeed. But then pressures mount in the opposite direction. High interest rates cut into home building. A slowdown in investment causes unemployment to rise. Tight government budgets mean that programs with important constituencies have to be cut back; Army bases are closed; social assistance programs abandoned. Business chafes under controls. Hence pressures mount for a relaxation. The red light changes to green. The money supply goes up again; investment is encouraged; public spending resumes its former upward trend; controls are taken off. Before long the expected happens: prices begin to move ahead too rapidly once more, and the pendulum starts its swing in the opposite direction.

Inflation as a way of life   Does this mean that inflation has become a chronic fact of life, uncurable except at levels of unemployment that would be socially disastrous or by the imposition of severe and unpopular wage, price, and income controls?

Probably. One fact of great significance is that inflation has been a worldwide experience. It has ravaged underdeveloped countries, where prices have often risen by 20 to 50 percent per year. **Inflation has appeared in every industrialized nation, even though those nations did not participate in the Korean or** Indochinese wars. As Table 16·3 shows, the United States' inflationary problem has generally been much *less* severe than the European or Japanese experience. In other words, contemporary inflation seems to be a new kind of economic problem that has appeared—and resisted attempts to remedy—in all industrialized nations.

Table 16·3   Worldwide inflation

	PRICE RISES IN INDUSTRIALIZED COUNTRIES *Average annual percentage*		
	1959—69	1969—72	1973—75
U.S.	2.2	4.5	11
Australia	2.4	5.3	16
Canada	2.4	3.7	12
France	3.7	5.8	13
Italy	3.6	5.1	19
Japan	5.0	6.1	19
Sweden	3.7	6.9	11
Switzerland	3.0	5.6	9
U.K.	3.4	7.6	22
W. Germany	2.4	4.9	7

Global inflation   To what can we ultimately trace this global phenomenon? Here our knowledge becomes even less certain, and we are forced to resort to more or less plausible hypotheses that refer to social and political as much as economic causes.

In Chapter 1 (pp. 8–10) we mentioned some likely reasons for this endemic condition. One of them, we will recall, is a shift from high-productivity goods output to lower-productivity services output, a trend visible in all nations. Another is the worldwide growth of market power, in the hands of giant corporations, powerful labor unions, and government marketing agencies. A third is the rise of expansionist government policies in almost all nations. A fourth is the advent of new attitudes of high aspiration, coupled with greater "staying power," evinced by citizens of the more developed countries.

For these reasons it seems that we will have to live with inflation for a very long period.

What economists hope for is that a middle ground can be reached where the frictions generated by inflation and the real damage done by unemployment can be reduced to reasonable proportions. A price rise of 1 or 2 percent a year, for example, can be fairly easily tolerated, since a year-to-year increase in the quality of goods can be said to justify such an increase. Similarly, 3 or 4 percent unemployment (which includes voluntary unemployment and a hard core of "unemployables") is also socially acceptable,

especially since both kinds of unemployment can be remedied by generous policies of unemployment compensation or by programs for retraining labor.

But it is one thing to announce such a goal and another to attain it. The simple fact remains that in no industrialized nation has anything like such an acceptable balance been achieved. In most nations, the claims of high employment quite properly take priority over those of inflation, and the rate of annual price increase has accordingly ranged from roughly 4 to 10 percent a year. As we have seen, in this chronicle of inflationary failure, the record of the United States is by no means the worst. Unhappily, its record in combating unemployment, as we shall see in our next chapter, is by no means the best.

Focus   There is a basic problem to be thought about in this chapter: the choice between the costs of unemployment and the frictions of inflation. This central dilemma affects all market economies. We can do no more than suggest that you read over the pages devoted to the subject (252–257) and review the main elements we stress.

Second, we hope you will bring from this chapter an understanding of both what we do and what we don't understand about inflation. You should clearly see why inflation must have some demand pull; that is, why it must have rightward moving demand curves in most markets. You should also see why it must have cost-push elements—bottlenecks or upward sloping demand curves. Do you understand why we could not have an inflation unless both conditions were present, regardless of which was the more "active" at the moment?

It is a little disconcerting to study a subject to find out what we don't know. Nonetheless, a knowledge of ignorance is a necessary part of wisdom. The elusive Phillips curve is a case in point. So is the unreliable guide of monetary policy, the happenstance of accidents, and the curious role of expectations. Can you see that we do not have a theory of inflation that compares in simplicity and explanatory power to the theory of underemployment equilibrium?

This brings us to the question of policy. When theory is weak, policy is apt to be catch-as-catch can. That is exactly what we find. You should try to understand the failures or partial successes of policy in terms of our inadequate theory. And you might look into the "Extra word" for two daring attempts to formulate much more effective policies than any that we discuss.

WORDS AND CONCEPTS YOU SHOULD KNOW

QUESTIONS

1. Distinguish between a change in prices in an individual market and an inflationary change. What is meant by calling inflation a "process"?

2. What is meant by "demand pull"? By "cost push"? What explanations can we give for the increase in demand? For the rise in costs? Can you have an inflationary *process* if both costs and demand are not rising?

3. What kind of event might give rise to a hyperinflation in the United States? Might a defeat in war trigger such an event? A victory? If we were to experience a runaway inflation, what measures would you counsel?

4. What is the importance of productivity in determining whether wage increases add to cost? Suppose that wages go up by 5 percent and that productivity goes up by 4 percent. Will there be an increase in costs per unit? Might this increase be absorbed by a fall in profits? Under what conditions is it likely to be passed on to consumers?

5. Is a war always inflationary? Does it depend on how it is financed? How should it be financed to minimize inflation? Does the same reasoning apply to an investment boom? (HINT: since corporations cannot tax, they must depend on savings for their expenditures.)

6. What is meant by the Phillips curve? Is it a concept that is useful for a general understanding of the inflationary process? Why is it of little use for prediction?

7. Suppose that you could add up the costs of unemployment in terms of income lost. Suppose that you could add up the losses incurred just by those groups who are left behind in inflation (forget about the "winners"). Suppose further, that the losses imposed by inflation were greater than those imposed by unemployment. Does this mean that inflation is necessarily a worse economic disaster than unemployment? Must personal values enter into such a calculation? (If you simply compare amounts, is this also a value judgment?)

8. Why have measures to control inflation been so unsatisfactory? Why are price controls more difficult to monitor than wage controls?

9. Suppose that unemployment and inflation rise again to about 10 percent a year. What measures would you propose?

Incomes policy and indexing

One of the most ambitious efforts to bring inflation under control is incomes policy, an effort to form a "social contract" that will establish the shares of national income going to each major power group. England, Sweden, and a few other European countries have been trying to bring labor and capital and other major interests (such as farmers and civil service employees) into an agreement about how much each will receive from the national income.

Incomes policies are not only efforts to deal with inflation but are, in fact, implicit theories of inflation. They assume that inflation is the result of power groups striving to outdo one another when the expansion of demand cannot be matched by a comparable increase in supply. The hope is that by bringing the free-for-all to a halt, all groups will gain secure shares of the national income, without the inflation-breeding struggle of the past.

Incomes policies have not yet been attended with great success. In part, the reason is that inflation is not always caused by domestic jockeying for place, but sometimes by outside factors, such as the "oil shock" that dealt European economies a fierce inflationary blow. Second, the idea of a social contract assumes that all groups can agree on "fair shares," and this is often difficult to do. Third, it also assumes that all members of society will be represented in a social contract. Otherwise the weak will simply be trampled on by the well-organized. And not least, the theory takes for granted that a bargain, once reached, will be respected by all.

Thus an effective incomes policy based on a "social contract" has very great problems. It is possible that some European nations where there already exists a high degree of social organization (such as Sweden) may succeed in forging such a new approach to inflation control over the coming years. In the United States, where most of the big economic interest groups are relatively unorganized, a social contract seems very unlikely, at least for the immediate future.

INDEXING

An entirely different approach to inflation has been suggested by Milton Friedman, whom we have already encountered as the leading protagonist of monetarism and as a staunch defender of a laissez-faire approach to economics (Chap. 15, p. 247). As we know, Friedman believes that inflation is wholly caused by excess money supply. He proposes, however, that if we cannot bring our money supply under strict control for political reasons, we can at least learn to live much less painfully with inflation by "indexing."

Indexing means that as many contracts or institutional arrangements as possible, such as wages and interest and rent and bond values and welfare payments, should have "escalator" provisions that would regularly adjust their nominal money price in terms of some index of prices. Suppose you were hired at $200 a week and had a $2,000 savings account in Year 1. If prices doubled in Year 2, your pay would automatically jump to $400 a week, and your savings account would be revalued at $4,000. If all prices were indexed in this fashion, it would make very little difference if inflation were fast or slow. Your relative position in society, your relative wealth and income would be unaffected, although of course you could try to get ahead faster than your neighbor, as so many now do.

Indexing has two major problems. First, it presents an array of difficult questions about how to index certain kinds of wealth or income. How do you index a lawyer's income? An artist's fees? The wages of the nonunionized? The price of foreign raw materials? The value of stocks, land, houses?

More troubling is that indexing would remove any reason whatever to oppose inflation. The inertia that is built into our system because some contracts are not indexed would disappear. As long as everyone is protected, what difference how high the prices go? With this philosophy might come the beginning of a self-fulfilling prophecy in which expectations of an ever faster rising rate of inflation in fact brought into being just such a state of affairs. From there to hyperinflation is too close for comfort. And though hyperinflation in a perfectly indexed world theoretically would not make any difference, no one is very eager to put the theory of indexing to such a test.

Unlike the social contract, however, indexing will certainly be used to some extent in the United States. Already much of the American economy is indexed. Social Security payments, many union pay arrangements, most long-run business supply contracts have built-in cost-of-living adjustments or some other form of indexing. These arrangements are likely to be extended to more groups in society. One idea that has long been urged is the indexing of government bonds for small savers, so that when the bond comes due, an investor in U.S. Savings Bonds will get back the full real purchasing power invested. Such a step would be a useful means of lessening the erosion of wealth (especially of small wealthholders) that *is* one of the real costs of inflation.

The problem of unemployment

We have already looked briefly into the problem of unemployment in Chapter 1 (on pp. 10–13), and the reader might do well to begin by looking back over those pages. Now, however, we are ready to examine the question in a much more searching and detailed manner than before. And we begin by acquainting ourselves with the meaning of the word "unemployment" itself.

The meaning of unemployment

The measure of unemployment is determined by a household-to-household survey conducted each month by the Bureau of the Census among a carefully selected sample. An "unemployed" person is thereupon defined not merely as a person without a job—for perhaps such a person does not *want* a job—but as someone who is "actively" seeking work but is unable to find it. Since, however, the number of people who will be seeking work will rise in good times and fall in bad times, figures for any given period must be viewed with caution.

267

As employment opportunities drop, unemployment will not rise by an equivalent amount. Some of those looking for work when job opportunities are plentiful will withdraw from the labor force and become part of *hidden unemployment*. When job opportunities expand, these "hidden unemployed" will reenter the labor force, so that unemployment will not fall as fast as employment rises. Thus the ups and downs in the measured unemployment rate reflect the state of the economy, but the swings are not as large as they would be if the term "unemployment" measured the hidden unemployed.

The elastic labor force

This gives rise to a curious and important result. Measured unemployment is not simply the difference between the number of people working and a fixed labor force. It is the difference between the number working and an elastic, changeable labor force.

The result of measuring unemployment is seemingly paradoxical. It is that employment and unemployment can both rise and fall at the same time, as workers (mainly youths and women) enter the labor market in good times, or as they withdraw in discouragement in bad times. Table 17·1 shows us this parallel rise in both the number working and the number without work. Look at the change from 1970 and 1971 or again between 1973 and 1974.

Participation rates

We call this elasticity of the labor force its *short-run participation rate*. In Chapter 5 (on pp. 64–66) we learned something about long-run participation rates, marked by historical changes in the ratios of men and women in the labor force, or in the proportions of the young and the old at work. Now we see that short-run changes play a significant role in determining the meaning of the phenomenon we call unemployment. The average number of hours worked per week also varies with good and bad times because employees can or cannot get overtime work or can or cannot "moonlight" (take on a second job).

These considerations mean that economists do not judge the severity of a given unemployment rate just by the percentage of the jobless. They also look to participation rates and hours of work. Relatively low participation rates and a fall in average hours worked per week indicate that the impact of a given unemployment rate is more serious than it appears to be.

Severity of unemployment

How serious is unemployment as a national economic problem? Table 17·2 shows us the record of the past few years and gives us the data for earlier, benchmark years to serve as a point of comparison. (In this discussion we ignore participation rates, to concentrate on more deep-lying problems.)

Table 17·1   Short-run changes in the labor force (millions)

	1970	1971	1972	1973	1974	1975	1976
Number in civilian labor force	82.7	84.1	86.5	88.7	91.0	92.6	94.8
Civilian employment	78.6	79.1	81.7	84.4	85.9	84.8	87.5
Unemployment	4.1	5.0	4.8	4.3	5.1	7.8	7.3

Table 17·2   Unemployment in the U.S.

Year	Unemployed (thousands)	Percent of civilian labor force
1929	1,550	3.2
1933	12,830	24.9
1940	8,120	14.6
1944	670	1.2
1960–65 av.	4,100	5.5
1966	2,875	3.8
1967	2,975	3.8
1968	2,817	3.6
1969	2,832	3.5
1970	4,085	4.9
1971	4,993	5.9
1972	4,840	5.6
1973	4,304	4.9
1974	5,076	5.6
1975	7,530	8.5
1976	7,288	7.7

The terrible percentages of the Depression years speak for themselves. At the very depth of the Depression, a quarter of the work force was jobless, at a time when unemployment insurance and welfare was largely nonexistent. Note, too, that massive unemployment persisted until 1940. Only the advent of World War II finally brought unemployment below 1929 levels.

The record of the 1960s and 1970s is mixed. During the early 1960s, unemployment was at a level considered to be uncomfortably high—roughly between 5 and 6 percent of the labor force. This percentage dropped in the second half of the decade, partly as a consequence of higher spending on armaments. At the end of this chapter we will ask whether arms spending is necessary to absorb unemployment in capitalism.

It is the record of the 1970s that is disturbing. First, we watched the number of unemployed soar to a peak of over 8 million in May 1975. Second, we saw unemployment rates approach 9 percent of the labor force, a rate more serious than any recession (barring only the 1933–1940 collapse) in this century.

Impact of unemployment

Moreover, as we recall from Chapter 1, the impact of an unemployment rate of, say, 7 percent does not mean that everyone who works will be laid off for 7 percent of the year, or about two weeks. Rather, the effect of unemployment hits very hard at particular groups, as Table 17·3 allows us to see in considerable detail.

Table 17·3   Composition of the unemployed

	1969	1975
Total	**3.5**	**8.5**
Male	2.8	7.9
16–19	11.4	20.4
20–24	5.1	14.3
25–64	1.7	5.2
65 up	2.2	5.4
Female	4.7	9.3
16–19	13.3	19.7
20–24	6.3	12.7
25–64	3.2	7.1
65 up	2.3	5.1
Black, total	**6.4**	**13.9**
16–19	23.9	37.4
White, total	**3.1**	**7.8**
16–19	10.7	18.1
White collar	2.1	4.7
Blue collar	3.9	11.7
Service	4.2	8.6
Farm	1.9	3.5

Duration (weeks)	Percent of unemployed	
0–5	57.5	37.0
6–10	22.2	22.2
11–14	7.1	9.1
15–26	8.5	16.5
27 and over	4.7	15.2

An analysis of unemployment

The table is long and complicated, but it repays some careful study. Let us begin by comparing total unemployment in 1969 and 1975. The year 1969 was the last year of a long period of real growth in GNP; 1975 was the bottom of the sharpest decline since the Great Depression. The effect on unemployment was to raise the national rate by more than 100 percent.

First look at the data for 1969. Notice that the seemingly low rate of 3.5 percent unemployment for the nation as a whole was a weighted average of very low rates (1.7 percent) for male workers between the ages of 25 and 64 and horrendous rates (23.9 percent) for black teenagers. Notice something else. At every age level, female unemployment rates exceeded male rates by substantial margins; and approximately twice as many blacks were jobless as whites. We can also see that unemployment hits different occupations differently. Service and blue-collar workers were twice as likely to be unemployed as white-collar or farm workers.

Now switch to 1975. With the rise in the national rate to 8.5 percent, unemployment rates for blacks and women have skyrocketed. Blue-collar rates are also relatively worse, compared with white-collar rates. And perhaps the most dramatic change has been in the duration of unemployment. In 1969 only 4.7 percent of the population had been without work for more than half a year. In 1975, as we noted in Chapter 1, this proportion had risen to 15.2 percent.

Easing the cost of unemployment

To some extent, this concentrated cost of unemployment is offset by transfer payments made to some of the unemployed.

Because these payments come from taxes that are mainly paid by employed persons, transfers help to some small degree to spread the burden.

Unemployment compensation in the United States differs widely among the states. In general, it provides for payment of one-half of an unemployed person's income, up to some maximum weekly benefit. Actual weekly benefits range from $99 in Washington, D.C. to $48 in Mississippi. There is also a limit on how many weeks' unemployment compensation can be claimed. Usually 20 weeks can be collected, although that was temporarily upped to 65 weeks by federal legislation during the 1975–1976 recession.

However, many individuals, such as new entrants into the labor force or employees of government and nonprofit institutions are not eligible for any benefits at all. If a person is not eligible or has exhausted his or her benefits, there is welfare, which also varies from state to state in terms of benefits and eligibility.

Causes and Cures

What causes unemployment, and what will cure it? We have already more than once studied the principal reason for joblessness—a lack of sufficient aggregate demand. For reasons that we understand very well, when total spending declines, employers let workers go. Thus the first cause of unemployment lies in too little demand, and the first cure lies in restoring demand to a "full employment level."

Level of demand

This is only the first step in our analysis, however, for we must recognize that a level of demand adequate to produce "full" or high employment in one year will not be adequate the next. First, there is a normal growth of the labor force as a consequence of population growth. This growth may accelerate if an unusually large number of young people, products of an earlier "baby boom," are leaving school. In the 1960s there was a flood of such young entrants; now, fortunately, the flood has ebbed (see box).

Second, even if there were no increase in the labor force, we experience a normal growth in productivity as the consequence of adding capital equipment, of improving our techniques of production, and of increasing our stock of skill and knowledge. This year-to-year increase in per capita productivity is about 3 percent. Therefore, unless GNP grows by at least that amount, there will not be enough demand to absorb the output of the given labor force.

Full employment growth

Thus we need a growth of GNP equal to the increase in the labor force, plus the increase in productivity, to insure a constant rate of employment. In ordinary times, this means that GNP, in real terms, must grow at about 4 to 4½ percent per year to give us steady high employment.

But suppose that we have too much unemployment and want to grow fast

enough to absorb it? Now comes an important twist that results from the elasticity of the labor force. As employment grows, more people enter the labor force, and hours lengthen. This means that we have to increase the level of GNP enough to absorb the "original" unemployed, plus the addition to the labor force that results from higher participation rates and more hours worked. Arthur Okun, former Chairman of the Council of Economic Advisors, has estimated that it takes a 2½ percent increase in GNP just to hold the unemployment rate constant, and a 3½ percent increase in GNP to bring about a 1 percentage point fall in unemployment.

The difficulty with revving up GNP to eliminate unemployment is that we rapidly run into inflationary bottlenecks, once unemployment reaches the 5 to 6 percent level. This brings us to familiar terrain, where we must fight out the battle between unemployment and inflation. **We know how to reduce unemployment by raising aggregate demand, but we do not know how to do so without creating unacceptable levels of inflation.**

Technological unemployment

Aggregate demand— or rather, the lack of it—is the prime cause of unemployment, but it is not the only cause. Let us now begin to take up a series of subsidiary reasons for the existence of unemployment—conditions that may create unemployment or make difficult its cure, even if the level of national spending is high.

The first candidate on our list is technological unemployment, the joblessness caused by the introduction of machines. This is a problem that vexes and worries us, partly because it is real, partly because we do not understand it very well. For example, we constantly hear references to "automation" as a great unemployment-creating force, although in the very next breath we speak of the need for "growth industries" (like automation!) to *create* employment. In this next section, therefore, we shall try to sort out the different effects that technology can have on employment. And the reader will note a box just after the questions at the end of the chapter, in which we look into automation from a different, historical angle.

Technology and the demand for labor

We should begin by realizing that not all technology economizes on labor. Fertilizer, for example, saves land; miniaturization saves capital; new technologies may save labor *and* capital to make the "same" product (e.g., a mass-produced Volkswagen and a hand-tooled Rolls-Royce are both cars). But the inventions that interest us here are *labor-saving* inventions or innovations, changes in technique or technology that enable an entrepreneur to turn out the same output as before, with less labor, or a larger output than before, with the same amount of labor.

Do such inventions "permanently" displace labor? Let us trace an imaginary instance and find out.

We shall assume that an inventor has perfected a technique that makes it possible for a local shoe factory to reduce its production force from 10 men to 8 workers, while still turning out the same number of shoes. Forgetting for the moment about the possible stimulatory effects of buying a new labor-saving machine,* let us see what happens to purchasing power and employment if the shoe manufacturer simply goes on selling the same number of shoes at the same prices as before, utilizing the new lower-cost process to increase profits.

Suppose our manufacturer now spends the increased profits in increased consumption. Will that bring an equivalent increase in the total spending of the community? If we think twice we can see why not, for the increased spending of the manufacturer will be offset to a large extent by the decreased spending of the two displaced workers.

Exactly the same conclusion follows if the entrepreneur used the cost-cutting invention to lower the price of shoes, in the hope of snaring a larger market. Now it is *consumers* who are given an increase in purchasing power equivalent to the cut in prices. But again, their gain is exactly balanced by the lost purchasing power of the displaced workers.

Incomes vs. employment

Thus we can see that the introduction of labor-saving machinery does not necessarily imperil *incomes;* it merely shifts purchasing power from previously employed workers into the hands of consumers or into profits. But note also that *the unchanged volume of incomes is now associated with a smaller volume of employment.* The fact that there

---

*This is not an unfair assumption. The labor-saving technology might be no more than a more effective arrangement of labor within the existing plant, and thus require no new equipment; or the new equipment might be bought with regular capital replacement funds.

is no purchasing power "lost" when a labor-saving machine is introduced does not mean that there is no employment lost.

Is this the end to our analysis of labor-displacing technology? It can be. It is possible that the introduction of labor-saving machinery will have no effect other than that of the example above: transferring consumer spending from previously employed labor to consumers or to entrepreneurs.

But it is also possible that an employment-generating secondary effect may result. The entrepreneur may be so encouraged by higher profits from the new process that he uses them to invest in additional plant and equipment and thereby sets in motion, via the multiplier, a rise in total expenditure sufficient to reemploy the displaced workers. Or in our second instance, consumers may evidence such a brisk demand for shoes at lower prices that, once again, our employer is encouraged to invest in additional plant and equipment, with the same salutary results as above.

Do not fall into the trap of thinking that the new higher demand for shoes, will, *by itself*, suffice to eradicate unemployment. To be sure, shoe purchases may now increase to previous levels or even higher. But unless their incomes rise, consumer spending on other items will suffer to the exact degree that spending on shoes gains.

The moral is clear. *Labor-saving technology can offset the unemployment created by its immediate introduction only if it induces sufficient investment to absorb the unemployed.*

New demands

Now let us take a second case of technology. Suppose that an inventor patents a new product—a stove that automatically cooks things to perfection. Will such an invention create employment?

We will suppose that our inventor personally assembles and sells original models in local stores, and we will ignore the small increase in spending (and perhaps in employment) due to the inventor's orders for raw materials. Instead, let us fasten our attention on the consumer who first decides to buy the new product in a store, because it has stimulated her demand.

Will the consumer's purchase result in a *net* increase in consumer spending in the economy? If this is so—and if the new product is generally liked—it is easy to see how the new product could result in sizeable additional employment.

But will it be true? Our consumer has, to be sure, bought a new item. *But unless her income has increased, there is no reason to believe that this is a net addition to her consumption expenditures.* The chances are, rather, that this unforeseen expenditure will be balanced by lessened spending for some other item. Almost surely she will not buy a regular stove. (When consumers first began buying television sets, they stopped buying as many radios and going to the movies as often.) But even where there is no direct competition, where the product is quite "new," everything that we know about the stability of the propensity to consume schedule leads us to believe that *total* consumer spending will not rise.

Thus we reach the important conclusion that new products do not automatically create *additional* spending, even though they may mobilize consumer demand for themselves. Indeed, many new products emerge onto the market every year and merely shoulder old products off. Must we then conclude that demand-creating inventions do not affect employment?

Employment and investment

We are by no means ready to jump to that conclusion. Rather, what we have seen enables us to understand that if a new product is to create employment, it must give rise to new *investment* (and to the consumption it induces in turn). If the automatic stove is successful, it may induce the inventor to borrow money from a bank and to build a plant to mass-produce the item. If consumer demand for it continues to rise, a very large factory may have to be built to accommodate demand. As a result of the investment expenditures on the new plant, GNP rises, consumers' incomes rise, and more employment will be created as they spend their incomes on various consumer items.

To be sure, investment will decline in those areas that are now selling less to consumers. At most, however, this decline can affect only their replacement expenditures, which probably averaged 5 to 10 percent of the value of their capital equipment. Meanwhile, in the new industry, an entire capital structure must be built from scratch. We can expect the total amount of investment spending to increase substantially, with its usual repercussive effects.

When we think of a new product not in terms of a household gadget but in terms of the automobile, airplane, or perhaps the transistor, we can understand how large the employment-creating potential of certain kinds of inventions can be. Originally the automobile merely resulted in consumer spending being diverted from buggies; the airplane merely cut into railroad income; the transistor, into vacuum tubes. But each of these inventions became in time the source of enormous investment expenditures. The automobile not only gave us the huge auto plants in Detroit, but indirectly brought into being multibillion-dollar investment in highways, gasoline refineries, service stations, tourism—all industries whose impact on employment has been gigantic. On a smaller, but still very large scale, the airplane gave rise not alone to huge aircraft building plants, but to airfields, radio and beacon equipment industries, international tourism, etc., whose employment totals are substantial. In turn, the transistor offered entirely new design possibilities for miniaturization and thus gave many businesses an impetus for expansion.

Industry-building inventions

What sorts of inventions have this industry-building capacity? We can perhaps generalize by describing them as inventions that are of sufficient importance to become "indispensable" to the consumer or the manufacturer, and of sufficient mechanical or physical variance from the existing technical environment to necessitate the creation of a large amount of supporting capital equipment to integrate them into economic life.

Demand-creating inventions, then, can indeed create employment. They do so indirectly, however—not by inducing new consumer spending, but by generating new investment spending.*

Unfortunately, there is no guarantee that these highly employment-generative inventions will come along precisely when they are needed. There have been long periods when the economy has not been adequately stimulated by this type of invention and when employment has lagged as a result.

---

*We should stress another effect of demand-creating inventions on consumption. It is probable that without the steady emergence of new products, the long-run propensity to consume would decline instead of remaining constant, as we have seen in Chapter 8. In this way, demand-creating technology is directly responsible for the creation of employment, by helping to keep consumer spending higher than it would be without a flow of new products.

Automation and employment   This discussion brings us to that cluster of new, versatile inventions we call automation. We have discussed the squeeze that these inventions might exert on employment in our long box at the end of the chapter. But we can see that a crucial aspect of the question is whether the technology of automation will be industry-building or labor-saving. We do not yet know. It is possible that the computer, the transistor, the myriad new possibilities in feed-back engineering will play the same role as the automobile and the railroad, not only giving rise to an enormous flow of investment, but opening new fields of endeavor for other new industries that will also expand. If this is the case, the demand for labor will grow fast enough to match the increase in the productivity of labor, and there will be nothing unusual to worry about.

But it is also possible that the impact of automation will make itself felt like our labor-saving shoe invention, cutting costs where it is used, but not giving an immediate expansionary push to investment. In that case, the new equipment would be likely to create unemployment in those industries in which it was used, and we would be in the anxious position of seeing unemployment mount without a strong new expanding industry to offer new jobs.

Other Causes of Unemployment

If automation does bring about unemployment, could we not take care of it through demand management? The question opens up new aspects of the unemployment problem that we have not yet studied. **Unemployment is not solely a** matter of people losing jobs, but of people not being able to find new jobs. As we saw in our first glimpse of the problem (pp. 12–13 and accompanying box), we can have unemployment that results from a lack of skills or from a mismatch between existing skills and required skills or because workers looking for jobs do not have the characteristics (such as literacy, or ethnic backgrounds, or education) that employers want.

Structural unemployment   This kind of unemployment is called *structural unemployment*. Because it is lodged so strongly in specific attributes of the individual, it resists the "easy" cure of higher aggregate demand. Business may be better for an employer, but he may prefer to pay his existing work force overtime, rather than to take on a new labor force that does not meet his specifications.

The remedy for structural unemployment is more difficult than for general lack-of-demand unemployment. New skills or new attributes (such as punctuality) are needed by the "structurally" unemployed, and these are expensive to impart. The Job Corps program of the 1960s, for example, found that it cost about $10,000 to $12,000 to make an unemployed person—often a member of a ghetto group—acceptable to employers. Society was not willing to pay so large a fee, and employers also resisted (or asked large subsidies for) programs to hire and train "unemployables."

The high cost of retraining or of imparting desired work characteristics is one reason why structural unemployment is a difficult problem. Perhaps even more difficult is the question: for what jobs shall the unemployed be trained? **Unless we very clearly know the shape of future de-**

mand, the risk is that a retraining program will prepare workers for jobs that may no longer exist when the workers are ready for them. And unless the *level* of future demand is high, even a foresighted program will not effectively solve the unemployment problem.

Employer of last resort

One solution to this problem would be to create a program aimed at creating permanent jobs in specific areas of the public sector, such as the repair, maintenance, and beautification of our inner cities, or the care of the aged. Once again, however, we encounter public resistance. The use of the government as the "employer of last resort" is a potentially powerful weapon for the alleviation of unemployment, but it is a departure that does not yet have the wholehearted endorsement of the public. Because this is likely to become a lively political issue in the future, we discuss it in "An extra word" at the end of this chapter.

Frictional unemployment

We should not leave this discussion of the causes of unemployment without mentioning the "normal" unemployment that occurs when workers voluntarily leave one job in search of a better one. This kind of unemployment is actually a source of benefit for the economy, because it is one of the ways in which productivity is enhanced, as workers move from declining industries to growing ones.

Nonetheless, we can increase the efficiency of this productivity-promoting flow of labor by reducing the period of "frictional" unemployment as much as possible. The most frequently suggested means of doing so is to provide a nationwide employment service that would make job information available to job searchers, so that a carpenter, wishing to leave an area where work was slow, would know what areas were booming; or a secretary who felt there was no room for promotion in a sluggish business would have available a roster of many other possibilities.

Want ads are a partial, but incomplete kind of employment service. A full-scale national information service would provide much more complete information; and a full national commitment to minimizing frictional unemployment would even help defray the costs of relocating. Sweden and some other European countries run such labor exchanges, but we have yet to establish one in the United States.

Capitalism and Unemployment

This is by no means a full discussion of all the causes of, or cures for, unemployment. We have, for example, ignored the problem of wage policy, although it must be obvious that unemployment can be generated if unions succeed in pushing up wage rates for certain jobs above the jobs' marginal productivity. And we have paid no heed to the long-run remedy for unemployment played by lengthening the years of schooling, lowering the age of retirement, liberalizing vacation policies, and other changes in social institutions.

But we have covered enough to enable us to draw up a preliminary report on the performance of the economy as a generator of employment. As we saw, when we first examined the data for the 1960s and 1970s, that report is not good.

Unemployment has ranged from 3.5 percent in the war-boom years to nearly 9 percent in the 1975 recession. Some of this was frictional unemployment—perhaps 2 to 3 percent of the labor force. All the rest was structural unemployment or the unemployment that resulted from inadequate levels of aggregate demand.

"Reserve Army of the Unemployed"

Is this a consequence of the inherent sluggishness of a capitalist system incapable of attaining high levels of employment except under armaments spending?

Marxists have argued that this is the case and have pointed to the very large workless bottom layer of the American economy. First there are the officially acknowledged unemployed—7.8 million in 1975. Then there are the underemployed, those who want full-time work but can get only part-time. These are another 3.7 million. Then there are 1 million who are not looking for work because they think they cannot find it. This gives us a very large "reserve army of the unemployed," to use Karl Marx's term for the jobless whose presence, he argued, served to keep down the wages of those who were employed. Really full employment, a Marxist would claim, would raise wages so high that profits—and capitalism—would disappear.

This is not an analysis to be lightly brushed aside. In Europe, for example, a similar "reserve army" has been created by importing cheap labor from Greece, Spain, Yugoslavia, and Turkey to man the great factories of the Continent. When times are bad, many of these "guest workers" are encouraged to return to their countries of origin; so that the European nations, in fact, export some of their unemployed.

U.S. vs. European performance

It may well be, in other words, that some unemployment above the frictional level is needed to prevent wages from squeezing out profits or sending prices skyhigh. Leaders in many countries speak candidly of the need to keep labor "in line," and unemployment is openly acknowledged to be a disciplinary force toward that end. Some degree of unemployment may indeed be inseparable from the operation of a capitalist system.

But what degree? It is also clear that the levels of unemployment that have been generated and tolerated in the United States are not necessary. In Western Europe the levels of unemployment have been far below that of the United States, as Table 17•4 shows—a record of years in which European nations were not "exporting" unemployment but were enjoying a strong boom.

Table 17•4   Unemployment rates 1960–1974

Country	Highest	Lowest	Average
United States	6.7%	3.5%	4.9%
Canada	7.1	3.9	5.4
Japan	1.7	1.1	1.3
France	3.0	1.6	2.3
West Germany	2.1	0.3	0.8
Italy	4.3	2.7	3.6
United Kingdom	5.3	1.2	3.2
Sweden	2.7	1.2	1.9

Source: Eva Christina Horowitz, "Unemployment Rates—An International Comparison," *The Nordic Economic Outlook,* mimeographed series B12 of the Federation of Swedish Industries, June 1975.

European nations have generally gone much further than we have in providing labor exchanges or in seeking to remedy structural unemployment, and they have been willing to accept a higher level of inflation as a lesser evil than a high level of unemployment.

What is lacking in our nation, to date, is a willingness to place employment at the very head of all the benefits that we expect from an economy, a willingness to bend every effort to achieve the right to work for all. We may still not wholly eliminate structural or aggregate demand employment. but at least we could not then be faulted for having failed to try to do so.

Focus   The most thought-provoking question of this chapter is the one that we raise at the very end. Is unemployment necessary for capitalism to function? Would really full employment bring such inflation or such a squeeze on profits that the system could no longer operate, at least not on the basis of free markets? This opens a question of much greater depth than we can explore in this text. But our quick look suggests that whereas, indeed, some unemployment may be necessary to maintain a working capitalist system, it is far less than the rates that we have permitted in the United States.

That leads us to a consideration of the causes of unemployment. Here we cover some ground that is familiar, some that is new. We learn about necessary, frictional unemployment. We look into structural unemployment. And we study, above all, the need for GNP to grow, merely to maintain a given rate of unemployment, because the labor force swells and productivity rises. In turn, this ties in with what we have learned about the elasticity of the labor force, resulting from variable short-run participation rates. To reduce a given level of unemployment, we must raise aggregate demand by an amount large enough both to create the new jobs we want and to create jobs for those who enter the labor force because jobs are more plentiful.

A side theme that runs through this chapter is the problem of technological unemployment or, rather, the impact of machines on work. Here the crucial thing to understand is that a new process or a new product does not directly create new employment. Its first effect is to change the flow of incomes or expenditures, not to augment them. Only if the technology creates a wave of investment will it bring strong employment effects in tow.

This is useful to keep in mind when thinking about the problem of automation, a recurrent worry of our times. It will help you also to think about the interplay between the entrance of technology (of any kind, automation or not) in different sectors and the elasticity of demand for the outputs of different sectors. (This is covered in the long box that follows.) This problem will have an important bearing on the severity of U.S. unemployment in the years ahead.

WORDS AND CONCEPTS YOU SHOULD KNOW

QUESTIONS

1. Suppose that an inventor puts a wrist radio-telephone on the market. What would be the effects on consumer spending? What would ultimately determine whether the new invention was labor-attracting or labor-saving?

2. Suppose that another new invention halved the cost of making cars. Would this create new purchasing power? What losses in income would have to be balanced against what gains in incomes? What would be the most likely way that such an invention could increase employment? Would employment increase if the demand for cars were inelastic, like the demand for farm products—that is, if people bought very few more cars despite the fall in prices?

3. Unemployment among the black population in many cities in the late 1960s was worse than it was during the Great Depression. What steps would you propose to remedy this situation?

4. Do you believe that there exists general support for large public employment-generating programs? Why or why not? What sorts of programs would you propose?

5. Do you think that the computer, on net balance, has created unemployment? How would you go about trying to ascertain whether your hunch was accurate? Would you have to take into account the indirect effects of computers on investment?

6. How much inflation would *you* willingly accept, to lower unemployment to, say, 3 percent?

7. Why is frictional unemployment useful, and structural unemployment not? If frictional unemployment is useful, why try to reduce it?

8. Explain why we need a rising GNP to maintain a constant level of employment. Would this be true if we had zero population growth, but rising productivity? Zero productivity growth but rising population? If we have both, will the target be constant employment? Constant unemployment? Constant unemployment rates?

For years, men have feared the effect of machinery on the demand for labor. The first-century Roman emperor Vespasian turned down a road-building machine, saying "I must have work for my poor." Shortly after Adam Smith's time, revolts of workers led by a mythical General Ludd smashed the hated and feared machines of the new textile manufacturers, which they believed to be stealing the very bread from their mouths.

In our own day, this lurking fear of machinery has focused on that extraordinary technology that "reads" and "hears" and "thinks" and puts human dexterity to shame. We call it automation. One of its characteristics is a feedback loop, by which the machine corrects itself, rather like a thermostat maintains a constant temperature. When such machines can make an engine block for a car almost without human supervision, it is understandable that thoughtful men should worry. There is a well-known story of Henry Ford II showing his newly automated engine plant to the late Walter Reuther, the famed head of the United Auto Workers, and asking, "Well, Walter, how will you organize these machines?" Reuther replied, "How will you sell them cars?"

Does automation impose a wholly new and dangerous threat to employment? Let us begin to answer the question by using the tried and true method of supply and demand.

MACHINES AND SUPPLY

What has the introduction of machinery done to the supply of labor? We know that its main effect has been vastly to increase the *productivity* of labor: a man with a tractor is incomparably more productive than a man with a shovel, not to speak of one with his bare hands.

But the effect of capital on productivity has not been evenly distributed among all parts of the labor force. On the contrary, one of the most striking characteristics of technology has been its *uneven entry* into production. In some sectors, such as agriculture, the effects of technology on output have been startling. Between

THE PROBLEM OF AUTOMATION

1880 and today, for instance, the time required to harvest an acre of wheat on the Great Plains has fallen from 20 hours to 3. Between the late 1930s and the mid-1960s, the manhours needed to obtain a hundredweight of milk were slashed from 3.4 to 0.9; a hundredweight of chickens from 8.5 to 0.6.

Not quite so dramatic but also far-reaching in their effect have been technological impacts in other areas. Output per worker has roughly doubled or tripled in most manufacturing industries over the last 20 years.

By way of contrast to the very great advances of productivity in the agricultural and manufacturing sectors, we must note the laggard advance in productivity in the tertiary sector of activity. Output per manhour in trade, for instance, or in education or in the service professions such as law or medicine or, again, in domestic or personal services such as barbering or repair work or in government has not increased nearly so much as in the primary and secondary sectors.

INFLUENCE OF DEMAND

These strikingly different rates of increase in productivity begin to suggest a way of analyzing the effects of automation, or for that matter, any kind of labor-saving machinery. Clearly, capital equipment increases the *potential output* of a given number of workers. But will increased output be absorbed through expanded demand, allowing the workers to keep their jobs? Let us look at the question first in its broadest scope. We have seen that productivity has increased fastest in agriculture, next in manufacturing, least in services. What has happened to demand for the output of these sectors? The table shows us the answers.

DOMESTIC DEMAND FOR OUTPUT

| | Distribution of demand (%) | |
	1899–1908	1976
Primary sector (agriculture)	16.7	3.2
Secondary sector (mining, construction, mfg.)	26.0	32.3
Tertiary sector transportation, communication, govt., other services)	57.2	64.5

What we see here is a shift working in a direction different from that of supply. As the productivity and potential output of the agricultural sector has risen, the demand for agricultural products has not followed suit but has lagged far behind. Demand has risen markedly for output coming from the secondary sector, but has remained roughly unchanged, in percentage terms, for the output of the tertiary service sector.

SQUEEZE ON EMPLOYMENT

If we now put together the forces of supply and demand, it is easy to understand what has happened to employment. The tremendous increase in productivity on the farm, faced with a shrinking proportionate demand for food, created a vast army of redundant labor in agriculture. Where did the labor go? It followed the route indicated by the growth of demand, migrating from the countryside into factory towns and cities where it found employment in manufacturing and service occupations. As the next table shows, the distribution of employment has steadily moved out of the primary and secondary, into the tertiary sector.

What we see here is the crucial role of technology in distributing employment among its various uses. As income rose, purchasing power no longer used for food was diverted to manufactured goods and homes. We would therefore expect that the proportion of the labor force employed in these pursuits would have risen rapidly. Instead, as we can see, it has fallen slightly. This is because technological improvements entered the secondary sector along with manpower, greatly increasing the productivity of workers in this area. Therefore a smaller portion of the national labor force could satisfy the larger proportional demands of the public for output from this sector.

DISTRIBUTION OF EMPLOYMENT

	Distribution of all employed workers (%)	
	1900	1976
Primary sector	38.1	3.8
Secondary sector	37.7	29.7
Tertiary sector	24.2	66.5

Most important of all is the service sector. As the first table shows us, the public has not much changed the share of income that it spends for the various outputs we call services. But technological advances have not exerted their leverage as dramatically here as elsewhere, so that it takes a much larger fraction of the work force to produce the services we demand.

IMPORTANCE OF THE TERTIARY SECTOR

The conclusion, then, is that the demand for labor reflects the interplay of technology (which exerts differing leverages on different industries and occupations at different times) and of changing demand for goods and services. Typically, the entrance of technology into industry has a twofold effect. The first is to raise the *potential* output of the industry, with its present labor force. The second is to enable the costs of the industry to decline, or its quality to improve, so that actual demand for the product will increase. But normally, the rise in demand is not great enough to enable the existing labor force to be retained along with the new techniques. Instead, some labor must now find its employment elsewhere.

There are exceptions, of course. But taking all industries and all technological changes together, the net result is unambiguous. **As our next table reveals, technology has**

THE PROBLEM OF AUTOMATION
(cont.)

steadily **increased our ability to create goods, both on the farm and on the factory floor, more rapidly than we have wished to consume them, with the result that employment in these areas has lagged behind output.**

OUTPUT AND EMPLOYMENT INDICES

	1950	1975
Agricultural output	100	130
Agricultural employment	100	47
Manufacturing output	100	206
Manufacturing employment	100	120
1950 = 100		

Note how agricultural output has increased rapidly in this period, while agricultural employment has shrunk by over 50 percent; and notice that whereas manufacturing output has more than doubled, employment in manufacturing is up by only 20 percent.

During this same period, however, our total civilian labor force increased by over 20 million. Where did these millions find employment? As we would expect, largely in the service sector. Figures for employment in various parts of the service sector appear in the fourth table. We might note that comparable shifts from agriculture "through" manufacturing into services are visible in all industrial nations.

SERVICE EMPLOYMENTS

	1950	1976	Increase
	(in millions)		1950–1976
Trade	9.4	17.5	86%
Services	5.4	14.6	170
Government	6.0	15.1	152
Finance and other	1.9	4.3	126
Total tertiary sector	22.7	51.5	127

IMPACT OF AUTOMATION

How does automation enter this picture? Our analysis reveals the threat that this new complicated technology may hold. It is that the whole complex of paper-handling, decision-making, service-generating devices we lump under the name of automation may represent the belated entry of technology into areas of economic activity that until now have been largely spared the impact of technical change. These are the areas of service and administrative tasks that we have previously marked as an important source of growing employment. *Thus the danger inherent in the new sensory, almost humanoid equipment is that it may put an end to the traditional employment-absorptive effects of the tertiary service and administrative sector.*

The implications of such a development would be very great. It would mean the end of the "safety valve" function provided by traditional service employments, and a corresponding need to find new ways to absorb labor that was rendered jobless in agriculture or manufacturing. What these methods might be we shall discuss further in the text.

But our analysis of the squeeze that machines have put on employment in some sectors and the absorption of employment in other sectors allows us to put the problem of automation in a historic perspective. We must wait to see if automation does indeed mean the full-scale invasion of the store and the office by machinery. If so, we shall have to find new ways of coping with a problem that an "old-fashioned" service sector has previously solved for us.

Government as employer of last resort

At the end of our chapter we broach a question of very great importance: can capitalism function with very low rates of unemployment? The danger, as we have mentioned, is that low unemployment would remove the "reserve army of the unemployed" and would create an upward pressure on wages. Prices would skyrocket; profits plummet.

There is a strong possibility that we will face a decisive test of that question in the reasonably near future. For on the agenda of possible legislation, there is the Humphrey-Hawkins bill, named after its principal cosponsors, Sen. Hubert H. Humphrey (D., Minn.) and Rep. Augustus F. Hawkins (D., Calif.), whose purpose is to assure that we make really full employment an official objective of U.S. economic policy.

We do not have such a policy today. The Employment Act of 1946, much heralded at its time of passage, commits the United States to the attainment of only "maximum feasible" employment. It makes no effort to define what this level might be or to designate the means of achieving it. The Humphrey-Hawkins bill, as it now stands, goes far beyond this. First, it defines "full employment" as 3 percent unemployment— barely above the frictional level. Second, it directs the government to attain this level by a number of fiscal and monetary means, but above all by the creation of permanent, desirable jobs open to all who want to work but cannot find acceptable work in the private sector. That is what is meant by making the government the employer of last resort. In effect, it makes the government a guarantor of full employment.

What sorts of problems will the Humphrey-Hawkins bill present if it is enacted into legislation? Here are some of them:

1. Will a guaranteed job program be limited to periods of recession or maintained during good times as well? The aim of the sponsors is certainly to maintain the program in operation year in, year out. But this means that during good times, the public and private sectors will compete for workers. As conditions improve, business will have to bid workers away from jobs, not from unemployment. This will raise the costs of creating new private employment—and may dampen the possibility for sustaining booms.

2. A related question has to do with the sorts of jobs that the public sector will offer. Will they be unskilled jobs, such as sweeping the streets or relaying the nation's roadbeds? This will hardly make them attractive to the skilled unemployed. Or will the jobs be creative, career-oriented work, such as redesigning the inner city, rehabilitating the handicapped, tending the young and the old? In that case, public jobs may be more attractive than private ones.

3. What will be the pay relation between similar jobs—say, a crane operator, a key punch operator, an office manager—in the public sector and the private sector? If we make the two sectors equal, will not the public sector, with its tradition of civil service, "outpull" the private? If we make public sector jobs pay less, are we really creating public employment or merely a fancy kind of public dole?

4. How will we determine what public jobs are worth creating? (This takes us into the question of national planning, a problem we examine in our next "Extra word.")

5. The biggest question of all: can we run an effective full-employment program without pushing wage rates up, accelerating inflation, and pushing down profits? This last crucial question ties back into some of the previous ones. If we keep the public service jobs at pay levels moderately below the private level—say 10 percent— then we could use public employment as a means of finding useful work for the "reserve army of the unemployed," adding to our output of needed goods and services with a minimal effect on the general level of wages.

But we can also see that this use of the public sector openly relegates public sector jobs beneath private sector jobs. It implies that we will use the public sector as a means of providing something better than unemployment insurance or welfare, but not that we are prepared to embark on imaginative, creative projects for which we would require first-rate talents who would not accept second-rate pay. In turn, this use of the public sector opens the dreary prospect of a public work force without morale or incentive.

We do not know, at this writing, whether the Humphrey-Hawkins bill or some similar bill will be passed. Our own inclinations strongly favor such a bill. The right to work strikes us as a fundamental element of a good society. But as this "Extra word" should make clear, we are far from blind to the range and difficulty of the problems that this new policy would create.

Problems of economic growth

Almost from the first pages of this book, growth has been at the center of our focus. Now, in this final chapter on that subject, we must return explicitly to the problem, adding to our previous knowledge and reflecting on issues that we have not yet had an opportunity to explore in depth.

The Business Cycle

Let us begin by investigating an aspect of growth that we have heretofore ignored. It is the uneven pace at which the historic trajectory of growth proceeds. If you will take a moment to look back at the chart of national growth on p. 2, you will notice its long, almost uninterrupted upward slope; or again, a glance at p. 4 will show the same thing.

18

Short vs. long run

But these long-run charts, on which only very large movements are visible, conceal from our view another aspect of the growth process that is of very great importance. In any short-run period,

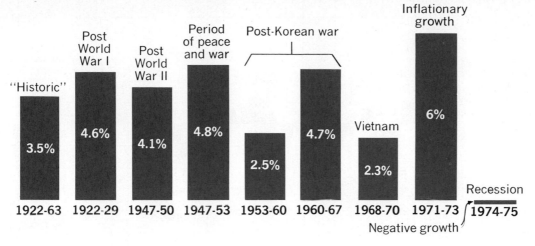

FIG. 18·1 Short-term variations in the rate of growth

the long-run consistency fades from view and the economy is marked by sharp ups and downs in the growth in output.

Take the years 1895 to 1905, very smooth-looking on the chart on p. 60. As Table 18·1 reveals, those years were, in fact, anything but steady.

Table 18·1 U.S. rates of growth 1895–1905

1895–1896	−2.5%	1900–1901	+11.5%
1896–1897	+9.4	1901–1902	+ 1.0
1897–1898	+2.3	1902–1903	+ 4.9
1898–1899	+9.1	1903–1904	− 1.2
1899–1900	+2.7	1904–1905	+ 7.4

Source: *Long Term Economic Growth* (U.S. Dept. of Commerce, 1966), p. 107.

Or examine a more recent period, not year by year, but in groups of years. As we can see in Fig. 18·1 the rate of growth has varied greatly over the last fifty years. At times, such as the 1974–1975 recession, the economy has even shown negative rates of growth. These episodes may show up only as small dips in the graph of our long-term advance, but they have meant suffering and deprivation for millions of persons who were robbed of work or income as a consequence of these dips.

Cycles

This sequence of ups and downs, riches of growth followed by doldrums, introduces us to the question of business cycles. For if we inspect the profile of the long ascent carefully, we can see that its entire length is marked with irregular tremors or peaks and valleys. Indeed, the more closely we examine year-to-year figures, the more of these tremors and deviations we discover, until the problem becomes one of selection: which vibrations to consider significant and which to discard as uninteresting.

The problem of sorting out the important fluctuations in output (or in statistics of prices or employment) is a difficult one. Economists have actually detected dozens of cycles of different lengths and amplitudes, from very short rhythms of expansion and contraction that can be found, for example, in patterns of inventory accumulation and decumulation, to large background pulsations of 17 or 18 years in the housing industry, and possibly (the evidence is unclear) swings of 40 to 50 years in the path of capitalist development as a whole.

Generally, however, when we speak of "the" business cycle we refer to a wavelike movement that lasts, on the average,

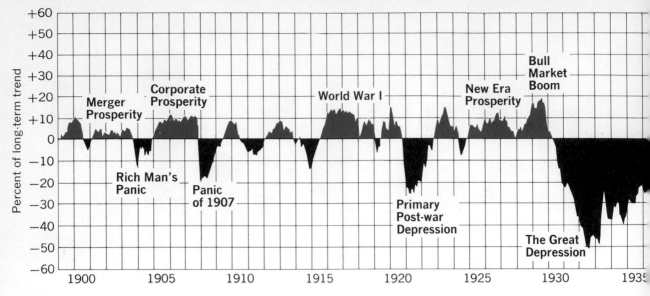

FIG. 18·2   The business cycle

about 8 to 10 years. In Fig. 18·2 this major oscillation of the American economy stands forth very clearly, for the chartist has eliminated the underlying tilt of growth, so that the profile of economic performance looks like a cross section at sea level rather than a cut through a long incline.

Reference cycles   In a general way we are all familiar with the meaning of business cycles, for the alternation of "boom and bust" or prosperity and recession (a polite name for a mild depression) is part of everyday parlance. It

will help us study cycles, however, if we learn to speak of them with a standard terminology. We can do this by taking the cycles from actual history, "superimposing" them, and drawing the general profile of the so-called *reference* cycle that emerges. It looks like Fig. 18·3. This model of a typical cycle enables us to speak of the "length" of a business cycle as the period from one peak to the next or from trough to trough. If we fail to measure from *similar* points on two or more cycles, we can easily get a distorted picture of short-term growth—for instance, one that begins at the upper turning point of one cycle and measures to the trough of the

FIG. 18·3   The reference cycle

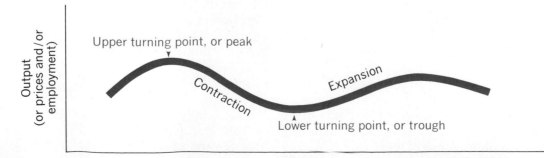

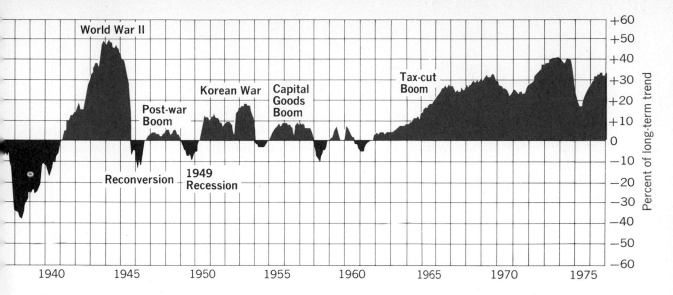

World War II

Korean War

Capital Goods Boom

Tax-cut Boom

Post-war Boom

Reconversion

1949 Recession

Percent of long-term trend

+60
+50
+40
+30
+20
+10
0
−10
−20
−30
−40
−50
−60

1940   1945   1950   1955   1960   1965   1970   1975

Courtesy Cleveland Trust.

next. Much of the political charge and countercharge about growth rates can be clarified if we examine the starting and terminating dates used by each side.

Causes of cycles

What lies behind this more or less regular alternation of good and bad times?

Innumerable theories, none of them entirely satisfactory, have been advanced to explain the business cycle. A common business explanation is that waves of optimism in the world of affairs alternate with waves of pessimism—a statement that may be true enough, but that seems to describe the sequence of events rather than to explain it. Hence economists have tried to find the underlying cyclical mechanism in firmer stuff than an alternation of moods. One famous late-nineteenth-century economist, W. S. Jevons, for example, explained business cycles as the consequence of sunspots— perhaps not as occult a theory as it might seem, since Jevons believed that the sunspots caused weather cycles that caused crop cycles that caused business

cycles. The trouble was that subsequent investigation shows that the periodicity of sunspots was sufficiently different from that of rainfall cycles to make the connection impossible.

Other economists have turned to causes closer to home: to variations in the rate of gold mining (with its effects on the money supply); to fluctuations in the rate of invention; to the regular recurrence of war; and to yet many other factors. There is no doubt that many of these events can induce a business expansion or contraction. The persistent problem, however, is that none of the so-called underlying causes itself displays an inherent cyclicality—much less one with a periodicity of 8 to 10 years.

The multiplier accelerator cycle

Then how do we explain cycles? Economists no longer seek a single explanation of the phenomenon in an exogenous (that is, external) cyclical force. Rather, they tend to see cycles as our own eye first

287

saw them on the growth curve—*as varia-tions in the rate of growth that tend to be induced by the dynamics of growth itself.*

We can gain considerable insight into this uneven pace of growth if we combine our knowledge of the multiplier and the accelerator—the latter, we recall, showing us the investment induced by the growth of output.

Boom and bust　　Let us, then, assume that some stimulus such as an important industry-building invention, has begun to increase invest-ment expenditures. We can easily see how such an initial impetus can generate a cu-mulative and self-feeding boom. As the multiplier and accelerator interact, the first burst of investment stimulates additional consumption, the additional consumption induces more investment, and this in turn reinvigorates consumption. Meanwhile, this process of mutual stimulation serves to lift business expectations and to en-courage still further expansionary spend-ing. Inventories are built up in anticipa-tion of larger sales. Prices "firm up," and the stock market rises. Optimism reigns. A boom is on.

What happens to end such a boom? There are many possible reasons why it may peter out or come to an abrupt halt. It may simply be that the new industry will get built, and thereafter an important stimulus to investment will be lacking. Or even before it is completed, wages and prices may have begun to rise as full em-ployment is neared, and the climate of ex-pectations may become wary. ("What goes up must come down," is an old adage in business, too.) Meanwhile, perhaps tight money will choke off spending plans or make new projects appear unprofitable.

Or investment may begin to decline because consumption, although still ris-ing, is no longer rising at the earlier *rate* (the acceleration principle in action). We

have already noticed that the action of the accelerator, all by itself, could give rise to wavelike movements in total expenditure (see p. 148). The accelerator, of course, never works all by itself, but it can exert its upward and downward pressures within the flux of economic forces and in this way give rise to an underlying cyclical im-petus.

Contraction and recovery　　It is impossible to know in advance what particular cause will retard spending—a credit shortage, a very tight labor market, a saturation of de-mand for a key industry's products (such as automobiles). But it is all too easy to see how a hesitation in spending can turn into a general contraction. Perhaps warned by a falling stock market, perhaps by a slowdown in sales or an end to rising profits, business begins to cut back. Whatever the initial motivation, what follows thereafter is much like the preced-ing expansion, only in reverse. The multi-plier mechanism now breeds smaller rather than larger incomes. Downward re-visions of expectations reduce rather than enhance the attractiveness of investment projects. As consumption decreases, unemployment begins to rise. Inventories are worked off. Bankruptcies become more common. We experience all the economic and social problems of a recession.

But just as there is a "natural" ceiling to a boom, so there is a more or less "natural" floor to recessions. The fall in in-ventories, for example, will eventually come to an end: for even in the severest recessions, merchants and manufacturers must have *some* goods on their shelves and so must eventually begin stocking up. The decline in expenditures will lead to easy money, and the slack in output will tend to a lower level of costs: and both of these factors will encourage new investment projects. Meanwhile, the countercyclical effects of government fiscal policy will slowly make their effects known. Sooner or later, in other words, expenditures will cease falling, and the economy will tend to "bottom out."

Government-caused cycles

We have spoken about business cycles as if they were initially triggered by a spontaneous rise in investment or by natural cessation of investment. But our acquaintance with the relative sizes of the components of GNP should make us wary of placing the blame for recessions solely on industry. More and more, as government has become a major source of spending, cycles have resulted from variations in the rate of government spending, not business spending. Cycles these days, more often than not, are made in Washington.

Take the six recessions (periods of decline in real GNP lasting at least six months) since World War II. Every one of them can be traced to changes in government budgetary policies. The first four recessions—in 1949, 1954, 1957–1958 and 1960–1961—resulted from changes in the military budget. In each case, the federal government curtailed its rate of military expenditure without taking compensatory action by increasing expenditure elsewhere or by cutting taxes. The result in each instance was a slackening in the rate of growth.

The 1969–1970 and the 1974–1975 recessions are even more interesting. They represent the first cases in which the federal government deliberately created a recession, through fiscal and monetary policies aimed at slowing down the economy. The purpose, as we know, was to dampen inflation. The result was to reverse the trend of growth. Thus, it is no longer possible, as it once was, to discuss business cycles as if they were purely the outcome of the market process. *There is no*

doubt that the market mechanism has produced cycles in the past, and would continue to produce them if the government were miraculously removed from the economy. But given the size of the public sector these days, we need to look first to changes in government spending as the initiating source of a cycle.

Curbing the business cycle

Can we do something about the cycle? Of course. All of our previous discussion of fiscal and monetary policy can be readily viewed in the context of trying to eliminate the fluctuations around a steady growth path.

Unhappily, the same problems that we have discussed at length in demand management and monetary policy also apply in the area of lessening the severity of the business cycle. The lags in time before we recognize a given situation, the delay before a remedy takes hold, the difficulty of measuring the appropriate dosage of our economic medicines, the continuous shifts in the spontaneous forces of investment spending or in government budgeting—all these enormously complicate the task of anti-business-cycle policy.

Nonetheless, difficult as it is to mitigate cycles, at least we have a clear picture of what we are doing. We know the basic causes, but our problems are in the difficulties of applying theory in the turmoil of real world events.

Long-Run Stable Growth

However difficult in practice, the aim of a fluctuation-free path of growth directs our attention once again to our long historic trajectory. Anti-business-cycle policy merely tries to iron out the wrinkles in our path of growth. But what about the path it-self? What determines how rapid our historic advance should be?

Potential vs. actual growth

This brings us again to a consideration in our previous chapter—the need for GNP to grow in order to accommodate a growing labor force and a rising level of productivity. If we multiply the rise in our year-to-year hours of labor input by an index of the rising productivity of that labor, we can easily derive a curve showing our *potential output over time*. The question is therefore how much of that potential output we do in fact produce.

As Fig. 18 • 4 shows, all through much of the 1950s, 1960s, and the mid-1970s, potential output ran well ahead of the output we actually achieved. Indeed, between 1958 and 1962 the amount of lost output represented by this gap came to the staggering sum of $170 billion. Even in 1972, a prosperous prerecession year, we could have added another $55 billion to GNP—$1,000 per family—if we had brought unemployment down from the actual level of 5.6 percent to 4 percent. In 1975, the total of lost output was immense—$136 billion in 1958 dollars.

Demand vs. capacity

The idea of a potential growth rate opens an aspect of the investment process that we have not yet considered. Heretofore, we have always thought of investment primarily as an income-generating force, working through the multiplier to increase the level of ex-

FIG. 18 • 4   Actual and potential GNP

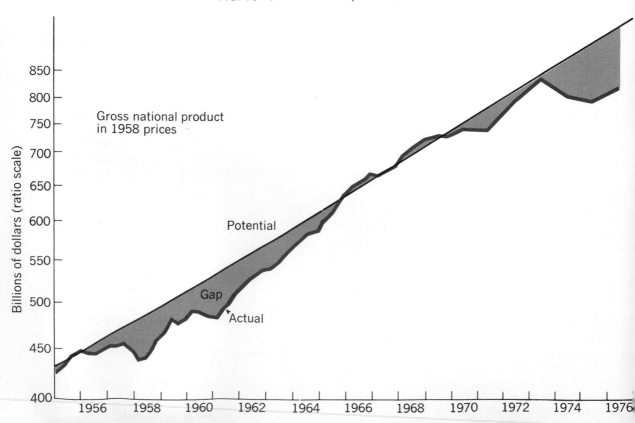

penditure. Now we begin to consider investment also as a *capacity-generating force*, working through the actual addition to our plant and equipment to increase the productive potential of the system.

No sooner do we introduce the idea of capacity, however, than a new problem arises for our consideration. *If investment increases potential output as well as income, the obvious question is: will income rise fast enough to buy all this potential output? Thus at the end of our analysis of macroeconomics we revert to the question we posed at the beginning, but in a more dynamic context. At first, we asked whether an economy that saved could buy back its own output. Now we must ask whether an economy that grows can do the same.*

Marginal capital-output ratio

The question brings us to a new concept. The *marginal capital-output ratio*, as the formidable name suggests, is not a relationship that describes behavior, as the multiplier does. It describes a strictly technical or engineering or organizational relationship between an *increase in the stock of capital and the increase in output that this new capital will yield.*

Note that we are not interested in the ratio between our entire existing stock of capital (most of which is old) and the flow of total output, but only in the ratio between the *new* capital added during the period and the *new* output associated with that new capital. Thus the marginal capital-output ratio directs our attention to the *net investment* of the period and to the *change in output* of the period. If net investment was $60 billion and the change in output yielded by that investment was $20 billion, then the marginal capital-output ratio was 3.

Income vs. output

The marginal capital-output ratio gives us a powerful new concept to bring to bear on the problem of attaining and maintaining a high, steady rate of growth, for we can now see that the problem of steady growth requires the balancing out of two different economic processes. Investment raises productive capacity. *Increases* in investment raise income and demand. What we must now do is investigate the relationship between these two different, albeit related, economic variables.

Let us begin with a familiar formula that shows how a change in investment affects a change in income. This is

$$\Delta Y = \left(\frac{1}{\text{mps}}\right) \times \Delta I$$

which is nothing but the multiplier. For brevity, we will write it

$$\Delta Y = \left(\frac{1}{s}\right)\Delta I$$

where s stands for all leakages.

Now we need a new formula to relate I, the rate of new investment (not ΔI, the *change* in new investment), and ΔO, the change in dollar output. This will require a symbol for the marginal capital-output ratio, a symbol that expresses how many dollars' worth of output comes from a dollar's worth of investment. If we use the symbol σ (sigma), we can write this relationship as follows:

$$\Delta O = \left(\frac{I}{\sigma}\right)$$

showing that increased output (ΔO) is determined by investment (I) divided by the marginal capital/output ratio, σ.

For example, if we have $10 of new investment, and σ is 2, output will rise by $5.00. If σ is 3, output will rise by $3.33.

(Note that the smaller σ is, the larger is the addition to output of a given investment.)

Balanced growth in theory

We now have two formulas. The first tells us by how much *income* will rise as investment grows. The second tells us by how much *output* will rise from a given rate of investment. Thus we are ready to take the last and most important step. We can discover *by how much investment must rise each year, to give us the additional income we will need to buy the addition to output that has been created by this selfsame investment.*

Our formulas enable us to answer that question very clearly. Increased income is ΔY. Increased output is ΔO. Since $\Delta Y = \left(\dfrac{1}{s}\right)\Delta I$, and $\Delta O = \dfrac{I}{\sigma}$ then ΔY will equal ΔO if $\left(\dfrac{1}{s}\right)\Delta I = \dfrac{I}{\sigma}$. This is the formula for balanced growth.

If we now multiply both sides of the equation by s, and then divide both sides by I, we get

$$\frac{\Delta I}{I} = \frac{s}{\sigma}$$

Balanced growth in fact

What does this equation mean? It tells us what *rate of growth of investment* $(\Delta I/I)$ is needed to make $\Delta Y = \Delta O$. In words, it tells us by what percentage investment spending must rise to make income payments keep pace with dollar output. That rate of growth is equal to the marginal savings (or leakage) ratio divided by the marginal capital-output ratio. Suppose, for instance, that the marginal leakage ratio is ⅓ and that the marginal capital-output ratio (σ) is 3. Then s/σ is ⅓ ÷ 3 (or ⅑), which means that investment would have to grow by ⅑ each year to create just enough income to match the growing flow of output. If the rate of investment grew faster than that, income and demand would tend to grow ahead of output and we would be pushing beyond the path of balanced growth into inflation. If the rate of growth of investment were smaller than that, we would be experiencing chronic overproduction with falling prices and sagging employment.

What is the rate at which investment should rise for balanced growth in the United States? To determine that, we would have to deal with tricky statistical problems of marginal capital-output ratios; we would have to calculate *net* investment—not easy to do; and marginal leakages would have to behave as tamely as they do in textbooks—not always the case. Moreover, to include public as well as private capital formation in the terms "investment" and "marginal capital output ratio" would also greatly complicate our computations.

Therefore we shall sidestep here the difficult empirical problems posed by the requirements for balanced growth and concentrate on the general issue that the formulation opens up. For the purpose of our discussion is to explain that there is a complex relationship between the growth in income and the growth in output. **Our analysis shows that we can have a** *growth gap* **if our leakages are too high, so that increases in injections do not generate enough new purchasing power, or if our marginal capital-output ratio is too low, so that a given amount of investment increases our potential output (our capacity) too fast.***

---

*One question may have occurred to the reader. Aren't incomes and outputs *identities*? Isn't it true that GNI ≡ GNP? Then how can a growth "gap" occur? The answer lies in our familiar ex ante and ex post perspectives (see page 198). Ex post, incomes are always the same as outputs. Ex ante they are not. The question, then, is not whether or not GNI will be equal to GNP, but *whether their identical values will be equal to potential output*. Our formula for balanced growth tells us which critical variables must be taken into account when we ask whether ex ante spending plans will bring us to a level of income and output that corresponds with *potential production*.

Policy for balanced growth

Suppose that we are not generating income fast enough to absorb our potential output. Suppose, to go back to Fig. 18·4, that we have a persistent growth gap similar to that of the late 1950s or middle 1970s. How can we bring the economy up to its potential?

Our formula for balanced growth gives us the answer. The relationship between the growth of incomes and the growth of output depends above all on the rate at which investment *increases*. Thus, if expenditures fall short of the amount needed to absorb potential output, the answer is to raise the rate of investment or, perhaps more realistically, to raise the rate of growth of all expenditures, public and private. Conversely, of course, if we find ourselves pushing over the trend line of potential growth into inflation, as in the late 1960s, the indicated policy is to lower the rate of growth of investment (or of investment and government and consumption) to bring the flow of rising incomes back into balance with the rise of output.

Thus the critical element in balancing a growing economy is not the *amount* of investment needed to fill a given demand gap, but the *increase* in investment (or other injection-expenditure) needed to match a growing output capacity with a large enough demand.

Here, one final time, we encounter the techniques and the problems familiar to us from our glance at anti-business-cycle policy and, before that, from our analysis of the means to combat unemployment and inflation. Demand management, through fiscal or monetary measures, remains the principal weapon at our disposal, supplemented in the future, perhaps, by measures for economic goal-setting (planning) that we will shortly discuss. And all the difficulties that we have considered heretofore remain to plague us in the pursuit of a policy of minimizing the growth gap.

Necessity for adequate growth

Nevertheless, the concept of a growth gap or a growth surplus enables us finally to put anti-business-cycle policy into a dynamic perspective. For we can now see that the objective of national economic policy is not merely to even out the ups and downs of a cycle but to assure a rate of expansion as close as possible to the line of our potential growth.

Here, of course, we come once again to the seemingly inescapable problem of choosing between inflation and unemployment. **The line of potential growth gives us our target if we want to put full employment at the head of our list of priorities.** But we know that the public does not want to do so. It prefers unemployment to inflation, hoping that the one will cure the other. *Nevertheless, the line of a rising potential GNP makes it clear that unless we grow at a sufficiently rapid rate, our unemployment will worsen. Even if we do not fully match income and potential output, income must grow to keep our condition of economic well-being unchanged. Growth is a prime essential for the healthy functioning of a capitalist system.*

The dangers of growth

But what about the dangers of growth that we discussed at the beginning of our studies (pp. 14f.)? Is there not a fundamental dilemma posed by the need to assure steady, high-level economic growth, on the one hand, and the dangers of resource stringency and pollution damage on the other?

There is indeed such a dilemma, and in the long run—over the next two or three generations—it may well be that we shall have to take drastic steps to curtail or monitor growth, unless we achieve dramatic technological breakthroughs. Even in the middle run—say during the next generation—there are likely to be conflicts between the need for growth and the dangers of growth. There is likely to be a scramble for certain kinds of resources, especially as the underdeveloped nations exert their claims for goods and tighten their hold on minerals. There is certain to be a series of assaults on the environment—chemical wastes poisoning fish, fertilizers endangering water supplies, smogs affecting health.

We hope that we can use this middle period to lessen these risks, learn how to recycle materials, utilize less toxic processes, harness the forces of the sun and the tides, bring population growth to zero. If we could achieve these ends, we may learn how to maintain a high level of employment and a better distribution of output with a slower rate of growth, or without any reliance on dangerous growth. Further into the distance lies the possibility of approaching a stationary state, although that is a problematic question (see box, above).

All this will take time, however. *For another decade or two we shall need growth to assure a high level of employment, and we shall also have to cope with the particular dangers that growth may bring, in squeezes on certain resources or the disturbance of the environment.*

Growth and national planning

These two requirements strongly suggest that we will be moving in a direction of more national economic planning.

Planning is a word that disturbs many

people. This is not the place to discuss all its pros and cons or to spell out the ways in which planning might be carried out within a capitalist system. We shall look into some of these matters in the "Extra word about national economic planning," pp. 298–99. Here we want to take up only two aspects of this very large and important question.

Plan or market?

The first has to do with the need for planning. Can we not assure ourselves of safe and satisfactory growth without planning? Cannot the market mechanism, by itself, accomplish these objectives without more intrusive government activity?

Of course, in such matters, one can never be sure. But neither our historical record nor our analytical understanding gives us much reason to believe that an unsupervised and undirected market system would bring about growth that was either steady or adequate. The instability of the investment process (and of the government budget, as it is now used), the cumulative tendencies of the business cycle, the unpredictable effects of technology—now creating labor displacement, now building new industries—these and many other familiar problems make the present system a poor guarantor of steady economic growth. And we have seen that the market system is no guarantor at all of full employment growth.

The same doubts apply to the market's capacity to provide safe growth. To some extent, as we know, the market acts as a safety mechanism, using the signal of high prices to discourage the use of scarce resources. But the market has no way at all of signaling the presence of many dangerous processes. Nor can the market serve to set into motion research and development activities that may be needed today to forestall a resource squeeze 25 years off—the very situation we face in our energy crisis.

Therefore, it seems probable that we shall extend our efforts to assure the pace and monitoring of growth. This will likely take the form of widening and strengthening our existing measures for demand management, and integrating these with democratically-chosen general macro and micro targets for the economy as a whole. National economic planning will not be so much a radical departure from present ways as it will be a coordination of existing institutions for the attainment of clearly articulated goals.

Planning and freedom

A second issue is whether planning, even for such benign purposes as the promotion and protection of growth, is compatible with economic and political freedom.

This is not a question to which quick answers ought to be given, positive or negative. There are assuredly risks in planning, no matter how mild the institutions of planning may be. There are always dangers inherent in the expansion of government authority, no matter for what good end. It would be wrong to deny that planning might lead toward a more statist regime.

But it would be foolish to assert that planning *must* bring such unwanted changes. We have a long history of government authority within the economy, from the days of Theodore Roosevelt, through Franklin Roosevelt, down to present times; but it would be hard to claim that this expansion of government has come at the expense of capitalism or freedom. Rather, one can make a good case that the continued functioning of liberal capitalism has required government to extend its authority into new economic fields to forestall or remedy economic or social problems. Planning for safe, stable growth could well be another instance of that same process.

Then, too, for every risk associated with planning one must weigh the risk of not planning. Suppose that we consistently fail to reach high employment, through a lack of planning. What consequences, economic or political, might that bring? Suppose that we encounter resource or pollution crises because we have not taken the measures to avert them. What results could that bring?

A *last word*

There is no final judgment to be rendered in these matters. Some economists will remain opposed to planning because they believe that the economic system, more or less as it is presently constituted, will give us good enough growth and fewer risks of bureaucracy or oppression. Others, including the authors of this book, expect and welcome the development of planning to sustain and safeguard growth. In "An extra word" we shall discuss what such a plan might look like in operation.

What is important in these matters is not to overstate the case, either for or against one's judgment. In our view, planning will be an important step in making capitalism capable of better meeting the challenges of our time, but we want to emphasize that planning is certain to bring as many new problems as solutions to old ones. In economics, as in daily life, there are no lasting solutions. There is only the never-ending effort to cope with a changing reality as best we can.

FOCUS

This chapter takes us from business cycles through balanced growth into full-potential expansion and economic planning. Of all the topics, probably the last is the most important, although it is the least "technical." We suggest that you read "An extra word" to follow and that you try to think hard about the side opposite from that which you tend to favor. There are certainly cogent arguments to be raised against economic planning, and good or better arguments (we think) in its favor. You should know both.

The main technical points of the chapter are two. The first has to do with the idea of "balanced" growth—growth that balances the generation of additional income with that of additional output. The formulas that state this balance are very difficult to translate into actual statistical measurements, so that balanced growth is an idea rather than a working tool. But it is an idea that we need if we are to understand why a growing economy will not run out of purchasing power, provided its growth of investment is high enough. This is a concept as useful as that of closing a static demand gap.

Balanced growth also helps us grasp the idea of a growth gap—the loss we suffer from failing to grow up to our productive capacity—and of the measures needed to remedy it. Unlike balanced growth, the line of "potential output" is easily fleshed out with statistics, so that we can measure the loss in man-years of production from a failure to grow at an adequate rate.

Finally, business cycles. We do not have time or space fully to discuss the fascinating question of the periodicity of cycles—why they have lasted about eight to ten years—or of the many cyclical rhythms that can be discovered in the economy.

That is better reserved for an advanced course on business cycles. But you ought to understand how the multiplier-accelerator interaction acts to swell the recovery phase and to add momentum to a contraction. These are processes that lie behind the newspaper descriptions of "booms" and "recessions," and you should be sure that you can describe them clearly.

WORDS AND CONCEPTS YOU SHOULD KNOW

QUESTIONS

1. Explain how the interaction of the accelerator and the multiplier can give rise to booms and busts. Why does a multiplier-accelerator model not tell us anything about the periodicity of cycles? Have you any ideas why the average cycle has been 8 to 10 years long? Suppose that capital goods tend to wear out and need to be replaced in about a decade. Would this by itself give rise to a cycle if the replacement (or original investment) were not bunched in time? Would it, if that were the case?

2. Try to get hold of a time series, such as a chart of stock market prices or GNP over a long time—say 10 years. Can you spot a cycle in the data? More than one?

3. What are the sources of growth for potential GNP? Explain why potential GNP is a kind of production possibility curve through time.

4. Investment adds both to capacity and the income. How does it add to capacity? Is this a behavioral function? What about the addition to income? Write the formula for balanced growth, carefully explaining to yourself the difference between the marginal capital-output ratio and the multiplier.

5. List the major policy problems in achieving balanced growth. Are they the same as those in minimizing business cycles?

6. How do you feel about the idea of national economic planning? Do you think it will infringe on economic liberty substantially? In what areas? What measures, if any, would you suggest instead?

National economic planning

For the reasons that we have seen, national economic planning is likely to become a reality—and is certain to be a topic of discussion—within the near future. What would such planning actually be like?

It is a great deal easier to say what American planning would *not* mean than to describe what it will be like. The first necessity is to disabuse ourselves of the idea that planning would mean the establishment of a giant apparatus resembling the cumbersome central planning system of the Soviet Union. Soviet planning, which attempts to substitute computerized calculation and ministerial direction for the mechanism of the market, can launch a stagnant society on a course of economic growth; but it is ill-adapted to the needs—not to speak of the traditions and values—of societies such as those of Europe or the United States.

Instead of central planning, we can expect that national economic planning in America will follow the course that is already emerging in Europe and Japan. This is an effort to use the market as a planning instrument and to confine the operation of planning to the establishment of long-term objectives, such as the national rate of growth or the level of unemployment or the rate of inflation or big micro objectives such as transportation, energy, or urban rehabilitation.

HOW PLANNING WORKS

How could this be done? As the planning process is currently envisaged by most economists, the first step is the formulation of a number of alternative micro and macro targets by a small group of economists and statisticians within the Executive branch. The initial task of planning is thus to work out a series of different "menus" of economic possibilities extending forward 3 to 5 years. Of course these menus will be political. They will present the preferences of the planners, or more realistically, of the Administration for whom the planners work.

But the menus are not just expressions of political preference. They are also efforts to discover what possibilities lie within the economy's grasp, given its labor force, its capital resources, its known technology, and so forth. In a sense, this first exercise is a translation of the idea of a production possibilities curve into reality.

How is such a set of menus drawn up? The first requirement is an extensive and reliable flow of economic statistics. Large as our present base of knowledge is, it is not large enough to allow us to make many economic calculations with much accuracy. (Just as an example: until the Arab oil crisis, there was no official statistical information regarding the size of total gasoline stocks in the country!)

These statistics would then be coordinated within an input-output matrix (see "An extra word" at the end of Chapter 6). This would give us the first general test of the feasibility of menus that might seem attractive. It could well turn out, for instance, that we could not undertake two major building programs simultaneously, although either one by itself would be feasible, just as in the case of the production possibility curve on p. 63 where we could not attain a desired output of both milk and wheat.

In making up our menus of choices, the big problem, however, is not so much apt to be the reconciliation of overambitious micro targets, but the reconciliation of macro targets; above all, targets for employment levels and rates of inflation. For the rate of growth will hinge, in the first instance, on the level of employment that we target; and that level, we know from experience, may not be easily matched with a desired rate of inflation, at least not without economic controls of various sorts.

Thus the planning economists are apt to offer us a range of two or three alternatives that might, for instance, include an option for 6 percent growth, 3 percent unemployment, and 5 percent inflation; or for 4 percent growth, 5 percent unemployment, and 4 percent inflation. In all likelihood the alternatives will not be so ambitious that we could realize them only by near-wartime measures (e.g., 10 percent growth and 1 percent unemployment with 2 percent inflation); or so unambitious that planning would be pointless—minus 2 percent growth, 9 percent inflation, and 8 percent unemployment, the combination we actually had in 1975.

FURTHER REVIEWS

In currently envisaged legislation, these alternative plans would then be reviewed by a standing committee, also within the Executive office. There the heads of the main departments and agencies, together with representatives from industry, labor, and the public, would voice their approval or disapproval of the various alternatives or perhaps ask the economists to devise still another feasible set of targets.

Thereafter, the plans, now perhaps reduced to one or two favored alternatives, would be presented to Congress, to be reexamined by the Joint Economic Committee of the House and Senate. Congress would then select a preferred plan or might even write a new one, heeding the advice of its own experts and the testimony it would gather from governors or other persons it might wish to consult.

The final plan would then be passed by both Houses and sent to the President for his signature. It would encompass both a set of targets and a set of means for achieving these targets—let us say 5 percent growth, 3 percent unemployment, 4 percent inflation, to be attained by new tax provisions, a major budget authorization for urban renewal, a general directive to the Fed, and so on. The plan might also include a number of environmental directives, accelerating research or investment in certain processes, discouraging it in others.

To a large extent, as we can see, this kind of planning resembles the process of law-making, with all its compromises, reconciliations, and efforts to achieve a workable consensus. The skepticism or faith that one holds out for planning is therefore closely related to that which one has for our capacity to produce just and workable laws. For those who hold democratic representative government in low esteem, there is no reason to assume that economic planning will rise above the level of a bureaucratic tangle or a sub rosa "takeover" by powerful groups.

But for those who hold a more sanguine view of the self-governing capabilities of a capitalist democracy, there is no reason to believe that a national planning effort could not achieve as acceptable a level of economic performance as our general legislation achieves for our political and social performance. The main purpose of economic planning, as we have seen, is to diminish the gap between potential output and actual output, and to achieve growth in ways that will not endanger the future.

Gains
from
trade

Americans have had the fortune to be extraordinarily sheltered from the currents of international economics that wash against other shores. British students are brought up knowing about exports and imports, because a quarter of their national income derives from foreign trade. A Canadian knows about international economics, because one Canadian dollar in five is earned or spent beyond Canadian borders. Any educated person in the underdeveloped world will tell you that the future of his country is critically affected by the exports it sells to the developed world and the capital it brings in from that world. Only the United States, among the nations of the West, is generally unconcerned and uneducated about foreign trade, for the general opinion is that we are relatively self-sufficient and could, if we had to, let the rest of the world go hang.

Could we? It is true that less than 10 percent of our gross national product is bought or sold overseas. Yet it is worth considering what would happen to our own economy if some mischance severed our ties with the rest of the world.

The first impact would be the loss of certain critical products needed for industrial production. In the earlier years of the country, we were inclined to treat our

19

300

natural resources as inexhaustible, but the astounding rate of our consumption of industrial raw materials has disabused us of that notion. Today the major fractions of our iron ore, our copper, and our wood pulp come to us from abroad. Ninety percent of the bauxite from which we make aluminum is imported. Ninety-four percent of the manganese needed for high-tempered steels, all our chrome, virtually all our cobalt, the great bulk of our nickel, tin, platinum, asbestos, a rising fraction of our petroleum is foreign-bought. Many of these materials are so strategic that we stockpile them against temporary disruption, but in a few years the stockpiles would be used up and we should be forced to make radical changes in some of our technology.

Then there would be other losses, less statistically impressive but no less irksome to consumer and industry: the loss of Japanese cameras, of British tweeds, of French perfume, of Italian movies, of Rolls Royce engines, Volkswagen cars, Danish silver, Indian jute and madras. Coffee and tea, the very mainstays of civilized existence, would no longer be available. Chocolate, the favorite flavor of a hundred million Americans, would be unobtainable. There would be no bananas in the morning, no pepper at supper, no Scotch whiskey at night. Clearly, shutting down the flow of the imports into America, however relatively self-sufficient we may be, would deal us a considerable blow. One can imagine what it would mean in the case of, say, Holland, where foreign products account for as much as 45 percent of all goods sold in that country.

But we have still not fully investigated the effects of international trade on the United States, for we have failed to consider the impact of a collapse of our exports. The farm country would feel such a collapse immediately of course, for a fifth of our cotton, almost a quarter of our grains, and more than a quarter of our tobacco go overseas. Mining country would feel it because a fifth of our coal and a third of our sulphur are sold abroad. Manufacturing enterprises in cities scattered all over the nation would feel the blow, as a quarter of our metalworking machinery and of our textile machinery, a third of our construction and mining machinery could no longer be sold overseas—not to speak of another thirty to forty industries in which at least a fifth of output is regularly sold to foreign buyers. In all, some three million to four million jobs, three-quarters of them in manufacturing or commerce, would cease to exist if our foreign markets should suddenly disappear.

Many of those jobs would be replaced by new industries that would be encouraged if our overseas markets and sources of supply vanished. If we could not buy watches or watch parts in Switzerland, we would make more of them here. If we could not sell machine tools to the world, we would no doubt try to use our unemployed skills to make some product or service that could be marketed at home—perhaps one of the items we no longer imported. With considerable effort (especially in the case of strategic materials) we *could* readjust. Hence the question: Why don't we? What is the purpose of international trade? Why do we not seek to improve our relative self-sufficiency by making it complete?

The bias of nationalism

No sooner do we ask the question of the aims of international trade than we encounter an obstacle that will present the single greatest difficulty in learning about international economies. This is the bias of nationalism—the curious fact that relationships and propositions that are perfectly self-evident in the context of "ordinary" economics suddenly appear suspect, not to say downright wrong, in the context of international economics.

For example, suppose that the governor of an eastern state—let us say New Jersey—wanted to raise the incomes of his constituents and decided that the best way to do so was to encourage some new industry to move there. Suppose furthermore that his son was very fond of grapefruit and suggested to him one morning that grapefruit growing would be an excellent addition to New Jersey's products.

The governor might object that grapefruit needed a milder climate than New Jersey had to offer. "That's no problem," his son might answer. "We could protect our grapefruit by growing them in hothouses. That way, in addition to the income from the crop, we would benefit the state from the incomes earned by the glaziers and electricians who would be needed."

The governor might murmur something about hothouse grapefruit costing more than ordinary grapefruit, so that New Jersey could not sell its crop on the competitive market. "Nonsense," his son would reply. "We can subsidize the grapefruit growers out of the proceeds of a general sales tax. Or we could pass a law requiring restaurants in this state to serve state grapefruit only. Or you could bar out-of-state grapefruit from New Jersey entirely."

"Now, my boy," the governor would return, "in the first place, that's unconstitutional. Second, even if it weren't, we would be making people in this state give up part of their incomes through the sales tax to benefit farmers, and that would

never be politically acceptable. And third, the whole scheme is so inefficient it's just downright ridiculous."

But if we now shift our attention to a similar scene played between the prime minister of Nova Jersia and his son, we find some interesting differences. Like his counterpart in New Jersey, the son of the prime minister recommends the growing of hothouse grapefruit in Nova Jersia's chilly climate. Admittedly, that would make the crop considerably dearer than that for sale on the international markets. "But that's all right," he tells his father. "We can put a tariff on foreign grapefruit, so none of the cheap fruit from abroad will undersell ours."

"My boy," says the prime minister after carefully considering the matter, "I think you are right. It is true that grapefruit in Nova Jersia will be more expensive as a result of the tariff, but there is no doubt that a tariff looks like a tax on them and not on us, and therefore no one will object to it. It is also true that our hothouse grapefruit may not taste as good as theirs, but we will have the immense satisfaction of eating our *own* grapefruit, which will make it taste better. Finally, there may be a few economists who will tell us that this is not the most efficient use of our resources, but I can tell them that the money we pay for hothouse grapefruit—even if it is a little more than it would be otherwise—stays in our own pockets and doesn't go to enrich foreigners. In addition to which, I would point out in my television appearances that the reason foreign grapefruit are so cheap is that foreign labor is so badly paid. We certainly don't want to drag down the price of our labor by making it compete with the cheap labor of other nations. All in all, hothouse grapefruit seems to me an eminently sensible proposal, and one that is certain to be politically popular."

Source of the difficulty Is it a sensible proposal? Of course not, although it will take some careful thinking to expose all of its fallacies. Will it be politically popular? It may very well be, for economic policies that would be laughed out of court at home get a serious hearing when they crop up in the international arena. Here are some of the things that most of us tend to believe.

Trade between two nations usually harms one side or the other.

Rich countries can't compete with poor countries.

There is always the danger that a country may sell but refuse to buy.

Are these fears true? One way of testing their validity is to see how they ring in our ears when we rid them of our unconscious national bias by recasting them as propositions in ordinary economics.

Is it true that trade between businesses or persons usually harms one side or the other?

Is it true that rich companies can't compete with poor ones?

Is it true that one company might only sell but never buy—not even materials or the services of factors of production?

What is the source of this curious prejudice against international trade? It is not, as we might think, an excess of patriotism that leads us to recommend courses of action that will help our own country, regardless of the effect on others. For, curiously, the policies of the economic superpatriot, if put into practice, would demonstrably injure the economic interests of his own land. The trouble, then, springs from a root deeper than mere national interest. It lies in the peculiarly deceptive problems posed by international trade. What is deceptive about them, however, is not that they involve principles that apply only to relations between nations. **All the economic arguments that elucidate international trade apply equally well to domestic trade.** The deception arises, rather, for two reasons:

1. **International trade requires an understanding of how two countries, each dealing in its own currency, manage to buy and sell from each other in a world where there is no such thing as international money.**

2. **International trade requires a very thorough understanding of the advantages of and arguments for, trade itself.**

Gains from trade In a general way, of course, we are all aware of the importance of trade, although we have hardly mentioned it since the opening pages of our book. *It is trade that makes possible the division and specialization of labor on which our productivity is so largely based.* If we could not exchange the products of our specialized labor, each of us would have to be wholly self-supporting, and our standard of living would thereupon fall to that of subsistence farmers. Thus trade (international or domestic) is actually a means of *increasing productivity*, quite as much as investment or technological progress.

Gains from specialization The importance of trade in making possible specialization is so great that we should take a moment to make it crystal clear. Let us consider two towns. Each produces two goods: wool and cotton; but Wooltown has good grazing lands and poor growing lands, while Cottontown's grazing is poor, but growing is good. Suppose, moreover, that the two towns had equal populations and that each town employed half its people in cotton and half in wool. The results might look like Table 19 • 1.

Table 19·1 Unspecialized production: Case 1

Production	Wooltown	Cottontown
Wool (lbs)	5,000	2,000
Cotton (lbs)	10,000	20,000

As we can see, the same number of grazers in Wooltown turn out two-and-one-half times as much wool as they do in Cottontown, whereas the same number of cotton farmers in Cottontown produce double the amount of cotton that they do in Wooltown. One does not have to be an economist to see that both towns are losing by this arrangement. If Cottontown would shift its woolworkers into cotton, and Wooltown would shift its cotton farmers into wool, the output of the two towns would look like Table 19·2 (assuming constant returns to scale).

Table 19·2 Specialized production

Output	Wooltown	Cottontown
Wool	10,000	0
Cotton	0	40,000

Now, if we compare total production of the two towns (see Table 19·3), we can see the gains from specialization.

Table 19·3 The gain from specialization

Output	Mixed	Specialized	Gain from specialization
Wool	7,000	10,000	3,000
Cotton	30,000	40,000	10,000

In other words, specialization followed by trade makes it possible for both towns to have more of both commodities than they had before. No matter how the gains from trade are distributed—

and this will depend on many factors, such as the relative elasticities of demand for the two products—both towns can gain, even if one gains more than the other.

Unequal advantages

If all the world were divided into nations, like Wooltown and Cottontown, each producing for trade only a single item in which it has a clear advantage over all others, international trade would be a simple matter to understand. It would still present problems of international payment, and it might still inspire its prime ministers of Nova Jersias to forego the gains from trade for political reasons that we will examine at the end of this chapter. But the essential rationale of trade would be simple to understand.

It is unfortunate for the economics student as well as for the world that this is not the way international resources are distributed. Instead of giving each nation at least one commodity in which it has a clear advantage, many nations do not have such an advantage in a single product. How can trade possibly take place under such inauspicious circumstances?

To unravel the mystery, let us turn again to Cottontown and Wooltown, but this time call them Supraville and Infraville, to designate an important change in their respective abilities. Although both towns still enjoy equal populations, which are again divided equally between cotton and wool production, in this example Supraville is a more efficient producer than Infraville in *both* cotton and wool, as Table 19·4 shows.

Table 19·4 Unspecialized production: Case II

	Supraville	Infraville
Wool output	5,000	3,000
Cotton production	20,000	10,000

Is it possible for trade to benefit these two towns when one of them is so manifestly superior to the other in every product? It seems out of the question. But let us nonetheless test the case by supposing that each town began to specialize.

Trade-off relationships

But how to decide which trade each town should follow? Figure 19 · 1, p. 306, may give a us a clue. The production possibility diagrams are familiar to us from Chapter 5, where we used them to clarify the nature of scarcity and economic choice. Here we put them to use to let us see the results of trade.

What do the diagrams show? First, they establish maximums that each town could produce if it devoted all its efforts to one product. Since we have assumed that the labor force is divided, this means that each town could double the amount of cotton or wool it enjoys when it divides its workers fifty-fifty. Next, a line between these points shows the production frontier that both towns face.* We see that Supraville is located at point A where it has 5,000 lbs of wool and 20,000 lbs of cotton, and that Infraville is at B, where it has 3,000 lbs of wool and 10,000 lbs of cotton.

But the diagrams (and the figures in the preceding table, on which they are based) also show us something else. It is that each town has a different "trade off" relationship between its two branches of production. When either town specializes in one branch, it must, of course, give up the output of the other. *But each town swaps one kind of output for the other in different proportions*, as the differing slopes of the two *p-p* curves show. Supraville, for example, can make only an extra pound of wool by giving up 4 pounds of cotton. That is, it gets its maximum potential output of 10,000 lbs of wool only by surrendering 40,000 lbs of cotton. Infraville can reach its production maximum of 6,000 lbs of wool at a loss of only 20,000 lbs of cotton. *Rather than having to give up 4 lbs of cotton to get one of wool, it gives up only 3.3 lbs.* Thus, in terms of how much cotton it must surrender, wool actually costs less in Infraville than in Supraville!

Not so the other way round, of course. As we would expect, cotton costs Supraville less in terms of wool than it costs Infraville. In Supraville, we get 40,000 lbs of cotton by relinquishing only 10,000 lbs of wool—a loss of a quarter of a pound of wool for a pound of the other. In Infraville, we can get the maximum output of 20,000 lbs of cotton only by a surrender of 6,000 lbs of wool—a loss of ⅓ lb of wool rather than ¼ lb of wool for each unit of cotton.*

Comparative advantage

Perhaps the light is beginning to dawn. Despite the fact that Supraville is more productive than Infraville in terms of output per man in both cotton and wool, it is *relatively* more productive in cotton than in wool. And despite the fact that Infraville is absolutely less productive than Supraville, man for man, in both cotton and wool, it is *relatively* more productive in wool. To repeat, it requires a smaller sacrifice of wool to get another pound of cotton in Infraville than in Supraville.

---

*Why are these lines drawn straight, not bowed as in Chapter 5? As we know, the bowing reflects the law of increasing cost, which makes the gains from a shift in resource allocation less and less favorable as we move from one extreme of allocation to another. Here we ignore this complication for simplicity of exposition. We have also ignored the problem of variable returns when we assumed that each town could double its output of cotton or wool by doubling its labor force.

*It takes long practice to master the arithmetic of gains from trade. Practice on questions 2 through 5 will help. It is more important, at this point, to "get the idea" than to master the calculations.

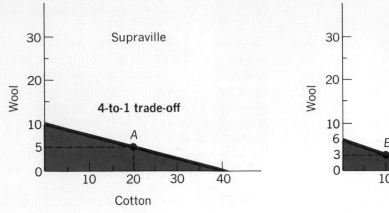

FIG. 19 · 1   Production possibilities in the two towns before trade

We call this kind of relative superiority *comparative advantage*. It is a concept that is often difficult to grasp at first but that is central to the reason for trade itself. When we speak of *comparative* advantage, we mean, as in the case of Supraville, that among *various* advantages of one producer or locale over another, there is one that is better than any other. *Comparatively* speaking, this is where its optimal returns lie. But just because it must abandon some lesser opportunity, its trading partner can now advantageously devote itself in the direction where *it* has a comparative advantage.

This is a relationship of logic, not economics. Take the example of the banker who is also the best carpenter in town. Will it pay him to build his own house? Clearly it will not, for he will make more money by devoting all his hours to banking, even though he then has to employ and pay for a carpenter less skillful than himself. True, he could save that expense by building his own house. But he would then have to give up the much more lucrative hours he could be spending at the bank!

Now let us return to the matter of trade. We have seen that wool is *relatively* cheaper in Infraville, where each additional pound cost only 3.3 lbs of cotton, rather than 4 lbs as in Supraville; and that

cotton is *relatively* cheaper in Supraville, where an additional pound costs but ¼ lb of wool, instead of ⅓ lb across the way in Infraville. Now let us suppose that each side begins to specialize in the trade in which it has the comparative advantage. Suppose that Supraville took half its labor force now in wool and put it into cotton. Its output would change as in Table 19 · 5.

Table 19 · 5   Supraville

	Before the shift	*After the shift*
Wool production	5,000	2,500
Cotton production	20,000	30,000

Supraville has lost 2,500 lbs of wool but gained 10,000 lbs of cotton. Now let us see if it can trade its cotton for Infraville's wool. In Infraville, where productivity is so much less, the entire labor force has shifted to wool output, where its greatly inferior productivity can be put to best use. Hence its production pattern now looks like Table 19 · 6;

Table 19 · 6   Infraville

	Before the shift	*After the shift*
Wool	3,000	6,000
Cotton	10,000	—

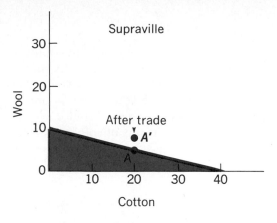
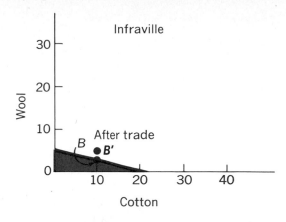

FIG. 19 · 2 Production possibilities in the two towns after trade

Infraville finds itself lacking 10,000 lbs of cotton, but it has 3,000 *additional* lbs of wool. Clearly, it can acquire the 10,000 lbs of cotton it needs from Supraville by giving Supraville *more* than the 2,500 lbs of wool it seeks. As a result, both Infraville and Supraville will have the same cotton consumption as before, but there will be a surplus of 500 lbs of wool to be shared between them. As Fig. 19 · 2 shows, *both towns will have gained by the exchange, for both will have moved beyond their former production frontiers* (from A to A' and from B to B').

This last point is the crucial one. If we remember the nature of production-possibility curves from our discussion of them in Chapter 5, any point lying outside the production frontier is simply unattainable by that society. In Fig. 19 · 2, points A' and B' do lie beyond the pre-trade *p-p* curves of the two towns, and yet trade has made it possible for both communities to enjoy what was formerly impossible.

Opportunity cost Comparative advantage gives us an important insight into all exchange relationships, for it reveals again a fundamental economic truth that we have mentioned more than once before. It is that *cost, in economics, means opportunities that must be foregone.* The real cost of

wool in Supraville is the cotton that cannot be grown, because workers are engaged in wool production, just as the real cost of cotton is the wool that must be gone without. In fact, we can see that the basic reason for comparative advantage lies in the fact that opportunity costs vary, so that it "pays" (it costs less) for different parties to engage in different activities.

If opportunity costs for two producers are the same, then it follows that there cannot be any comparative advantage for either; and if there is no comparative advantage, there is nothing to be gained by specializing or trading. Suppose Supraville has a two-to-one edge over Infraville in *both* cotton and wool. Then, if either town specializes, neither will gain. Supraville may still gain 10,000 lbs of cotton for 2,500 lbs of wool, as before, but Infraville will gain only 2,500 lbs of wool (not 3,000) from its shift away from cotton. Thus, the key to trade lies in the existence of *different* opportunity costs.

Are opportunity costs usually different from country to country or from region to region? For most commodities they are. As we move from one part of the world to another—sometimes even short distances—climate, resources, skills, transportation costs, capital scarcity, or abundance all change; and as they change, so do opportunity costs. There is every

307

possibility for rich countries to trade with poor ones, precisely because their opportunity costs are certain to differ.

Exchange ratios

But we have not yet fully understood one last important aspect of trade—the *prices* at which goods will exchange. Suppose that Supraville and Infraville do specialize, each in the product in which it enjoys a comparative advantage. Does that mean they can swap their goods at any prices?

A quick series of calculations reveals otherwise. We remember that Supraville needed at least 2,500 lbs of wool for which it was going to offer some of its extra production of cotton in exchange. But how much? What price should it offer for its needed wool, in terms of cotton?

Suppose it offered 7,500 lbs of cotton. Would Infraville sell the wool? No, it would not. At home it can grow its own 7,500 lbs of cotton at a "cost" of only 2,273 lbs of wool, for we recall that Infraville traded off one pound of wool for 3.3 lbs of cotton (7,500 ÷ 3.3 = 2,273).

Suppose, then, that Infraville counter-offered to sell Supraville 2,500 lbs of wool for a price of 12,000 lbs of cotton. Would Supraville accept? Of course not. This would mean the equivalent of 4.8 lbs of cotton for a pound of wool. Supraville can do better than that by growing her own wool at her own trade-off ratio of only 4 lbs to one.

We begin to see, in other words, that the price of wool must lie between the trade-off ratios of Infraville and Supraville. Infraville wants to import cotton. If it did not trade with Supraville, it could grow its own cotton at the cost of one pound of wool for every 3.3 lbs of cotton. Hence, for trade to be advantageous, Infraville seeks to get *more* cotton than that, per pound of wool.

Supraville is in the opposite situation. It seeks to export cotton and to import wool. It could make its own wool at the sacrifice of 4 lbs of cotton per pound of wool. Thus it seeks to gain wool for a *lower* price than that, in terms of cotton. Clearly, any ratio between 3.3 and 4.0 lbs of cotton per pound of wool will profit both sides.

The role of prices

Let us put this into ordinary price terms. Suppose that cotton sells for 30¢ per pound. Then wool would have to sell between 99¢ and $1.20 (30¢ × 3.3 and × 4) to make trade worthwhile.* Let us say that supply and demand established a price of $1.10 for wool. Supraville can then sell its 10,000 lbs of extra cotton production at 30¢, which will net it $3,000. How much wool can it buy for this sum? At the going price of $1.10 per lb, 2,727 lbs. Therefore Supraville will end up with the same amount of cotton (20,000 lbs) as it had before specialization and trade, and with 227 *more* lbs of wool than before (2,500 lbs produced at home plus 2,727 lbs imported from Infraville—a total of 5,227 lbs). It has gained by trade an amount equal to the price of this extra wool, or $249.70.

How has Infraville fared? It has 3,273 lbs of wool left after exporting 2,727 lbs to Supraville from its production of 6,000 lbs, and it also has 10,000 lbs of cotton imported from Supraville in exchange for its wool exports. Thus it, too, has a gain from trade—the 273 lbs of wool (worth $300.30) over the amount of 3,000 lbs that it would have produced without specialization and trade. In brief, *both* sides have profited from the exchange. To be sure, gains need not be distributed so evenly between the trading partners. If the price of wool had

---

*Obviously, these prices are used for illustrative purposes only. And once again, let us reassure you: these calculations are easy to follow but not easy to do by yourself. Familiarity will come only with practice.

been $1.00, trade still would have been worthwhile, but Supraville would have gained almost all of it. Had the price of wool been $1.19, both sides again would have come out ahead, but now Infraville would have been the larger beneficiary by far. The actual price at which wool would sell would be determined by the supply and demand schedules for it in both communities.

The Case for Free Trade

Would the prime minister of Nova Jersia be convinced by these arguments? Would his son? They might be weakened in their support for hothouse grapefruit, but some arguments would still linger in their minds. Let us consider them.

1. "Our workers cannot compete with low-wage workers overseas."

This is an argument one hears not only in Nova Jersia, but in every nation in the world, save only those with the very lowest wage rates. Swedish workers complain about "cheap" American labor; American workers complain about sweatshop labor in Hong Kong. And indeed it is true that American labor is paid less than Swedish and that Hong Kong labor is paid a great deal less than American. Does that not mean that American labor will be seriously injured if

we import goods made under "sweatshop" conditions, or that Swedish labor is right in complaining that its standard of living is undermined by importing goods from "exploited" American workers?

Like the answers to so many questions in economics, this one is not a simple yes or no. The American textile worker who loses his job because of low-priced textile imports *is* hurt; and so is the Swedish worker in an electronics company who loses his job because of American competition. We will come back to their legitimate grievances later. But we must note that both workers would also be injured if they lost their jobs as a result of domestic competition. Why do we feel so threatened when the competition comes from abroad?

Because, the answer goes, foreign competition isn't based on American efficiency. It is based on exploited labor. Hence it pulls down the standards of American labor to its own low level.

There is an easy reply to this argument. The reason Hong Kong textile labor is paid so much less than American textile labor is that *average* productivity in Hong Kong is so much lower than *average* productivity in America. To put it differently, the reason that American wages are high is that we use our workers in industries where their productivity is very high. If Hong Kong, with its very low productivity, can undersell us in textiles, then this is a clear signal that we must move our factors of production out of textiles into other areas where their contribution will be greater; for example,

309

in the production of machinery. It is no coincidence that machinery—one of the highest wage industries in America—is one of our leading exports, or that more than 75 percent of our manufactured exports are produced by industries paying hourly wage rates above the national average for all manufacturing industries. In fact, all nations tend to export the goods that are produced at the highest, not lowest, local wages! Why? Because those industries employ their labor most effectively.

This fact opens our eyes to another. Why is it that the American garment industry is worried about competition from Hong Kong, but not the American auto industry or the electrical machinery industry or the farm equipment industry? After all, the manufacturers of those products could also avail themselves of low wages in Hong Kong.

The answer is that American manufacturers can make these products at much lower cost in America. Why? Because the technical skills necessary to produce them are available in the U.S., not in Hong Kong. Thus, if Hong Kong has a comparative advantage over us in the garment trade, we have a comparative advantage over her in many other areas.

But suppose Hong Kong accumulated large amounts of capital and became a center for the manufacture of heavy equipment, so that it sold *both* garments and electrical generators more cheaply than we sold them. We are back to Supraville and Infraville. There would still be a *comparative* advantage in one or more of these products in which we would be wise to specialize, afterward trading with Hong Kong for our supplies of the other good.*

---

*Newspapers in Southeast Asia carry editorials seeking protection from American imports because, they say, we do not use labor in our production, and it is unfair to ask its citizens to compete with our machines that do not have to be paid wages.

2. "Tariffs are painless taxes because they are borne by foreigners."

This is a convincing-sounding argument advanced by the prime minister of Nova Jersia (and by some other prime ministers in their time). But is it true? Let us take the case of hothouse grapefruit, which can be produced in Nova Jersia only at a cost of 50 cents each, whereas foreign grapefruit (no doubt produced by sweated labor) can be unloaded at its ports at 25 cents. To prevent his home industry from being destroyed, the prime minister imposes a tariff of 25 cents on foreign grapefruit—which, he tells the newspapers, will be entirely paid by foreigners.

This is not, however, the way his political opponent (who has had a course in economics) sees it. "Without the tariff," she tells her constituency, "you could buy grapefruit for 25 cents. Now you have to pay 50 cents for it. Who is paying the extra 25 cents—the foreign grower or you? Even if not a single grapefuit entered the country, you would still be paying 25 cents more than you have to. In fact, *you are being asked to subsidize an inefficient domestic industry.* Not only that, but the tariff wall means they won't ever become efficient because there is no pressure of competition on them."

Whether or not our economic candidate will win the electoral battle, she surely has the better of the argument. Or does she? For the prime minister, stung by these unkind remarks, replies:

3. "But at least the tariff keeps spending power at home. Our own grapefruit growers, not foreigners, have our money."

There are two answers to this argument. First, the purchasing power acquired by foreigners can be used to buy goods from efficient Nova Jersia producers and will thus return to Nova Jersia's economy. Second, if productive resources are used in inefficient, low-productivity industries, then the resources available for use in efficient, high-productivity industries are less than they otherwise would be, and the total output of the country falls. To keep out foreign grapefruit is to lower the country's real standard of living. The people of Nova Jersia waste time and resources doing something they do not do very well.

4. "But tariffs are necessary to keep the work force of Nova Jersia employed."

An investigation of macroeconomic policies, however, would reveal that the governments of Nova Jersia and every other country can use fiscal and monetary policies to keep their resources fully employed. If textile workers become unemployed, governments can expand aggregate demand and generate domestic job opportunities in other areas.

Classical argument for free trade

Are there no arguments at all for tariffs? As we shall see, there are some rational arguments for restricting free trade. *But all of these arguments accept the fact that restrictions depress world incomes below what they would be otherwise. If world production is to be maximized, free trade is an essential ingredient.* Free trade must therefore be considered a means of increasing GNP, a means not essentially different from technological improvement in its effect on output and growth. We may not want to maximize GNP, but we need to understand that to advocate restrictions on trade is to advocate lower real incomes. These arguments apply cogently to developed countries. They are less persuasive when applied to underdeveloped countries.

The Case for Tariffs

Are *all* arguments against tariffs? Not quite. But it is essential to recognize that these arguments take full cognizance of the inescapable costs of restricting trade. They do not contest the validity of the theory of free trade, but the difficulties of its application. Let us familiarize ourselves with them.

Mobility

The first difficulty concerns the problem of mobility. Explicit in Bastiat's case (see box) is the ease with which Crusoe and Friday move back and forth between hunting and gardening. Implicit in the case of Supraville and Infraville is the possibility of shifting workers and resources from cotton to wool production. But in fact is is sometimes exceedingly difficult to move resources from one industry to another.

Thus when Hong Kong textiles press hard against the garment worker in New

York, higher wages in the auto plants in Detroit are scant comfort. She has a lifetime of skills and a home in New York, and she does not want to move to another city where she will be a stranger and to a new trade in which she would be only an unskilled beginner. She certainly does not want to move to Hong Kong! Hence, the impact of foreign trade often brings serious dislocations that result in persistent local unemployment, rather than in a flow of resources from a relatively disadvantaged to a relatively advantaged one. If Crusoe had suggested that it was very difficult (perhaps because of the noonday sun) to work in the gardens in the morning when they usually went hunting, Friday would have been harder put for a reply.

ROBINSON CRUSOE

The beclouding effect of national bias on our thinking was never more charmingly or effectively presented than in this argument by Frédéric Bastiat, a delightful exponent of mid-nineteenth-century classical economic ideals, in a little book entitled *Social Fallacies*.[1]

In Bastiat's book, Robinson Crusoe inhabits an island with Friday. In the morning, Crusoe and Friday hunt for six hours and bring home four baskets of game. In the evening, they garden for six hours and get four baskets of vegetables. But now let Bastiat take over:

One day a canoe touched at the island. A goodlooking foreigner landed and was admitted to the table of our two recluses. He tasted and commended very much the produce of the garden, and before taking leave of his entertainers, spoke as follows: "Generous islanders, I inhabit a country where game is much more plentiful than here, but where horticulture is quite unknown. It would be an easy matter to bring you every evening four baskets of game, if you will give me in exchange two baskets of vegetables."

At these words, Robinson and Friday retired to consult, and the debate that took place is too interesting not to be reported in extenso.

FRIDAY: What do you think of it?
ROBINSON: If we close with the proposal, we are ruined.
FRIDAY: Are you sure of that? Let us consider.
ROBINSON: The case is clear. Crushed by competition, our hunting as a branch of industry is annihilated.

FRIDAY: What matters it, if we have the game?
ROBINSON: Theory! It will no longer be the product of our labour.
FRIDAY: I beg your pardon sir; for in order to have game we must part with vegetables.
ROBINSON: Then, what shall we gain?
FRIDAY: The four baskets of game cost us six hours' work. The foreigner gives us them in exchange for two baskets of vegetables, which cost us only three hours' work. This places three hours at our disposal. . . .
ROBINSON: You lose yourself in generalities! What should we make of these three hours?
FRIDAY: We would do something else.
ROBINSON: Ah! I understand you. You cannot come to particulars. Something else, something else—that is easily said.
FRIDAY: We can fish, we can ornament our cottage, we can read the Bible.
ROBINSON: Utopia! Is there any certainty we should do either the one or the other? . . . Moreover there are political reasons for rejecting the interested offers of the perfidious foreigner.

FRIDAY: Political reasons!
ROBINSON: Yes, he only makes us these offers because they are advantageous to him.
FRIDAY: So much the better, since they are for our advantage likewise. . . .
ROBINSON: Suppose the foreigner learns to cultivate a garden and that his island should prove more fertile than ours. Do you see the consequences?
FRIDAY: Yes; our relations with the foreigner would cease. He would take from us no more vegetables, since he could have them at home with less labour. He would bring us no more game, since we should have nothing to give him in exchange, and we should then be in precisely the situation that you wish us in now. . . .
The debate was prolonged, and, as often happens, each remained wedded to his own opinion. But Robinson possessing a great influence over Friday, his opinion prevailed, and when the foreigner arrived to demand a reply, Robinson said to him: "Stranger, in order to induce us to accept your proposal, we must be assured of two things: the first is, that your island is no better stocked with game than ours, for we want to fight only with equal weapons. The second is, that you will lose by the bargain. For, as in every exchange there is necessarily a gaining and a losing party, we should be dupes, if you were not the loser. What have you got to say?"
"Nothing," replied the foreigner; and, bursting out laughing, he regained his canoe.

[1]Translated by Frederick James Sterling (Santa Ana, Calif.: Register Publishing, 1944), pp. 203f.

Transition costs   Second, we have seen that free trade is necessary to maximize world incomes and that it increases the incomes and real living standards of each country participating in trade. *But this does not mean that it increases the income and real living standards of each individual in each country.* Our New York textile worker may find herself with a substantial reduction in income for the rest of her life. She is being economically rational when she resists "cheap" foreign imports and attempts to get her congressman to impose tariffs or quotas.

There is, it should be noted, an answer to this argument—an answer, at any rate, that applies to industrial nations. Since the gains from trade are generally spread across the nation, the real transition costs of moving from one industry, skill, or region to another should also be generally spread across the nation. This means that government (the taxpayers), rather than the worker or businessman, should bear the costs of relocation and retraining. In this way we spread the costs in such a manner that a few need not suffer disproportionately to win the benefits of international trade that are shared by many.

We should also be aware of the possibility that transition costs may actually exceed the short-term benefits to be derived from international trade. Transition costs thus place a new element in the system, since the standard analysis of competitive systems—national or international—ignores them. A country may be wise to limit its international trade, if it calculates that the cost of reallocating its own factors is greater than the gains to be had in higher real income. Remember, however, that transition costs tend to be short-lived and that the gains from trade tend to last. Thus it is easy to exaggerate the costs of transition and to balk at making

changes that would ultimately improve conditions.

Full employment   Third, *the argument for free trade rests on the very important assumption that there will be substantially full employment.*

In the days of the mid-nineteenth century when the free trade argument was first fully formulated, the idea of an underemployment equilibrium would have been considered absurd. When Crusoe asks what use they should make of their free time, Friday has no trouble replying that they should work or enjoy their leisure. But in a highly interdependent society, work may not be available, and leisure may be only a pseudonym for an inability to find work. In an economy of large enterprises and "sticky" wages and prices, we know that unemployment is a real and continuous object of concern for national policy.

Thus, it makes little sense to advocate policies to expand production via trade unless we are certain that the level of aggregate demand will be large enough to absorb that production. **Full employment policy therefore becomes an indispensable arm of trade policy.** Trade gives us the potential for maximizing production, but there is no point in laying the groundwork for the highest possible output, unless fiscal and monetary policy are also geared to bringing about a level of aggregate demand large enough to support that output.

National self-sufficiency   Fourth, *there is the argument of nationalism pure and simple.* This argument does not impute spurious economic gains to tariffs. Rather, it says that free trade undoubtedly encourages production, but it does so at a certain cost. This is the cost of the vulnerability that comes from extensive and extreme specialization. This vulnerability is all very well within a nation where we assume that law and order will prevail, but it cannot be so easily justified among nations where the realistic assumption is just the other way. Tariffs, in other words, are defensible because they enable nations to attain a certain *self-sufficiency*—admittedly at some economic cost. Project Independence, the United States' effort to gain self-sufficiency in energy, is exactly such an undertaking.

When Crusoe argued that trade might cease, Friday properly scoffed. But the argument is much more valid for an economy of complex industrial processes and specialized know-how that cannot be quickly duplicated if trade is disrupted. In a world always threatened by war, self-sufficiency has a value that may properly override considerations of ideal economic efficiency. The problem is to hold the arguments for "national defense" down to proper proportions. When tariffs are periodically adjusted in international conferences, an astonishing variety of industries (in all countries) find it possible to claim protection from foreign competition in the name of national "indispensability."

Infant industries   Equally interesting is the nationalist argument for tariffs advanced by so-called infant industries, particularly in developing nations. These newly-formed or prospective enterprises claim that they cannot possibly compete with the giants in developed countries while they are small; but that if they are protected by a tariff, they will in time become large and efficient enough no longer to need a tariff. In addition, they claim, they will provide a more diversified spectrum of employments for their own people, as well as aiding in the national transition toward a more modern economy.

The argument is a valid one if it is applied to industries that have a fair chance of achieving a comparative advantage once grown up (otherwise one will be supporting them in infancy, maturity, and senility). Certainly it is an argument that was propounded by the youthful industries of the United States in the early nineteenth century and was sufficiently persuasive to bring them a moderate degree of protection (although it is inconclusive as to how much their growth was ultimately dependent on tariff help). And it is being listened to today by the underdeveloped nations who feel that their only chance of escaping from poverty is to develop a nucleus of industrial employment at almost any cost in the short run.

Producers'   Finally there is an
welfare   argument that comes
down to desired life styles and the quality of life. Economists tend to think entirely of consumers' welfare and to ignore producers' welfare. They define work as a "disutility" that must create pain. But in fact, the quality of an individual's productive life may be as important to him as, or more important than, the quality of his consumptive life. Individuals can and do choose to have lower standards of consumption in exchange for a job that they enjoy. Whole countries may make the same choice.

Assume for the moment that the U.S. has a comparative advantage in agricultural production vis-à-vis France, but Frenchmen enjoy being farmers. In a world of free trade, Frenchmen would be driven out of farming. They would work in the cities and have more goods and services than they would have on their farms. But they would no longer be able to enjoy their farms. Is it irrational for France to place high tariffs and quotas on

American agricultural exports in this case? Clearly not. The only irrationality occurs when countries pretend that such actions do not impose costs and when they do not tell their populations that the whole country (farmers and nonfarmers) must reduce its material standard of living so that some can enjoy their work.

The problem of producers' welfare—the quality of work rather than consumption—is one with which neither economists nor society has adequately come to grips. It may become a key area in raising real standards of living.

The basic argument

Thus there are arguments for tariffs, or at least rational counterarguments against an extreme free trade position. Workers *are* hurt by international competition; and in the default of proper domestic plans for cushioning these blows, modest tariffs can buffer the pains of redeployment. Free trade *does* require a level of high employment; and when unemployment is already a national problem, tariffs may protect additional workers from losing their jobs. Strategic industries and development-stimulating industries *are* sometimes essential and may require protection from world competition. People may enjoy their jobs even though they work with less efficiency than they would in other jobs. All these arguments are but qualifications to the basic proposition on which the economist rests

his case for the freest *possible* trade, but they help to define "possible" in a realistic way.

Nonetheless it may help if we sum up the classical argument, for there is always a danger that the qualifications will take precedence over the main argument.

Free trade brings about the most efficient possible use of resources, and any interference with free trade lessens that efficiency.

Note that international trade is in no way different from interregional domestic trade in this regard. We recognize that we would suffer a loss in higher costs or smaller output by imposing restrictions on the exchange of goods between New York and Chicago. We suffer the same loss when we interfere with the exchange between New York and Hong Kong, whether by tariffs, quotas, or other means.

Frictional problems

International trade may indeed bring frictional problems, such as unemployment in an industry that cannot meet foreign competition. But the answer is not to block the imports but to cure the unemployment by finding better uses for our inefficiently used resources.

Once again, international trade is no different in this regard from domestic trade. When low-price textiles from the South cause unemployment in New England, we do not prevent the sale of southern goods. We try to find new jobs for New Englanders, in occupations in which they have a comparative advantage over the South.

Trade and welfare

Finally we must remember that the purpose of all trade is to improve the well-being of the consumer by giving him the best and cheapest goods and services possible. Thus imports, not exports, represent the gains from trade.

The whole point of trade is to exchange things that we make efficiently for other things in which our efficiency is less. Anything that diminishes imports will reduce our standard of living, just as anything that blocks a return flow of goods from Chicago to New York will obviously reduce the benefit to New Yorkers of trade with Chicago.

Actually, free trade works to improve total (national) income and may not serve the interests of every person in a nation. Under certain conditions, free trade can raise national income by favoring capital over labor or by raising the incomes of some groups at the expense of others. Thus this "welfare" argument must be taken with a certain caution, and in our last sec-

tion, when we turn to the troubles of the underdeveloped world, we will see some of these problems illustrated not in textbook example, but in reality.

However, it is encouraging that since 1948 the total value of world exports has risen from $54 billion to over $250 billion, and that the volume of world trade has been increasing at the rate of 6 percent a year since the 1960s.* For all its difficulties, trade is still "indirect production"; and in a world that needs production, trade is still very welcome.

---

*A considerable part of the impetus to the growth of world trade must be credited to the spread of more rational—i.e., lower and fewer—tariff barriers. The General Agreement on Tariffs and Trade (GATT), an international body formed in 1947 to work for wider world trade, has succeeded in steadily reducing tariff levels and in dismantling import quotas. It is pleasant to record that the United States initially played a major role in this movement. During the 1930s we had the unenviable reputation of being one of the most restrictive trading nations in the world, but our tariff wall has been far reduced since those irresponsible days. Today our average level of duties on dutiable imports is roughly 10 percent, compared with 53 percent in 1930; and in addition, a third of all our imports are admitted duty-free. On the negative side, however, it must be noted that we continue to discriminate against imports that affect our manufacturing interests. For example, coffee comes in free, but not instant coffee, so that the underdeveloped nations who would like to process coffee within their own economies are gravely disadvantaged. Moreover, in recent years there has been a revival of U.S. protectionism, resulting in "voluntary" agreements on the part of foreign producers to restrict certain kinds of exports, such as TV sets, to us, and (until very recently) in quotas on oil imports. The lessons of free trade continue to persuade economists more than business people.

FOCUS

Here is one of the central ideas of economics—the idea of the gains from trade. You will not really understand this idea until you have mastered the concept of comparative advantage. That is always a tricky and confusing idea because it forces us to think in terms of "tradeoffs" as costs (opportunity costs), rather than in our accustomed dollars-and-cents terms. There is no short cut to mastering this idea. We suggest you work through questions 2 to 5 carefully.

The arguments for and against free trade or tariffs hinge on a prior understanding of the gains from trade. These gains are entirely gains of efficiency—gains represented by a movement outward of production possibility frontiers. The arguments against free trade mainly have to do with the irrelevance of production (e.g., the very real importance of producers' welfare rather than consumers') or with the frictions that a movement of the p-p frontier generates or with other criteria such as the need to promote full employment or to protect national independence. The arguments for free trade—above all the arguments that counter the threats of "cheap foreign labor"—rest their case on the greater welfare of consumers, after the necessary production adjustments have been made.

You should approach this argument to understand both sides, because neither free trade nor protectionism rules the roost today. It must be clear there is something to be said for both sides. Your job is to know what that "something" is, so that you could intelligently take either side in a debate. Where your own preferences fall is, once again, a matter that will be determined by your values—which groups in society do you favor?—and not by an appeal to economic "science."

WORDS AND CONCEPTS YOU SHOULD KNOW

Specialization of labor, 303–4
Trade-off relationships, 305
Comparative advantage, 305–7
Opportunity cost, 307
Exchange rates, 308
Classical argument for free trade, 309–311

Mobility, 311–12
Transition costs, 313
Self-sufficiency, 313–14
Infant industries, 314
Producers' welfare, 314–15

QUESTIONS

1. What do we mean when we say that trade is "indirect production"?

2. Suppose that two towns, Coaltown and Irontown, have equal populations but differing resources. If Coaltown applies its whole population to coal production, it will produce 10,000 tons of coal; if it applies them to iron production, it will produce 5,000 tons of iron. If Irontown concentrates on iron, it will turn out 18,000 tons of iron; if it shifts to coal, it will produce 12,000 tons of coal. Is trade possible between these towns? Would it be possible if Irontown could produce 24,000 tons of iron? Why is there a comparative advantage in one case and not in the other?

3. In which product does Coaltown have a comparative advantage? How many tons of iron does a ton of coal cost her? How many does it cost Irontown? What is the cost of iron in Coaltown and Irontown? Draw a production-possibility diagram for each town. Show where the frontier lies before and after trade.

4. If iron sells for $10 a ton, what must be the price range of coal? Show that trade cannot be profitable if coal sells on either side of this range. What is the opportunity cost of coal to Irontown? Of iron to Irontown?

5. Is it possible that American watchmakers face unfair competition from Swiss watchmakers because wages are lower in Switzerland? If American watch workers are rendered unemployed by the lowpaid Swiss, what might be done to help them—impose a tariff?

6. Is it possible that mass-produced, low-cost American watches are a source of unfair competition for Switzerland? If Swiss watchmakers are unemployed as a result, what could be done to help them—impose a tariff? Is it possible that a mutually profitable trade in watches might take place between the two countries? What kinds of watches would each probably produce?

7. Are the duties on French wines borne by foreigners or by domestic consumers? Both? What, if any, is the rationale for these duties? How would you go about estimating the transition costs if we were to abolish the tariff on all wines and spirits? Who would be affected? What alternative employment would you suggest for the displaced labor? The displaced land?

Trade adjustment assistance

We have seen that free trade can increase the average real standard of living in a nation but that it may not increase the real living standard of every person. In fact, it usually will not do so. The losses are real, sharp, and concentrated. A textile mill goes out of business because it cannot meet foreign competition. Perhaps from the overall point of view, the gains outweigh the losses—the rise in purchasing power of the nation is greater than the loss in income to the workers and owners of the mill. But the workers and owners are outraged, and the consumers are largely unorganized or uninformed. Hence it is far from unusual that the minority interest prevails over the majority interest. Intensity overwhelms numbers, as in the case of tax reform. Thus we get special tariff preferences or protections—informally negotiated quotas on the amounts of textiles that low-cost countries will send us, limitations on imports of cheap steel, tariffs on French wine, and so on.

Can we find a way out? Economic theory suggests one. Because economic gains exceed economic losses, it should be possible for the winners to compensate the losers and still come out ahead. Our Trade Adjustment Act, modified in 1974, is exactly such an effort. Under the Trade Adjustment Act, producers who can demonstrate injury from foreign competition are entitled to special compensation from the "winners"; that is, from the United States Treasury. Workers are provided with retraining allowances, moving allowances, and extra unemployment benefits. Companies are helped financially and technically to move into new kinds of enterprise. The assistance is not enough to remove all the losses from those who have been hurt, but it mitigates the injury.

The problem is that it is often difficult to determine whether an industry has been damaged by international competition or by other factors. Shoes are a good example. In the past decade American shoe manufacturers have seen imports take an ever larger share of the American shoe business. But was this because of low-wage foreign competition? The shoe companies say so. But some students of the industry argue that the American manufacturers lost their markets because they were slow to recognize that men had become style conscious, and because American companies were poorly managed. These are difficult questions to resolve. In the past, the Trade Adjustment Act has been narrowly interpreted, and few workers or companies have benefited. Recently, the interpretations have been more generous.

Yet, this raises a question. If winners can compensate losers from international trade, why should not the same principle apply to domestic trade? Why should not the winners from environmental clean-up programs compensate the companies and workers who have been economically hurt because of stricter pollution standards? The difficulty is that we cannot apply the principle of compensation to *every* economic change. Perhaps you can see the complexities to which this would lead, if we extended it far enough.

Mechanism of international transactions

We have learned something about one of the sources of confusion that surrounds international trade—the curiously concealed gains from trade itself. Yet our examples of trade have thus far not touched on another source of confusion—the fact that international trade is conducted in two (or sometimes more) currencies. After all, remember that Infraville and Supraville both trade in dollars. But suppose Infraville were Japan and Supraville America. Then how would things work out?

Foreign Money

The best way to find out would be to price the various items in Japan and America (assuming that Japan produces both wool and cotton, which she does not). Suppose the result looked like Table 20·1.

Table 20·1

	United States	*Japan*
Price of wool (lb)	$1.10	¥ 300
Price of cotton (lb)	.30	¥ 100

What would this tell us about the cheapness or dearness of Japanese products compared with those of the U.S.? Nothing, unless we knew one further fact: *the rate at which we could exchange dollars and yen.*

Suppose you could buy 400 yen for a dollar. Then a pound of Japanese wool imported into America (forgetting about shipping costs) would cost 75¢ (¥300 ÷ 400), and a pound of Japanese cotton in America would cost $0.25 (¥100 ÷ 400). Assuming that these are the only products that either country makes for export, here we have a case in which Japan can seemingly undersell America in everything.

But now suppose the rate of exchange were not 400 to one but 250 to one. In that event a pound of Japanese wool landed in America would cost $1.20 (¥300 ÷ 250); and a pound of cotton, $0.40. At this rate of exchange everything in Japan is more expensive than the same products produced in the United States.

The point is clear. *We cannot decide whether foreign products are cheaper or dearer than our own until we know the rate of exchange*, the number of units of their currency we get for ours.

Mechanism of exchange: imports

How does international exchange work? The simplest way to understand it is to follow through a single act of international exchange from start to finish. Suppose, for example, that we decide to buy a Japanese camera directly from a Tokyo manufacturer. The price of the camera as advertised in the catalog is ¥20,000, and to buy the camera we must therefore arrange for the Japanese manufacturer to get that many *yen*. Obviously we can't write him a check in that currency, since our own money is in dollars; and equally obviously we can't send him a check for dollars, since he can't use dollars in Tokyo any more than we can use a check from him in yen.

Therefore, we go to our bank and ask if it can arrange to sell us yen to be delivered to the Tokyo manufacturer. Yes, our bank would be delighted to oblige. How can it do so? The answer is that our bank (or if not ours, another bank with whom it does business) keeps a regular checking account in its own name in a so-called correspondent bank in Tokyo. As we might expect, the bank in Tokyo also keeps a checking account in dollars in *its* own name at our bank. If our banker has enough yen in his Tokyo account, he can sell them to us himself. If not, he can buy yen (which he will then have available in Japan) from his correspondent bank in exchange for dollars which he will put into their account here.

Notice that two currencies change hands—not just one. Notice also that our American banker will not be able to buy yen unless the Japanese banker is willing to acquire dollars. And above all, note that banks are the intermediaries of the foreign exchange mechanism because they hold deposits in foreign banks.

When we go to our bank to buy ¥20,-000 the bank officer looks up the current exchange rate on yen. Suppose it is 385. He then tells us that it will cost us $51.95 (20,000 ÷ 385) to purchase the yen, plus a bank commission for his services. We write the check, which is deducted from our bank balance and added to the balance of the Tokyo bank's account in this country. Meanwhile, the manufacturer has been notified that if he goes to the Tokyo bank in which our bank keeps its deposits of yen, he will receive a check for ¥20,000. In other words, the Tokyo bank, having received dollars in the United States, will now pay out yen in Japan.

Exports

Exports Exactly the opposite is true in the case of exports. Suppose that we were manufacturers of chemicals and that we sold a $1,000 order to Tokyo. In Japan, the importer of chemicals would go to his bank to find out how many yen that would cost. If the rate were 385, it would cost him ¥385,000 which he would then pay to the Japanese bank. The bank would charge his account and credit the yen to the Tokyo account of an American bank with which it did business, mean-time advising the bank here that the transaction had taken place. When the appropriate notice arrived from Japan, our U.S. bank would then take note of its increased holdings of yen and pay the equivalent amount in dollars into our account.

Foreign exchange Thus the mechanism of foreign exchange involves the more or less simultaneous (or anyway, closely linked) operations of two banks in different countries. One bank accepts money in one national denomination, the other pays out money in another denomination. Both are able to do so because each need the other's currency, and each maintains accounts in the other country. Note that when payments are made in international trade, money does not physically leave the country. It travels back or forth between American-owned and foreign-owned bank accounts *in America*. The same is true in foreign nations, where their money will travel between an American-owned account there and the account of one of their nationals. *Taken collectively, these foreign-owned accounts (including our own overseas) are called "foreign exchange." They constitute the main pool of moneys available to finance foreign trade.*

Exchange Rates

Thus the mechanism of foreign exchange works through the cooperation of banks. But we must go beyond an understanding of the mechanism to see the actual forces of supply and demand at work. And this is confusing because we have to think in two money units at the same time.

Buying and selling money We are used to thinking of the price of shoes in terms of dollars. We don't turn around and ask what is the price of dollars in terms of shoes, because consumers don't use shoes to buy dollars.

When we buy pounds or francs or yen, however, we are buying a commodity that is indeed usable to buy the very money we are using. Dollars buy francs and marks and yen; and marks, francs and yen buy dollars. We will have to bear this in mind when we seek to understand the supply and demand curves for international exchange.

Now let us consider an exchange market, say the market for yen (Fig. 20·1). The demand curve for yen is easy to understand. It shows us that we will want to acquire larger amounts of yen as they get cheaper. Why? Because cheap yen means relatively cheaper Japanese goods and services. Really our demand curve for foreign exchange is a picture of our changing demand for foreign goods and services as these goods get cheaper or dearer because the money we use to buy them gets cheaper or dearer.

Now the supply curve. We can most easily picture it as the changing willingness and ability of Japanese banks to offer yen as we pay high or low prices for yen. (There is a better way of explaining the

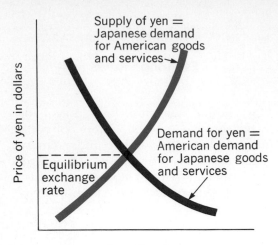

Supply of yen =
Japanese demand
for American goods
and services

Demand for yen =
American demand
for Japanese goods
and services

Price of yen in dollars

Equilibrium
exchange
rate

Quantity of yen

FIG. 20·1   The market for exchange

supply curve, but it takes some hard thought. Those who want to penetrate the mysteries of foreign exchange should look at the box, p. 323.)

Equilibrium prices

What is important is that our diagram shows that there is an equilibrium price for yen that just clears the market. At that price, the amounts of yen that Americans want are exactly equal to the amounts of yen that Japanese want to supply. If we look through the "veil of money," we can see that at this price the value of all Japanese goods and services that we will buy must also be equal to the value of all American goods and services that they will buy!

Appreciation and depreciation of exchange rates

From this, a very important result follows. Suppose that you are a U.S. importer who is eager to buy Japanese automobiles priced at ¥1 million per car. You go to the bank to finance the deal. Here you have an unpleasant surprise. Your banker tells you that exchange is very "tight" at the moment, meaning that the banker's own yen

balances in Japan are very small. As a result, the American banker can no longer offer yen at the old price of, say, 350 to the dollar. The Japanese banks with whom he does business are insisting on a higher price for yen—offering only 325 or perhaps even 300 yen for a dollar. Because of supply and demand, the yen has risen in price, or *appreciated;* and the dollar has fallen in price, or *depreciated.*

You now make a quick calculation. At 350 yen to the dollar, a Japanese car that costs ¥1 million will cost $2,857 (¥1,000,000 ÷ 350). At an exchange rate of 300, it would now cost $3,333 (¥1,000,000 ÷ 300). The new higher price is too steep for the American market. You decide not to place the order. Exactly the opposite situation faces the Japanese importer. Suppose he wants to buy a $50,000 IBM computer. How much will it cost *in yen* if he has to pay 350 yen for a dollar? 300 yen?

The principle is very clear. Movements in exchange rates change relative prices among countries. At different relative prices, imports will rise or fall, as will exports. If the price of the dollar falls, American exports will be increased and its imports diminished. If the price of the yen rises, Japanese exports will fall and its imports will rise.

Thus a moving exchange rate will automatically bring about an equilibrium between the demand for, and the supply of, foreign exchange, exactly as a moving price for shoes will bring about an equality between the value of the dollars offered for shoes and the value of the shoes offered for dollars! In one case as in the other, there may be time lags. But the effect of a moving price in both cases is to eliminate "shortages" and "surpluses"; that is, to bring about a price at which quantity demanded (of a particular currency or any other commodity) equals quantity supplied.

Let us trace the exchange process once more, very carefully. The chart of the New York market shows the demand for English pounds in dollars. When it costs $3 to buy £1, our demand is for one million pounds (we can think of them as commodities, like one million shoes). This is point A. When the price falls to $2 for £1, our demand rises to 2 million pounds, point B. The broken line AB is our demand curve for pounds.

Now we move to the London market on the right. We are going to show that the New York demand curve AB becomes a London supply curve A'B'. To do so, remember that when it costs $3 to buy £1, from the London point of view the price of $1 is 33 pence (one-third of a pound). What is the supply of dollars at this price? It is equal to the number of dollars spent for pounds in New York. At the $3 price, we bought one million pounds. Our supply of dollars is therefore $3 million. This gives us point A' in the London market.

It is now simple to get point B' When £1 falls to $2 in New York, $1 rises to 50 pence (one-half pound) in London. How many dollars are supplied at this price? We can see in the New York diagram that we bought £2 million at $2 each, spending $4 million. Hence in the London market, we locate point B' at a price of 50 pence and a quantity of dollars equal to 4 million.

Now we have a demand curve in New York and a supply curve in London. We need a supply curve in New York and a demand curve in London. We'll start in London, with a high price for dollars. Point C shows us that when it costs £1 to buy $1, the

ANOTHER LOOK AT THE EXCHANGE PROBLEM

demand for dollars is small—only $.5 million are demanded. But this point on the demand curve also gives us a supply of pounds: .5 million "units" of dollars at £1 each, or a total of £.5 million. Back in New York this shows up as point C'. (Remember: $1 = £1.)

Now back to London. The price of dollars falls to 33 pence or ⅓ of a pound. At that price, suppose Britishers demand $4 million, point D. To buy $4 million at 33 pence each, Britishers will have to spend 132 million pence, or £1.32 million. This gives us the supply of pounds in the New York market at the price that corresponds to $1 = 33 pence. This price is $3 = 100 pence (one pound). Point D' locates the supply curve at that price. We suggest you draw the two new curves: CD, the demand for

dollars, and C'D', the supply of dollars.

Each panel now has an equilibrium price. In London it is a little over 33 pence, say 37 pence. But the New York price must be the very same price, expressed in dollars instead of pounds. If 37 pence = $1 in London, then in New York £1 must equal $2.70 ($1.00 ÷ .37). And if we look at the equilibrium price in New York, so it does.

This is not really surprising. The price of pounds in dollars is the same thing as the price of dollars in pounds "upside down." It is as if pounds were shoes and we were saying that a pair of shoes that cost $10 is the same thing as 10 dollars costing 1 pair of shoes. But it takes a while to get used to the idea of two markets in which supply and demand are linked, as in the case of international exchange. With a little practice, the mystery begins to evaporate.

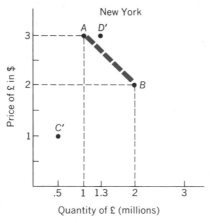

New York

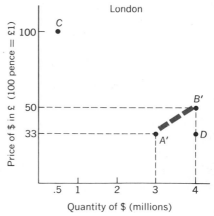

London

Balance of Payments

What does all this have to do with the U.S. balance of payments? To understand the answer, we first have to understand what we mean by the "balance" of payments. We don't speak of a "balance" of payments in, say, a market for shoes. Why, then, is there one in the market of foreign exchange?

Disaggregating the balance of payments

The first part of the answer lies in an important attribute of this market. In a shoe market, all buyers want shoes, presumably to wear. In an exchange market, there are many kinds of buyers (or sellers) who want to buy or sell exchange for different purposes. That is, the so-called balance of payments represents supplies and demand for foreign exchange by *different groups* in each economy. When all supplies and all demands are added together, the two totals must balance because we then have an identity: Purchases ≡ Sales (i.e., the purchases of any currency, such as dollars, must equal the sales of that currency). But they need not balance for any particular group in the economy. As a result, deficits and surpluses refer to groups that are demanding more foreign exchange than they supply, or supplying more than they demand.

Items in the U.S. balance of payments

Let us learn more about these groups by examining the actual balance of payments for the United States for 1975 (Table 20•2). We begin with some obvious and self-explanatory figures—the exports and imports of *merchandise*. As we can see, in 1975 exporters sold 107.3 billion, earning that many dollars (foreign buyers had to supply us with dollars to that amount). U.S. importers bought $98.3 billion worth of foreign goods, supplying that many dollars to the foreign exchange market. On net balance, the merchandise trade showed a balance of $9.0 billion—a surplus arising from an excess of exports over

Table 20 • 2   The United States balance of payments, 1975 (billions of dollars)*

1. *Merchandise*		
Exports	+107.3	
Imports	−98.3	
Balance on merchandise	+9.0	
2. *Services*		
Military transactions	−0.9	
Travel & transportation	−2.5	
Investment income	+6.0	
Other	+4.7	
Balance on services	+7.3	
Balance on goods and services		+16.3
3. *Unilateral transfers*		
Remittances	−1.7	
Government transfers	−2.9	
Balance on transfers	−4.6	
Balance on current account		+11.7
4. *Capital outflow*		
Private	−27.1	
Government	−4.0	
Balance on long-term capital	−31.1	
5. *Capital inflow*	−0.5	
Private	+8.5	+28.0
Government	+6.4	
	+14.9	
6. *Statistical discrepancy*	+4.6	

*Based on first 3 quarters.

imports. This creates a net demand for dollars on the foreign exchange market.

The second group of items consists of supplies and demands for exchange to pay for *services* rather than goods. In our table we note a few of these major transactions. Note that *military transactions* gave rise to a small demand for foreign exchange to pay for expenses at U.S. bases abroad, a wind-up of the Indochina war, and the like. *Travel and transportation* mainly shows us that American tourists were demanding more foreign currencies to voyage abroad than foreigners were demanding dollars to travel here. It also shows the net balance between U.S. payments for foreign carriers (for example, a flight on Lufthansa or the charter of a Greek freighter) and foreign payments for U.S. transportation (flights on PanAm or cargo on a U.S. owned ship).

More interesting is the item for *investment income.* This reflects the flow of profits from U.S. companies in foreign nations to their home offices in the United States, minus the flow from foreign companies in the United States to their home offices abroad. When IBM in Italy sends profits back to its U.S. headquarters, it buys dollars with its local bank balances of lire, creating a demand for dollars. When Nestlé sends profits back to *its* headquarters country, it uses its dollar balances to buy Swiss francs. From this large inflow of earnings we must subtract a small outflow of government interest payments going abroad. When we net out these flows, we can see that investment income was a strong source of dollars for the United States in 1975, amounting to $6.0 billion.

Two partial balances

If we now sum up all items on the merchandise account and all items on service account we get the so-called *balance of goods and services.* In 1975 this showed a surplus of $16.3 billion.

Next we move to two further items, under the category of *unilateral transfers.* Here we find remittances, or the sums that persons residing in America send to private individuals abroad, less any sums coming the other way from Americans residing abroad and sending their pay home. The pay that an American working abroad might send home would be a remittance that would earn us dollars; the sums sent home by a Britisher working in the United States would require the purchase of pounds. As we can see, remittances cause a further deficit in our accounts.

This is augmented by *government unilateral transfers*—sums "sent abroad" by the government for foreign aid, emergency relief, and so on. Of course, these sums are not actually sent abroad; rather, the U.S. government opens a dollar account for the recipient nation, which then uses these dollars. But in using them, the recipient country again sells dollars for other currencies.

Summing up again, we now reach a new partial balance—*the balance on current account*, which showed a surplus of $11.7 billion in 1975.

Items on capital account

The next items reflect supplies and demands for foreign exchange associated with capital investments (not *income* from these investments, which we have already counted). This may include investment by U.S. companies in plant and equipment abroad, less investment by foreign companies in plant and equipment here; or purchases of foreign long-term securities by Americans less American stocks or bonds bought by foreigners. These *private capital* flows cost us a net $18.6 billion in 1975 (an outflow of $27.1 billion less an inflow of $8.5 billion). That outflow was slightly offset, however, by *government capital transactions*—the purchases of foreign government securities by the U.S. government, less any purchases of U.S. bonds by foreign governments. The net balance on *both* private and public capital account gave rise to a deficit or net supply of $16.2 billion ($31.1 billion of public and private outflow less $14.9 billion of inflow).

Capital inflows and outflows can also be divided into short-term and long-term capital inflows and outflows. (Not shown in Table 20·2.) In 1975 there was a short-term capital outflow of $11 billion. The most important of these consists of the transfer from one country to another of private balances, belonging to individuals or companies, that are moved about in response to interest rates or for speculative reasons. The treasurer of a multinational company may "park" his extra cash in Sweden one year and in the United States the next, depending on where he can earn more interest in short-term securities or special bank accounts. Some individuals and even some small governments move their bank balances from country to country in search of the best return or in anticipation of a move in exchange rates that will benefit them. This movement of short-term capital tends to be volatile and can on occasion give rise to speculative "flights" from one nation to another. In 1971, for example, when there was a general distrust of the American dollar, well over $7 billion was withdrawn from American accounts and "sent abroad," creating a deficit of that amount on short-term capital account.

Summing up the accounts   As we have seen, very different motivations apply to these different actors on the foreign exchange markets. Exports and imports reflect the relative price levels and growth of output of trading countries. Tourism is also affected by prices abroad, as well as by the relative affluence of different countries. Flows of corporate earnings arise from investments made in the past. Long-term private capital items reflect estimates of the *future* earning power of investments home or abroad. Short-term capital is guided by interest rates and speculative moods. Government flows hinge largely on foreign policy decisions.

Whatever the different motives affecting these flows, each gives rise to supplies of, or demands for, dollars. Thus we can sum up the net outcome of all these varied groups to discover the overall demand and supply for dollars. As must always be the case, they are in balance. The balance on current account plus the positive statistical discrepancy are exactly equal to the deficit on the capital account.

The "Balance"

What we have traced thus far are the various groups whose economic (or political) interests caused them to supply dollars to or demand dollars on the exchange market. But we have arrived at a curious stopping point.

Our description has shown that it is entirely possible that the quantity of foreign exchange demanded by one country will be larger (or smaller) than the quantity of foreign exchange supplied to it. In fact, only by chance would the total requirements of foreign exchange of importers and exporters of goods and services and capital balance out. But the existence of a difference between the total quantities supplied and demanded should present no problem. Just as in a market for shoes, the price of foreign exchange should change, exactly as we described it on page 321, altering the quantities that different groups would want to buy or sell. An equilibrium price for foreign exchange should clear the exchange market just as an equilibrium price for shoes clears the shoe market. No "balance" of exchange would remain, any more than there is a "balance" of shoes.

That will happen, however, only if the exchange market is as free as the shoe market. In fact, it is not quite so free, so that "balances" do remain, as we will see in our next chapter. In order to understand how these balances remain, we will have to take a moment to learn what happens in a foreign exchange market in which exchange rates are not free to move but are "fixed" in price by international agreements.

Fixed exchange rates

Suppose, for example, that the British pound is "pegged" at a price of $2.00 (we will soon learn how this is accomplished). This means that all transactions—all purchases or sales of pounds and dollars—will take place at that price, plus or minus a small fee for transaction costs. We can easily see that the quantity of pounds demanded at $2.00 may be greater than the quantity supplied at that price, or vice versa. In that case, some agency must provide the "missing" pounds to settle up any shortage that arises from market transactions, or it must provide some other currency to make up for the deficiency of some other currency, if more dollars (for example) are offered for pounds than are made available by the sale of pounds.

We call this a *fixed exchange rate system*. It is the system under which all international exchanges took place until

quite recently. In our next chapter we shall review the dramatic events that led to its abandonment. But it is clear that under fixed rates our accounts do not necessarily "balance." How are accounts "settled" in such a case?

Central banks

The question leads us to a critically important group of institutions in international exchange called central banks. Central banks are the national banks we find in all countries. One of their functions, as we know, is to play a role in the determination of the appropriate quantity of money for domestic purposes. But a second role is equally important. Central banks are agencies of their governments, who buy or sell foreign exchange, making their own currencies available to foreigners when they buy foreign exchange and absorbing their own currency from foreigners when they sell foreign exchange. By buying at a price established by agreement, they "peg" the exchange of their currencies.

How do central banks acquire the capacity for these transactions in foreign exchange? The answer is that private banks in all countries have the option of transferring their own supplies of foreign exchange to their central bank, receiving payment in their own currency. For example, let us suppose that the Chase Manhattan Bank finds itself with large and unwanted supplies of francs. It can exchange these francs for dollars with the Federal Reserve. The Chase Manhattan Bank will then get a dollar credit at the Federal Reserve, and the Federal Reserve will be the owner of the francs formerly belonging to Chase. In the same way in their home countries, the Bank of Yokohama or Barclay's Bank or the Swiss Bank can exchange their holdings of dollars for yen or pounds or Swiss francs, in each case receiving a credit at their central bank in their own currencies and transferring their holdings of foreign currencies to their government bank.

How central banks work

Thus central banks are the holders of large amounts of foreign exchange, which they acquire indirectly from the activities of various groups in their own nations. The central banks are therefore the last "group" whose own actions must balance out the unbalanced flows that arise under "fixed" rates. There are two ways in which this can be done.

1. Gold flows

For many years, any balances "left over" were settled by the shipment of gold from one central bank to another. For example, all through the early 1960s, the United States balanced its accounts partly by selling gold to cover any deficit in its Official Reserve Transactions Balance. The sale of gold was exactly like an export. Foreign central banks paid us in dollars from their holdings of dollar exchange, and this dollar inflow offset any deficit of dollars arising from other transactions. (Recently, a new kind of "paper gold" called Special Drawing Rights has also served as another *reserve asset* available to balance accounts. We will learn more about SDRs in our next chapter.) For reasons that we will also investigate there, gold shipments have been discontinued since the international monetary crisis of 1971.

2. Holding reserve currencies

The second means by which the central banks balanced out the difference between demand and supply was to hold a foreign currency *as if it were a reserve asset*. This is exactly what the central banks of the world (reluctantly) agreed to do all through the 1960s and early 1970s in the case of the United States. The central banks of France, Germany, Japan and other nations allowed their dollar holdings to mount as a "reserve currency" without converting those holdings into gold.

Thus the major balancing item in the past consisted of increases in holdings of dollars owned by foreign governments. How did this increase in dollar holdings formally balance out the accounts? *The answer is that increased dollar holdings were counted in the overall balance of payments as a short-term credit for the United States.* They were, after all, foreign claims on U.S. wealth that have been "loaned" to us. In the official books they counted as a "plus" item that offsets the "minus" items.

Importance of liquidity

Our analysis has shown us a very important fact. Under fixed rates of exchange, we can run an unbalanced foreign exchange account only if we can "finance" it by one or the other of the two means described above. Suppose, for example, that we had no gold and that foreign central banks refused to hold any more dollars. Then an American importer or tourist who went to buy francs or marks would soon discover that there weren't any, because no bank would accept any more dollars. Since there weren't any, he or she could not finance imports or a trip abroad.

The balance of payments would then be brought into balance at the cost of a lower level of international transactions. Americans would have to do with fewer Toyotas. Fewer Americans could visit

THE GOLD STANDARD

Until the Great Depression, the international monetary system was run on a gold standard, under which any citizen at any time could demand gold for paper money. This led to two problems. One was the risk of a "run" on gold in times of panic. It was this that provided the rationale for the gold "backing" of currency in the original Federal Reserve System.

The second problem was that anyone at any time could convert his money into gold and then ship the gold abroad to buy francs or marks or any other currency, if that was profitable. This international ebb and flow

of gold kept all currencies tightly tied together. The difficulty was that the gold link among currencies made it impossible for any nation to launch an expansionary program *if the rest of the world was experiencing a recession*. As a result of its expansion program, its prices would rise. As prices rose, its citizens found it profitable to turn their money into gold, to send the gold abroad and to

buy cheaper foreign goods or assets. This drained gold from the expanding economy, caused credit to contract, and promptly brought the boom to a halt.

After World War II, nations used a gold-exchange standard. Under this standard, gold was reserved for foreign exchange use. The U.S. Treasury sold gold only to foreign official holders of dollars, such as central banks. No gold was sold to foreign private citizens or to domestic U.S. citizens. As we shall see, even this attempt to safeguard the system did not work.

Paris. No doubt more Fords would be sold instead, and Yellowstone Park would be more crowded. But the level of consumer well-being would be lower than if trade could have occurred; and the total of world production, as we saw in our preceding chapter, would suffer because countries could not take full use of their comparative advantages.

Thus the willingness of central banks to hold one another's currencies and the quantity of reserve assets that they can use to "settle up" was of the greatest importance in determining the level of world trade. That is the meaning of the phrase that was often heard as to the importance of having enough "liquidity" in the world. Not having enough liquidity means that the ability to finance imports is crippled because a country has no gold or SDRs or because no central bank is willing to accept its currency in the way that dollars have been accepted. This absence of liquidity is particularly difficult for poor nations that desperately need imports and cannot pay for them.

Why fixed rates? Why were exchange rates fixed? We shall look into some of the practical advantages

of a fixed rate in our next chapter. But the basic cause must be sought in history and psychology. For centuries, the only commodities that have universally commanded the magic of belief have been gold and silver. No nation in the past would accept the curious pieces of paper that another nation called money. This led nations to "declare" the value of their paper monies in terms of their gold "content" and to agree that any foreign holder of its paper money (or of a checking account) could "redeem" that money in gold. In the United States, the value of a dollar from 1933 until very recent years was 1/35th of an ounce of gold.*

Numerous suggestions were put forward by economists for other international standards of value, and many economists urged that exchange rates should be cut loose entirely from any "fixed" value—that they should fluctuate like any other price. Until recent years, however, these proposals have been stubbornly resisted by most governments. But that leads us into the problems discussed in our next chapter.

*Nations that owned very little gold declared the value of their currencies in terms of a major "reserve currency" such as dollars or pounds.

FOCUS This is certainly a difficult chapter, mainly because it deals with things that are unfamiliar to most of us. Therefore it may help to keep in mind two main objectives:

1. You must learn how imports and exports (or other transactions) give rise to demands for, and supplies of, foreign exchange. This is best done by tracing through the series of transactions that accompany a given import and the corresponding export from abroad; or reversing the coin and watching the chain of transactions that finances a given export (and the corresponding import abroad). This will show you how money in each country leaves domestic accounts to enter foreign owned accounts in that country, or vice versa. It will also show you the role of the banks in making possible the coordinated activities taking place simultaneously in two countries.

2. Once the mechanism of foreign exchange is understood, you must learn about the balance of payments. That is not so hard, once you see that "the" balance of payments is nothing but a collection of quite different demands for and supplies of foreign exchange—some for trade, some for tourism, some for military purposes, some for long-term capital investment, some for short-term capital investment. The "total" balance of payments always balances, just as a balance sheet always balances. Indeed, a balance of payments is a balance sheet of a kind, showing who has gained and who has lost claims on foreign exchange.

What complicates matters is *how* it balances. If exchange rates are free to move, the balance is achieved exactly the way it is in a market for shoes. Prices (foreign exchange in this case) rise or fall until quantities demanded and supplied are equal. There is no "surplus" or "shortage." Nothing has to be added to, or absorbed by, any institution. The marketers themselves pick up the tab.

This is not the case when rates are fixed. We then have a situation that is exactly analogous to shortages or surpluses in commodity markets. Just as the government has to buy the "surplus" of wheat offered in a price-supported market, so the government (through its central bank) has to buy the surplus of foreign exchange that arises when foreign exchange is officially priced too dearly vis-à-vis the dollar. In our next chapter we shall go into the history of the dissolution of this method of providing international liquidity.

WORDS AND CONCEPTS YOU SHOULD KNOW

Foreign exchange, 321
Appreciation of exchange, 322
Depreciation of exchange, 322
Balances in the balance of payments, 323–327
Current account, 325

Capital account, 325–26
Fixed exchange rate system, 327
Role of central banks, 327–28
Liquidity, 328–329

QUESTIONS

1. If you wanted to buy a Swiss watch and discovered that it cost 200 francs, what would you need to know to discover if it were cheaper or more expensive than a comparable American watch? Suppose that the price of francs was 20¢ and the American watch cost $50? What if the price of francs rose to 30¢?

2. If you now bought the watch, to be sent to you, how would you pay for it? What would happen to your bank check? How would the Swiss watchmaker be paid?

3. Suppose that the Swiss, in turn, now decided to buy an American radio that cost $40. He finds the rate of exchange is 5 Swiss francs to the dollar. Explain how he makes payment.

4. Now suppose that the rate of exchange rises for the Swiss, so that he has to pay 6 francs for a dollar. What happens to the price of the radio in Swiss terms? Suppose the rate cheapens, so that he pays only 4 francs? Now what is the price of the radio to him?

5. How is an exchange rate determined in a free market? Can you explain why the demand for a foreign currency increases as its price decreases? Why the supply increases?

6. Is the appreciation of the mark versus the franc the same thing as the depreciation of the franc versus the mark?

7. Show the relation between a "deficit" in the balance of payments and a surplus in a commodity market.

8. Suppose there were no central banks. Could a fixed exchange system work? A flexible exchange system?

The international monetary problem

In our preceding chapter we learned something about how the international monetary system works. Now we are going to use that knowledge in tracing the ups and downs of monetary affairs over the last several years. We shall divide our analysis into two parts. First we will watch the deterioration of the U.S. international trade position up to the middle of 1972. Then we will see the outcome of that great monetary crisis in the last few years.

The Pre-1972 Crisis

Bearing in mind that we are dealing only with the first act of the drama, let us watch what was going on in the international economic arena from 1967 to 1972.

Deterioration of trade

21

Figure 21•1 gives us a first clue to the problem. It shows the irregular but eventually precipitous fall in our earnings on current account. At the beginning of the period we were earning almost $1.5 billion in exchange. By the middle of 1972 we were running a deficit at almost the same rate. What was the cause of this fall?

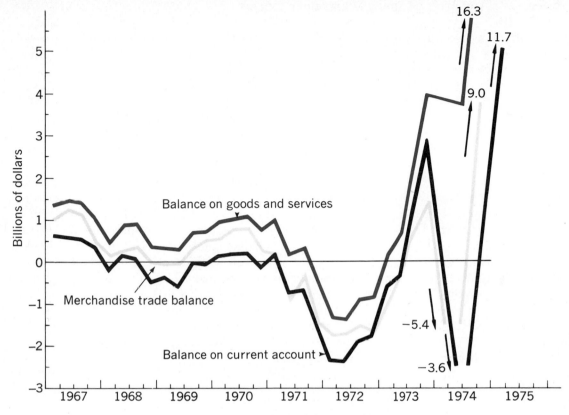

FIG. 21·1 Balance on current account

We can find the answer by examining the main components of our balance on current account. The largest of these are our transactions on merchandise account. Here we find an immediate reason for the deterioration of the balance on current account.

Table 21·1 Balance on current account

	Exports	Imports (billions)	Net balance*
1967	$30.7	$26.9	$+3.8
1968	33.6	33.0	+0.6
1969	36.4	35.8	+0.6
1970	42.0	40.0	+2.1
1971	42.8	45.4	−2.7
1972	48.8	55.7	−6.8

*Figures are rounded.

The fall on current account

What was the cause of this tremendous decline in merchandise earnings? Many people tend to ascribe it to the inflation that was then rampant in the United States. Inflation in one country can indeed be a cause of balance of payment problems. But during the 1960s, inflation was even more pronounced in the lands of our major customers than at home. American export prices were actually cheapened on the international markets by the forces of inflation!

The real cause of the long-term decline was a much more rapid growth of productivity in Europe and Japan than in the United States (see "An Extra Word" to Chapter 5.) Productivity grew approximately twice as fast in Europe and three times as fast in Japan as in the United States. As a result, during the late 1960s we became importers of commodities such as steel and autos, although we had traditionally been the major suppliers for many nations in the world.

Travel and transportation

This was not, however the only cause for the fall on current account. Travel and transportation added their drains to those of imports. At the beginning of the period, Americans were spending, net, $1.7 billion abroad for travel and transportation. By the end of the period, this figure had risen to $2.8 billion. Here, an enormous increase in tourism played a central role. A million and a half Americans traveled abroad in 1960 (creating a demand for foreign exchange). By 1971, this number had risen to 5.7 million, and the rise was not counterbalanced by an equivalent rise in foreign tourism in the U.S.

Military expenditures

These two large drains on American exchange were augmented by a third, this time originating from government rather than private persons. Every year, during the six-year period we are examining, the government ran up a large deficit for military purposes. In 1965 we were spending $3.0 billion in net foreign exchange to support U.S. military activities abroad. By 1972 this had risen to $4.7 billion, largely because of the Vietnam War. Notice that this is not the full cost of our military activities. Much of the war and nonwar military expenditure, such as the maintenance of U.S. troops in foreign bases, is paid in dollars and creates no demand for foreign exchange. The bombers we build or fly and the pay for soldiers (in U.S. dollars) create no exchange problems. But inextricably connected with foreign military activity is a need to make large expenditures in other currencies. Non-U.S. personnel must be paid in their currencies, not in ours. Supplies such as food or local supplies must also be paid for in foreign currencies.

Investment income

If we add up the deficits for 1972 (the worst year) on merchandise account, travel and transportation, and military, we get a total of $13 billion—far larger than the actual deficit of some $8 billion on current account for that year. What accounted for the difference?

Part of the difference is to be found in the other items we learned about in our last chapter, some of which helped and

---

EURODOLLARS

A student in international economics sooner or later hears about a mysterious currency called Eurodollars. Eurodollars are simply European bank accounts denominated in dollars rather than in the currency of the country. They represent a pool of funds that can be borrowed—*a pool of funds that are essentially unregulated by any government.* Since they are not held in the U.S., they are outside of the jurisdiction of the U.S. government. Since they are held in dollars and not in local currency, they are outside the jurisdiction of the local government.

Their main impact is to make it much more difficult for any country to control its own monetary policies. Suppose a firm wants to invest during a period when its own government is restricting the money supply and making it difficult to obtain loans. Unable to borrow in local currency, the firm borrows Eurodollars and exchanges these borrowed dollars for local currency. It now has the funds that it wished to have for investment purposes, and its government has been frustrated in its efforts to retard lending. In the United States credit crunch of 1969–1970, large U.S. firms were substantial borrowers of Eurodollars, to circumvent the Federal Reserve Board's policy of making it harder and harder to obtain local loans. Eurodollars are therefore one of the reasons for the uneven impact of monetary policies that we noted earlier.

Finally, Eurodollar accounts serve as a ready source of funds for speculating on international exchange rates. They are highly mobile and acceptable everywhere.

Table 21 · 2 Net private investment income (billions)

1967	1968	1969	1970	1971	1972	1973	1974	1975
$+5.8	$6.2	$5.8	$6.4	$9.0	$9.8	5.2	10.2	6.0

some of which hurt our balance on current account. During the 6-year period, for example, our remittances abroad increased, worsening our balance, whereas our sales of other services (such as insurance on cargoes), improved, helping the situation. But the main source of dollars to offset the huge total of our merchandise, travel, and military expenditures was a large and growing income from United States private investments abroad, mainly the flow of profits of U.S. corporations. Table 21 · 2 shows the substantial rise in these sources of foreign exchange for the United States (remember that every time a foreign branch of a U.S. company sends profit home, it must buy dollars).

Trends on capital account

We have still to look into the activities on capital account which, as we know, also enter into our official reserve transactions balance—the "balance" being achieved by sales of gold or other reserve assets or by holdings of currency by foreign central banks.

Table 21 · 3 shows the trends in both long-term and short-term capital.

What do these figures show? We see, first, that there has been a steady drain on the balance of payments from long-term government transactions. These largely reflect foreign aid loans, which are counted as claims against the U.S., although they are mainly spent *in* the U.S., creating additional exports.

More important, we see in the next column an irregular deficit earned on long-term private account. This is partially the result of companies purchasing foreign exchange to build plants and equipment abroad—a flow that ran between $1 billion and $2 billion all during the early 1960s. It is also partly the result of companies and individuals investing in long-term foreign securities in the early 1970s. They invested because they thought growth prospects were good for these companies, or because they wanted to protect themselves against a change in the value of the dollar, or were speculating that such a change would take place.

For example, a person who bought a World Bank Bond in Swiss francs in 1970 would have paid the fixed rate of exchange, then about 25¢ per franc. If the dollar then fell in price, so that each franc now cost 35¢ instead of 25¢, an owner of a

Table 21 · 3 Long- and short-term capital flows (billions)

	1967	1968	1969	1970	1971	1972
Long term						
Gov't.	$-2.4	$-2.2	$-1.9	$-2.0	$-2.4	$-1.3
Private	-2.9	+1.2	-0.1	-1.4	-4.1	-0.1
Short term	+1.2	+3.5	+8.8	-6.0	-7.8	-0.5

10,000 franc bond that cost $2,500 would be able to sell the bond for $3,500. (After the very large outflow of private capital in 1971, the United States placed a tax of 18 percent on purchases of most foreign securities, to deter just such speculative transactions. This tax has since been removed.)

Short-term trends

Finally, we come to the column of short-term capital flows. As we know, these are sums that travel from nation to nation in search of profitable short-term investment. They are partly guided by interest rates, partly by speculative considerations of the kind we have just considered. Note how volatile this item is. Between 1969 and 1970, there was a difference of $14 billion—$8 billion entering this country in the first year, $6 billion leaving it the next. Here was another serious cause for the crisis that finally erupted in 1971.

Now let us sum up our partial balances, to look at the trend in the official reserve transactions balance. As we can see in Table 21·4, this balance worsened seriously in 1970, "collapsed" in 1971, and remained badly in deficit in 1972.

The gold drain

How did the United States meet its worsening foreign exchange situation? As we have seen, there are only two ways to finance a deficit: by selling gold (or other reserve assets) or by persuading foreign central banks to hold the currency of the deficitary nation, in this case dollars.

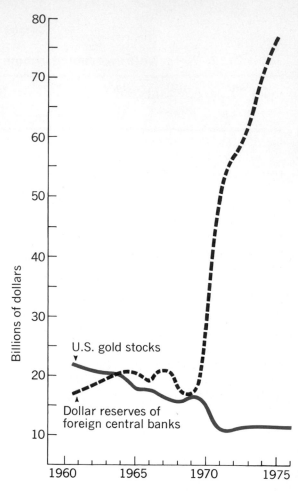

FIG. 21·2   Changes in U.S. gold stocks

Figure 21·2 shows that this is exactly what happened in the case of the United States. Beginning in the 1960s, our gold stock steadily declined, and the dollar reserves of foreign central banks rose. As we can see, as early as 1964 the holdings of dollars were so large that if foreign central banks had exercised their legal claims to gold, the entire gold stock of the nation would have been wiped out!

Table 21·4   Official reserve transactions balance (billions)

1967	1968	1969	1970	1971	1972
$−3.4	$+1.6	$+2.7	$−9.8	$−29.8	$−10.3

336

This would have been a major economic catastrophe—not because we would have no gold "behind" our currency, but because we would have cheated foreign nations out of hundreds of millions or billions worth of purchasing power. For if the gold supply ran out, foreigners could no longer repatriate their dollar holdings at a known exchange rate. Instead, their dollar holdings would now have to find their own price vis-à-vis their own currencies; and since dollars are held in very large quantities, this price might be very low.

Take, for example, a Netherlands bank that had allowed $1 million to remain in America, because it was confident that it could always get 28,571 ounces of gold for it (at $35 per ounce) *with which it could then purchase other currencies whose value in gold was also firmly fixed.* Suddenly it would find that its million-dollar deposit would be worth only as many ounces of gold as the market decreed—very possibly much less than the quantity it thought it owned. In turn, the amounts of other currencies available to the Netherlands bank would also fall, since it would have less gold to buy them with. *Thus, countries that had cooperated with us by allowing their dollars to remain here would be penalized.* They would never again allow dollars to pile up in U.S. banks.

Not less important in staying the hand of the central banks who might have claimed our gold was the fear of a terrible slump in trade that could have followed. Since World War II, the dollar had been *the* unit for settling balances among nations. If the dollar were no longer—at least in theory—convertible into gold, a main instrument for international "liquidity" would be wiped out. Unless another means of settling balances was put in its place, a straitjacket of gold could be placed on the volume of international trade, with an almost certain consequence of a drastic fall in the volume of trade.

The gold rush of 1967–68

Just because the consequences of a "run" on gold would be so disastrous, the central banks of foreign nations agreed not to demand their dollar balances in gold. This did not, however, prevent *private* speculators abroad from taking their holdings of dollars and converting them into gold. For many years there has been a perfectly legal market in gold in London and elsewhere, where private individuals could exchange their holdings of dollars or other currencies for gold bullion. The gold they bought was sold to them at the fixed price of $35 an ounce by an international gold pool comprised of the main goldholding nations. In the pool, the United States, as the largest

---

GOLD "FLOWS"

When the United States "loses" gold, the metal is not usually shipped abroad, as one might think. Instead, it is trucked to a vault many feet below the street surface in the Federal Reserve Bank of New York, where it is stacked in dull yellow bricks about the shape (but half the thickness) of a building brick. It is possible to visit this vault, which now holds some $13 billion of foreign gold, neatly separated into bins assigned to different countries. To see this modern equivalent of Montezuma's treasure is an astonishing sight. Gold may well be, as many have said, a kind of international psychosis, but its power over the imagination, no doubt the result of its traditional association with riches, is still remarkable. It is amusing to note that the Federal Reserve Bank, as custodian of this foreign gold, once suggested to its binholders that they might save a considerable sum if, instead of actually weighing the bricks and moving them from bin to bin whenever gold was bought and sold, both parties agreed to move the gold just on the books, the way bank balances are moved about. All governments demurred. They wanted the actual gold bricks in their bins. Hence, when gold moves from nation to nation to help settle up accounts, it is still actually pushed across the floor of the Fed's vault and carefully piled in the proper bin.

holder of gold in the world, was committed to providing 59 percent of all bullion supplied to the market.

In March, 1968, the gold pool suddenly faced a crisis. Alarmed at the shrinkage of U.S. gold reserves, private speculators converged on the London market to convert their dollars into bullion. On the first day of that month, the pool, which had normally sold 3 to 4 tons of gold per day, suddenly found itself obliged to sell 40 tons. A week later the demand had risen to 75 tons. On March 13, it was 100 tons; the next day, 200 tons.

At this rate of drainage, the United States Treasury was being forced to put $1 million of gold into the pool every two to three minutes. Officials in Washington nervously figured that if the gold hemorrhage were not checked, the nation's entire gold reserves would be used up in a few weeks. To prevent such a crisis, the world's central bankers hurriedly convened in Washington and after a weekend of continuous conferences, announced that the gold pool was to be discontinued and that a new "two-price" system would immediately begin. All *official* holders of dollars (i.e., governments and central banks) would still be able to buy gold at $35 an ounce from the Treasury. But there would no longer be any effort to maintain the price of gold at an "official" level in the private market by supplying whatever gold was needed there at that price. Instead, there would be no sales from any national reserve of gold into the private market, and "private" gold would be allowed to find its own price.*

*By late 1974, the price of gold on these private markets reached the astronomical price of $198 per ounce. This was far beyond any reasonable calculation of the equilibrium price of the dollar. It was simply an index of the capacity of that extraordinary metal to command belief in itself and, of course, evidence of the international private speculators' continuing feelings that the existing exchange rate structure was still untrustworthy. By 1976, the price was back to around $110.

The system worked fairly well for a while. But the continuing imbalance of American accounts made it clear that such a means of avoiding an international currency crisis was at best a stopgap.

Curing the Balance of Payments Deficit

Before we look into the next episode of the international monetary crisis of the early 1970s, let us take a moment to reflect on the problem. As we have seen, the United States had run a persisting deficit on its official reserve transactions balance—a deficit that had caused a drastic fall in its holdings of gold and an even more marked increase in the holdings of dollars by foreign central banks. American officials and businesspeople—especially bankers—were increasingly convinced that something should be done. What were the possibilities?

1. The classical medicine

One much-discussed option was to apply a stiff dose of what was called "the classical medicine." This consisted of higher interest rates and restrictive fiscal policies whose purpose was *to deflate the economy—forcing down our price level to make our exports more attractive, and lowering incomes to reduce imports.*

The problem with the classical medicine was twofold. In the first place, no one was sure that prices would fall, even if GNP did drop. The second was that few wanted to impose so drastic a remedy on the economy. Unemployment seemed too high a price to pay for a mistaken international exchange rate.

2. Restraints on capital flows

A second remedy was to discourage American spending abroad on capital account. Indeed, domestic short-term interest rates were raised to attract foreign short-term capital, and a tax was imposed on the American purchase of foreign securities.

This was a less deflationary solution to the balance of payments problem. But the difficulty with the solution was that capital exports, in the long run, earned us money on current account. Hence, discouraging the export of American capital (other than speculative capital) was killing the goose that laid the golden eggs of dividends and interest.

3. Cutting the government international deficit

A third possibility was to pare down the heavy government deficit on international account. Here there were two candidates for cutting. One was the flow of American foreign aid to the underdeveloped world. But as many economists pointed out, over 90 percent of this aid was directly "tied" to the purchase of American goods by its recipients and therefore cost us nothing in terms of a dollar drain. In addition, the spectacle of the richest nation on earth extricating itself from its international problems at the expense of the poorest nations on earth was not an attractive one.

The second candidate was the large American deficit on military account. In the eyes of many observers this was the real villain in the piece—the ultimate cause of our international economic (and political) problems. But the remedy of the military drain necessitated a change in our Vietnam and European military postures, and this was a course beyond the competence of economists to recommend or effect.

4. Devaluation

Another course of action, much talked about, was devaluation, a declaration that the gold content of the dollar had been reduced. Rather than an ounce of gold being worth $35, the President would state that henceforth it would be worth $45 or $75 or any other price that seemed likely to establish a balance in the supply and demand for American currency.

Devaluation had staunch advocates—and equally strong opponents. The advocates pointed out that it was an instant and painless cure. By devaluating the dollar sufficiently, the gold in America's possession could immediately be worth enough to cover all America's obligations to other central banks. A shipment of only a small quantity of our gold would then wipe out all of America's international obligations.

The opponents pointed to the obvious difficulties in this "solution." America would get rid of its problem by handing it to its creditors. Countries that had helped the United States by not demanding gold during the exchange crisis would now be penalized for their cooperation by receiving a much smaller amount of international purchasing power than they had expected and were originally entitled to.

Moreover, devaluation was a two-edged sword. If the United States devalued, so could its trading partners. If France, Germany, Japan, and other major nations also lowered the gold content of their currencies, there would be no gain to anyone, but a considerable friction and animosity shared by all. Finally, opponents pointed out that even if the United States' devaluation was tolerated, the cost of devaluation was a rise in the price of imports to the devaluing country. Imports were a strategic element in many aspects of America's economy. To devalue meant to raise their prices, and to give another boost to American inflation.

5. Creating new reserve assets: SDRs

A fifth method was more imaginative. It consisted of finding a reserve asset other than gold to enable central banks to "cover" any deficits. As we have seen, for many years the dollar itself was such an asset. Many foreign nations, especially in the less affluent nations, counted their holdings of dollars as if they were "as good as gold." But with the loss of faith in the ability of the United States to maintain the fixed exchange value of dollars, dollars ceased to become an acceptable reserve currency. Hence the effort was made to create a new reserve currency.

This effort was mounted by the International Monetary Fund (IMF), an institution which serves as a kind of central bank for many nations. Into the IMF, subscriber nations deposit both both gold and their own currencies. From the bank, they can borrow gold or other currencies to meet temporary shortages of reserve assets. In turn, the fund serves as a kind of monitor of exchange adjustments, because it will not lend reserves unless it approves of the borrower's exchange rates and overall economic policies.

To meet the growing crisis of liquidity, the IMF in 1970 took the very important step of creating a new reserve asset called Special Drawing Rights or SDRs. These new assets were, in fact, created out of thin air (as all money ultimately is); but because SDRs had the backing of the fund, they were just as "good" as gold in settling international accounts.

SDRs were a creative and important step in breaking the gold psychosis. The problem was the extreme difficulty in persuading the richer nations to accept this new form of international liquidity, and numerous technical difficulties in finding an acceptable formula for creating and distributing SDRs. The new step was promising, but very limited in its impact.

6. Flexible exchange rates

The sixth method was the simplest of all. It was simply to abandon the mechanism of fixed rates and to allow the price of exchange to fluctuate like any other price. As we have seen, under a "floating" exchange rate, a shortage or surplus of exchange could not develop, any more than under a free market price for shoes we find either shortages or surpluses of shoes.

Why was not this method tried at once? Partly the reasons have to do with the nationalistic feelings that obscure common sense in so many areas of international trade. Money is the very symbol of national sovereignty. To relinquish command over the international price of our money seemed tantamount to relinquishing a certain portion of sovereignty itself. And of course this was true. What was not considered was that sovereignty was also diminished by allowing the development of a balance of payments problem that, in the end, forced us to take actions against our best interests—a clear loss of sovereign powers.

There were also more thoughtful reasons for a general unwillingness to let rates "float." Most international transactions are not concluded immediately across a counter but extend over weeks or even months between the time that a sale is agreed upon and the time when the goods arrive and payment is due. If exchange rates changed during this period, either the importer or the exporter could be severely penalized. Although it is possible to insure oneself to some extent against exchange variations by buying "forward exchange," most traders would rather not deal in exchange rates that are likely to alter over the course of a transaction. More important, international investors who put money overseas for long periods have no way of protecting themselves against changes in rates, and they were even more concerned about the risks of flexible exchange.

In addition, many monetary experts feared that fluctuating rates would lead to speculative purchases and sales of foreign currencies just for the purpose of making a profit on swings in their price—and that these speculative "raids" would have the effect of self-fulfilling prophecies in still further aggravating those swings.

The Great Monetary Muddle

Now let us return to the situation of worsening tensions that we have traced up to 1971. *Between 1968 and August 1971, none of the six measures above was effectively applied.* The United States was unwilling to swallow the classical medicine. It tried to restrain capital outflows but with scant success. It did not cut down overseas government spending—in fact, it stepped up its military expenditures. It steadfastly opposed raising the number of dollars that an ounce of gold would buy (devaluation). It was unable to create a major addition to reserve assets, which in any case would not have solved the problem of persistent deficits. It did not allow the fixed exchange system to lapse and a new flexible exchange system to take over.

The Crisis of August 1971

Inevitably, therefore, the U.S. balance of payments deficit worsened, and foreign holdings of dollars grew. As they grew, so did fears that the U.S. would eventually be *forced* to devalue as the only way out of its dilemma. This brought worries that foreign governments who held dollars would suffer large losses.

To forestall this possibility, in August 1971 the British government apparently asked for a guarantee that our government would compensate the British Treasury for any losses on its dollar reserves in case we devalued. This placed the American government in a quandary. If it granted the English request, it would be forced to make similar concessions to other governments. This would have transferred the losses from devaluation from foreign governments to ourselves, since we would have had to give foreign central banks additional dollars to compensate for the fall in purchasing power of their "old" dollars.

Faced with this cost, and with the rapidly worsening climate of confidence, the United States government chose a drastic step. *It announced that it would no longer sell any gold to foreign central banks at any price.* In effect, it severed the tie of dollars to gold. Since dollars could no longer be "valued" in gold, in effect the United States allowed dollars to find their own market price. The dollar was "floated." To show that the United States meant business in correcting its balance of payments deficits, it imposed a temporary 10 percent tax on all imports.

Painful options   This immediately led to acrimonious debates as to what should be done next. The trouble was that all possibilities were painful. If nothing were done, foreign countries would be "stuck" with unwanted dollar holdings. If the dollar were formally devalued, then foreign currencies would appreciate. In that case, American goods would become cheaper, and foreign goods more expensive for Americans. Foreign producers who competed with American exporters, (such as French farmers) feared they would be flooded with cheap American goods; and foreign exporters, such as automobile makers, feared they might be priced out of America's enormous market.

Moreover, if the dollar were devalued in terms of gold, by raising the number of dollars that an ounce of gold was worth, this action would reward all the less cooperative countries in the world who had refused to allow their reserves to be held in American dollars, while penalizing the very countries that had worked with us by agreeing not to exercise their option to exchange dollars for gold.

The fight to hold fixed rates

Out of such conflicts of interest no happy solution could ever emerge, and none did. After long negotiations, European countries and Japan agreed to revalue (appreciate) their currencies vis-à-vis the dollar; the United States agreed to devalue its dollar in terms of gold, changing the price from $35 per ounce to $42, *and the nations of the world attempted to return to a new system of fixed exchange rates,* albeit rates that were different from those of the immediate past.

FIG. 21·3

How parities have changed

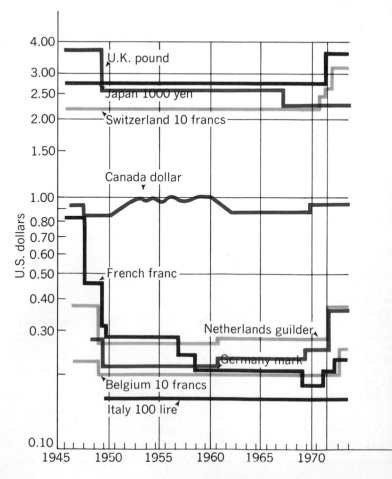

This patchwork lasted only a short time. Many individuals and corporations doubted that the exchange adjustments were large enough to correct the persisting deficit in America's balance of payments. Accordingly, they sought to buy currencies that were most likely to rise in value in the expected next round of devaluation. Once again a self-fulfilling prophecy fulfilled itself. During January and February of 1973, German reserves rose by $8 billion, or almost 50 percent, as speculators sought to buy German marks, the most obviously undervalued international currency (the Germans had been running persistent balance of payments *surpluses*). The German government then decided that it did not want its already huge dollar balances to rise further and announced that the mark would be allowed to "float." Once again the world was forced off a fixed exchange rate system and onto a floating one.

And once again the world tried to find a system of fixed rates that would hold up. The dollar was devalued again; calm was restored for a few weeks; but the rush into marks resumed, and the governments of

the world were again forced to abandon their fixed rates and to allow their currencies to float.

Figure 21•3 shows the gyrations of currencies during the turbulent years from 1946 to 1972. Note the dramatic fall in most currencies vis-á-vis the dollar just after the war, and the swing upward during the 1970 crisis years.

Recent Events

Dirty floating   The outcome of the long period of trial and error was thus a movement from fixed to floating rates. But as we have seen, the movement was resisted at each step along the way. Partly for reasons of international "prestige," partly because international bankers feared the possibility of diminishing trade, or of speculative raids, the world tried again and again—albeit unsuccessfully—to find a system of fixed rates that would withstand the pulls and tugs of

---

A heartening note. The need for liquidity—reserves of currency (or gold) that will be accepted by other nations as payment for their goods—remains a matter of anxious concern for the world, especially for the poorer nations whose currencies are not acceptable as international currencies. Hence the importance of raising the international supply of liquidity, and of distributing it among the needier nations, remains as great as ever, despite the advent of a more workable system of determining international currency prices.

Here we have seen a new development of promise. We have already traced the origin of Special Drawing

REJUVENATED SDRs

Rights (SDRs) as man-made equivalents of gold, to augment international buying power. The original SDRs were "backed" by gold and by "hard" currencies whose prices were established in terms of gold.

After the general abandonment of gold, the SDR had to be reconstituted. The new SDR consists of a "basket" of the currencies of the 16 IMF nations that accounted for at least 1 percent of world trade in 1968–1972. The value of an SDR on any day is found by valuing the basket on that day's exchange rates. Thus one SDR can rise or fall in

terms of the value of any given currency, although it tends to remain very stable in terms of an average of the world's major currencies.

Little by little the SDR is becoming a genuine international currency, rivaling gold in acceptability. OPEC has discussed stating the price of oil in SDRs; Suez Canal tolls have been set in SDRs, and similar action is being contemplated for international air transport rates. The day may come when tourists going abroad will buy SDR traveler's checks; and the day has arrived when corporations in international trade are beginning to write contracts in SDR-denominated amounts.

changes in international economic strength.

Today we have a system that is nominally free, but not entirely free—a system called "dirty floating." The major central banks have agreed not to intervene in the exchange market, except to stabilize it against speculative raids. They are supposed to offset short-run fluctuations that would make business difficult, but not to alter long-run trends.

Intervention of central banks

In fact, however, some central banks have intervened considerably beyond this point. The Japanese have frequently been accused of buying foreign currencies, thereby keeping down the price of the yen to encourage Japanese exports. Other countries have also intervened at crucial moments. The result is that exchange rates float, but they do not float all the way to the equilibrium price that a wholly free market would yield.

As a result, shortages and surpluses still appear in international accounts, evidenced by changes in the amounts of liquid liabilities (foreign-held bank accounts) held by most governments. We can see these in the case of the United States in 1975, when foreign liquid balances rose by $6.3 billion. If the liquid liabilities of any government are persistently large and positive, we can be sure that its central bank is intervening to buy foreign exchange in order to hold the price of its own currency down. If the balances are large and negative, we can be certain the bank is selling foreign exchange, in order to hold the value of its currency above the price that the free market would enforce.

The OPEC crisis

Will the new system work? There seems reason to be modestly hopeful. The near disastrous imbalance of the fixed-exchange crisis cannot recur under a regime of floating rates, even if the float is not quite "pure." And the new system has managed to weather some very serious blows.

The most serious was the OPEC oil crisis following the Arab-Israeli war of September 1973. Acting as a cartel, the Organization of Petroleum Exporting Countries (OPEC), largely concentrated in the oil-rich Middle East, dramatically raised the taxes imposed by its members on oil produced within their countries. In September 1973 every barrel of oil exported from an OPEC nation brought in $1.77 to the exporter. Within a year this had increased to $9.75. With transportation and other costs added, plus oil company profits, this increased the cost of oil to most Western nations to over $12—a four- to fivefold increase in a single year.

The OPEC price squeeze meant an enormous change in the world's balance of payments. The industrialized nations were forced to pay over $100 billions *a year* to the OPEC producers. Of this sum the OPEC nations utilized about half, mainly to pay for additional imports from the industrial nations and to provide some assistance to the underdeveloped world. But the remaining half—roughly $50 billion a year—simply piled up as "petrodollar" balances, largely deposited in German and American banks.

Considerable concern was raised by these balances, for had the OPEC countries shifted them about carelessly or tried to convert them all into the currencies of one or two preferred nations, this huge sum could have worked international financial havoc. In fact, the OPEC nations have sought to reinvest most of their petrodollar balances in the oil-buying industrial world, thereby "recycling" the money spent for oil and preventing a major financial crisis.

A workable system?

Meanwhile the American position has recovered considerably. Shortly after the *de facto* abandonment of fixed rates, the dollar fell by an average of about 21 percent relative to the value of the currencies of its major trading partners. It then regained strength during the oil crisis. Because the United States is still a very large producer of oil within its own borders, the OPEC squeeze was a much smaller drain on our foreign exchange reserves than on those of our major Western allies. The dollar recovered about half of its relative fall after the "oil shock" began. In the last year or two, the dollar has essentially held its own, neither rising nor falling with respect to the average value of its trading partners' currencies, although some currencies, such as the pound, have fallen vis-à-vis the dollar. Others, such as the mark, have risen.

Even with the intervention of central banks, the system of floating rates should allow currencies to reflect the two basic forces that we have already identified as crucial in determining the international economic position of governments. One of these is the *relative rate of inflation* of different nations; the other is *the relative gain in productivity* among them. Other factors, such as threats of war, fears about certain governments, and similar political events, may cause a national currency to fall or rise temporarily, but the long-run trend should be governed by these underlying factors.

Thus a persistent "excess" rate of inflation, coupled with a persistent lag in productivity, will create serious problems for any nation. *But these problems will exist under any system of international payments.* To the extent that such a nation must sell abroad or provide inputs from abroad, its standard of living must fall, and no monetary arrangement in the world can prevent that.

But a system of floating rates can mitigate the damage by "signaling" its advent, as the price of the beleagured country's currency slowly falls, and a drastic and politically unmanageable sudden "crisis" can thereby be avoided. Thus there seems a fair change that the new system will work better than the old. In the imperfect world of international economic arrangements, that is perhaps as much as we can ask.

Focus

We do not ask you to learn a complicated story of monetary history, whose twists and turns read at times like a suspense novel. Rather, we suggest that you study the chapter as a "case history" of the difficulties that can develop when exchange rates are fixed at levels markedly divergent from those the free market would impose.

Today we live under a regime of "dirty" floating exchanges that, in all likelihood, will persist for a long time. The difficulties of going back to fixed exchange rates (and of determining those rates) now seem greater than the difficulties of living with free exchange rates, partially disturbed by the interventions of governments. Because the float seems here to stay, much of this chapter—such as the discussion of devaluation, the "classical medicine," and other cures for the pre-1971 chronic crisis—seems academic. It is a discussion of economic problems that were pressing at one time, but that are not likely to recur unless we go back to the system that got us into such trouble. Perhaps we should study them to understand why we should not try to resurrect the past.

No chapter on international monetary problems can ever come to a satisfactory end, because international monetary flows can change rapidly. The thing to understand is the mechanism by which these flows are generated and the way in which the supply and demand for foreign exchange establishes a price that clears the market for exchange. It will repay the time if you review the material of the previous chapter in the light of the more dynamic analysis of this one.

WORDS AND CONCEPTS YOU SHOULD KNOW

Flights of short-term capital, 336
The "classical medicine," 338–39
Devaluation, 339

SDRs, 340
Flexible exchange rates, 340–41
Dirty floating, 343–44

QUESTIONS

1. In the tables below we show the price of British pounds from 1971 to 1975. We also show the cost of living index in the two countries. Can you deduce what probably happened in the relationship of productivity between the U.S. and the U.K.? Are there other factors that could account for the slippage of the British pound?

	U.S. price of £	Rise in cost of living	
		U.S.	U.K.
1971	$2.44	4.3%	9.4%
1972	2.30	3.3	7.1
1973	2.45	6.2	9.2
1974	2.34	11.0	16.0
1975	2.22	9.1	24.2

2. Does gold or do SDRs serve a purpose under a system of free exchange rates if there is no intervention on the part of banks? If gold and SDRs were eliminated, what would provide "liquidity"?

3. Assuming that there was a general demand to return to fixed rates, what would you recommend as the proper basis for establishing the relation of various currencies to one another?

4. Can dirty floating persist in one direction only unless there is agreement to use some currency (or some asset) as a reserve currency?

Index

A

B